THE FIRST WORLD EMPIRE

This book offers a comprehensive overview of the early modern military history of Portugal and its possessions in Africa, the Americas, and Asia from the perspective of the military revolution historiographical debate. The existence of a military revolution in the early modern period has been much debated in international historiography, and this volume fills a significant gap in its relation to the history of Portugal and its overseas empire. It examines different forms of military change in specifically Portuguese case studies but also adopts a global perspective through the analysis of different contexts and episodes in Africa, the Americas, and Asia. Contributors explore whether there is evidence of what could be defined as aspects of a military revolution or whether other explanatory models are needed to account for different forms of military change. In this way, it offers the reader a variety of perspectives that contribute to the debate over the applicability of the military revolution concept to Portugal and its empire during the early modern period. Broken down into four thematic parts and broad in both chronological and geographical scope, the book deepens our understanding of the art of warfare in Portugal and its empire and demonstrates how the military revolution debate can be used to examine military change in a global perspective.

This is an essential text for scholars and students of military history, military architecture, global history, Asian history, and the history of Iberian empires.

Hélder Carvalhal is a researcher at the Interdisciplinary Centre for History, Culture and Societies (CIDEHUS), University of Évora. He is a PhD candidate in early modern history at the Inter-University Doctoral Programme in History (PIUDHist), between Évora and Lisbon. He is interested in global economic and social history since the 1500s. He has published in journals such as *Gender & History* and *Journal of Iberian and Latin American Economic History*.

André Murteira is a researcher at Centre for the Humanities – CHAM (FCSH, Universidade NOVA de Lisboa). His MA dissertation was the basis for his published book *A Carreira da Índia e o Corso Neerlandês, 1595–1625* (2012). He has published in journals such as the *Journal of Military History*. He is interested in the history of Dutch-Iberian conflicts outside of Europe in the seventeenth century.

Roger Lee de Jesus is a researcher at Centre for the Humanities – CHAM (FCSH, Universidade NOVA de Lisboa). He is a PhD candidate at the University of Coimbra interested in the history of Portuguese presence in Asia, from political to military history, especially in the implementation of European institutions and warfare in the Portuguese *Estado da Índia* (sixteenth century).

Warfare and History

General Editor: Jeremy Black

European Warfare in a Global Context, 1660–1815
Jeremy Black

Warfare, State and Society on the Black Sea Steppe, 1500–1700
Brian L. Davies

War in the Modern World
Jeremy Black

Israel's Wars
A History since 1947, 4th edition
Ahron Bregman

The Spanish Civil War
A Military History
Charles J. Esdaile

Military Thought of Asia
From the Bronze Age to the Information Age
Kaushik Roy

The First World Empire
Portugal, War and Military Revolution
Edited by Hélder Carvalhal, André Murteira and Roger Lee de Jesus

For more information, or to place orders visit Routledge, Warfare and History www.routledge.com/Warfare-and-History/book-series/SE0417

THE FIRST WORLD EMPIRE

Portugal, War and Military Revolution

Edited by Hélder Carvalhal, André Murteira and Roger Lee de Jesus

Routledge
Taylor & Francis Group
LONDON AND NEW YORK

First published 2021
by Routledge
2 Park Square, Milton Park, Abingdon, Oxon OX14 4RN

and by Routledge
52 Vanderbilt Avenue, New York, NY 10017

Routledge is an imprint of the Taylor & Francis Group, an informa business

British Library Cataloguing-in-Publication Data
A catalogue record for this book is available from the British Library

Library of Congress Cataloging-in-Publication Data
A catalog record for this book has been requested

ISBN: 978-0-367-36550-9 (hbk)
ISBN: 978-0-367-36548-6 (pbk)
ISBN: 978-0-429-34696-5 (ebk)

Typeset in Bembo
by Apex CoVantage, LLC

CONTENTS

ILLUSTRATIONS

Figures

Maps

Tables

PREFACE

Excitement for reading this collection will be readily appreciated by all those working both in military history and in global studies. From the fifteenth century to the mid 1970s, Portugal was the longest lasting of the transoceanic empires, but this role and its military history have been underplayed in the general literatures on imperialism and on war. There are a host of reasons, including linguistic skill, access to archives, and the dominance of Hispanicists and their perspectives in most appointments in the field of Iberian history,[1] but the net consequences are unfortunate. In relative terms, we see too little discussion of the empire and of the continual role of conflict in its history, while Portugal's history plays an insufficient role in the global account. There are obviously significant exceptions, notably the recent work of Gabriel Paquette,[2] but the trend is apparent. Too often, accounts of military development are in part "constructed" from a questionable list of examples.

In contrast to the widespread underplaying of Portugal, the chapters here all contribute greatly to the discussion of the putative early modern European military revolution, not least by providing a widespread basis for assessing different aspects of interactions with non-Western states. The collection offers a tremendous amount for evaluating the current controversy, whether on artillery fortresses, as with the chapters by Lopes and Correia, Conceição and Araújo, and White; hybrid warfare, as with Murteira;[3] or the direction of influence, as with Mostert and Noordam. Carvalhal, Costa, and Cruz provide powerful chapters on the military-political dimension; Cossart adds to Noordam on artillery; and Lee de Jesus and Andrade contribute significant but different assessments of the extent and nature of the situation from an East Asian perspective. This excellent collection throws light both on more-general military developments and on the history of Portugal and its empire. It also brings attention to how far later-Portuguese military history can be scrutinized for similar reasons.

The coverage in this collection is helpful when considering how to move the subject forward. The original military revolution thesis has been both criticized and contextualized,[4] but we still require an intellectual structure within which to signpost and assess developments in this period. As far as the criticism is concerned, it is best to consider, as with all analysis by historians, the scholarly context in which the idea emerged. Academic theories in the humanities and social sciences gain traction not so much because of any inherent intellectual merit, because that is of course contextual, but rather because they are readily usable and useful. The "pull" dimension, the usefulness of a thesis, and especially its usefulness in a particular context, is one that can be approached in materialist terms, whether filling textbooks and lecture slots or advancing academic careers, but also with reference to the value of an argument at a specific moment. Indeed, from that perspective, the unoriginal thesis generally does best, because "thinking within the box," or at least a similar box, helps to make a proposition readily digestible. The "push" dimension is an aspect of the same factors, of material and ideological import. The major one is the ability to appear cutting edge but in terms that can be in practice somewhat predictable.

In this way grew the idea of an early modern military revolution, a proposition that drew heavily on already-established ideas and literatures of modernization and, eventually, globalization. These ideas had a long genesis, but the key origin was that of progress as measured in and by social development, an approach that put to one side religious notions of time as leading towards a millenarian outcome. If Montesquieu, Smith, and Robertson are all key names in this intellectual project, it was in practice one of a longer pedigree, with notions of improvability in human life accompanied by that of development.

These ideas lent themselves to nineteenth-century interest in scientific formulation and application. Darwinism is part of the mix, as evolutionary ideas provided metaphors and concepts, notably what was to be termed *functionalism*, in the shape of serving goals necessary for survival and therefore strength. These ideas affected new, developing sciences such as sociology, geopolitics, and anthropology and were brought into academic history through a shared concern with modernity and therefore modernization. Rational choice was seen as at play, from biological preference to economic and political practice, but there was a difference between an emphasis on constraints, as with Durkheim, or with contingent outcomes, as with Weber. There was a parallel with the geographical ideas of determinism or "possibilism."

Weber's approach to modernity led him to define it in terms of rationality and standardization, with motivation in terms of instrumental behaviour as opposed to traditional action. Weber also linked the prudent rationality related to capitalism with Protestantism. Taken into US thought by Talcott Parsons, Weber was the forbear of what was to be called the structural-functional approach, and modernization theory became a key tool in the social sciences, a theory emphasising rational abstract principles and an abandonment of past practices. Key texts included Walt Rostow's *The Stages of Economic Growth: A Non-Communist Manifesto* (1960) and

Francis Fukuyama's *The End of History and the Last Man* (1992), the latter a work propounded around the means, goals, and modernity of liberal democracy and free market capitalism. In the 1960s and again in the 1990s, modernization was regarded as a form of a global "New Deal," able to create a new world order, and information and theory were deployed accordingly.[5]

Modernization theory, however, was often advanced with insufficient attention to practicalities, let alone reality, as with the failure to understand Vietnamese society and resilience. On a related but separate point, the attempt to produce "modern," quantifiable criteria of military success fell afoul of the ability of the Viet Cong and North Vietnamese to soak up heavier casualties and, accordingly, to defy US equations of success with their emphasis on quantification. It would be easy to draw a line between these (and other) modernization writers and the proponents of, and even more response to, the thesis of a military revolution.

While that is apposite, there are other elements of modernization theory that should first be addressed. A key one was that of secularization, as the analysis, means, and goal of development. Durkheim, Weber, and many others argued that modernization meant a decline in religious practice and significance, and this approach affected a broad tranche of writing in the social sciences and humanities and affected discussions of historical change.[6] The cult of reason, understood as inherently secular, with faith banished to the private sphere, meant that the present necessarily understood the past better than the latter did: reason could reveal the prospectus to a better future and a better-understood past. The significance of religion, from the fifteenth century to Salazar, to the Portuguese imperial project, ensured that this was a particularly inappropriate approach when assessing Portugal.

A circularity in thought and selectivity in evidence were inherent to this process, and both, indeed, were very much to be seen in the work by the proponents of a military revolution. As far as the first was concerned, functions were presented in a quasi-automatic fashion, with needs and drives readily ascribed to states and effects ascribed to functions, and those functions were defined by the effects they produced.[7]

A key aspect of the cult of a modern reason, in terms of secularism and of other elements, can be a failure not only to understand the military cultures of the past (and even arguably the present), but also to appreciate the nature of development. Failing to perceive the values of the past and to understand its practices understandably leads to a neglect of key factors in the evaluation of proficiency, capability, and success, both individual and collective. Honour is misleadingly disparaged as conservative, if not redundant, and practices of aristocratic officership are often misunderstood.[8]

Revolution was a fashionable term in the twentieth century, not only reflecting political commitment but also reflecting that it became the standard way to describe and explain structural change. This practice owed much to the *Industrial Revolution*, a term first used in 1799 but popularized by Arnold Toynbee in 1881, with apposite capitals and in part particularly significant because of the growing competition between industrial powers in the late nineteenth century. This term also became the basis for subsequent revolutions, as with the Agricultural Revolution,[9] so it was not surprising that the term was deployed in military history. There were precursors, but the most influential argument was advanced in 1955 by Michael Roberts in a work published in 1956[10] that liberally employed the idea of fundamental change and the term *Military Revolution*, and it closed with a clear affirmation of transformation: "By 1660, the modern art of war had come to birth. Mass armies, strict discipline, the control of the state, the submergence of the individual had already arrived" and so on, culminating with "The road lay open, broad and straight, to the abyss of the twentieth century." From the perspective of Portugal, however, there were problems with Roberts's work, not least his failure to grasp the nature of pre-1560 or post-1660 warfare and his neglect of navies and the global dimension.

Parker was far more impressive with his inclusion of the naval dimension, his wider-ranging chronology, and his engagement with the world scale. Initially, Parker focused on the Spanish dimension, but he broadened his approach with his hugely influential book *The Military Revolution: Military Innovation and the Rise of the West, 1500–1800* (Cambridge, 1988). For Portugal, it is particularly instructive that Parker addressed the global question, employing "the Military Revolution of the sixteenth century"[11] to in effect explain both the rise (and multipolarity) of the West and why it was to provide the most successful of the *gunpowder empires* to employ a term probed by William H. McNeill.

The undoubted strengths of Parker's work, however, can be scrutinized empirically, not least and not only, by questioning the idea of a three-century revolution or by referring to the limitations of Western success, the nature of late medieval circumstances, the importance of the post-1660 period, and, despite the brilliance of the footnotes, the selection and deployment of evidence to establish apparent significance. For example, an emphasis on Dutch proficiency from the 1590s needs to address more the failure of the Dutch, despite a major effort, to prevail over the Portuguese in Brazil.

There are also debatable assumptions in theses of modernization and in the characterization of capability. The emphasis on particular notions of proficiency, and the embrace of the proposition of change that is fundamental because it is described as revolutionary and that is described as revolutionary because it is fundamental, fits within a practice of historical writing that increasingly looks very much like that of a particular period. Alluding earlier to Fukuyama was deliberate: there are instructive parallels between the mindsets represented in these two works. Each appears qualified at the very least by the more varied presentation of modern warfare that the subsequent three decades would offer.

Parker very much takes modernization theory on board:

> the Muslim states . . . could no longer meet and defeat the expanding repertory of innovations developed by their Christian adversaries, because the Westernisation of war also required replication of the economic and social structures

and infrastructures, in particular the machinery of resource-mobilisation and modern finance, on which the new techniques depended.[12]

This, however, does not quite explain either the varied success of Portugal over the period covered in this volume or, in different contexts, the same for Israel and the United States in the Islamic world over the past three decades. Instead, the specificity of conflict and individual conflicts and the multivalent character of war emerge, and the language of modernity, modernization, and revolution is misleading as an account, narrative or analytical, of this phenomenon.

The Portuguese position in the eighteenth century exemplifies the broad-spectrum nature of the Atlantic European militaries of the early modern period. The Portuguese fought other European powers (e.g., France and Spain), had to be able to engage on land and on the sea with Morocco, and were opposed on land and on the water by a wide range of non-European forces, from the Marathas in India to the Muras in Amazonia. These wars proved very testing. Thus, in India, the Portuguese, having failed in their 1722 campaign against the strongholds of the Maratha naval leader, Kanhoji Angria, were hard hit in 1737–40, when they were involved in a disastrous war with the Marathas. Despite the concept of the superiority of the European artillery fortress, Salsette, Bassein, and Chaul fell, and Goa was nearly lost. The Marathas combined their cavalry with an infantry drawn from a disaffected peasantry. In India, expansion from Angola and Mozambique was limited, and, having failed in 1744, as in 1683, in a campaign against the Kingdom of Matamba to the east of Angola, Portugal became more cautious in its military activity and focused on gaining slaves by trade, not war.[13] In Amazonia, the Portuguese found the Muras adept with their bows and arrows and effective because of their mobility.[14]

These and other case studies are most valuable not only for looking at the current discussion but also for considering how best to advance the subject. To this end, this collection deserves widespread attention as a major contribution to the empirical and conceptual development of early modern military history.

Jeremy Black

Notes

1 See, for example, the relative treatment of Portugal and Spain in B. Yun-Casalilla, *Iberian World Empires and the Globalisation of Europe, 1415–1668* (Basingstoke: Palgrave Macmillan, 2019).

2 G.B. Paquette, *Imperial Portugal in the Age of Atlantic Revolutions* (Cambridge: Cambridge University Press, 2013); G.B. Paquette, *The European Seaborne Empires: From the Thirty Years' War to the Age of Revolutions* (New Haven, CT: Yale University Press, 2019). It is also a great pleasure to draw attention to the work of my former colleague Malyn Newitt, including *A History of Portuguese Overseas Expansion, 1400–1668* (London: Routledge, 2004).

3 See also A. Murteira, "The Military Revolution and European Wars Outside of Europe: The Portuguese-Dutch War in Asia in the Frist Quarter of the Seventeenth Century," *Journal of Military History* 84 (2020): 511–35.

4   See, most recently, C. Paoletti, *Military Revolution, Military Evolution, or Simply Evolution* (Rome, 2020), www.commissionestoriamilitare.it.

5   M.E. Latham, *Modernisation as Ideology: American Social Science and 'Nation Building' in the Kennedy Era* (Chapel Hill, NC: The University of North Carolina Press, 2000); M.E. Latham, *The Right Kind of Revolution: Modernisation, Development, and U.S. Foreign Policy from the Cold War to the Present* (Ithaca, NY: Cornell University Press, 2011); N. Gilman, *Mandarins of the Future: Modernization Theory in Cold War America* (Baltimore, MD: Johns Hopkins Press, 2003); D.C. Engerman, "American Knowledge and Global Power," *Diplomatic History* 31 (2007): 599–622.

6   For a critique, J.C.D. Clark, "Secularisation and Modernisation: The Failure of a 'Grand Narrative,'" *Historical Journal* 55 (2012): 161–94.

7   A. Hawkins, "Modernity and the Victorians," unpublished paper. I am grateful to Angus Hawkins for providing me with a copy.

8   For a more rounded account, see G. Hanlon, *Italy 1636: Cemetery of Armies* (Oxford: Oxford University Press, 2016); G. Hanlon, *European Military Rivalry, 1500–1750: Fierce Pageant* (Abingdon: Routledge, 2020).

9   J.D. Chambers and G.E. Mingay, *The Agricultural Revolution* (London: Routledge, 1966).

10 M. Roberts, *The Military Revolution, 1560–1660* (Belfast: M. Boyd, 1956).

11 G. Parker, "In Defense of *The Military Revolution*," in *The Military Revolution Debate*, ed. C.J. Rogers (Boulder, CO: Westview Press, 1995), 356. For a liberal progressivism at Christ's College, Cambridge on the part of Jack Plumb, Geoffrey Parker's teacher, to whom Parker referred as having 'such an immense impact,' D. Cannadine, "Historians in the 'Liberal Hour': Lawrence Stone and J.H. Plumb Re-Visited," *Historical Research* 75 (2002): 316–54; D. Cannadine, "John Harold Plumb 1911–2001," *Biographical Memoirs of Fellows, III, Proceedings of the British Academy* 124 (2004): 269–309 at 286–96.

12 Parker, "In Defense," 355.

13 J.K. Thornton, "Firearms, Diplomacy, and Conquest in Angola," in *Empires and Indigenes: Intercultural Alliance, Imperial Expansion, and Warfare in the Early Modern World*, ed. W.E. Lee (New York: New York University Press, 2011), 187.

14 D. Sweet, "Native Resistance in Eighteenth-Century Amazonia: The 'Abominable Muras' in War and Peace," *Radical History Review* 153 (1992): 49–80.

ACKNOWLEDGEMENTS

The present volume was inspired by the international congress "The Military Revolution in Portugal and Its Empire (15th–18th Centuries)," organized and held by CIDEHUS, University of Évora (UID/HIS/00057/2019) during 29–30 May 2018, with the support of the Portuguese Foundation for Science and Technology (FCT, I.P.), the Portuguese Economic and Social History Association (APHES), and the Portuguese Commission for Military History (CPHM, Ministry of Defence). Without the support of these institutions, the congress would not have been possible.

We also thank Ana Teresa de Sousa and the technical staff of CIDEHUS – Carla Malheiro, Sónia Bombico, and Francisco Brito – for their cooperation on the organization of the event. Seven of the thirteen chapters in this volume are reworked versions of papers presented during the aforementioned congress. The remaining contributions were solicited especially for the purposes of improving the geographical and chronological coverage of the topics under debate.

We thank a number of people for their help and manifestations of support in the making of this book. Lorraine White helped us to review some of the content of this volume, for which we are very grateful. Peter Lorge, Tonio Andrade, and Phillip Williams have provided advice and encouragement since the beginning of this project. A word of gratitude is also due to the editorial team at Routledge – Eve Setch and Zoe Thomson, along with the series editor, Jeremy Black – for patiently answering all our questions. Lastly, we thank all the institutions that provided their permission for the reproduction of illustrations – Nationaal Archief and the Koninklijke Bibliotheek, both in The Hague, Netherlands; Badische Landesbibliothek in Karlsruhe, Germany; and the Royal Library in Brussels, Belgium.

Hélder Carvalhal, André Murteira, and Roger Lee de Jesus

CONTRIBUTORS

Tonio Andrade has degrees from Reed College (BA in anthropology), the University of Illinois Urbana–Champaign (MA in history), and Yale University (PhD in history). He is currently a professor of history at Emory University, where he writes on global history and the history of China. His most recent book, *The Gunpowder Age*, is a work of global military history that explores gunpowder warfare in Europe and China from 900 to 1900. He is also author of *How Taiwan Became Chinese* (Columbia University Press, 2008), which focuses on the early history of Taiwan, and *Lost Colony: The Untold Story of Europe's First War with China* (Princeton University Press, 2011), which explores the Military Revolution in Europe with data from East Asia. His articles have appeared in the *Journal of World History*, *Late Imperial China*, *International Journal of Maritime History*, *Canadian Journal of Sociology*, *Itinerario*, *Journal of Asian Studies*, and various other publications.

Renata Malcher de Araujo is graduated in architecture and urbanism. She has a PhD from FCSH, Universidade NOVA de Lisboa in art history (2001) and from University of São Paulo in history and foundations of architecture and urbanism (2005). Her research has mainly been developed within the areas of the history of colonial urbanization, the history of cartography, and heritage studies. She is currently a professor at University of Algarve and an integrated researcher of CHAM (FCSH, Universidade NOVA de Lisboa), and she co-coordinates the project TechNetEMPIRE | Technoscientific Networks in the construction of the built environment in the Portuguese Empire (1647–1871), funded by Portuguese Foundation for Science and Technology (FCT, I.P.). She is also a professor in the PhD programme heritage of Portuguese influence at the Institute of Interdisciplinary Research of University of Coimbra.

Hélder Carvalhal has a BA in history (University of Minho) and is a PhD candidate in early modern history at the inter-university doctoral programme in history

(PIUDHist), where he is working on a thesis about power, political patronage, and external relations in sixteenth-century Portugal. He is a researcher of CIDE-HUS, University of Évora. While generally focused in global economic and social history since 1500, his research agenda is diverse and includes gender, labour, and military history. Over the past few years, he has been affiliated with projects of labour relations and occupational structures (at the International Institute for Social History, Amsterdam) and living standards in a global world (Wageningen University and Research). He has published in journals such as the *E-Journal of Portuguese History*, *Gender & History*, and the *Journal of Iberian and Latin American Economic History*.

Margarida Tavares da Conceição holds degrees from University of Lisbon – BA in history of art, 1989; from FCSH, Universidade NOVA de Lisboa – MA in history of art, 1998, with the dissertation *Urban space Evolution in Almeida (16th–18th Centuries)* and from the University of Coimbra – PhD in architecture, variant theory, and history of architecture, 2009, with the dissertation *On the City and Fortification in Portuguese Texts (1540–1640)*. She has been a researcher at the Institute of Art History at NOVA School of Social Sciences and Humanities since 2013 and an invited assistant professor at the same university. She has also been an invited assistant professor at the Architecture Department of University Autónoma of Lisbon since 2015. She is a team member of the research project TechNetEMPIRE | Technoscientific networks in the construction of the built environment in the Portuguese Empire (1647–1871). Her main research interests are the city and fortifications in the early modern period and treatises on architecture, town planning, and related areas.

Jorge Correia holds a degree in architecture and a PhD from the School of Architecture/University of Porto, Portugal, with a thesis on Portuguese settlements in North Africa. Currently, he is an associate professor at the School of Architecture/University of Minho, deputy director of the Landscape, Heritage and Territory Lab (Lab2PT) and vice-president of the European Architectural History Network (EAHN). His main research interests are devoted to the Portuguese early modern colonial sphere's built environment, particularly in the Maghreb and the Middle East, the cultural faces/challenges of heritage, and traditional Islamic cities, and he regularly publishes books or book chapters and papers in such fields. Recently, he was a visiting scholar at the Canadian Centre for Architecture (CCA), where he curated the exhibition "Photographing the Arab city in the 19th century," and has been a guest professor or a staff fellow at several universities in Iberia, Brazil, the Balkans, and the Middle East.

Brice Cossart is a French researcher who obtained his PhD in history at the European University Institute in Florence (Italy) in 2016, with a dissertation on the gunners at the service of the Habsburg Monarchy (1560–1610). He is currently a Marie Skłodowska-Curie fellow at the University Pablo de Olavide in Seville

(Spain), with a project financed by the European Union (grant agreement No. 845675), titled "GLOBALGUNS," about the circulation of military technology and experts in the Spanish and Portuguese colonial space during the Iberian Union (1580–1640). He has published various articles and book chapters in English, French, and Spanish about gunners and schools of artillery. His PhD dissertation has received two scientific awards (the Turriano-ICOHTEC prize and the Military History prize from the French Ministry of Armies) and will soon be published as a book in *Classiques Garnier* with the title *Guerre, Savoirs techniques, état: les artilleurs et la Monarchie hispanique (1560–1610)*.

Fernando Dores Costa has since 1985 researched various subjects on Portuguese social history during the seventeenth, eighteenth, and nineteenth centuries, changing the interpretation of issues related to liberal agrarian legislation, public finances, and the social modelling of the army in Portugal, a privileged place for observing social structuring and modes of governance. Since 1995, he has been working on adopting the methods of the social history of war, the results of which can be found in his books *A Guerra da Restauração (1641–1668)* (2004) and *Insubmissão: aversão ao serviço militar no Portugal do século XVIII* (2010) and in other publications, such as on the role of Portugal during the Peninsular War (1808–14) and the Liberal Revolution (1820–34). He is also a coauthor of the biography of King João VI (r. 1792–1826).

Miguel Dantas da Cruz is an assistant researcher at the Institute of Social Sciences – University of Lisbon. He has PhD in history, variant empires, colonialism, and postcolonialism. He has a diverse research agenda, which includes the military, institutional, and cultural aspects of the early modern Portuguese Empire. He has published on the evolution of imperial and martial imaginaries and about the circulation of military personnel in the seventeenth-century Portuguese Empire. Recently, he has been exploring petitionary drives of the early-nineteenth-century Liberal Revolution. He participates in several ongoing international projects, like RESISTANCE (Rebellion and Resistance in the Iberian Empires) and RITUALS (Public Rituals in the Portuguese Empire [1498–1822]). He organizes and coordinates several permanent seminars. He also teaches at the University of Lisbon and at the University of Coimbra, both undergraduate and postgraduate courses.

Roger Lee de Jesus is a PhD candidate at the University of Coimbra, finishing a thesis on the governance of the *Estado da Índia* by João de Castro, the governor and viceroy between 1545 and 1548. His MA thesis (2012) analyses the second Gujarati siege of the Portuguese fortress of Diu, in India (1546). He is interested in the history of Portuguese presence in Asia, from political history to military history, especially in the implementation of European institutions and warfare in the Portuguese *Estado da Índia* (sixteenth century). His publications include the edited volume (with Bruno Lopes) *Finanças, Economia e Instituições no Portugal Moderno* *(séculos XVI–XVIII)* (Coimbra University Press, 2019). He is currently a researcher at CHAM (FCSH, Universidade NOVA de Lisboa) and contributes there on the international project *De Re Militari: From Military Literature to the Battlefield Imagery in the Portuguese Space (1521–1621)*.

Ana Lopes is a PhD candidate, developing a thesis titled "Military architecture of Portuguese origin in the Arabian Peninsula: the fortifications in Muscat (16th and 17th centuries)" at the School of Architecture/University of Minho, under the supervision of professors Jorge Correia and André Teixeira. She earned a master's degree in architecture (2009) at the same institution. Since then, she has been a guest lecturer at that institution as well as a researcher at CHAM (FCSH, Universidade NOVA de Lisboa), studying Portuguese military architecture in Morocco and, more recently, at Lab2PT, integrating the SpaceR research group. Her interests include studies in history of architecture and in civil and military architecture and its urban settlements, with a special interest in the architecture produced by the Portuguese maritime expansion between the fifteenth and the eighteenth centuries. In this context, she has worked on several research projects, participating in scientific meetings and publishing articles and book chapters in this field.

Tristan Mostert is a PhD candidate at Leiden University. His dissertation focuses on conflicts over access to the clove trade in the eastern Indonesian archipelago in the seventeenth century. His earlier publications include *Silk Thread: China and the Netherlands from 1600* (coauthored with Jan van Campen, Rijksmuseum, 2015), and the edited volume *The Dutch and English East India Companies: Diplomacy, Trade and Violence in Early Modern Asia* (coedited with Adam Clulow, Amsterdam University Press, 2018).

André Murteira is a researcher at CHAM (FCSH, Universidade NOVA de Lisboa). He has an MA in the history of Portuguese overseas expansion from the New University of Lisbon on the subject of Dutch privateering against Portuguese navigation between Europe and Asia from 1595 to 1625. His MA dissertation was the basis for his published book *A Carreira da Índia e o Corso Neerlandês, 1595–1625* (2012). He has recently finished his PhD in history at the New University of Lisbon on the subject of Dutch privateering against Portuguese navigation in Asia in the first quarter of the seventeenth century (2016). He benefited from a grant from *Fundação Oriente* (Portugal) to do his MA and from another from the Portuguese Foundation for Science and Technology (FCT, I.P.) for his PhD. He has published in journals such as the *Journal of Military History*, *Tijdschrift voor Zeegeschiedenis*, *Análise Social*, and *Anais de História de Além-Mar*. He is interested in the history of Dutch-Iberian conflicts outside of Europe in the seventeenth century.

Barend Noordam's PhD research analysed the connections between the Neo-Confucian movement of Wang Yangming (1472–1529) and the military revitalization of the Chinese Ming dynasty, as exemplified by General Qi Jiguang's (1528–88) career. Besides creating social networks of civil and military elites, Wang's movement mediated access to military knowledge and career opportunities. Noordam's earlier research focused on the transfer and appropriation of military technology between European actors and Ming-Qing China, as well as the history of transcultural perceptions and military intelligence. Other interests include the sociocultural and intellectual aspects of the simultaneous upsurge of military knowledge production in both Europe and China in the sixteenth and early seventeenth centuries. At present, as part of the project *Aftermath of the East Asian War of 1592–1598* at the Autonomous University of Barcelona, Barend Noordam is tracing the development, application, and diffusion of military technological innovation in Ming China resulting from the Imjin War (1592–8) in Korea.

Miguel Geraldes Rodrigues is an integrated researcher at CHAM (FCSH, Universidade NOVA de Lisboa), where he obtained his MA degree. For his PhD in history at the European University Institute (EUI), Florence (2019), he focused on the transatlantic slave trade in the South Atlantic, the colonial history of Angola, and Iberian financial networks during the early modern period.

Lorraine White completed a PhD on the war of 1640–68 from the Spanish perspective in terms of the army, warfare, and government on the main war front in Extremadura. While teaching in Australia for a number of years at the University of Wollongong, she expanded her research, first into aspects of the Military Revolution and the war of 1640–68 and then into the war from the Portuguese perspective. She has published several articles on the war of 1640–68 in the *Journal of Military History, War in History, War and Society, Studia Histórica – Historia Moderna, Manuscrits*, and others. She has also published a book chapter and articles on the Portuguese India Company and Dom Jorge Mascarenhas, *Marquês de Montalvão*, in Disney and Booth (eds.) *Vasco da Gama and the Linking of Europe and Asia, Portuguese Studies, Portuguese Studies Review*, and *Oriente*.

INTRODUCTION

This book debates the applicability of the military revolution (henceforth, MR) concept to Portugal and to its empire during the early modern period (fifteenth to eighteenth centuries). It seeks to explore whether the assumptions that support the concept conceived by Michael Roberts and later developed by Geoffrey Parker (among others) are relevant to the Portuguese case or whether other explanatory models can be put together from the analysis of several chronologically and geographically diverse case studies.[1] The book fills a notable gap regarding in-depth studies dealing with Portugal and its empire. The absence of such studies is especially surprising given Portugal's priority in European overseas expansion, the coexistence between such expansion and the period where the effects of MR were allegedly felt more intensely, and the fact that the Portuguese came into contact with what some historians view as other "forms" of MR in their connections with other military powers in Asia, Africa, and South America.

Over recent decades, the concept of MR has been useful as a framework for the debate about military change. Lately, it has even been updated in the modern military world in the debate around the revolution in military affairs (RMA). The idea of this book is to place military change in Portugal and its empire in a more globalized debate. The debate of the topics in which the concept of MR was underpinned allows for Portugal's national military historiography, traditionally closed in upon itself, to overcome barriers and to benefit from different perspectives. Discussing the MR concept does not have to imply an adherence to it. On the contrary, it can be a way to go *beyond the Military Revolution*, as Jeremy Black puts it, to "focus on capability, change and continuity, and only at close to consider whether the Military Revolution is still a relevant concept."[2] Black has certainly been critical of the concept, arguing that it fails to take account of the diversified reality of early modern warfare. Pointing out its debt to theories of modernization, he sees it as a product of the particular period when it was developed.[3] Thus, he explicitly compares Geoffrey Parker's volume on the MR to the roughly contemporary well-known book of Francis Fukuyama on "the end of history," suggesting that it partook of the same belief in a modernization narrative that subsequent decades have questioned. Nevertheless, probably no other concept in military history has generated such extended and productive discussions in recent decades between experts on different regions and periods.

One of the reasons for the origin of this book is the near absence that the MR debate registered in Portugal as opposed to that in neighbouring Spain, where discussion of the concept and its application started early on.[4] While minor works on some features of Portuguese military history and, to a certain extent, on some Portuguese topics connected with the MR do exist, there is a notable lack of in-depth studies dealing with the concept and its topics regarding Portugal and its empire. From our perspective, two factors contributed to this paradigm: the idea of naval superiority and the impact of a more conservative history on the period of the composite monarchy. Both factors deserve some detailed attention.

First, the swift Portuguese expansion through Asia during the sixteenth century – the best-known period in Portuguese early modern military history by far – allowed for a simplistic interpretation of what should be seen as a complex and irregular process – the idea that "guns and sails," as Carlo Cipolla puts it, were responsible for the hegemony of the Portuguese navy on the Indian Ocean.[5] This provided historians with a simple and convenient explanation which, for the most part, they did not feel the need to challenge or at least to elaborate on as, for example, did Geoffrey Parker. Regarding the second factor, for many decades, Portuguese historiography had a troubled time when interpreting the period 1580 to 1640, when Portugal was under Habsburg rule – precisely one of the periods where literature on military change is most concentrated. While legal and social historians were able to overcome this issue easily, military historians had a hard time conceiving the role of Portugal within the composite monarchy. The incorporation of the Kingdom of Portugal was seen as a period of decline. Moreover, several defeats in the Portuguese Empire were also ascribed to Habsburg dominion, which further added to this general portrait of decadence and submission.

The gradual renovation of Portuguese historiography has shown that this period was not linear and that serious and critical evaluations of sources reveal a different history. At that moment, Portuguese military historiography embarked on a broad view of Portugal and its empire in relation with Europe and the world.[6] New studies also initiated interest in recruitment and finances, especially for seventeenth- and eighteenth-century mainland Portugal.[7]

However, the literature still has a long way to go, regardless of a few notable efforts on the dissemination of new tactics.[8] Even in one of the most debated fields – war on sea – little effort has been made to frame the mass of empirical research of recent decades into the set of questions that the MR concept raises.[9] Thus, no substantial advances have been made to assess, for instance, the validity of Geoffrey Parker's claims about European naval superiority.[10] A recent profusion of Portuguese military history titles concerning both mainland Portugal and its empire do not provide adequate answers to the problems debated here, as their focus is directed more towards politics or general considerations about the art of war.[11]

Interested as we are in a non-Eurocentric type of military history, we must stress the existence of other literature that deals with the MR concept in different geographical areas and its connection with the Portuguese Empire. Among them, one can include the works by Tonio Andrade and Peter Lorge, both of which deal with the MR from a Eurasian perspective.[12] Although both authors criticize the Eurocentric perspective by suggesting that some kind of MR occurred in Asia before there was any contact with Western technological developments, the impact of the latter is also debated. Among those, the impact of Portuguese weaponry and the dissemination of knowledge appear quite relevant.[13]

Lastly, we consider not only how criticism of Eurocentric perspectives has grown during the past three decades but also how the MR concept has been criticized from a more evolution-oriented perspective.[14] However, few works in this vein include Portugal and its empire when arguing this. Several works by Jeremy Black and the recent book by Frank Jacob and Gilmar Vinosi-Alonzo are exceptions.[15] Even in these cases, we cannot speak of in-depth analysis but rather of a set of observations that deserve to be explored further and updated according to recent scholarship.

The present book is divided into four key sections: fortifications and military revolution; the size of armies and the rise of the fiscal state; tradition and innovation in warfare; and cultural exchange and the circulation of military knowledge. They deal with aspects where military change was visible during the early modern period. From their own perspective, all chapters reflect in turn whether something could be termed a *military revolution* or whether one could imagine an alternative scenario.

Given the geographical and chronological amplitude of this book and the variety of societies and polities with which the Portuguese had contact, it is not realistic to expect a single, unified, and definitive answer to this question. On the contrary, the reader will be presented with different points of view, some of them exploring the Portuguese case by comparing it with European counterparts, while others examine it from a non-Western perspective. This book should therefore be considered as a way of keeping the debate alive by providing more food for thought for economic, political, and military historians and for political scientists whose penchant for the topic has been clear over the past decades.[16]

The first section, "Fortifications and Military Revolution," consists of three chapters. Some common issues are worthy of mention, such as the impact of foreign personnel on the dissemination of new ideas and practices, the training of native experts, or, even more relevant, the emergence of innovations in fortifications outside Europe. The first chapter, by Ana Lopes and Jorge Correia, explores the renovation of the fortress of Azemmour (Morocco) during the first half of sixteenth century from a cross-disciplinary perspective. It argues that change and readaptation in Portuguese African overseas outposts was following the theoretical precept circulating in Europe. Thus, the empire was simultaneously a laboratory and a centre of diffusion for early modern transitional architecture.

A similar idea is observable in the second chapter, by Margarida Tavares da Conceição and Renata Malcher de Araujo, which deals with the Portuguese experience regarding early modern fortification, its connection with the education of engineers, and the dissemination of knowledge. At different moments over time, the ability to maintain engineering training structures was the key to the existence of a technical network between mainland Portugal and the empire. While knowledge transfers provided by foreign engineers did take place, especially in the first stages, the tendency was for a gradual implementation of a Portuguese "perspective" supported by the aforementioned training project and also by the diffusion of Portuguese technical manuals. The authors rely on evidence not only from the Portuguese metropolis but also from the empire, focusing especially on the Brazilian case study.

The third chapter, by Lorraine White, is also connected to fortifications and their construction, but it returns to the mainland because it explores the provenance, recruitment, and deployment of military engineers in Portugal against Habsburg Spain during the Restoration War (1640–68). By examining the role that both native and foreign military engineers played in the design and construction of the new style of fortifications, White stresses that there was no clear and linear development in the conception and construction of modern fortifications. Necessity fostered the adaptation of pre-existent structures. Although the transition to modern fortification in Portugal – as elsewhere in Western Europe – may not have been smooth and rapid, it was profound, and it ultimately ensured success against Spanish attempts at seizing control.

Section two is dedicated to the relation between growth in army size and state building from the late fifteenth century until the Age of Revolutions. The three chapters in this section deal with topics such as what resources the state allocated to war and how relevant the major stakeholders (e.g. the nobility) actually were to warfare in the long run. In chapter four, Hélder Carvalhal argues that Portugal did not go through a military revolution in the sixteenth century, given the absence of a growth in army effectives, lack of evidence that more resources were allocated to war, and the obvious continuities with the late medieval period regarding military recruitment. Military change in mainland Portugal was thus of little significance. By establishing comparative points with other case studies, the author stresses that despite the ongoing costs of maintaining an overseas empire, Portugal did observe a recruiting capacity that was in line with that of its European counterparts. This followed a tendency which was already apparent in the mid 1400s.

Following this chronology, Fernando Dores Costa (chapter five) examines whether there was an MR at all in Portugal in the early modern period. The author maintains that there is no clear answer to this matter. On the one hand, it is not possible to make a case for a "revolution." No significant increase in army size is visible, there is no substantial proof of a higher extraction of resources from the society by the state, and military change is not as considerable in the long term. On the other hand, the author recognizes a set of innovations that progressively penetrate Portuguese society, even if the effect produced by those in the medium to long term is short and its consequences are weak. In a different geographical sphere, Miguel Dantas da Cruz (chapter six) explores the relation between war efforts and the development of a fiscal and bureaucratic apparatus in colonial Brazil. He argues that the increase of taxation for war purposes did not imply a higher intervention by the state. Instead, the development of local institutions and the increase of power of colonial elites were the two driving forces behind major warfare episodes in the region, at least until the eighteenth century. Only in the latter period did the state gradually replace the functions of these local powers. The chapters in this section point to the inexistence of a military revolution, as it were. Instead, military change was discontinuous and heavily driven by local powers as much as it was by context and circumstances regarding international trade, politics, and diplomacy.

Section three deals with the topic of tradition and innovation in warfare. Its contributions allow us to perceive the impacts of military change both in Portugal and in the empire. To a certain extent, all chapters debate whether naval technology or artillery permitted Portugal to achieve military dominion over a third party or to attain a superior degree of power and engagement in warfare. This is a highly relevant topic given the outdated Eurocentric visions of Western superiority that also impacted Portuguese historiography until recently. Brice Cossart (chapter seven) attempts to overhaul military literature in the period of the Habsburg composite monarchy (1580–1640) by debating the impact of the annexation of Portugal on military technology, especially artillery. He argues that this period benefited Portugal by allowing the kingdom to reach the forefront of artillery innovation. Cossart stresses that change in the institutions and the circulation of knowledge and specialized personnel helped to integrate Portugal into the Habsburg military organization, with its consequent technological improvements.

For this same period in Iberian history, André Murteira (chapter eight) approaches Portuguese–Dutch War in Asia in the light of the discussion of the MR. More specifically, he focuses on the issue of whether an MR in Europe produced a European military exceptionalism that gave Europeans military superiority over non-Europeans. He concludes that Asian actors and Asian circumstances contributed in no small measure to Portuguese defeats. This goes against the argument that traditionally explained the victories of the Dutch exclusively in terms of their superior experience of European warfare. Thus, these findings fit well with the more recent historiography questioning traditional assumptions about European military superiority, which is also debated by Roger Lee de Jesus in chapter nine. The author argues here that despite an initial European superiority in Asia during the early 1500s due to the combination of gunpowder technology with highly effective naval support, the long sixteenth century saw a gradual fading of Portuguese military power. Indicators such as the use of gunpowder weapons, the degree of adaptation of fortresses, and the supply of men to Indian garrisons are used to test this hypothesis. The author discusses its conclusions while proceeding to re-evaluate what the most recent literature has conveyed about the topic and pointing to the perils of generalized assumptions and less-informed interpretations.

Section four deals with an important factor for military change, especially given the context in which early Portuguese overseas endeavours took place: cultural exchange and the circulation of military knowledge. The four chapters in this section explore the role of Portuguese individuals in different regions around the world as technological brokers and relevant actors of a much more complex process of change. Chapter ten, by Miguel Geraldes Rodrigues, explores the extent to which the technological and military innovations brought by the Portuguese to overseas affairs succeeded and does so through an examination of the conquest of Angola in the sixteenth and seventeenth centuries. The failure to adapt European tactics and the fact that the state did not support warfare in the conquest of Angola does not suggest the existence of a "military revolution." As the alleged innovations failed to adapt to the west African reality, a new hybridized way of conducting warfare gradually emerged. This double process of adaptation and intercultural exchange would benefit both Portuguese and west central African armies. Similar to Spanish efforts in Central America, the only way that the Portuguese army was able to hold fast involved precisely the considerable integration of Indigenous troops.

In chapter eleven, Tristan Mostert explores the role of the Portuguese in the military development of Makassar (actual Indonesia). Exploration of this role is threefold: the involvement of the Portuguese in the evolution of fortifications; their role in the dissemination of European-based weapons and expertise; and the participation of the Portuguese community living on the island at the time of the Dutch invasion (mid seventeenth century). The exploration in this case study highlights that, while not as relevant in the evolution of fortifications, the Portuguese were conspicuous in the supply of gunpowder weapons and in disseminating technological innovations to the rulers of Makassar. In turn, the Portuguese community was sufficiently established to participate briefly in the defence against the Dutch until the negotiations between the Vereenigde Oost-Indische Compagnie (VOC) and locals resulted in their subsequent expulsion.

In chapter twelve, Barend Noordam also examines the impact of Portuguese military technology but in relation to Ming dynastical Chinese warfare. According to the literature, the Portuguese cannons were not very interesting to the Chinese, given that the size and thickness of their walls discouraged any attempt to develop anti-fortification artillery, Noordam argues in a different direction. Portuguese cannons did influence their Chinese counterparts throughout the sixteenth century as they increased in size and weight. Enemy combatants lost their exclusivity as targets, and the artillery started to aim for armoured and unarmoured enemy equipment and secondary fortifications. Although intrastate warfare in China may have been the driving force behind military innovation, the Portuguese seem to have played their role as disseminators of knowledge.

Taking a broader view, and to conclude this section, Tonio Andrade reassesses the MR debate by examining different perspectives offered by a case study of East Asia. Andrade highlights that, as in European warfare, East Asian powers (namely Chinese states) experienced periods of both innovation and stagnation in the late medieval and early modern periods, when the Portuguese provided one of the waves of innovation in the mid sixteenth century. Andrade also advocates the Parkerian argument of a "double spiral of causation" regarding whether state centralization was fostered by military competition, or vice versa. Thus, the author calls for an improved awareness of the dissemination of guns as an index of measuring the globalization of the MR between 1400 and 1800. As these chapters argue, military change was not always provoked by the arrival and interaction of the Portuguese with other European and non-European peoples. Many European innovations were already known in other regions of the globe. Nevertheless, they played a role when local powers experienced periods of confrontation, creating synergies that eventually led to military change.

Despite the disparity of the questions broached by the various chapters and their different perspectives, this book widens our knowledge about the state of art of warfare in Portugal and its empire. Additionally, it shows how the MR debate can be used to examine military change, from a global perspective. While the wide context under scrutiny here does not allow for a single firm conclusion, it seems that the Portuguese played a role, even if only secondary, in how war was being waged in many geographical spheres of the globe. Nevertheless, their intervention did not always directly provoke military change or innovation. This might, however, have more to do with either the absence or backwardness of the intervention provided by mainland Portugal, which we know faced several complex challenges as the early modern period unfolded.

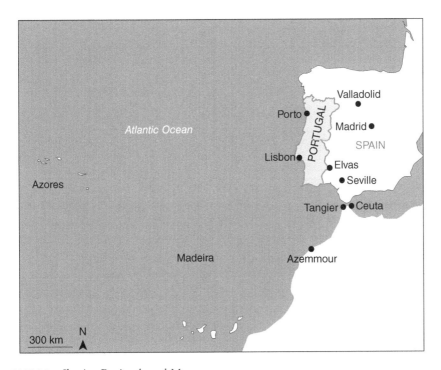

MAP 0.1 Iberian Peninsula and Morocco

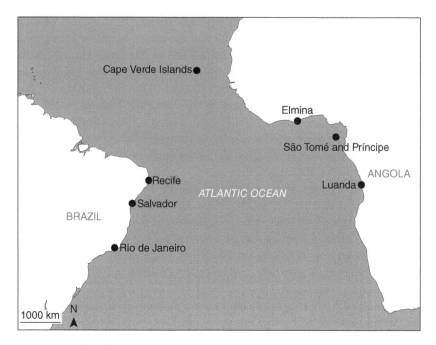

MAP 0.2   South Atlantic

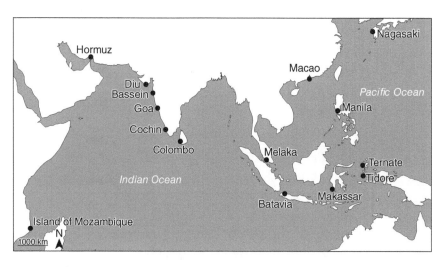

MAP 0.3   Asia

Notes

1 Michael Roberts, *The Military Revolution, 1560–1660: An Inaugural Lecture Delivered Before the Queen's University of Belfast* (Belfast: M. Boyd, 1956); Geoffrey Parker, *The Military Revolution: Military Innovation and the Rise of the West*, 2nd ed. (Cambridge: Cambridge University Press, [1988] 1996).

2 Jeremy Black, *Beyond the Military Revolution: War in the Seventeenth Century World* (London: Palgrave Macmillan, 2011), 7.

3 Jeremy Black, "Modernisation Theory and (some of) the Conceptual Flaws of the Early-Modern Military Revolution," *Nuova Antologia Militare* 1, no. 3 (2020): 3–7.

4 Among others, see Parker, *The Military Revolution*, 24, 52, 62–63; I.A.A. Thompson, "'Money, Money, and Yet More Money!' Finance, the Fiscal-State, and the Military Revolution: Spain 1500–1650," in *The Military Revolution Debate: Readings on the Military Transformation of Early Modern Europe*, ed. Clifford J. Rogers (Boulder, CO: Westview Press, 1995), 273–98.

5 Carlo Cippola, *Guns, Sails and Empires: Technological Innovation and the Early Phases of European Expansion 1400–1700* (New York: Pantheon Books, 1965).

6 Francisco Contente Domingues, "Em guerra com o Mundo, por todo o Mundo (1580–1668)," in *História Militar de Portugal*, ed. Nuno Severiano Teixeira (Lisbon: Esfera dos Livros, 2017), 273–90.

7 António M. Hespanha, *As Vésperas do Leviathan. Instituições e poder político: Portugal, século XVII* (Coimbra: Almedina, 1994); António M. Hespanha, "Introdução," in *Nova História Militar de Portugal*, ed. Manuel Themudo Barata and Nuno Severiano Teixeira, vol. II (Lisbon: Círculo de Leitores, 2004), 9–33; Fernando Dores Costa, "Os problemas do recrutamento militar no final do século XVIII e as questões da construção do Estado e da nação," *Análise Social* XXX, no. 130 (1995): 121–55; Fernando Dores Costa, "Formação da força militar durante a guerra da Restauração," *Penélope* 24 (2001): 87–119; Pedro Puntoni, "'The Barbarians War': Colonization and Indigenous Resistance in Brazil (1650–1720)," in *Resistance and Colonialism: Insurgent Peoples in World History*, ed. Nuno Domingos, Miguel Bandeira, and Jerónimo Ricardo Roques (Cham, Switzerland: Palgrave Macmillan, 2019), 153–73.

8 Pedro de Brito, "Knights, Squires and Foot Soldiers in Portugal During the Sixteenth-Century Military Revolution," *Mediterranean Studies* 17 (2008): 118–47; Luís Costa e Sousa, *A arte na guerra: A arquitectura dos campos de batalha no Portugal de quinhentos* (Lisbon: Tribuna da História, 2008); Luís Costa e Sousa, *Construir e desconstruir a guerra em Portugal (1568–1598)* (Lisbon: IESM, 2016).

9 Vitor Luís Gaspar Rodrigues, "A evolução da arte da guerra dos portugueses no Oriente (1498–1622)" (PhD diss., vol. 2, IICT, Lisbon, 1998); João da Rocha Pinto, *Marte no Oceano Índico: Antropologia da arte da guerra dos portugueses no Oriente, 1497–1525 (Afonso de Albuquerque, a invenção do poder naval e a construção do primeiro sistema mundial)* (PhD diss., New University of Lisbon, Lisbon, 1997).

10 Parker, *The Military Revolution*, 92–94, 104–8.

11 Domingues, "Em guerra com o Mundo"; Luís Costa e Sousa and Vítor Rodrigues, "The 16th Century (1495–1600)," in *War in the Iberian Peninsula*, ed. Francisco García Fitz and João Gouveia Monteiro (London and New York: Routledge, 2018), 241–66.

12 Tonio Andrade, *The Gunpowder Age: China, Military Innovation, and the Rise of the West in World History* (Princeton, NJ: Princeton University Press, 2016); Peter Lorge, *The Asian Military Revolution: From Gunpowder to the Bomb* (Cambridge: Cambridge University Press, 2008).

13 Lorge, *Asian Military Revolution*, 45–63, 79–99.

14 Tonio Andrade, Hyeok Hweon Kang, and Kirsten Cooper, "A Korean Military Revolution? Parallel Military Innovations in East Asia and Europe," *Journal of World History* 25, no. 1 (2014): 51–84.

15 From Jeremy Black, "European Overseas Expansion and the Military Revolution," in *Technology, Disease, and Colonial Conquests, Sixteenth to Eighteenth Centuries: Essays*

Reappraising the Guns and Germs Theories, ed. George Raudzens (Leiden: Brill, 2001), 1–30; Jeremy Black, *European Warfare, 1494–1660* (London and New York: Routledge, 2002); Frank Jacob and Gilmar Vinosi-Alonzo, *The Military Revolution in Early Modern Europe: A Revision* (London: Palgrave Macmillan, 2017).

16 See, for instance, J.C. Sharman, *Empires of the Weak: The Real Story of European Expansion and the Creation of the New World Order* (Princeton, NJ: Princeton University Press, 2019), 4–18.

PART 1

Fortifications and military revolution

1

NEGOTIATING EARLY MODERNITY IN AZEMMOUR, MOROCCO

Military architecture in transition

Ana Lopes and Jorge Correia

Motto

On the left bank of the Oum er-Rbia, one of the major rivers of Morocco, Azemmour is around 3 kilometres inland from the mouth and is today a laid-back town. This city was the last big Portuguese conquest in the Maghreb, marking a strategic stage for the expansion of the Crown between the fifteenth and the sixteenth centuries (Map 1.1). The Portuguese presence here, which lasted from 1513 to 1542, would irreversibly influence the town's image, dimension, and limits because of a drastic downsizing procedure undertaken. This technique was joined by important phases of military architecture experiments as its defences would play a key role in the early 1500s renovation that all the other Portuguese possessions in North Africa were witnessing.

This chapter aims to expose the key phases of the changes in military architecture that this short European presence introduced in this city in the first half of the sixteenth century. Such actions were central to the Military Revolution within the Portuguese's overseas sphere, particularly an almost constant war effort in the Maghreb. One of the most interesting aspects for the analyses of the Portuguese fortifications in Azemmour is the degree of revision of pre-existing structures and the newly built defensive architectural elements. Azemmour's works epitomize the laboratorial character of Portuguese military architecture interventions in new, coeval conquests, as pioneer models for full bastioned developments later in the century in the region or in revisions of obsolete defences in older Portuguese possessions in North Africa.

Indeed, this was a time to negotiate novel early modern winds of reform and atavistic late medieval affirmations of power, which were rather based on cavalry ways of making war. Given recent architectural surveys, a detailed analysis of drawn material and historic archival research, the argument in this chapter seeks

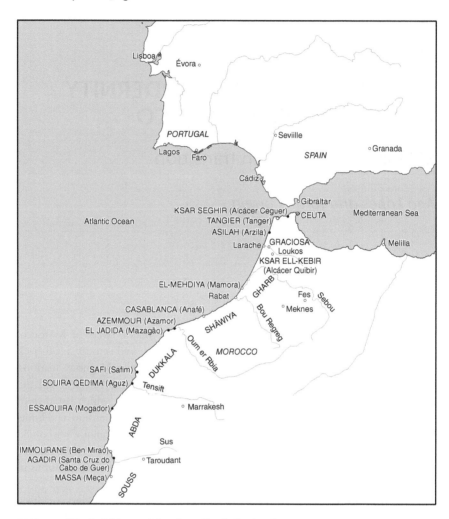

MAP 1.1   North Africa and Southern Iberia Peninsula

to evaluate the urban impact of the Portuguese presence and its military architectural achievements in Azemmour. Furthermore, it looks for interpretations that can position this case study as a central development between neuro and pyroballistic discussion in Portugal at the time.

Beyond morphological and typological analyses that convey a panorama of the physical metamorphosis, Azemmour is part of important cultural exchanges and the circulation of military knowledge, which is reflected in the work of Diogo and Francisco de Arruda. These master builders managed to bridge experiences in the metropolis and the Maghreb through an extensive network of interventions in fortifications and even international contacts.

Context

The Portuguese presence in North Africa lasted from 1415, when King João I (1385–1433) started what would become a series of conquests, to 1769. This last date represents the epilogue of a political, military, and commercial investment in the Maghreb, when the evacuation of the last stronghold was decided in Lisbon. For more than three and a half centuries, the Portuguese main expression of its territorial expansion consisted in isolated enclaves along the Strait of Gibraltar and Atlantic coasts, which corresponds today to a long seashore stretch along the Kingdom of Morocco, with the exception of the Spanish city of Ceuta. This territory was never treated as a full colony, with autonomous jurisdiction, by the Crown. It was rather based on the conquest and occupation of pre-existing Arab and Muslim cities, meaning a network of isolated possessions ruled directly by the king through local captains and governors. The time span covers an important shift in ideas and ways of making war, transitioning from late medieval images to early modern conceptions on the verge of the year 1500.

Traditionally, historiography has divided Portuguese military conquests and the establishment of commercial outposts in North Africa into two important areas. On the northern tip of the territory, the military takeover of Ceuta, followed by Ksar Seghir in 1458 and both Assilah and Tangier in 1471, defined what was then called *Algarve de Além-mar* [Overseas Gharb]. These former Muslim cities were integrated into the Portuguese Crown even though their influence only occasionally went beyond the limits of their walls. A peace treaty with the Kingdom of Fez allowed the European power to extend their administration towards the hinterland for a period of a few decades at the end of the fifteenth century.

Further south, Portuguese ambition was to prevent Marrakesh from accessing its sea ports. The establishment of suzerainties in cities such as Azemmour (1486) and Safi (1488) in exchange for military protection clearly shows how vulnerable these places were, being caught between internal Moroccan disputes. As a consequence, a few years later, both cities were militarily conquered (Safi in 1508 and Azemmour in 1513) as a part of a broader plan by King Manuel I (1495–1521) to ensure a stronger Portuguese presence in this southern area and a leading position in reaping the commercial benefits of its harbours. Furthermore, several castles were built at strategically important sites along the coast, to provide additional protection for recently conquered cities, such as Mazagão, 15 kilometres south of Azemmour, in 1514.

Overall, the arrival of a new power and faith also led to a reconfiguration of the urban fabric, reducing its area. The most frequent military approach was conquest. Urban appropriations shrank cities, erased suburbs, and promoted the opening of new streets and squares, closer to a Portuguese identification of the built environment. In the cities occupied by the Portuguese, a pragmatic attitude was the rule, oriented towards sustainability in a hostile environment. Significant reductions in perimeter and surface were carried out, in a procedure known as *atalho* (downsizing).[1] In some cases, opportunities to experiment with more-elaborate systems left an urban heritage that remains today. The establishment of new settlements was another paradigm for expanding the Portuguese presence, if less successful. The foundation of Mazagão (today the neighbourhood of the *Cité Portugaise* in El Jadida), in 1541, is an exemplary case study, representing the climax of all the urban and military architecture experiences acquired in a region where city walls generally meant a frontier for faith and possession. Mazagão also embodies an epistemological shift owing to all the previous experience, notably in neighbouring Azemmour.

Azemmour: historical background

By the time the Portuguese took the city in 1513, it had already had a long history to tell regarding its past urban history and recent Portuguese interactions. While it is only possible to speculate about Azemmour's Roman and even pre-Roman origin, its importance during the Islamic period is historically documented.[2] In the twelfth century, its commercial connection with the Iberian Peninsula remained active, especially with the port of Cádiz. The city's apogee came during the rule of the Almohad dynasty (1130–1269), when the maritime dimension of the Maghreb had increased and ties between the region and the Iberian Peninsula were strengthened. It was at the time a regional capital,[3] and its description by Ibn al-Khathib in the mid-fourteenth century gives an image of a wealthy and prosperous city.[4] Recent archaeological work carried out in Azemmour has led to the identification of remains related to this description.[5]

Curtain walls and rammed-earth towers describe a mostly circular perimeter clearly beyond the current medina's wall (Figure 1.1). Today's urban display of modern Azemmour registers a perfectly visible contour that follows the archaeological data. Such a medieval dimension was anchored on a street that still today houses the market and leads to the sanctuary of the city's patron Moulay Bouchaib, a mausoleum of the eleventh and twelfth centuries. This evidence indicates that Azemmour had a walled circuit enclosing a larger area. Furthermore, excavations performed next to that wall uncovered a pottery production zone, whose artefacts were attributed to the Marinid.[6] This discovery helps to date the last stage of occupation around the beginning of the fifteenth century, approximately one century before the Portuguese occupation.

Due to its location and good resources, Portuguese interest in Azemmour grew. At the same time, political and military instability in the region, along with the need of protection from extensive external plundering (mostly by Europeans, including the Portuguese), led Azemmouri authorities to request Portuguese suzerainty.[7] The city and the Portuguese signed a treaty in 1486 setting the deal. In exchange for military protection and the continuation of trade, local inhabitants would pay an annual tribute that included an enormous catch of fish, and the Portuguese were exempted from ship taxes, authorized to buy horses, and granted a house in the city to be used as a commercial factory.

This advantageous position in the northern Doukkala region was fundamental to reinforcing and guaranteeing the lordship of the "peaceful moors" whose

FIGURE 1.1 Plan of Azemmour 1. Kasbah/Mellah neighbourhood; 2. Medina neighbourhood; 3. Former medieval Islamic surface; 4. Portuguese *atalho* wall;
5. Former medieval Islamic wall; 6. Mausoleum of Moulay Bouchaib.

territory was centred in Safi. Manuel I's 1507 expedition to scout the river mouths, including Oum er-Rbia's, was a sign of the Portuguese greed over a series of maritime outposts.[8] Suzerainty led to military campaigns to conquer the city. In 1508, the first military expedition against Azemmour failed, only to succeed five years later. On 3 September 1513, the city was taken, without much resistance.[9] Upon the Portuguese approach, the inhabitants fled, terrified by the power displayed by the Portuguese forces. Therefore, when the Duke of Braganza made his triumphal entrance, he found a deserted city. Nevertheless, the real happenings were not echoed correctly in the official speech. As soon as the news of conquest arrived in Portugal, Manuel I displayed it as a great military victory and announced it to other European nations and, particularly, the Holy See.[10]

On the field, however, the conquerors of Azemmour faced a more realistic mission: the appropriation of a Muslim city and its maintenance as a Portuguese stronghold. Several measures were about to be undertaken in order to comply with the celebrated dream. Situated in a geostrategic position between the Shâwiya region to the north and the Doukkala to the south, where it actually belonged, about 75 kilometres away from what is currently Casablanca, this port city benefited from the economic potential of these two provinces, from agricultural and fishing resources. Nonetheless, by the time of the Portuguese settlement, its harbouring duties were starting to be undermined by the silting of sea access. For the new settlers, the challenge comprised a profound revolution of the built environment of Azemmour. Because Europe was evolving from late medieval conceptions to early modernity, the city serves as an example for understanding the Portuguese urban establishment and building processes in North Africa and as a study case for the reading of the transitional style as far as military architecture is concerned.

In this regard, Braun's engraving in the world atlas *Civitates Orbis Terrarum* is the only coeval, existing visual representation of Azemmour from this period[11] (Figure 1.2).

FIGURE 1.2   *Azaamurum*, in Braun G., Hogenberg F. and Novellanus S., *Civitatis Orbis Terrarum*, I, fl. 57.

Most certainly, it was made after an original of the early-sixteenth-century drawing made during the 1507 Portuguese expedition to scout river mouths.[12] It represents the image of the city immediately before the Portuguese military assault, displaying an urban wall interrupted by several towers and encircling an urban fabric with an exaggerated number of minarets. This means that the city had meanwhile witnessed an urban contraction right before the establishment of the Portuguese. The reduction of the surface, from a former medieval broader area to the long rectangle along the river shore the Portuguese encountered, must have occurred during the course of the fifteenth century. Even though the city that the Portuguese conquered was of smaller scale, its glorious past, large surface, and heydays were still referred to in the beginning of the sixteenth century and justified the political and economic appetite for it.[13]

Urban impact

With a surface of around 9 hectares, the urban area conquered by the Portuguese exceeded the military capacities of the available garrison. Thus, after the takeover, the Portuguese found it necessary to reorganize and refortify the township. One of the strategies, carried out in almost all Portuguese-controlled cities in the Maghreb, was the downsizing of the inherited Islamic cities, to better sustain the military. This operation, called *atalho*, shortened the fortified contour and led to a radical review of the cities, regularizing them geometrically, directing them towards the sea, and reassessing their internal displays.[14] One or more new curtain walls were introduced in order to narrow down the former Islamic perimeter, meaning that the *atalho* constituted the most important tool for spatial control. As a political consequence, it would determine the abandonment and subsequent razing of all areas outside the new defensive limits, erasing all built structures that could potentially favour enemy hideouts, skirmishes, and counterattacks.

Such was the practice undertaken in Azemmour. Immediately after the Portuguese conquest, the establishment of an *atalho* was a serious proposal on the table.[15] The reduction of the urban surface implied the reuse of several segments of the former Muslim walls but also of several civil and religious buildings, due the shortage of material and human resources.[16] There were divergent views among the conquerors of the effective characteristics of the downsizing. The debate dragged on for years, but finally, in 1517, the monarch enacted a statute to build the *atalho* wall. The *Regimento da obra do muro e atalho da cidade dezamor* [Statute of the wall's works and downsizing of the city of Azemmour] was approved in Lisbon[17] with such a detailed description that it can still be read in the remaining walled structures of the city. The materials used also respected the statute. The foundation was built with stone and mud, while most of the superposed curtain wall, including the battlements, was constructed of mud, a curious adoption by the Portuguese of techniques traditionally used in the Maghreb, though these were not obviously strange to them. The urban surface to be kept was the northern part of the old fortified perimeter as it was by the early-sixteenth century, where the former Islamic headquarters and a mosque must have stood, later transformed into

House of the Captains and church, respectively. In general, there was an interest in saving the sector closest to the sea, the major communication canal with the metropolis, which corresponds nowadays to the Kasbah/Mellah neighbourhood, approximately one-third of the original 9-hectare area of the conquered medina (Figure 1.3). The new wall had a linear design that started at the inflection point of the old Islamic wall (where the bastion of *São Cristóvão* [Saint Christopher] would be erected) and ran directly to the former mosque. Here it drew an elbow to the north, marked by the new town bastion/gate, running again straight up to the river, where it formed another bastion (bastion R). The curtain wall of the *atalho* was safeguarded by flanking fire from neighbouring military structures, and it was reinforced by a battered wall and an external ditch. In fact, the construction of the wall, reinforced by a strong talus, imposed a deep and strategic visual boundary between the protected Portuguese zone and the "excluded" section of the former medina called *vila velha* [old town]. Besides the *atalho* wall, one of the main priorities was the strengthening of defensible points and limits, adapting some of the pre-existing towers along the former Arab perimeter and reinforcing the walls with new bastions.[18]

The Portuguese endured inside the perimeter of the area defined by the *atalho* downsizing, especially its new or former inflections or corners. This area was from then on called *castelo* [castle], meaning that no separate military structure was erected, as was common in all the other Portuguese possessions in the Maghreb. An almost nonurbanized area before the Portuguese arrival, houses were to be erected there to accommodate new European settlers.

Simão Correia, captain since 1516, devised an intervention for an overall urban plan in Azemmour, organized on several fronts, with special focus on the internal disposition of the new walled area of the castle. The proposal became effective in a letter to King Manuel I (1495–1521), announcing the layout of paved streets for houses with good door sills and special care devoted to the town's cleansing and public health.[19] Such a proposal regulated the urban design, displaying a pioneering effort of early modern public space legislation. Moving away from the narrow street system that the Portuguese had observed in their Maghribi conquests, the new urbanism was more attentive to street layout, matching the Manueline tendency of the time.[20] Presumably, therefore, there were conditions for the establishment of a new town on almost empty ground or ground with just a few built constraints (Figure 1.4).

Overall, the *atalho* procedure, the new military structures, the adaptation of former Islamic ones, and the urban experiment were the result of the knowledge of their master builders, under the patronage of Captain Simão Correia. Contracts for Azemmour were adjudicated to the Portuguese brothers and master builders Diogo and Francisco de Arruda, who would have to work closely with the town captains.[21] The work carried out in the city (1513) and its neighbour Mazagão (1514), 15 kilometres to the south, and the previous presence of Diogo in Safi contributed to putting the brothers Arruda among the most relevant and key agents of the transition period in built environment as far as military architecture is concerned.

FIGURE 1.3   Plan of the walled city of Azemmour: 1. Kasbah/Mellah neighbourhood: 2. Medina neighbourhood; 3. Portuguese *atalho* wall; 4. *Vila* [town] bastion/gate; 5. *São Cristóvão* [Saint Christopher] bastion; 6. *Raio* [Thunderbolt] bastion; 7. Bastion N; 8. *Ribeira* [river] gate; 9. Bastion R; 10. River Oum er-Rbia.

N

0 10   50 m

FIGURE 1.4 Plan of the Kasbah/Mellah neighbourhood, with evidence of the Portuguese urban stratum.

Military architecture

Siblings Diogo and Francisco de Arruda were indeed the master builders who conducted a significant Manueline operation in Azemmour that can be described as the application of a transitional style of military architecture. Fortified structures reveal their knowledge about the newly developing architectural expertise in the use of pyroballistic, the calculation of gun ranges, and designs according rational geometry. Their work proposed a technological revolution, bridging an increasing refusal of the neuroballistic systems, still indexed to medieval battle strategies, and an irreversible use of pyroballistic techniques.

The two most important military structures designed by both Arruda were *São Cristóvão* [Saint Christopher] and *Raio* [Thunderbolt] bastions. They were considered to be the most robust elements of the defensive system and enough to protect the castle area once they had been appropriately equipped with large-calibre guns in their embrasures.[22] On the one hand, the circular bastion of *São Cristóvão* was built at the countryside edge of the *atalho* wall, attached to the House of the Captains with which it formed a political and military cluster. On the other hand, *Raio* bastion was an important reinforcement on the northwestern corner of the former Islamic contour. It was described by the town captain as being one of the most beautiful things in the world.[23]

São Cristóvão presents a cylindrical drum typology, with an internal 22-palm radius (4.84 m) and an external 31-palm radius (6.84 m),[24] and comprises three platforms for embrasures and a distinct topmost feature of balconies for vertical shot.[25] Due to its location and its peculiar round shape, so different from the other bastioned structures, this bastion is a unique example of Manueline architecture.[26] Such features position this bastion as an almost independent structure of the abutting walls on its northern and western sides, thus increasing its fire range due to its projection to the exterior. It is a solid and compact look that combines innovative elements of military strategy with atavistic decorative ones. In fact, above the two lower levels of gun embrasures, there is a series of quite large bays that introduce the idea of sculpting a sort of corbels all around,[27] meaning a wish to furnish the top of the bastion with a kind of machicolated battlement, yet not too protuberant. Originally, this bastion would have had rhythmic corbelled elements all around the bastion in a clearly retro vision intended to convey a message rather than to really sustain the notion of a "drop on the head" defensive mechanism[28] (Figure 1.5).

The Portuguese castle of Azemmour did not possess a donjon, and the location of *São Cristóvão* bastion would have worked as a substitute, standing at the crossroads of the *atalho* and the hinterland-approaching ways. There was no point in building high towers and donjons when a technological revolution based on gunpowder fire was taking place. Therefore, this bastion is not very tall and tries to articulate itself with the adjacent walls, making the Arruda brothers prominent agents of the early modernization of Portuguese military architecture, even if sticking to some aesthetic values seen before.[29] An archaeological reading of the wall surface indicates the radial distribution of the embrasures, similar to other bastions in Azemmour, allowing a comfortable area of fire coverage. The embrasures show a careful design, indicating that the Arruda brothers also aimed at aesthetics. Bays present a kind of flat, bell-shaped neck, wider in the interior and narrower towards the exterior, which clearly was the right way to design them. The embrasures would have had roundish vaulting as well,[30] and they were most likely to be closed by shutters on the inside. *São Cristóvão* still preserves elements that can be identified as fixings for that purpose.

The other distinguished military architectural element, *Raio* bastion, is considered one of the most relevant achievements of Manueline architecture,[31] and it is, indeed, a fundamental structure for the understanding of the transitional style of

FIGURE 1.5 *São Cristóvão* bastion.

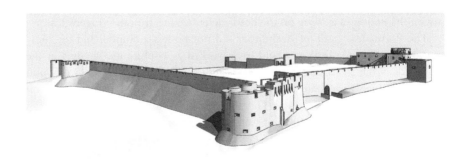

FIGURE 1.6 *Raio* bastion.

Portuguese military architecture. Like *São Cristóvão*, it represents the most avant-garde symbol of the use of artillery in the early sixteenth century, allying that capacity with a decorative language in an unknown and original combination.[32] For the *Raio* bastion, there is a detailed description regarding its highly developed fire capacity, able to dominate the whole surrounding city[33] (Figure 1.6). Indeed, this bastion is an imposing structure, the biggest and most remarkable bastion of those that punctuate the fortified Portuguese perimeter of Azemmour. It is formed by simple geometrical forms: two juxtaposed 45-palm (9.9 m) side squares – adapting a former Islamic tower – and a semicircle with the same diameter. The square module generates the height of the bastion and the beginning of a talus. Above it, the vertical faces of the bastion show a slight obliqueness, a rather disguised feature intended to add to its strength.[34] The elevations show multiple options: arrow slits on top and lower levels of rectangular gun embrasures,[35] especially active in the round section of the bastion, where they are organized alternately in two platforms of radial fire, thus contributing to complete coverage of the immediate hinterland. It also possesses the same kind of topmost feature as the *São Cristóvão*: a machico-lated battlement with an exuberant decorative effect. The same comments apply to this solution that actually digs holes in the surface at the top of the bastion rather than projecting corbels or consoles as a balcony.[36]

Given the locations of the *São Cristóvão* and *Raio* bastions, they were considered sufficient to ensure the city's protection, but there were other significant structures. To the west of *Raio*, the bastion that interrupts the northern curtain wall, here called bastion N,[37] is another imposing yet rather plain structure. It has a projected U-shaped volume over the ditch in a classical plan[38] and included a talus to deflect enemy fire.[39] It could have held several levels of fire through embrasures, as minor details and eroded marks on its sides still suggest, although the only remaining firing level is the upper platform. The distribution of slits and crenels is quite regular, alternating wider bays and loopholes with narrow necks for the protection of archers.[40]

Showing a similar plan, another bastion projected to the exterior at the river corner of the *atalho*, here called bastion R, was erected over a strong talus partially carved in the natural rock scarp. The gun embrasures would have mainly pointed at the river upstream direction and along the new *atalho* curtain wall, in a radial distribution commonly used in Azemmour. Although they are partially blocked today, it is possible to reconstruct their original shape; at the base of the bastion, the battered wall was the object of a thorough archaeological dig.[41] It presents a section formed by two superposed talus-shaped slopes, showing an obvious concern for oblique surfaces and the ricochet effect of possible enemy fire.

The *atalho* wall's intermediate zone, between bastion R and *São Cristóvão's* is worth mentioning too. Interrupted by a less exuberant rectangular bastion called *Vila*, it also worked as a gate, designed according to an elbow-shaped plan. This bastion/gate looked very much like a rectangular tower mass with the approximate height of the *atalho* wall in which it creates a serrated edge. It included embrasures that could shoot parallel to the walls and a wooden door that was backed by a sliding vertical grid protecting the castle entrance.[42] Another gate can be identified along the castle contour: the *Ribeira* [river] gate. Of smaller dimensions yet describing the same elbow-shaped passage as the *Vila* gate, it opens to the river and to the town through round arches, in a tunnelled and vaulted structure.

Complementing this strategy of newly built and up-to-date military architecture devices, the digging of a ditch was also started immediately after the conquest of

Azemmour. It was mainly carved out of the existing rock.[43] Today, the remains of the ditch do not show its original scale. Filled up on all sides to a considerable extent, it also disguises the depth of the battered wall which helped to form the ditch.

The town's defensive efficiency depended on the combination of the architectural display and its fire range. The castle of Azemmour acted as one cohesive structure. Embrasures and arrow slits allowed for the total coverage of the surroundings[44] (Figure 1.7). Fire could occur not only from bastions but also from walls, where different kinds of bays were positioned along the wall parapets. These long linear segments concentrated gun embrasures next to the bastions and loop windows elsewhere, for the use of bows and maybe crossbows. Altogether, the system would guarantee a completely inaccessible area at the bottom of the fortress, hence preventing mining and sabotage schemes.

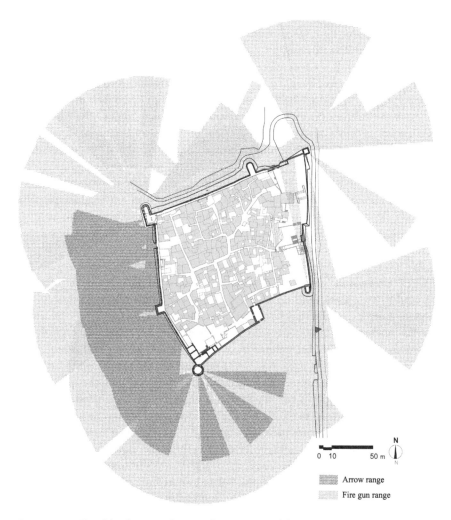

FIGURE 1.7 Combined gun and arrow fire capacity of the Portuguese castle.

Resilience versus revolution

Azemmour is both a cause and a product of the Portuguese project for Morocco. On the one hand, the territory in which the city played a fundamental role slowly became a fundamental part of an overseas expansion that would shift Portugal towards modernity. On the other hand, Azemmour was also part of a new paradigm for its architectural and urban dimensions. The area chosen for the Portuguese forces to gather was the top north of the ancient Islamic city, closer to the river's mouth, taking advantage of the pre-existing fence segments on the east, the north, and partially the west. The *atalho* cutting wall on the south side drew an imperfect quadrilateral shape which now constitutes the Kasbah/Mellah neighbourhood in present-day Azemmour, as mentioned earlier, roughly one-third of the area of the former medina. Urban conceptions joined rational and Cartesian geometries in its street display, clearly clashing with Muslim urban concepts.

Furthermore, military architecture built by the Portuguese after the 1513 conquest clearly shows experimental attempts to adapt itself to new gunpowder innovations even if profiting from former structures. Following the coeval avant-garde design of fortresses in Europe, the Moroccan project functioned as a laboratory for new construction. These cutting-edge experiences, conducted by master builders Diogo and Francisco de Arruda, clearly demonstrate the rejection of neuroballistic systems and the irreversible embracement of pyroballistic techniques, a technological revolution.[45] Moreover, they also attest to increasing cultural exchanges and the circulation of military knowledge in the first decades of the sixteenth century, not only within the Portuguese realm but also amid a network of artistic contacts that the commercial position of Portugal fostered in that period.

In fact, Diogo had previously been in contact with Francesco di Giorgio Martini and might have worked with him on the fortifications of Naples.[46] From the beginning, the architectural plans of the Italian master were careful to include new artillery apparatus, assigning it to a useful location for the defence of the fortification. For him, new establishments should take advantage of the natural conditions on-site, managing the role of each tower/bastion in a joint action. Actually, this showed the practical use of the principles of flanking and enfilading fire, noted in Francesco di Giorgio's *Tratatto di architettura ingegneria e arte militare*.[47]

In that same spirit, Diogo and Francisco de Arruda applied such knowledge in careful design for Azemmour, where bastions show a preference for circular shapes. Their forms and shapes seem to derive from the Arruda's own experiences in Portugal, with a certain degree of influence from the instructions gathered in the writings by Giorgio Martini. Notably, they used geometrical patterns in the design and building processes.[48] Indeed, the work of the younger of the Arruda brothers in the kingdom was known for his intervention on the fortified enclosures of Moura, Mourão, and Portel back in 1510,[49] while the elder, Diogo, had just arrived from Safi, where he had coordinated the reform of its defences in 1512.[50] Even though all these contracts involved new military structural devices, updates, or solutions for Azemmour, the work carried out also aligns them with Manueline style's more expressive decoration applied to military architecture. The examples of the Belém tower in Lisbon or the Evoramonte castle are among the finest to understand their position.[51]

In fact, beyond technological, urban, and military innovations, the Portuguese presence in the city was affirmed by a symbolic rhetoric that often surpassed the mere political occupation itself and embraced a spiritual appropriation of the land. The construction and renovation of the Azemmour city walls, which ultimately corresponded to a new frontier of faith and power, were also engaged in a clearly medieval performance towards the hinterland. There was a common belief among European monarchies that the image of a novel and modern fortification advertised the new ruler's power. The fortified system aimed at transmitting a sensation of full security, persuading populations in the hinterland to obey the new sovereign.[52] Non-functional and decorative crowning on top of bastions, adorned with hoisted flags, attests to a chivalrous imaginary that the Portuguese wanted to convey to the exterior (Figure 1.8). Inside the walls, the Portuguese nobility was at the service of such a city image. In fact, the Moroccan project also functioned as a sort of military school for youngsters training for members of the nobility. Azemmour worked as a perfect base to perpetrate looting on surrounding Muslim communities in the countryside. Raids over neighbouring villages enabled young nobles to acquire fame and profits.

Oscillating between latent and explicit hostility, the Portuguese monarch desired to show off bastions ornamented with flags bearing the royal arms and the cross of Christ. This festive vision of floating flags on the top of the fortified barrier confirmed and emphasized the Portuguese Crown's rights and claims over conquered territories in North Africa and, thus, its Christian crusader legitimacy to the Papacy.

Besides the machicolation battlements of *São Cristóvão* and *Raio* bastions mentioned earlier, there are still traces of small sculptures with Manueline decorations in those bastions, including corded and torso elements and half spheres. Those

FIGURE 1.8   3D models of the Portuguese castle showing hoisted flags and details of the flag pole.

elements were, in fact, bracings supporting a continuous and paced distribution of flags allusive to the king's arms or to Christianity.[53] Moreover, in the bastion/gate of *Vila*, the arched passage was also complemented by some sort of drapery or flags, held by stone devices that can still be seen next to the upper bays.

On the one hand, such display, combined with firing power, would have strengthened the morale of the Portuguese soldiers. On the other hand, it would also cast fear into potential enemies approaching from the countryside. The defenders were aware that the entire atmosphere created around the fortification, plus the image of authority that it could emanate, would be more powerful than the mere impregnability of the military structures alone.[54] Cannon shots were fired without a specific target, just to display the gun's power, an action that would send a clear message of a permanent and active defensive stance. From a strictly functional point of view, the radial firing platforms alone were enough to control the surrounding field. Therefore, the combination of the top ornamentation design and the flag decoration reveal the symbolic message that the Portuguese wished to send outside the walls.[55] Plus, King Manuel I employed different means of propaganda, from the time of the conquest preparation up to the final disclosure of the king's victory. Such is the case of the tragicomedy *Exhortation to War* written by the Portuguese court playwright Gil Vicente and performed in Lisbon before the king's departure on the campaign of Azemmour. In this play, the author set as the ultimate goal the taking of Fez and the consecration of its mosque as a cathedral.[56] Hence, the visual representations depicted along the top of Azemmour's bastions constitute the "in situ tangible material" which echoed political and literary discourses at the Portuguese court.

The symbolic meaning of the Portuguese appropriation of Azemmour went beyond. On the one hand, the mosque was consecrated as a church. Its internal layout was kept, the mihrab turned into a main altar, and the minaret adapted into a belfry. On the other hand, the new urban space sought a more identifiable city image than the one left at home. Azemmour's new town, established inside the *atalho*-selected surface, was thought as a town made by Portuguese for Portuguese, whose limits were circumscribed to the walled space, isolated from the countryside.

Final considerations

Despite all the installed military capacity and affirmation of a political project, the Portuguese leadership of Azemmour was short-lived, dismantled by the middle of the sixteenth century, as the Moroccan political space became unified. The sheriff of Sus's takeover of Santa Cruz do Cabo de Guer, today Agadir, in 1541 irreversibly shook the Portuguese programme for North Africa. Drastic decisions were taken then that involved the voluntary abandonment of three towns and a city. Azemmour was among them, and the withdrawal needed to be immediate. The evacuation of the city was a dramatic event because three decades of occupation had rooted some families, who had invested all their possessions in this enterprise. It was concluded between September and October 1541. The Jewish community was split between Moroccan towns, especially Tangier; Christian women and children were transferred to Portugal, leaving the men in the defence of neighbouring castle of Mazagão, which would become one of the strategic investments made to prevent the Portuguese Crown from completely giving up Morocco.

Earlier, this point of the Moroccan coast, some 15 kilometres south of Azemmour and possessing a generous harbour which formed a long bay, had been claimed by the Portuguese Crown since the beginning of the Portuguese establishment at the mouth of river Oum er-Rbia. Here brothers Diogo and Francisco de Arruda[57] composed a quadrangular plan with curtain walls linking four cylindrical towers, one of them a pre-existing watch tower. This castle is yet another example of the up-to-date military architecture built by the Portuguese at that time in Morocco and witnessed the use of experimental artillery just like the coeval bastions in the Azemmouri complex.

However, siltation in the river that had eventually caused Azemmour to be included in the list of the places to be abandoned in North Africa pushed the Portuguese to further invest in Mazagão. By 1541, the Portuguese decided to build a modern bastioned fortification around the primitive Manueline castle, with the foundation of a town in its interior, submitted to a grid project. The royal initiative was managed by a team of architects led by Benedetto da Ravenna, Diogo de Torralva, and Miguel de Arruda and put into practice in loco by João de Castilho.[58] For more than two and a half centuries, the inexpungable Mazagão remained in the hands of the Portuguese Crown. Until 1769, we saw the consolidation of this project: the fortified perimeter was defined by five big bastions, long inflected curtain walls, and a surrounding moat; in the centre, the former 1514-castle was transformed into administrative headquarters, housing a church, a hospital, store houses for cereals and munitions, a jail, and a huge water reservoir.

If Mazagão represents the climax of the military architecture revolution conducted by the Portuguese in the Maghreb, indeed the first European modern fortification in Africa to be erected, then its first stage, along with the Manueline interventions in Azemmour, represents the most important step towards it. The works carried out there consist of a laboratorial phase integrating more-powerful uses of artillery and belonging to an international move towards the use of bastioned typologies in defensive structures, a move led by Italy. The occupation of Azemmour happened at the same time as changes in taste and architectural needs were being revised by novel warfare technologies and early modern ideologies in Europe.

The rushed 1541 evacuation prevented Azemmour from evolving even further, just like what happened to its close neighbour. Following the Portuguese withdrawal, the medina would recover its pre-Portuguese configuration, and the present-day urban assemblage continues its expansion into the countryside. In this sense, Azemmour is an exceptional case, unlike the rest of Portuguese *atalho* operations that irreversibly changed the other conquered cities' image. Partly ruined, partly renewed, the Azemmouri military built heritage still attests to its central role in the transitional architectural style between the Late Middle Ages and the early modern period, within a broad regional laboratorial experience in the Maghreb, when Portugal's overseas empire was at the centre of science experimentation and diffusion of knowledge in the field.

Notes

1 For further details on this matter, see Jorge Correia, *Implantation de la ville portugaise en Afrique du Nord: de la prise de Ceuta jusqu'au milieu du XVIe siècle*. (Porto: FAUP publicações, 2008), 353–57.
2 *Villes et Tribus du Maroc* (Casablanca: Éditions Frontispice, 2002), 24–28.
3 Christophe Picard, *L'océan Atlantique musulman: De la conquête arabe à l'époque almohade. Navigation et mise en valeur des côtes d'al-Andalus et du Maghreb occidental (Portugal-Espagne-Maroc)* (Paris: Éditions Maisonneuve & Larose, 1997), 119–20, 156–57; 172–73; Christophe Picard, *La Mer et les musulmans d'Occident au Moyen Age, VIII–XIIII siècle* (Paris: Presses Universitaires de France, 1997), 75–96.
4 "It rules all from above. Its minarets and its towers watch the river, which ensures its wealth, as well as the neighbouring sea. Its stores are filled with everything to feed everyone. Its stocks are full with every sorts of meat. People are rich and clothe themselves from their labour. Houses are elegant. And shad is a fish like no other." Boutaleb Brahim, "Azemmour," in *Regard sur Azemmour* (Rabat: Marsam, 2008), 24.
5 This study belonged to a broader research project FCT PTDC/HAH/71027/2006 titled "Portugal e o Sul de Marrocos – Contactos e Confrontos, séculos XV–XVIII" [Portugal and Southern Morocco: Contacts and Clashes between the 15th and the 18th Centuries], whose main researcher was Maria Augusta Lima Cruz. It also followed the archaeological mission (coordinated by André Teixeira and Azzeddine Karra) and the architectural study on the Portuguese-Moroccan heritage in the region of Doukkala-Abda, established by a protocol between the University of Minho, CHAM of the Nova University at Lisbon, and the Direction du Patrimoine Culturel, Morocco, in 2008.
6 Azzeddine Karra and André Teixeira, "Fouilles archéologiques à Azemmour: Questions historiques et premières Constatations," in *Portugal e o Magrebe: IV Coloque d'Histoire Maroco-Lusitanienne (Proceedings)* (Lisbon and Braga: Centro de História de Além-Mar, Centro de Investigação Transdisciplinar 'Culturas, Espaço e Memória,' 2011), 177–90.
7 Maria Augusta Lima Cruz, "Os Portugueses em Azamor (1513–1541)" (BA diss., University of Lisbon, Lisbon, 1967), 18–21.
8 Damião Góis, *Crónica do Felicíssimo Rei D. Manuel*, vol. II (Coimbra: Imprensa da Universidade, 1949–1955), 91.
9 Maria Augusta Lima Cruz, "Du discours euphorique à la réalité: la conquête portugaise d'Azemmour," in *La Présence Portugaise au Maroc et les relations actuelles entre les deux pays* (Mohammadia: Anajah Al Yadidah, 2009), 45–54.
10 Ibid. The echoes of an atmosphere of patriotic and religious exaltation were noted in the *Cancioneiro Geral*, of Garcia de Resende, a printed collection of poems in 1516, three years after the capture of Azammūr. Among others, the ballads of Luis Henriques to the Duke of Braganza link the conquest of the Moroccan city to the future triumphal entrance of his sovereign in the Holy Land, in a clear conformity with the Manueline imperial ideology. Ibid; Luís Matos, "La Victoria contro Mori e le presa di Azimur," *Boletim Internacional de Bibliografia Luso-Brasileira* I, no. 2 (1960): 214–22.
11 Georg Braun, Frans Hogenberg, and Simon Novellanus, *Civitates Orbis Terrarum*, vol. I. (Cologne: Philippus Galleus, 1572).
12 See Cruz, "Os Portugueses em Azamor (1513–1541)."
13 Valentim Fernandes, *Description de la côte d'Afrique de Ceuta au Sénegal par Valentim Fernandes (1506/1507)*, trans. Pierre de Cénival (Paris: Librairie Larose, 1938), 28.
14 Correia, *Implantation de la ville portugaise en Afrique du Nord*, 353–57.

15 Letter from King Manuel I to Dom João Meneses, 5 January 1514 (Pierre Cénival, ed., *Les Sources Inédites de l'Histoire du Maroc: Première Série – Dynastie Sa'dienne* [Paris: Paul Geuthner, 1934], 478). Being the last important conquest in Morocco, it beneficiated from the experience acquired from Ceuta to Safi for almost a century.
16 Correia, *Implantation de la ville portugaise en Afrique du Nord*, 294–303.
17 Maria Augusta Lima Cruz, *Documentos Inéditos para a História dos Portugueses em Azamor*, vol. II (Lisbon: Arquivos do Centro Cultural Português, 1970), 147–8.
18 Robert Ricard, "Sur la chronologie des fortifications portugaise d'Azammūr, Maza-gan et Safi," in *Congresso do Mundo Português*, vol. 3 (Lisbon: Comissão Executiva dos Centenários, 1940), 108. Although called bastions in this chapter, a direct translation of Portuguese *baluartes*, they were mostly gun towers rather than modern and fully artillery structures. See Martin Elb, "Portuguese Urban Fortifications in Morocco," in *The Urban Enceinte in Global Perspective*, ed. James D. Tracy (Cambridge: Cambridge University Press, 2000), 371.
19 Letter from Rui Barreto to King Manuel I, 1 April 1514 (Cénival, *Les Sources*, 538).
20 Correia, *Implantation de la ville portugaise en Afrique du Nord*, 305–6.
21 Francisco Sousa Viterbo, *Dicionário Histórico e Documental dos Arquitectos, Engenheiros e Construtores Portugueses*, fac-simile of 1899–1922 ed., vol. 1 (Lisbon: Imprensa Nacional, Casa da Moeda, 1988), 46–65.
22 Letter from Rui Barreto to King Manuel I, 21 February 1514 (Cénival, *Les Sources*, 489–501).
23 "hũa das formosas peças que no mundo pode ser." Letter from Nuno Gato to King Manuel I, 31 March 1514 (Cénival, *Les Sources*, 531).
24 In this chapter, we translate as "palm" the ancient Portuguese measure of *palmo* (22 centimetres), which corresponded to the width of a man's spread fingers (Rui Maneira Cunha, *As medidas na arquitectura, séculos XIII–XVIII. O estudo de Monsaraz* (Casal de Cambra: Caleidoscópio, 2003), 76).
25 Letter from Nuno Gato to King Manuel I, 31 March 1514 (Cénival, *Les Sources*, 530–3).
26 Rafael Moreira, *História das Fortificações Portuguesas no Mundo* (Lisbon: Alfa, 1989), 132.
27 "huas sacadas como quaes todo a rroda." Letter from Rui Barreto to King Manuel I, 21 February 1514 (Cénival, *Les Sources*, 489–501).
28 John Rigby Hale, *Renaissance Fortification: Art or Engineering?* (London: Thames and Hudson, 1979), 12.
29 Moreira, *História das Fortificações Portuguesas no Mundo*, 132.
30 Pedro de Alboim Inglez Cid, *A Torre de S. Sebastião da Caparica e a arquitectura militar do tempo de D. João II* (Lisbon: Edições Colibri, 2007), 225.
31 Moreira, *História das Fortificações Portuguesas no Mundo*, 130–1.
32 Ana Lopes, "(A)cerca de Azamor: Estruturas militares ao manuelino" (MA diss., University of Minho, Braga, 2009), 85, 125.
33 "que sujeita toda a cidade" [dominating the entire city]; "uma vista que não possa nin-guém chegar ao pé do baluarte" [a view that prevents anyone from getting closer to the bastion]. Letter from Nuno Gato to King Manuel I, 31 March 1514 (Cénival, *Les Sources*, 531).
34 This strategy can also be observed in several of Francesco di Giorgio Martini's draw-ings (Francesco di Giorgio Martini, *Tratatto di architettura ingegneria e arte militare* (Milan: Edizioni il Polifilo, 1967); Barbara Nazzaro and Guglielmo Villa, *Francesco di Giorgio Martini: Rocche, Città, Paesaggi* (Rome: Edizione Karpa, 2004).
35 This type of embrasure elevation, "*de vanguarda do ponto de vista militar*" [a vanguard work for military purposes] can also be spotted in other Portuguese fortresses, such as Portel and Belém Tower (Moreira, *História das Fortificações Portuguesas no Mundo*, 135).
36 One can observe one previous application of this feature in Porto de Mós castle, in a way that may have inspired the Arruda brothers, but it has not the exact same conformation.

The bottom of Belém Tower's *échauguettes* has the same kind of miniature corbels (Moreira, *História das Fortificações Portuguesas no Mundo*, 131). In that sense, the drawings by Francesco di Giorgio Martini delineate a topping for fortifications similar to that at Porto de Mós. It is not a machicolated battlement but an evolution of this feature with a similar function. However, they merge with the body of the bastion (Martini, *Tratatto di architettura ingegneria e arte militare*; Nazzaro and Villa, *Francesco di Giorgio Martini*), as observed in the *retardataire* tower at Mondavio, for example. These bays existed in the original tower of Mazagão castle (Torre da Boreja) too, also a work by the Arruda brothers built in 1514 (Correia, *Implantation de la ville portugaise en Afrique du Nord*, 363).

37 Due to the lack of original Portuguese names, letters were attributed to such notable structures.

38 Correia, *Implantation de la ville portugaise en Afrique du Nord*, 363.

39 Here the angle is 42 degrees, very much closer to the range between 45 degrees and 60 degrees, the appropriate assortment (Luís Mora-Figueroa, "Transformações artilheiras na fortificação tardo-medieval," in *Simpósio Internacional sobre Castelos*, ed. Isabel Cristina Ferreira Fernandes (Lisbon: Colibri, 2001), 651).

40 This kind of deep chamfer allowed the shooter to be protected while enabling them to get closer to the outer face of the wall. This configuration was an evolution from arrow slits to gun loops, and eventually, it led to more-developed splayed necks and the full design of a gun embrasure (Cid, *A Torre de S. Sebastião da Caparica*, 205).

41 See note 5.

42 This kind of door display was well known by the Portuguese, who had already developed this sort of knowledge during the Christian Reconquest. The space between the grid lock and the wooden door could be used to trap enemies.

43 The works were suspended just four months after their start, due to the difficulty of the task, especially on the northern side (Letters from Nuno Gato [5 December 1513], Francisco and Diogo de Arruda [31 March 1514], and again Nuno Gato [31 March 1514] to King Manuel I (Cénival, *Les Sources*, 455, 527, 531, respectively). It was eventually finished two years later (the letter from Vicente Rodrigues Evangelho to King João III, 10 April 1530 [Cénival, *Les Sources*, 511], refers to the existence of a ditch next to the House of the Captains).

44 Lopes, "(A)cerca de Azamor," 167–73.

45 Hale, *Renaissance Fortification*, 12.

46 Moreira, *História das Fortificações Portuguesas no Mundo*, 106–7.

47 Martini, *Tratatto di architettura ingegneria e arte militare*.

48 Luís Costa e Sousa, *A arte na Guerra: A arquitectura dos campos de batalha no Portugal de Quinhentos* (Lisbon: Tribuna da História, 2008), 95; Cid, *A Torre de S. Sebastião da Caparica*, 284–5.

49 Viterbo, *Dicionário Histórico e Documental*, vol. I, 55–59.

50 *Livro desbaratado do almoxarife de Safim Lourenço Mendes em que se carregou a despeza que fez com as obras da d.ª cid. no anno de 1512* [Book by Safi's ware keeper Lourenço Marques regarding the city works in 1512]. Arquivo Nacional da Torre do Tombo (Lisbon), *Núcleo Antigo*, no. 768, fls. 55–9v.

51 Moreira, *História das Fortificações Portuguesas no Mundo*, 130–1.

52 David Parrott, "The Utility of Fortifications in Early Modern Europe: Italian Princes and Their Citadels, 1540–1640," *War in History* 7, no. 2 (2000): 148.

53 Moreira, *História das Fortificações Portuguesas no Mundo*, 132.

54 Parrot, "The Utility of Fortifications," 133, 139.

55 Hale, *Renaissance Fortification*, 38.

56 Cruz, "Du discours euphorique à la réalité," 45–54.

57 *Letter from Francisco de Diogo de Arruda to King Manuel I* – Azamor, 31 March 1514. Arquivo Nacional da Torre do Tombo (Lisbon), *Corpo Cronológico*, 1ª parte, m. 15, n° 14.

58 *Letter from Luis de Loureiro to João III* – Mazagão, 25 August 1541. Arquivo Nacional da Torre do Tombo (Lisbon), *Corpo Cronológico*, 1ª parte, m. 70, n° 75.

2

EARLY MODERN FORTIFICATION

The Portuguese experience and engineer education[1]

Margarida Tavares da Conceição
and Renata Malcher de Araujo

Introduction

The general question that this book poses, about whether we can apply the concept of military revolution to Portugal and its empire during the early modern period, is not easy to answer. The question may not have a direct or single answer.

This chapter reflects on the extent to which the transformations, which took place in early modern fortification, had an impact on Portugal. The question contains an apparent paradox. On the one hand, the presence of early modern fortifications within the framework of the Portuguese Empire is undeniable – as is the role attributed to these structures, both from a strictly military point of view and from a symbolic point of view. On the other hand, this coexists with a background reading which places Portugal in a peripheral position in the context of the major transformations which took place in this field throughout the early modern period.

This text argues that within the area of fortification, the Portuguese were undoubtedly modern. They would even have participated in the initial steps which led to this modernity, and in this sense, they can be rightly associated them with the revolutionary process of change. The text follows the successive phases in which the measures taken by the Portuguese Crown aimed above all to guarantee continuous aggiornamento and to achieve critical mass in this matter. That process was consolidated after the Restoration, in 1640, but it started before that.

In this regard, two parallel ways have to be considered. One implies an attempt to obtain discursive autonomy, which was immediately shown in the choice of the titles of the main treatises produced in the seventeenth and eighteenth centuries, which deliberately invoked the Portuguese point of view: the *Método Lusitânico* (*Lusitanian Method* – 1680) of Luís Serrão Pimentel and *O Engenheiro Português* (*The Portuguese Engineer*) of Manuel de Azevedo Fortes (1728–9). The other attempts to reconcile this theoretical-methodological investment with the expanded training of engineers, to meet the continuous needs in the different areas of the empire. The "classes (*aulas*)" set up in different locations, in the metropolis and in the empire, were the solutions for this process. This choice has to be taken into account in more than one aspect. The main argument of this chapter is that the education of Portuguese engineers played a major role in the Portuguese Crown's strategy, and such an argument should be read in the context of the Military Revolution.

The debate about the Military Revolution and fortification

Geoffrey Parker identified what he called the *trace italienne* as a significant part of the Military Revolution, recognizing that the emergence of new fortification techniques was one of the most important changes in the ways of waging war.[2] The picture described by Parker, and by many others authors, made the perimeter defended through pentagonal bulwarks synonymous with early modern fortification.[3]

Although the notion of the modernity of fortification concentrated on the invention of the angular bastion, the formation of so-called bastioned architecture was happening as a process, and its perception as a new typology was visible only in the 1530s and 1540s in Europe. Recent studies[4] have demonstrated that even if the precedence and influence of Italian experiences is inescapable,[5] the coexistence of important contributions, both in the Flemish area and in the territories under Iberian dominance, must be considered.

This type of fortification is early modern not only because it is a new response to the violent impact of a technology which was constantly being updated but also because of its conceptualization. Indeed, the bastioned polygon is essentially a proportional geometric system, and its design implies a knowledge of arithmetic and geometry, through requiring the ability to calculate and design beforehand. Drawing, as an idea and as a tool for experimentation and visualization, forms the methodological (mathematical) basis of architectural culture and underlies the sense of design in modernity, which is common to engineering, architecture, and the visual arts. This geometric matrix transformed the bastion of an empirical or experimental conception (whatever its shape) into a significant part of a fortification system. Both the technical reality and the conceptual question of bastioned fortification were linked to the performance and training of new stakeholders – that is, the engineers.

Since the pioneering works of Rafael Moreira,[6] Portuguese military engineering has been increasingly studied. The overall views usually point to the successive aggiornamento to European novelties, identifying the primacy of Italian influence in the sixteenth century, followed by Flemish-Dutch development and French maturation in the seventeenth and eighteenth centuries. Although this is overall correct, and consensual even, this picture does not, however, do justice to the process – in particular because at this juncture, Portugal's role cannot be measured in terms of mere receptivity, but necessarily of trialling, especially in the broad geographical framework of the empire.[7]

Experimenting and circulating on the scale of an empire (1540–1640)

In the European world, until the 1530s, circular section bastions were the most used, because they had the most effective response against the impact of gunpowder artillery, despite experiences with polygonal structures. It was exactly this panorama, which was made known in Portugal through the drawings of Francisco de Holanda, which attested to the experimental period of early modern fortification,[8] where the *rocca* predominated with bastions that had a tapered section each.

It is important to have this information in order to understand the context of the start-up of the first fortified site with angular bastions built by the Portuguese Crown, namely the city fortress of Mazagão (present-day El Jadida, Morocco). The process started in April 1541, and the perimeter was closed in December 1542. The work involved the main Portuguese construction masters (Miguel de Arruda, João de Castilho, and Diogo de Torralva), who joined with an Italian engineer (Benedetto da Ravenna), about whom the word engineer was used for the first time in the Portuguese language.[9] Significant here was not only the arrival of the Italian technician who introduced a new solution (somehow feeding the idea of a "revolutionary" moment) but also how the collaboration with the Portuguese protagonists took place. The written documentation among those involved in the Mazagão process is illuminating and allows us to capture the moment of convergence, rarely so deeply documented, which embodied the technical turning point in the 1540s.[10]

Modern Portuguese bastioned fortification thus began outside Portugal. Following this process, two aspects deserve to be emphasized: the recognition of the sufficiency demonstrated by Miguel de Arruda in acquiring new knowledge and the dissemination of new fortifications in the Portuguese positions in four continents, proving the ability to recreate the learning obtained from Mazagão.

Indeed, in this sequence, Miguel de Arruda was in 1543 appointed master of the works of the king and in 1548 master of the fortification works of the kingdom and places beyond,[11] this new position marking specialization and wide-ranging geographical scope. He was not mentioned as an architect or engineer, even though he acted as such.[12]

Meanwhile, important geographically distant construction sites – Ceuta,[13] Diu,[14] Mozambique,[15] Salvador in Bahia,[16] São Julião da Barra (in the River Tagus),[17] and Lagos[18] in Portugal – have in common the reference and outlines sent by (or attributable to) Miguel de Arruda, although mention of this always appears associated with other protagonists (decision makers, the military, masters of works, and master fortifiers), reflecting the ambiguity and density of architectural production methods, which crosses oceans.

In the Portuguese world and in just over a decade, the fortification landscape had changed a lot in terms of the design and actual production of fortifications. In these two decades of activity by Miguel de Arruda (who died in 1563), an imperial logic can be observed, in which the founding of the city of Salvador was a cornerstone, despite of the vicissitudes of the walled belt, which was never definitively built. While the angular bastion model is common to all these sites, the testing of the fortified urban model was formalized only in Mazagão.

As regards the next cycle, corresponding to the reign of King Sebastião (1557– 78), there is common agreement in the identification of the tendency for substantial investment in military matters.[19] However, even in the Sebastian period, a clear transition towards strengthening the hiring of foreign technicians can be identified, despite the detection of continuous activity by Portuguese masters of works. We know that after Arruda's death, the position of master of the fortification works was successively occupied.[20] As for the importation of human resources, this was a clear general trend, with Italian engineers working in the most varied parts of the world, from Flanders or Sweden to the West Indies or the Indian Ocean. The Austrians had considerable ability to attract foreign technicians, who circulated throughout the imperial area. The list of those who worked in Portugal is long but the details of their works are not always well known.[21] However, the participation of Portuguese technicians indicates learning and exchange processes that have yet to be identified.

Two long-standing institutions linked to education, with roots from the sixteenth century, deserve a reference in this respect. One of them is the (historiographically) called *Aula do Paço* or *Aula de Riscar* (*Drawing Class*) organized around 1594, the master of which was also the Italian Filippo Terzi (hired during the reign of King Sebastião) and which consisted, according to several documents, of "three positions for the learning of architecture." Given this, the architectural treatise taught by Mateus do Couto the Elder,[22] although it does not go into detail on fortification, was one of the references where military architecture would be included in this hub restricted to the training of royal architects, some of whom carried out duties on military works.

Two aspects still need to be underlined: the designation *architect* became official, tending to become generalized, and apprentices were required to attend the "geometry class" of the head cosmographer (the starting of which dated back to the middle of the sixteenth century).[23] Given this, at least two names show us the importance of this training. First, Francisco Frias de Mesquita who was in 1598 an architecture apprentice and was afterwards referenced as the chief engineer of Brazil.[24] Another character who showed the continuity of that process and who was assigned responsibility for the fortifications of Brazil, was Diogo Pais, who in 1624 was also one of the architecture apprentices and who in 1629 left for Brazil, as a "military engineer,"[25] this being one of the first times that this professional qualification was applied to a Portuguese professional, as pointed out by Moreira.[26]

The second important institution in these areas was the *Aula da Esfera* (Sphere Class) at the *Santo Antão* College in Lisbon, which the Jesuits had been running since the 1590s as a scholastic institution in the true sense of the word. There, cosmography and associated mathematics were studied, within which the first books on fortification were identified, thus documenting the inclusion of this topic in formal learning networks.[27] Since the Jesuits are inherently a transnational institution, its contribution to fortification[28] must urgently be researched in more detail – in addition to the training issue. Some of these circumstances have been identified, with priests who knew the profession and art of fortification that have acted both in India[29] and Brazil.[30]

Rebuilding the frontier and training engineers: the *Lusitanian Method* (1640–1700)

With regard to early modern fortification in the Portuguese (metropolitan) context, no other event had an experience comparable to the cycle of the Portuguese Restoration War or Acclamation War (1640–68), by requiring the immediate reactivation of the continental and maritime borders. However, this cycle must also be understood within the European dilemma – that is, the Eighty Years' War or Dutch War of Independence (1568–1648) and the Thirty Years' War (1618–48) – involving the Habsburgs on several fronts and must take into account the preponderance which had meanwhile been acquired by Dutch and French fortification. On the main aspects of the understanding of this period, studies by Rafael Moreira remain a reference.[31]

In addition to the colonial territories under dispute and the defensive reinforcement of the main port entrances, the urgency began by focusing on the almost complete reorganization and renovation of the military facilities along the Portuguese border, which had not undergone any update since the beginning of the sixteenth century. This process was rooted in certain political and administrative conditions, which must not be lost sight of, such as the setting up of the Council of War, which made a more effective centralization of decision-making possible, at the same time as other dependent institutions ensured the management of various sectors. From a technical perspective, the success of this undertaking involved three main aspects, in sequence: the immediate recourse to the mathematical Jesuit priests, the hiring of (mostly) French engineers, and the training of Portuguese engineers, inevitably causing a greater intensity of international exchanges.

The immediate need for specialized human resources was ensured by the actions of Jan Ciermans (a Flemish individual known as João Cosmander). He was a mathematician at the *Santo Antão* College in Lisbon, where he arrived with his background of mathematical work linked to the teaching he had previously undertaken in Leuven, which included civil and military architecture.[32] He was the one who outlined the first proposals for Lisbon and Setúbal, but his activity ended up focusing on Alentejan garrisons.[33]

The list of contracts on the metropolitan border, between 1641 and 1644, showed the significant predominance of the French *ingénieurs du roy*, perhaps due to reasons involving a strategic alliance. We will not mention all those involved, but only those with the most relevant profiles from the point of view of this chapter: Charles Lassart, a veteran who was said to have come to serve as the chief engineer[34]; Jean Gilot, a disciple of Descartes and who studied in Leiden and was present at the fortification works for Lisbon, Setúbal, and the Alentejo but who disappeared early on;[35] and Michel de Lescol, who undertook considerable work in the province of Minho, where he settled.[36]

The various problems caused by the hiring of foreigners have been seen as the driving force for the response concerning the training of Portuguese engineers – Portuguese historiography having always underlined the setting up of the Fortification Class (*Aula de Fortificação*) in Lisbon, where it has been common to identify a specialized school hub. Its operation started from 1647, led by Luís Serrão Pimentel, who had been in the service of the Crown since 1641.[37] He almost certainly attended the Sphere Class of the Jesuits. Due to his duties as the interim chief cosmographer, he was inherently responsible for the mathematics class for seafarers, and the architecture apprentices were obliged to attend. Thus, Pimentel did not start this class as an engineer, but in affinity with the Jesuit school culture and nautical teaching, it was through the teaching of mathematics and as a cosmographer, that Pimentel introduced the classes involving fortification, castrametation, attack, and defence, just as had been the case in the Sphere Class.

Luís Serrão Pimentel became an engineer, with practical activity in the Alentejo. However, he stood out above all for his scientific work and as a teacher, "graduating engineers who are currently serving Your Majesty from the class," as was attested in 1657.[38] Despite the lengthy process, Pimentel was finally designated chief engineer (1671) and marked a generation of professionals who, from this cycle on, started to be explicitly referred to in documentation of the period as engineers. Pimentel, among other written materials,[39] produced the first published Portuguese treatise on fortification (albeit late and posthumously, in 1680), the title of which is revealing of its purpose: *Lusitanian Method of Designing Regular and Irregular Fortifications.*[40]

This contribution naturally raises the issue of the changes which took place in the design of fortifications. The Portuguese cycle, which started in 1640, had to deal with the obvious problem of updating early modern fortifications which, despite the constancy of their basic assumptions, had changed in half a century, especially in response to tactical and technical changes. However, the change that is easiest to recognize refers to the primacy of so-called outworks, some of which had already been invented but the use of which had become widespread. Such a development made military architecture even more expensive and complex. As Pimentel showed, an already vast corpus of treatises and manuals constituted abundant study material on what the most appropriate proportional design for each of the (many) elements of the fortification should be, generating (well-known) endless academic speculation.

At the same time, the idea of national schools or methods was developed, more ideologically than technically, which in reality (theoretical and practically) intersected in a considerable manner, as the early modern engineer shared identical design principles:[41] the ability to design a well-proportioned polygonal perimeter, specifying an appropriate dimensioning of the sides (and therefore of the distance between bastions) according to the shooting range and the desired lines of defence. Thus, one of the main aspects of the discussion involved choosing the position of the perimeter line from which the lines for drawing the bastion were taken, thereby generating variations in a chain.

On this level of dispute, Pimentel wrote his work – studying and collecting aspects from here and there, in the theory of the foreigner books and in the practice, which he also followed closely, in a truly international work environment. He was indebted to Flemish and Dutch authors (like all French authors in the 1640s). He adopted Antoine de Ville's "new" proposals for the design of flanks and the determination of the flanked angle. From Pagan (whose book he summarized and translated, placing it in an appendix to the *Lusitanian Method*), and despite some criticisms, he sought primarily the principle of simplifying design.[42]

However, from Dutch authors (Stevin and Marolois), he used the decimal system and calculation tables to determine angles and other proportional measurements. In a certain sense, Pimentel documented a moment of transition in geometry, taking into account the growing mathematical design in fortification, which was exactly the assumption that would gradually move design (by drawing) from the architect to design (through calculation) from the engineer. The *Lusitanian Method* as a treatise printed in Europe can be understood as not being innovative, particularly because it was late with regard to its publishing. However, such assessment has to be measured by Pimentel's previous activity, on the basis of the apostilles written by his followers and by the magisterium that the book effectively exercised through its reach throughout the empire.

The fortification class operated regularly in Ribeira das Naus, permanently offering (at least since 1693) ten positions for students or apprentices assigned to the engineering service.[43] Studies currently available do not yet allow us to unequivocally clarify some aspects of the functioning of the class. On the other hand, we assume that shortly afterwards there was a rapid spread of the *Lusitanian Method*, through other classes. Elvas was the first city to experience a royal fortification class instituted by the crown prince in 1651, taking advantage of the resources of the city's Jesuit college and the active presence of Cosmander.[44] In 1666, the intention to create a fortification class in Estremoz was documented, and it was even expected that Pimentel would teach there. The Viana nucleus was also noteworthy, where the French engineer Michel de Lescol started to instruct his aides early on.[45] This class later included the activity of Manuel Pinto Vilalobos[46] and continued in the eighteenth century with his son.[47]

A similar process was recognized in other cities. In 1686, Jerónimo Velho de Azevedo, who had been examined at the Lisbon Fortification Class in 1661,[48] was authorized by a royal licence to "to teach through a school" in Almeida and Penamacor.[49] In Almeida, the class continued with António Velho de Azevedo, who began to operate as his father's assistant. In fact, a hereditary succession in the teaching of fortification had also occurred in Ribeira das Naus, when Francisco Pimentel replaced his father, Luís Serrão Pimentel, who died in 1679. Significantly, the post of chief cosmographer was reserved for the other son, Manuel Pimentel, showing an (almost) definitive distancing between fortification teaching and nautical teaching.

In fact, during the reign of King Pedro II (1683–1706, but also regent since 1668), there was an interest in creating a network of teaching cells, which became operational after the appointment of engineers for the different areas of the empire. A set of royal letters issued at the end of his reign (between 1699 and 1705), all of similar content, determined that wherever there was a capable engineer, that person was obliged to teach people who wanted to learn.[50] At this same juncture, a decree in 1701 made official those classes that were in operation in the kingdom (Elvas, Viana, and Almeida).[51]

In Brazil, the royal letters went to the governors of Bahia, Pernambuco, Maranhão, and Rio de Janeiro and in all cases resulted in initiatives, which, however, had different levels of continuity. Similar orders were sent to the governors of Angola and Goa,[52] apparently without immediate results.

In Bahia, classes began as determined by the governor, in 1696, even before the royal charter of 1699, and continued until at least the end of the eighteenth century. In São Luís do Maranhão, Pedro de Azevedo Carneiro was appointed to teach in 1699.[53] In Recife, one can also identify the beginning of a class in 1701, with Pedro Correia Rebelo (1701–3) followed by Luís Francisco Pimentel (1703–7), grandson of Luís Serrão Pimentel. In Rio de Janeiro, some doubts remained regarding the effective installation of the school determined by the royal letter of 1699. Gregório Gomes Henriques provided a class since 1698, but there were a number of vicissitudes which prevented him from continuing. José Velho de Azevedo was appointed as his replacement, yet another son of Jerónimo, therefore son and brother of the teachers in Almeida, but he did not come from Pará, where he had been since 1693.[54]

The aim was to create a sustainable network of knowledge transmission, distributed throughout the empire. That was justified by the speed of immediate replacement of agents in loco, but it also had much greater reach, especially in the training adjusted to the constraints regarding effective action on the ground. The gradual consolidation of a flexible network of fortification classes became a pragmatic and effective process of the decentralization of knowledge, which was, in it, particularly important.

Educating by geometry: *The Portuguese Engineer* (1700–1800)

After the death of Serrão Pimentel in 1679, the continuity of the school was ensured not only by his son Francisco Pimentel but also by another key figure, namely Manuel de Azevedo Fortes.[55] After foreign academic training (Alcalá, Paris) and consequent contact with the European scientific vanguard, he had been the substitute director of the mathematics chair (from the Ribeira das Naus Class) since 1695,[56] when Francisco Pimentel (who passed away in 1706) was still the holder of that post.

Therefore, the beginning of Fortes's activity in the service of the Crown also coincided with the creation of fortification schools, somehow mixing with the continuance of teaching on the basis of the *Lusitanian Method* and the desire to introduce other requirements. His well-known professional curriculum shows that his training as a military engineer was Portuguese and took place largely in the traditional field of practical experience. Between the death of chief engineer Serrão Pimentel and the appointment of Manuel de Azevedo Fortes to the same position, in 1719, four decades of vacancy elapsed, showing the difficulties in consolidating the class within a true academy, which was a target of constant criticism by Fortes.

After his appointment to the highest position in military engineering, his theoretical work began to be published, with which he sought to globally reorganize the teaching of military engineering. In 1720, he published *Representation to His Majesty on the form and direction that Engineers must have*,[57] in which he argued for the expansion of specialized education as one of the first reforms to be undertaken. He argued mainly for the utility not only of the engineering profession but also of the training for engineers, as an educational process, which, in his view, was essential for all officers.[58] The two volumes of the compendium for the training of engineers date from 1728 and 1729, under the significant title *The Portuguese Engineer*.[59]

The first volume was dedicated to the practice of geometry and the second dealt with fortification itself. In the first place, in comparison with the *Lusitanian Method*, the reversed role given to geometry is obvious, which was how the manual began. There he extensively developed the methodological procedures indispensable to professional practice, including a systematization of the language of drawing and the practice of planimetric and topographic surveys, which had previously been the subject of his attention. In 1722, he published the *Treatise of the Easiest Way and the most accurate way of making Geographical Charts*,[60] a book that remained widely used in the second half of the eighteenth century, when in fact its guidelines began to bear fruit.

The second volume was explicitly intended to supplement the outdated manual of Pimentel, especially incorporating the contributions of Vauban and his disseminators, showing guidelines which can be detected at the same time in the French school. This work underwent a systematic critique of the generalized tendency of each author (and each nation) to present its own original method of fortification:

> Many Authors of this past century proposed methods, which they stated were their own invention, and with little change were imitations of other more ancient Authors; and so it should be, because this Art was perfected with experience, and military observations, and the same Monsieur Vauban, the Oracle of our times, did not fail to imitate the former Italian Engineers.[61]

When going through the issue of design in detail, *Outlining the Body of the Fortress, and Outworks* (book 4), he built a synthesis of the methods in terms of effective design. This synthesis was seen not as a search for a new theory but rather as increasing the adjustment to the best theoretical rules and their applicability. It was instead a purely technical discourse, which emphasized the requirement to calculate in engineering design, as a distinctive professional feature of amateurism.

To examine step by step the implications of "delineating" all the components of the fortified enclosure, including the outworks, the engineer is required to operate mathematically and not be limited to applying repetitive working formulas. The simplicity of the presentation of the scientific method did not result in expeditious simplification.

The Portuguese Engineer was both the result of and the engine for the reform in the school structure of military engineers, an institutional reform that was mainly pedagogical. In 1732, the efforts of Azevedo Fortes resulted in the wording of a royal decree institutionalizing – in addition to the royal academy in Lisbon and that of Viana – two academies in Almeida and Elvas (thus renovating the anterior classes). The decree determined that the doctrine would apply "uniform in all the Academies, in the apostilles to be dictated."[62] The requirements mentioned in this 1732 decree, like the previous one in 1701, influenced by the presence of Azevedo Fortes in the Fortification Class, were repeatedly mentioned in their texts, testifying to a desire for reform, which was at least partially achieved.

Under his management, the classes in Brazil were also renovated.[63] In the classes in Bahia and Recife, we can identify the first trainers with direct link to the Lisbon Fortification Class, followed by others who had already done their training in Brazil. Among twenty names, which had already been identified as trainers in these classes, two names are worthy of a special mention. First, José António Caldas, who graduated from the Bahia school, played an important role through his teaching.[64] A series of pedagogical drawings is known that were made by students of the school while he was in charge, which included theoretical references to Vauban and Bélidor.[65] Second, Diogo da Silveira Veloso (1720–50), in Recife, wrote a fortification treatise, which shows not only the continuous circulation of texts of diverse origin in the various training locations but also the role played by the treatises already published in Portuguese, namely those of Pimentel and Azevedo Fortes, widely cited in his book.[66]

The beginning of continuous training in Rio de Janeiro can be dated from the royal letter 19 August 1738, which determined that a class should be established in the recently created third artillery troop, naming José Fernandes Pinto Alpoim the master and setting up a five-year course. The main focus of the lessons was artillery, but fortification matters were also mandated. This was guaranteed by the training of Alpoim, which was carried out in the kingdom, initially at the Viana Class, together with his uncle Manuel Pinto de Vilalobos, and it continued at the Lisbon Fortification Class, with Manuel de Azevedo Fortes. Alpoim published *Examination of Artillerymen* in 1744[67] and *Examination of Firemen* in 1748,[68] treatises which summarized subjects taught in the school. Eusébio António de Ribeiro (1768–74) and António Joaquim de Oliveira (1774–95) succeeded him in the School of the Third Artillery Troop, which in 1792 was reformed and renamed the Royal Academy of Artillery, Fortification and Design and which António Joaquim de Oliveira continued to head. The Royal Academy of Artillery, Fortification and Design in Rio de Janeiro functioned until the setting up of the Royal Military Academy (1810), which replaced it and ensured its continuity.

In the state of Maranhão and Grão Pará, there are no reliable data on the continuity of training during the first half of the eighteenth century. Training, however,
resumed in 1757, in Belém, with the engineer Manuel Álvares Calheiros appointed
as master of the class by Governor Francisco Xavier de Mendonça Furtado.[69] Also
in India, the 1732 decree was published, but not until 1759 was the first navy class
opened. The Military Academy of Goa, the first educational institution to train
engineers in the Indian subcontinent, was founded in 1817.[70]

Such a technical learning network, reasonably consolidated in the middle
of the eighteenth century, in its disciplinary versatility and geographical scope,
proved to be suitable not only for the training of engineers who were experts
in defensive projects but also for urban design and civil architecture (which had
been part of their practice since the beginning). Furthermore, this Portuguese
approach was distinguished by how the programmes and the operational scheme
were reproduced, based on the metropolitan matrix of the Lisbon Fortification
Class's not intending that the subsidiary classes follow the contents of a strictly
colonial scope.[71] The chronology of the institutional organization of the teaching of military architecture and the process of its dissemination were presented as
truly pioneering data, both in comparison with the realities of the Castilian world
and with the institutionalization of the teaching of these subjects in France and
in the Anglo-Saxon world.[72] This was in addition to what this option implied in
terms of training an elite in a colonial environment and the connections that can
be established between the various points of this extended training/performance
network.

Manuel de Azevedo Fortes died in 1749, having been replaced as chief engineer
by Manuel da Maia, his close collaborator and the one responsible for the urban
planning of Lisbon after the 1755 earthquake.[73] In 1750, King João V signed the
Treaty of Madrid, initiating the process of demarcating the vast border along Spanish domains in South America.[74] The complications on the ground, which resulted
in the outbreak of the Guaraní War (1752–6), prevented the first demarcation
campaigns from concluding and led to the annulment of the Treaty of Madrid,
in 1761. The disputes would be pacified only in 1777, with the Treaty of Santo
Ildefonso, and new demarcation campaigns were envisaged, which took place in
the 1780s and 1790s.

The engineers trained in the various classes of the metropolis and the empire
were sufficient to send mostly nationals to the boundary campaigns of the Santo
Ildefonso treaty, practically dispensing with the hiring of foreigners (which had
still been necessary in the first campaigns). These men carried out the huge carto-
graphic creation, which then took place in Brazil. Its action on the ground served
both the purpose of demarcating the border and the actual design of the territory,
due to the establishment of new villages and the construction of new fortifications.
In addition, the entire reign of King José (1750–77), known for the reforms undertaken by his minister Sebastião José de Carvalho e Melo, was marked from the
military point of view by the arrival of Count Schaumburg-Lippe, who introduced
the greatest early modern reform of the Portuguese army.

Engineers' (con)science: revolution or education?

Indeed, from a disciplinary and tactical point of view, the picture that is normally presented of the Portuguese military organization in the early modern period is not easy to reconcile with the general narratives of the Military Revolution. The Restoration War (1640–68) led to the creation of a more centralized structure of regular bodies (paid or reserve troops), but it continued to coexist with various complementary forms of military organization, the modernization of which was late and would be consolidated only in the second half of the eighteenth century, during the Pombaline period.

In this context, could the process followed by military engineering be read in any way as a path which, at least in part, contradicts this reading of a systematic "delay"? The commitment of the Portuguese Crown in this regard is clear. The timing of perceiving the fundamental changes occurring in early modern fortification occurred in Portugal at the moment of its transformation. The notion of early modern fortification links it to processes that were inexorably undertaken as a sign of change. Fortification was no longer just the work to be built but also the diagnosis of the best conditions for defending the site, which might vary over time and require continuous reflection and review.

Though clearly conceptualized and critical, the Portuguese approach is also fundamentally pragmatic. What makes its discursive production genuinely autonomous is not its originality but its claiming for itself the thought concerning its object and not the use of already-tested formulas. The definition that Azevedo Fortes gives of what a good engineer should be is in this respect quite clear:

> A good engineer must be a brave soldier, created with doctrine, and military exercise; and in addition, he must have the science to undertake all the duties of war, such that if he does not find the means to attack or defend a Garrison, he himself invents them.[75]

But what is perhaps more significant is that when the procedure focused on the education of the engineer, it gained in two ways: first by protecting itself from the dependence on importing agents and knowledge and second by investing in training in situ, in the different parts of the empire, the peripheral condition was also somewhat overcome, because this transformed the peripheries into operational and reflection centres. However, beyond this, the educational project was broader.

In *Representation*,[76] Azevedo Fortes stated that military academies should be set up "so that not only those who were to be engineers but also most private soldiers, officers of the regiments, and nobility would attend them, and learn military doctrine from them."[77] The intention was that "[in] this way, in a short time, Your Majesty will have almost as many engineers (even if they are not by profession) as there are infantry officers."[78]

These aspects were especially significant because they clearly established the central point of Azevedo Fortes's academic project. Indeed, what was at issue was not simply the training of military engineering technicians. Although it seems contradictory, it was probably against this idea that the chief engineer was fighting, at least at first. In this sense, the defence of the incorporation of engineers in the military structure (in the infantry bodies) aimed to reinforce what was a priority in terms of discourse at that time – that is, that a military engineer was, above all, a soldier. In the words of Azevedo Fortes, he was "the most perfect soldier."

When admitting the existence of an "engineer by profession" and an "engineer by training" (in the absence of another term, as this in theory could be confused with the official), Azevedo Fortes argued for his unequivocal intention of forming a new soldier, the "soldier" par excellence, in a new vision of war (mental and practical), which was the war of intelligence and not the war of the body. This idea of the early modern and well-formed soldier sustained the entire academic project of Azevedo Fortes.

However, this investment in education showed another side of the issue which implies another internal cleavage that emerged during the process. It is that the speech of the engineers, made from mathematical knowledge of fortification and above all from the training methodology itself, somehow claimed a separate status, not so much "civil" (since the proposed efficiency was to be in the service of war) but rather "technical scientific" and in this sense outside the strictly "military" scope.

This reading appears in the characterization that Matias José Dias Azedo made of engineers, alluding to their *paisanice* (civilianness).[79] Even though he was recriminatory of civil exercises, "contrary to the true purpose of the profession," Azedo recognized that they were specially qualified for the "theoretical education of the officers of other bodies," which is interesting.[80] In this sense, the commitment to the training of engineers in the Portuguese case arguably represented a vision that can be associated in some way with the framework of the Military Revolution, although the impact of this revolution may have been less strictly military and more widely cultural.

Notes

1 Text written within the scope of the TechNetEMPIRE | Technoscientific networks in the construction of the built environment in the Portuguese Empire (1647–1871) PTDC / ART-DAQ / 31959/2017, FCT – Foundation for Science and Technology, I.P. This article had the support of CHAM (NOVA FCSH / UAc), through the strategic project sponsored by FCT (UID/HIS/04666/2019).
2 Geoffrey Parker, *The Military Revolution: Military Innovation and the Rise of the West, 1500–1800* (Cambridge: Cambridge University Press, 1988).
3 Simon Pepper and Nicholas Adams, *Firearms and Fortifications: Military Architecture and Siege Warfare in Sixteenth Century Siena* (Chicago: University of Chicago Press, 1986). Amelio Fara, *Il Sistema e la Città, Architettura Fortificata dell'Europa Moderna dai Trattati alle Realizzazioni, 1464–1794* (Génova: Sagep Editrice, 1989).
4 Fernando Cobos, "Una visión integral de las Escuelas y los escenarios de la fortificación española de los siglos XVI, XVII y XVIII," in *Actas IV Congreso de Castellología, Madrid 2012* (Madrid: Associacíon Española de Amigos de los Castillos, 2012), 1–48. Nicolas

Faucherre, Pieter Martens, and Hugues Paucot, eds., *La genèse du système bastionné en Europe, 1500–1550* (Navarrenx: Cercle Historique de l'Arribère, 2014), 21–30.

5 Under the impact of John R. Hale, "The Development of the Bastion, 1440–1534, an Italian Chronology," in *Renaissance War Studies* (London: The Hambledon Press, 1983), 1–31.

6 Rafael Moreira, "A Arquitectura Militar do Renascimento em Portugal," in *A Introdução da Arte da Renascença na Península Ibérica, Actas do Simpósio Internacional* (Coimbra: Epartur – Universidade de Coimbra, 1981), 281–305; Rafael Moreira, "Arquitectura Militar," in *História da Arte em Portugal, O Maneirismo*, ed. Vítor Serrão (Lisbon: Alfa, 1986), 137–52; Rafael Moreira, "Do Rigor Teórico à Urgência Prática: A Arquitectura Militar," in *História da Arte em Portugal, O Limiar do Barroco* (Lisbon: Alfa, 1986), 67–86.

7 Rafael Moreira, ed., *História das Fortificações Portuguesas no Mundo* (Lisbon: Alfa, 1989); Francisco Faria Paulino, ed., *Arquitectura Militar na Expansão Portuguesa* (Lisbon: CNCDP, 1994).

8 John Bury, "Francisco de Hollanda, a Little Known Source for the History of Fortification in the 16th Century," *Arquivos do Centro Cultural Português* 14 (1979): 163–202; John Bury, *Two Notes on Francisco de Holanda* (London: Warburg Institute, 1981); Fernando Cobos, "Dessins de Fortification dans 'Os desenhos das antigualhas' du Portugais Francisco de Holanda (1538–1540)," in *Atlas Militaires Manuscrits Européens (XVIe–XVIIIe siècles): Actes des 4es journées d'étude du Musée des Plans-Reliefs* (Paris: Ministère de la Culture et de la Communication, 2003), 117–32.

9 Margarida Tavares da Conceição, "Le langage militaire des ingénieurs et des fortificateurs portugais (c. 1480–1580)," in *Les mots de la guerre dans l'Europe de la Renaissance*, ed. Marie Madeleine Fontaine and Jean-Louis Fournel (Genève: Librairie Droz, 2015), 141–68.

10 Rafael Moreira, ed., *A construção de Mazagão: Cartas inéditas 1451–1542* (Lisbon: IPPAR, 2001); João Barros Matos, "Do mar contra terra: Mazagão, Ceuta e Diu, primeiras fortalezas abaluartadas da expansão portuguesa" (PhD diss., University of Sevilla, 2012), 81–162; Walter Rossa, "1514 El Jadida 1541: Le vicende della fondazione di una città marocchina," in *Il cantiere della città: strumenti, maestranze e tecniche dal medioevo al novecento*, ed. Aldo Casamento (Rome: Edizioni Kappa, 2014), 103–20. Jorge Correia, *Implantação da cidade portuguesa no Norte de África: Da tomada de Ceuta a meados do século XVI* (Porto: FAUP, 2008).

11 Francisco de Sousa Viterbo, *Dicionário Histórico e Documental dos Arquitectos, Engenheiros e Construtores Portugueses*, vol. 3 (Lisbon: INCM, 1988), 72–73.

12 Margarida Tavares da Conceição, *Da cidade e fortificação em textos portugueses, 1540–1640* (Lisbon: Nota de Rodapé Edições, 2015), 102–3.

13 Matos, "Do mar contra terra," 246–47.

14 Ibid., 335–36.

15 Nuno Gonçalves, "O projecto para a fortaleza da ilha de Moçambique atribuído a Miguel de Arruda" (MA diss., University of Coimbra, 2011).

16 Mário Mendonça de Oliveira, *As Fortificações portuguesas de Salvador quando cabeça do Brasil* (Salvador: Fundação Gregório de Matos, 2004).

17 Rui Carita, *O escudo do Reino: A Fortaleza de São Julião da Barra* (Lisbon: Ministério da Defesa Nacional, 2007), 36–40.

18 Daniela Pereira, *A evolução urbanística de Lagos (séculos XV–XVIII)* (Faro: Direcção Regional de Cultura do Algarve, 2017), 56–57. Rafael Moreira, "De la Méditerranée à l'Atlantique: Le succès du bastion dans le monde portugais," in *La genèse du système bastionné en Europe, 1500–1550*, ed. Nicolas Faucherre, Pieter Martens, and Hugues Paucot (Navarrenx: Cercle Historique de l'Arribère, 2014), 212–18.

19 Luís Costa e Sousa, *Construir e Desconstruir a Guerra em Portugal, 1568–1598* (Lisbon: IESM, 2015), 247–319.

20 Moreira, "Arquitectura Militar," 143–49.

21 Rafael Moreira and Miguel Soromenho, "Engenheiros Militares Italianos em Portugal (séculos XV–XVI)," in *Architetti e Ingegneri Militari Italiani all'estero dal XV al XVIII secolo: Dall'Atlantico al Baltico*, ed. Marino Viganò, vol. 2 (Rome and Livorno: Sillabe, 1999), 109–31.
22 Matheus do Couto, *Tractado de Architectura que leo o Mestre e Architecto Matheus do Couto o velho no Anno de 1631* (Lisbon: Biblioteca Nacional de Portugal, Códice 946).
23 Conceição, *Da cidade e fortificação*, 175–79, 221–41.
24 Viterbo, *Dicionário*, vol. 1, 376–80.
25 Ibid., vol. 2, 235–37.
26 Moreira, "A Época Manuelina," 91–142.
27 Henrique Leitão et al., *Sphaera Mundi: A Ciência na Aula da Esfera. Manuscritos científicos do Colégio de Santo Antão nas colecções da BNP* (Lisbon: BNP, 2008).
28 Denis De Lucca, *Jesuits and Fortifications: The Contribution of the Jesuits to Military Architecture in the Baroque Age* (Leiden: Brill, 2012).
29 Sidh Losa Mendiratta, "Dispositivos do Sistema Defensivo da Província do Norte do Estado da Índia, 1521–1739" (PhD diss., University of Coimbra, Coimbra, 2012), 573–76.
30 José Luis Mota Menezes, "Recife," in *Portuguese Heritage Around the World: South America* (Lisbon: FCG, 2010), 60–162.
31 Moreira, "Do Rigor Teórico," 67–86.
32 Jan Ciermans, *Disciplinae Mathematicae* . . . (Louanii: apud Euerardum de Vitte, 1640).
33 Edwin Paar, "O sistema fortificado de Elvas no panorama da arquitectura militar europeia da época," *Monumentos* 28 (2008): 52–57; Leitão et al., *Sphaera Mundi*, 175–78.
34 With poorly known activity (Moreira, "Do Rigor Teórico," 70–71).
35 Ibid., 72.
36 Miguel Soromenho, "Manuel Pinto de Vilalobos, da Engenharia Militar à Arquitectura" (MA diss., New University of Lisbon, Lisbon, 1991).
37 Nuno Ferreira, "Luís Serrão Pimentel (1613–1679): Cosmógrafo Mor e Engenheiro Mor de Portugal" (MA diss., University of Lisbon, Lisbon, 2009), 77–80.
38 Viterbo, *Dicionário*, vol. 2, 272.
39 On the manuscripts related to Pimentel see texts by Miguel Soromenho in *A Ciência do Desenho: A Ilustração na Colecção de Códices da Biblioteca Nacional* (Lisbon: Biblioteca Nacional, 2001), 64–71.
40 Luís Serrão Pimentel, *Methodo Lusitanico de Desenhar as Fortificaçoens das Praças Regulares, & Irregulares, Fortes de Campanha e Outras Obras Pertencentes a Architectura Militar Distribuido em Duas Partes Operativa, e Qualificativa* (Lisbon: Antonio Craesbeeck de Mello, 1680).
41 Cobos, "Una visión integral de las Escuelas."
42 António Castanheira da Silva, "Praça de guerra de Estremoz – a formação (1640–1690)" (MA diss., New University of Lisbon, Lisbon, 2019), 13–22.
43 Soromenho, "Manuel Pinto de Vilalobos," 18.
44 Paar, "O sistema fortificado de Elvas"; Soromenho, "Manuel Pinto de Vilalobos," 21.
45 Also leaving *Lições de Artelharia* (1676), a booklet copied by Sebastião de Sousa Vasconcelos. Soromenho, "Manuel Pinto de Vilalobos," 22–30.
46 Manuel Pinto de Vilalobos, *Tractado do Uzo do Pantometra de Desenhar as Forteficasoins . . . pello Methodo de Luís Serrão Pimentel. . .* (Lisbon: Biblioteca Nacional de Portugal, c. 1690, Códice 13201).
47 Soromenho, "Manuel Pinto de Vilalobos," 34.
48 Viterbo, *Dicionário*, vol. 3, 171.
49 ANTT, Conselho de Guerra, Livro 40, fl.s 232–33v; Soromenho, "Manuel Pinto de Vilalobos," 21–22; Margarida Tavares da Conceição, *Da vila cercada à praça de guerra. Formação do espaço urbano em Almeida* (Lisbon: Livros Horizonte, 2002), 285.

50 Christovam Ayres de Magalhães Sepúlveda, *História Orgânica e Política do Exercito Português: Provas*, vol. 5 (Lisbon: Imprensa Nacional, 1910), 87; Roberta Marx Delson, "Para o entendimento da educação colonial: O papel das academias militares no Brasil colonia," in *Coletânea de Estudos Universo Urbanístico Português 1415–1822* (Lisbon: CNCDP, 1998), 212; Beatriz Bueno, *Desenho e desígnio: O Brasil dos engenheiros militares, 1500–1822* (São Paulo: Universidade de São Paulo, 2011), 218–49.
51 Sepúlveda, *História Orgânica e Política do Exercito Português*, vol. 5, 104.
52 Ibid., 87–88.
53 Viterbo, *Dicionário*, vol. 2, 245.
54 Renata Malcher de Araujo, *As Cidades da Amazónia no século XVIII: Belém, Macapá e Mazagão* (Porto: FAUP, 1998), 313–14.
55 Mário Gonçalves Fernandes, ed., *Manuel de Azevedo Fortes (1660–1749) Cartografia, Cultura e Urbanismo* (Porto: GEDES, 2006).
56 Viterbo, *Dicionário*, vol. 1, 80.
57 Manuel de Azevedo Fortes, *Representação a Sua Magestade sobre a forma e direcção que devem ter os Engenheiros para melhor servirem ao dito Senhor neste Reyno, e nas suas conquistas* (Lisbon: Officina de Matias Pereira da Silva, 1720).
58 Renata Malcher de Araujo, "Manuel de Azevedo Fortes e o estatuto dos engenheiros portugueses," in *Manuel de Azevedo Fortes (1660–1749)* (Porto: GEDES, 2006), 24.
59 Manuel de Azevedo Fortes, *O Engenheiro Portuguez: dividido em dous Tratados, Tomo Primeyro que Comprehende a Geometria Pratica sobre o Papel, e sobre o Terreno: o Uso dos Instrumentos Mais Necessarios aos Engenheiros: o Modo de Desenhar e Dar Aguadas nas Plantas Militares e no Appendice a Trigonometria Rectilinea, Tomo Segundo que Comprehende a Fortificação Regular, e Irregular: o Ataque e Defensa das Praças; e no Appendice o Uso das Armas de Guerra*, vol. 2 (Lisbon: Officina de Manuel Fernandes da Costa, 1728–1729).
60 Manuel de Azevedo Fortes, *Tratado do Modo o mais Facil, e o mais exacto de fazer as Cartas Geográficas* (Lisboa Occidental: Officina de Pascoal da Sylva, 1722).
61 Fortes, *O Engenheiro Português*, vol. 2, 39.
62 Sepúlveda, *História Orgânica e Política do Exercito Português*, vol. 5, 109–11.
63 Delson, "Para o entendimento da educação colonial," 205–23; Bueno, *Desenho e desígnio*, 218–49.
64 Oliveira, *As Fortificações portuguesas*, 122–28.
65 Bueno, *Desenho e desígnio*, 218–49.
66 Diogo da Sylveyra Vellozo, *Arquitetura Militar ou Fortifcação Moderna* (Salvador: Edufpa, 2005).
67 José Pinto Alpoim, *Exame de Artilheiros* (Lisbon: Oficina de José Antonio Plates, 1744).
68 José Pinto Alpoim, *Exame de Bombeiros* (Madrid: Oficina de Francisco Martinez Abad, 1748).
69 Araujo, *As Cidades da Amazónia*, 111.
70 Alice Santiago Faria, "O papel dos luso-descendentes na Engenharia Militar e nas obras públicas em Goa ao longo do século XIX," in *Goa: Passado e Presente*, vol. 1 (Lisbon: CEPCEP – CHAM, 2012), 225–37.
71 Roberta Delson, "The Beginnings of Professionalization in the Brazilian Military: The Eighteenth Century Corps of Engineers," *The Américas* 51, no. 4 (April 1995): 555–74; Delson, "Para o entendimento da educação colonial," 225–42.
72 Delson, "Para o entendimento da educação colonial," 234 and ss.
73 Walter Rossa, *Beyond Baixa: Signs of Urban Planning in Eighteenth Century Lisbon* (Lisbon: IPPAR, 1998), 63–89.
74 Jaime Cortesão, *Alexandre de Gusmão e o Tratado de Madrid*, vol. 3 (Lisbon: Livros Horizonte, 1984); João Carlos Garcia, ed., *A Nova Lusitânia: Imagens Cartográficas do Brasil nas colecções da Biblioteca Nacional* (Lisbon: CNCDP, 2001).
75 Fortes, *Representação*, 7–8.

76 Ibid.
77 Ibid., 3.
78 Ibid., 10.
79 Matias José Dias Azedo, *Compendio militar: escrito segundo a doutrina dos melhores autores para instrusão dos discipulos d'Academia Real de Fortificasão, Artilheria, e Dezenho* (Lisbon: Regia Tipografia Silviana, 1796), Prefasão VII–VIII.
80 Ibid., 69.

3

MILITARY ENGINEERS, THE MILITARY REVOLUTION, AND THE DEFENCE OF PORTUGAL, 1640–68

Lorraine White

Introduction

On 18 June 1580, just hours before the expected launch of the Duke of Alba's invasion of Portugal to claim the vacant crown for Philip II of Spain, the frontier fort of Elvas surrendered without a fight. Where Alba did encounter resistance from towns along the invasion route, his artillery (or the threat of deploying it) overcame it in two or three days.[1] On 30 August, Alba proudly wrote to advise Philip that the military campaign to conquer the neighbouring kingdom had been completed "two days short of two months, for this army set out on 27 June and at midday on 25 August Your Majesty was master of all."[2] While not discounting the absence of a Portuguese army, adequate leadership, or the supporting maritime element of Alba's campaign, a key factor in the initial success of the 1580 invasion was the lack of effective "modern" fortifications on the border and elsewhere. In sharp contrast to 1580, even in the earlier stages of the 1640–68 War of Portuguese Independence, the presence on or near Portugal's border of fortified towns and strongholds initially incorporating simple, but increasingly more complex, hybridized modern-style fortifications succeeded for the most part in countering the advances of the invading Spanish forces. At no stage during the 1640–68 war did Elvas capitulate or fall, not even during the lengthy four-month artillery siege of 1658–59. The erection of such modern geometric fortifications required a "scientific" approach to their planning and design and saw the emergence of a cadre of engineers with specialist knowledge of military architecture.

This study explores the endeavours of Portugal's Restoration government to engage the military engineers needed to design and construct the new style of fortifications and those needed to undertake appropriate defensive measures to prevent their capture when attacked. It examines the provenance of some of these military engineers, their experience and recruitment, their role, and the growing debate over the use – and dangers – of employing foreign instead of native-born military engineers.

Between the later fifteenth century and the seventeenth century major changes took place across Western Europe in the design and construction of military architecture, a key element in what has been termed the *Military Revolution* (henceforth MR). The changes followed improvements in gunpowder artillery deployed by besiegers, which saw them more accurately fire harder-hitting, longer-range horizontal cannonballs capable of breaching the high, thin curtain walls and round or square towers of castles and fortified towns. This prompted defenders in active or potential war fronts to develop new forms of fortifications. Designers and builders of military architecture experimented with scarped, thick, and lower walls and towers filled with earth, timber, and rubble that presented smaller targets for artillery fire and that were better able to absorb the impact of cannonballs. The construction of forward-projecting gun platforms – bastions – on which heavier cannons and small arms could be deployed allowed for the switch from a passive to an aggressive defence system. Later, the building of a free-standing outwork, the ravelin, outside the curtain wall, and a covered way – a walkway part way up the contraescarpment of a ditch – along which the defenders could move hidden from the view of the besieger, combined to form a triple line of advanced, in-depth defence. The fortifications developed in Italy which had the angular bastion at its core gave the new style its name, the *trace italienne*, and its first school of military architects, the Italian School.[3] A new "school" emerged from the 1570s in the Netherlands, where a cadre of Dutch engineers further developed and improved the *trace italienne*. They broadened and deepened the ditch, widened the hidden way, and in a fourth line of works beyond this added other independent angular outworks such as demi-lunes crown-works, and horn-works to provide further forward-projecting defensive platforms on which musketeers could be positioned. Dutch reasoning was sound: the Dutch placed a greater stress on musketry to repel assaults, because muskets were cheaper than cannons and had a much faster rate of fire. Moreover, for speed and economy, their fortifications were built of fascines and packed earth – the "poor man's *trace italienne*."[4]

The introduction of modern fortifications that proved so vital for Portugal's defence during the 1640–68 war correlate closely with those associated with the MR.[5] They incorporated elements that were fundamental to both schools, but above all to the Dutch. All new fortifications featured ramparts (*trincheiras*, even if only partial in smaller settlements), while larger works incorporated bastions (*baluartes*), terrepleins (gun platforms or *terraplenos*), and often demi-lunes (*meias luas*), and the main strongholds added one or more covered way (*estrada cuberta*). Initially they too were simple earthworks (sometimes faced with turf, *tepe*).

Following the 1 December 1640 Lisbon uprising and overthrow of the Spanish viceregal government, the newly formed government of the native king, João IV, had to move quickly to defend Portugal against an expected Spanish invasion. The problem of defending against the anticipated invasion was truly enormous: around half of the country was exposed to direct attack overland from neighbouring Spain, while the other half was open to attack from the sea. A terrestrial invasion could be expected via four possible routes, the most probable being launched from the Castilian province of Extremadura and through the Alentejo (the route chosen by Alba in 1580); another could be initiated from the Castilian province of Salamanca and down through the Beira region (employed by Juan II of Castile in 1385); finally, an attack could be made from Andalusia and into the southern kingdom of the Algarve, though solely in terms of distance this, like the northern route from Galicia, was not suited to an attack on the capital, Lisbon.[6]

Organizing the defence of Portugal thus took priority for the new king and his advisors. Nobles with local ties were hastily appointed as frontier commanders (*fronteiros*) in the Minho, Trás-os-Montes, and Beira regions that bordered Spain, while the monarch's favourite, the Count of Vimioso, was appointed to lead the principal army in the Alentejo. On 11 December, only five days after arriving in Lisbon, the king established a Council of War. With the necessary administrative tools in place, attention turned to the modernization of Portugal's physical defence infrastructure. Although there were numerous castles along the border, they were almost all of medieval design[7] and in need of extensive repair. With their round and square towers and high, thin curtain walls – prime examples of the system of vertical defence – they were not just vulnerable to cannon bombardment but also were totally unsuited to the placement of artillery for defence. Changes to fortifications close to the border began quite modestly, with simple steps to improve existing defences. In Elvas, for example, existing walls were restored, and seven of the ten gates of the town were sealed up.[8] However, to protect against artillery attack, existing fortifications needed to undergo significant remodelling. For this, special expertise was required, but military officers or engineers with such knowledge in Portugal were few in number.

Provenance, recruitment, and role of military engineers

In the first weeks of war, lacking designated military engineers, the Council of War deployed a handful of native veteran soldiers who were familiar with the latest developments in European fortifications, though by indirect means. These veterans could draw on their experiences in Brazil, where they had been defending against foreign incursions and fighting to regain the territories captured by the Dutch in the 1620s and 1630s. A prime concern was coastal defence. Cascais took precedence, as it was from near here that the second phase of Alba's attack on Lisbon had been launched in 1580. The task of the veterans was to inspect the principal strongholds on the coast and design and oversee the necessary adaptations to their existing fortifications. Martim Afonso de Mello, newly appointed councillor of war and a veteran of Portuguese India (who had served as governor of Muscat and Cabo Comorim), was sent on 19 December to Cascais to review its fortifications.[9]

Not until January 1641, however, did attention turn to the terrestrial border with Spain. Matias de Albuquerque, the former governor and *capitão-mor* of Pernambuco in Brazil and *visitador e fortificador* of the captaincies of the north, being "very experienced in fortifications," was released from five years' imprisonment and sent without a formal appointment to the main war front in Alentejo. Albuquerque's initial assessment was that the construction of fortifications in Olivença, exposed on the far side of the river Guadiana, needed his attention before those of Elvas, headquarters of the army.[10] Just six months later, however, Albuquerque's focus was diverted with his appointment (short-lived, as it turned out) as governador of arms of the army and frontiers of the province of Alentejo (*governador das armas no exército e fronteiras da provincia de Alentejo*).[11] At the end of July 1641, Albuquerque was arrested on suspicion of participating in a plot to assassinate João IV.[12] A second Brazil veteran with expertise in fortifications, Sebastião Pereira de Frias, a native of Pernes, near Santarém, was then sent to Elvas.[13] Albuquerque was subsequently exonerated in December 1642 and, then aged 60, returned to his military duties, inspecting and assessing fortifications, as he was said to be "very knowledgeable in mathematics and fortifications."[14] Meanwhile, the newly appointed commanders of the secondary war fronts (the provinces of Entre Douro e Minho, Trás-os-Montes, and Beira), all of whom had some military experience, made tours of the border territory under their control and ordered the construction of fortifications in the major settlements and strongholds of their respective regions.[15]

The critical shortage of native Portuguese with expertise in constructing modern fortifications created an urgent need to seek out foreign military engineers with proven practical experience. Over the years, a small number of Dutch and Italian engineers were recruited and sent to the various war fronts and coastal forts to survey and draw up plans to modernize the fortifications of the main strongholds. However, thanks to the support of Spain's main enemy, France, and the activities of two of Portugal's ambassadors to the French court (Dom Francisco de Melo and the Count of Vidigueira), a much higher proportion of French military engineers were contracted to serve in Portugal. Though the focus here has been limited to just a few of the foreigners who served as military engineers during the war of 1640–68, an examination of their profiles reveals an interesting range in their background and careers.

The first influx of foreign military engineers arrived on 6 August 1641 in a group of some 250 volunteers who sailed in the French fleet commanded by Cardinal Richelieu's nephew, the Marquis of Brézé.[16] The contingent of six military engineers was headed by Charles de Lassart (personally recommended by Richelieu) and comprised four other French engineers – Nicolás de L'Isle (known in Portugal as Lila), Pierre Pellefigue, Pierre Gilles de Saint Paul (Pedro Gilles), and Georges Duponsel – and an Italian (from Genoa), Hierónimo Rosetti.[17]

Seven months later, being "much loved and esteemed by the King and by everyone," Lassart was appointed chief engineer (*engenheiro mór*). His work on the new style of fortifications began with Cascais and soon after included those of Porto, Évora, Elvas, and Olivença.[18] Lassart's time in Portugal, however, was intermittent and quite short (he left Portugal in early 1644, returned in 1657, and departed definitively around 1659). The tenure of another French engineer was even shorter: Blaise de Pagan, a native of Provence, was a veteran engineer with twenty-two years' experience of sieges and an author of a treatise on fortifications, subsequently published in Paris in 1645. He arrived in Portugal at the beginning of 1642 to take up a prestigious appointment as field marshal (*maestre de campo*). His appointment was brief, however, because having lost one eye twenty years earlier, he completely lost his sight while on campaign the year of his arrival.[19] In his place, another engineer, Nicolás de Langres (a resident of Charleville, capital of the French estates of the house of Gonzaga), was appointed on 31 March 1644.[20] Like the others, Langres was given a three-year appointment, but owing to the constant shortage of engineers, he succeeded in negotiating several new contracts which improved his conditions of appointment and pay. He remained for some seventeen years – the longest serving of all of the foreign engineers. Much of his time was spent on the main war front of the Alentejo, but he also worked on fortifications elsewhere, including Cascais.[21]

As a final profile, Pierre de Massiac, *seigneur* of Sainte-Colombe (1616–82), known in Portugal as Santa Colomba, was a native of Narbonne in Languedoc. Aged about thirty-two at the time of his arrival in Portugal in 1648, he had previously served in France and then under the Venetians for three or four years.[22] He, too, remained for some time in Portugal – around sixteen years – until (as we shall see) his capture by the Spanish in 1663. He also worked on more than one war front (notably the Alentejo and in the Algarve), as well as in Lisbon, and in 1656, he was appointed to the post of *tenente* (deputy) *de maestro de campo*.[23]

Given the length of the terrestrial border, the creation of four armies to defend it, and the shortage of engineers (and of money to employ them), demand would inevitably exceed supply. Priority was naturally given to the main war front in the Alentejo, where there was the greatest risk of invasion. In October 1641, of the five engineers who arrived with Lassart, one was allocated to Beira, one to Tras-os-Montes, and one to the Algarve, and two more (including Rossetti) were assigned to the Alentejo. Rossetti, however, was appointed sergeant major (*sargento mor*) of a regiment (*terço*), which left him unable to prioritize fortifications.[24] By April 1642, however, still preoccupied with his *terço*, only Rossetti remained in Elvas, prompting the then governor of arms, Martim Afonso de Melo, to claim that "under no circumstances can this city have fewer than a pair of engineers as it is the main one of this province."[25] By June 1645, in anticipation of a Castilian offensive, besides Joannes Cieremans (a Jesuit from 's-Hertogenbosch in the Low Countries, known in Portugal as João Pascácio Cosmander), three other engineers were based in Elvas: the Italian Piada, the French Langres, and Sebastião Pereira Frias.[26] Significantly, it seems that the number of engineers needed differed according to the type of campaign being undertaken: in 1650, some claimed that a defensive campaign responding to an enemy invasion required a minimum of three good engineers and four or five assistants. This was because when the enemy army went on campaign, the engineers and assistants had to be sent out to the principal strongholds of the Alentejo. For an offensive campaign where the Army of Alentejo crossed the border into Extremadura, fewer engineers and assistants would be needed.[27] Back in 1645, the rather inexperienced and ill-informed commander of the Army of Alentejo, the Count of Castelo Melhor, had asked the king why, if his ministers wanted to save money on army salaries, they did not begin by dispensing with the three engineers then resident in Elvas. In his opinion, only one engineer was needed to fortify the whole of the kingdom![28] Nevertheless, at times it was relatively unusual for even two engineers to be serving with the main army; there was often just one. With just one engineer on the main war front, however, one army commander lamented that if the engineer were to die, "we would be left with no one to attend to such a necessary job."[29]

The duties carried out by a military engineer were extensive and called for expertise in a number of sciences,[30] the foremost being mathematics and geometry. A major function was, of course, surveying and then drawing up designs for the construction of the new style of fortifications for existing castles and strongholds and for towns. Engineers were also expected to precede the army on its campaign and to make bridges across rivers. As there were few bridges in Portugal at this time,[31] this was potentially an important duty. Some engineers were also involved in the construction of *atalaias*, small watchtowers built to protect strategic locations such as bridges, river crossings, and the main roads to key villages. These *atalaias* eventually proliferated along the terrestrial border – by 1657, more than fifty had been constructed in the Alentejo region alone, and more were planned.[32]

In anticipation of or during an offensive campaign, engineers were dispatched to survey enemy fortifications and to draw up plans to attack an enemy town or position. At the end of August 1644, for example, Cosmander was sent with a contingent of Portuguese soldiers to reconnoitre the Castilian stronghold of Valencia de Alcántara (in Extremadura). After the enemy soldiers withdrew (presumably into the more heavily fortified inner castle), Cosmander was able to enter the outskirts of the town and collect sufficient information to draw up a detailed plan of the stronghold.[33]

The ultimate aim of examining the defences of an enemy stronghold and drawing up detailed plans of its fortifications was to assess and prepare for its attack and capture. In sieges of enemy strongholds, the military engineer played a key role. As French engineer Manesson-Mallet (1630–1706) indicated in his treatise, engineers were responsible, among other things, for the inspection of the masonry of strongholds to be besieged and for "drawing the [enemy's] batteries and other works."[34] They were to advise on where and how to make an attack, on the composition of "fireworks" (bombs and such like), and on siege works.[35] In particular, they determined how to breach fortifications through such things as mining and laying charges beneath them and how to place petards (*petardos*, commonly employed against the entrances to forts and towns).

Manesson-Mallet succinctly summarized the role of engineers when they were on campaign as:

> they who accompany an army, whether in battle or in sieges, who must have as much courage as prudence, for they are the first to plant the stake in the open before besieged towns to plot the trench, to mark the line of the battle

square, and the spot where one must construct the batteries and the redoubts, to accompany the dragoons when a palisade must be broken and crossed, make a *logement* on the top of a glacis or on a contraescarpment, to cross a dry moat or one full of water, to conduct a mine, or to entrench oneself at the foot or on the top of a breach, etc., which is not done without great peril.[36]

Once an enemy stronghold had been captured, the engineer was also responsible for improving and, where necessary, upgrading its fortifications to guard against its recapture. In October 1643, following the siege and capture of the Extremaduran stronghold of Villa Nueva del Fresno, Cosmander was ordered to "reduce its castle to modern fortifications" – that is, to convert its fortifications from a medieval style to the modern style.[37] Conversely, engineers were sometimes "parachuted" into strongholds that were threatened with or actually under siege. In 1663, for example, with news of the approach of the Castillian army led by Philip IV's illegitimate son, D. Juan de Austria, another French engineer, Sélincourt, was quickly moved into Évora in the hope that his skills would make up for the inexperience of the city's governor.[38] (Unfortunately, they did not: the city was captured.)

The more experienced senior engineers, and those formally granted the title of *engenheiro mór*, could also be invited to participate in meetings where plans for military campaigns were discussed. In war councils (*conselhos de guerra*) of the Army of Alentejo, for example, the engineers could comment and give expert advice and could join in debates about prospective targets for the forthcoming campaign. As Manesson-Mallet explained, engineers "have the honour of being called sometimes into the *conseil du general* [general's council], and to receive the order from him or from the Lieutenant general of the day."[39] Less frequently, the individual opinion of a senior engineer was discussed and taken into consideration by the Council of War in Lisbon. After the Army of Alentejo's aborted attack on Badajoz in July 1645, the king forwarded engineer Cosmander's letter in support of another attack on the city's adjacent fort of San Cristóbal to the Council of War for its consideration; the king then ordered the council to hear Cosmander in person and vote in his presence on the proposed attack.[40]

Military engineers had another significant role: they were often accompanied by assistants – in effect, apprentices – who were expected to learn from their respective "masters." Occasionally, the contract of an engineer specified that he was to train an assistant, a native Portuguese, who could then go on to be examined and qualified as a full engineer.

Given the critical shortage of military engineers in Portugal, early attempts were made to train more native engineers through the establishment by royal decree of 13 May 1641 of a School of Artillery and Cannon Science (*Aula de Artilharia e Esquadria*) and by appointing to its chair a young (only twenty-eight at the time) native Portuguese, Luís Serrão Pimentel (1613–79), a Jesuit from the College of São Antão, Lisbon. As a resident French diplomat observed upon its creation, "Artillery . . . almost completely escaped the ability of the Portuguese, and custom demanded that they called above all on Germans to manoeuvre it."[41] Military engineering was emerging as a highly respectable and honourable skill and, as one historian has pointed out, "one of the elements of a gentleman's education."[42] In a further effort to train native military engineers, in July 1647, the king decreed the establishment of a School of Fortification and Military Architecture (*Aula de Fortificação e Architectura Militar*) in the Ribeira das Naus in Lisbon. Once again, Pimentel, now thirty-four, was appointed as its chair.[43] Four years later, in 1651, the seventeen-year-old heir to the throne, Prince Teodósio (who had been instructed in the art of fortifications by Cosmander), combined the essence of the two schools with the establishment of a School of Fortification, Artillery, and Encampment (*Aula de Fortificações, Artilheria, e Castramentação*) in the Jesuit College of Elvas in the headquarters of the main Army of Alentejo.[44] As we shall see, the rationale behind producing more home-grown engineers was simple: not only were they more likely to remain loyal to their king, they were far cheaper to employ as well.

Problems and issues

The career and life of an engineer was far from easy, however, and was usually fraught with problems of both a professional and a personal nature. First was the question of whose jurisdiction the engineer fell under. This depended largely on the title and position that they held. Cosmander was appointed as colonel and required to report to the governor of arms of the Army of Alentejo. He was also obliged to ask for written permission to leave his post for whatever reason, but on at least one occasion, he ignored this and withdrew to Lisbon without permission. The engineer could also come into conflict with the army's general of artillery. In 1647, for example, the king was obliged to rule that Cosmander was exempted from the jurisdiction of the artillery general of the Army of Alentejo in matters relating to fortifications.[45]

A major problem for engineers, however, was the all-too-frequent challenge to their professional expertise and ability. Their designs were regularly questioned and criticized – most often by their peers than by others. While native Portuguese were generally attacked by foreigners for their lack of knowledge and expertise, foreign engineers often criticized each other for the same reasons. Though never formally appointed to an engineering position during the 1640 war, Matias de Albuquerque was criticized for initially constructing the *trincheiras* around Olivença with too large a circumference, thus making them impossible to man.[46] He was not the only engineer to face such criticism. As part of his tour of the border strongholds of Alentejo in 1662, one of French Marshal Turenne's secretaries declared of Campo Maior that "as far as its fortification is concerned the Portuguese have been led astray by unskilful engineers, who have begun (but not completed) several works which would require a great garrison."[47] The problem was that because no two engineers produced the same design or solution to defence, it was easy to question the competence of a professional rival. In cases where two or more engineers surveyed a major stronghold together and disagreed, it was generally left to the Council of War to determine which plan would be adopted.

As time went on, the criticism of foreign engineers grew louder. In 1658, the Council of War advised the king "to create native-born [engineers], as they are less costly and more reliable than foreigners."[48] Teodósio's earlier *álvara* establishing the School of Fortifications in Elvas in 1651 pointed out that "it is always necessary for us to use foreigners with high salaries and problems, which we can excuse by creating native-born engineers in the kingdom."[49] Foreign engineers had been brought to Portugal as experts in designing modern fortifications and paid significantly higher salaries and emoluments than native Portuguese. They were also despised for expecting to take precedence over local (i.e. native) military commanders. Moreover, not all arrived with practical experience. Francisco Manuel de Mello described Jean Gillot, a disciple (and former servant) of Descartes and teacher of mathematics at the Engineering School of Leyden, as "a studious young man of military architecture, with no experience of it."[50] Pimentel in particular was especially vitriolic in his criticism of foreign engineers, most notably of the French engineer Manesson-Mallet: Pimentel claimed in 1666 that far from being an engineer in Portugal, "he did not have any position, not even as assistant engineer," to which position he was only appointed ten months later, and that in any case, there were long-serving and experienced Portuguese engineers.[51] Moreover, as foreign engineers were hired on fixed-term contracts (usually three years), this provided them with leverage to negotiate better conditions when their contracts were about to expire. By threatening to leave the country, they were able to exert pressure on government to gain an increase in their remuneration, to obtain promotion to a higher military position or gain some other privilege. In July 1648, for example, after Langres threatened to return home at the end of his contract, he was granted the position and salary of 54,000 réis a month as a *tenente de mestre de campo geral* in the Army of Alentejo.[52] In an effort to persuade Gillot, whose contract expired at the end of May 1648, to remain in Portugal at least until the end October (which marked the end of the campaigning season), the king sent him a gift of a jewel.[53] Then, in 1651, taking advantage of the continued shortage of engineers, Gillot negotiated his return to Portugal with his appointment as *maestro do exército do Alentejo e engenheiro das fortificações.*[54]

At issue in terms of their high salaries was the cost to the treasury and to army finances. As one official declared, "the salaries of foreigners are much higher than ours, and they are very ruinous to accommodate."[55] While younger, less-experienced engineers like Bartolomé de Massiac, Robert de Fontaine, and Pierre Gilles de Saint Paul were appointed with a salary of 20,000–26,000 *réis* a month,[56] Langres was initially contracted at 40,000 *réis* a month,[57] though later he negotiated an increase to 54,000. Gillot, too, was paid 54,000 *réis*,[58] while Cosmander was paid 64,000. The highest paid of all was French engineer Sélincourt. As the Count of Mesquitela pointed out, for the same cost as paying him 80,000 *réis* a month, the king could engage ten disciples of Pimentel as engineers' assistants.[59]

Where the experience and expertise of foreign engineers was called into question, the fault usually lay in the manner of their recruitment: as we have seen, they were recommended to or rumoured to have experience and were given contracts by the Portuguese ambassadors resident in friendly foreign courts. Sélincourt, hired in England on the recommendation of Charles II, was singled out in 1662 as being "so old, that because of that, or laxity in these last few days, he has proved incapable of working." His greatest critic, Mesquitela (at that time governor of arms of the Army of Alentejo), complained in 1662 that

> if he has any [knowledge of] theory, he has no practice, nor experience, and none of the [veteran] foreigners say they know him in war to be an engineer, nor has he shown this by service papers when his patent was issued.[60]

In an attempt to address the potential issue of their lack of expertise, from around the 1650s foreign engineers began to be examined upon their arrival by a tribunal of fortifications specialists.[61]

For Manneson-Mallet, there was a significant difference between an engineer schooled solely in the theory and science of fortifications and one who had practical experience in war (like himself). The latter, he declared, is the *true* engineer! It was, perhaps, a subtle insult aimed at his greatest critic and professional rival, Luís Serrão Pimentel. Portugal's Council of War seemingly shared this view when in 1658 it advised the king that Pimentel was "very practised in theory, and someone of great promise if he was practised in war, and it would be very convenient if Your Majesty ordered him there, in the company of his disciples."[62] By 1680, Pimentel had wisely concluded in his own treatise that "neither science alone, nor experience alone are sufficient. Both of these are necessary to form a good engineer."[63]

A potential benefit of hiring foreign engineers was that they sometimes brought with them a brother or a son who served as their assistants, so the Portuguese effectively gained two engineers from the one engagement. Almost from its origins, engineering was a noticeably hereditary profession. Under the terms of his appointment, for example, Santa Colomba was accompanied by his brother, Bartolomé Massiac.[64] Langres's brother Claude, who had been working on fortifications in Malta, arrived in Portugal in 1650; in 1655, his son Jean Dentel was engaged as his assistant.[65] Similarly, Sélincourt's son was included as his assistant in his contract of 1661.[66]

As elsewhere in Western Europe, the life of a military engineer in war was, of necessity, a peripatetic one.[67] The few engineers present on Portugal's war fronts were often obliged to travel remorselessly from one town – or even one war front – to another, to the coast, or to Lisbon. Given the demands placed on them, at times their schedule could be gruelling. In 1661, Santa Colomba was given just ten to twelve days to survey and draw up the designs to fortify Beja; immediately afterwards, he was expected to return to Faro, in the Algarve, and begin the construction of the barbican of Vila Nova.[68] The frequent movement of military engineers, coupled with the relatively high casualty rate among their already-limited ranks,[69] resulted in a recurring problem throughout the war: a lack of consistency in the design, oversight, construction, and progression of the new style of fortifications. As the Count of Prado lamented in 1657, "with the continuous changes, one finds the strongholds of the kingdom with defective fortifications."[70] Once an engineer had died or moved on, a lack of motivation and urgency to continue the work at the same pace often ensued; as we have seen, his replacement often questioned and proposed altering his predecessor's work.

The competition for military engineers, however, was not just between war fronts in Portugal (though the Alentejo usually took precedence over the other fronts). In the wake of the "uprising" of 1645 against the Dutch in Brazil, there was an urgent demand for engineers there. From about 1647, at least five French engineers and two Portuguese sailed to Brazil: Pierre Ponsué (in 1647),[71] Pierre Pellefigue (in 1647),[72] Michel de l'École (known in Portugal as Miguel Lescol, around 1649),[73] Philippe Guiton (around 1650),[74] and Pierre Garsin (1653),[75] along with Portuguese engineers Diogo Paes and *maestro de campo* Gaspar Pinheiro Lobo (both in 1647).[76]

Apart from the depletion of the corps of engineers through deployment overseas, the dangers of serving in war also diminished the pool of available military engineers. A constant risk faced by engineers was capture by the enemy; it was also greatly feared by their masters, as it was common practice – "practically an obligation," as one historian asserts – for captured engineers to change sides. Vauban, generally recognized as the greatest of all military engineers of the early modern period, changed sides when he was captured in 1653 during the Fronde rebellion.[77] Early in September 1647, one of Portugal's key military engineers, Cosmander, was captured en route to the Alentejo. He was taken to Madrid, where he was persuaded to enter the service of the Spanish king. With his intimate knowledge of the fortifications of Portugal's key strongholds, especially those on the main war front, his capture and engagement by the enemy posed a major threat to the Portuguese: "practiced and experienced [as he is] in matters of [the Kingdom], Cosmander alone can do more damage to it than an army."[78] To their relief, however, less than a year after his capture by the enemy, Cosmander was killed while directing the (unsuccessful) Castilian siege of Olivença.[79] Some years later, French engineer Santa Colomba was captured by the Spanish during the battle of Ameixal on 8 June 1663. Despite Portuguese efforts to exchange him for a high-ranking Spanish officer, he remained captive in Spain until the end of the war (though reportedly cooperating with the authorities).[80]

However, the ultimate danger for military engineers was death in action. The risk was greatest while campaigning, and several engineers, both native and foreign, were killed on active duty. Portuguese engineer João Soares was killed in the battle of Montijo in May 1645.[81] However, most engineers met their demise during sieges. In the three-year siege of Ostend by the Spanish that began in 1601, seven of the twelve Dutch engineers employed died before its surrender.[82] In Portugal, Gillot was killed in May 1657, during the successful Castilian siege of Olivença.[83] And at the siege of Villa Viçosa in 1665, the veteran French engineer Langres died a day after being shot in the chest. Fortunately for the Portuguese, at the time of his death, he was fighting in the enemy army, having retired from service in Portugal in 1660 and negotiated his appointment by Spain a year later.[84]

Conclusion

Space constraints have limited this exploration of the provenance, recruitment, and deployment of military engineers in Portugal during the 1640–68 war, and of the role they played in defence through the design and construction of the new style of fortifications associated with the MR. Nevertheless, even from so brief a study, it is clear that there was no neat, linear development in the proposal, introduction, and construction of the new style of fortifications during this war. As elsewhere in Western Europe, of necessity – and certainly in the early years of the 1640–68 war – they were largely hybridized adaptations of existing medieval fortifications. The fortifications of the main strongholds – particularly those of the main triangle of the three artillery fortresses at Elvas, Campo Mayor and Estremoz, and of the provincial capital, Évora – were designed and constructed in an irregular and sporadic fashion over many years. This reflected the lack of stability (not to mention unpredictability) resulting from the constant change of engineers – whether through circulation both within and between the various war fronts or on the termination of their contracts and departure from Portugal, capture by the enemy, or death. Just as importantly, it also reflected changes in attitudes regarding the demands of civilians, the availability of finance, manpower and materials, and the nature and extent of the risk to which the various strongholds and locations were exposed. In the *Cortes* of 1653, the petition of the representatives of Campo Mayor encapsulated the issues in question and their consequences. They asked that the king complete the town's stone fortifications, criticized the successive alterations that various engineers had designed, and declared that

> experience has shown that engineers always propose different plans from those that others have laid down, and are only concerned with undoing what is already done, without finishing anything. With this confusion, much of the town has been torn down, much money has been spent, and the work has been in vain.[85]

Nevertheless, as Portugal's Council of War had repeatedly argued and as successive military commanders had reiterated in their letters to the king, fortifications ultimately proved vital to the defence of the kingdom. In its most developed form, in keeping with the MR paradigm, the "artillery fortress" constituted a formidable obstacle for any enemy army: first, although it required a large, well-equipped, and well-supplied force to attack it, there was no guarantee that it would fall, even if subjected to a protracted (and to the enemy, costly) siege; and second, its ability to withstand a protracted siege provided adequate time for a relief army to be raised and deployed in a counterattack against the besiegers. So, even though piecemeal in its introduction, the new military architecture, designed and constructed over the years under the direction of a small cadre of foreign and native military engineers, played a key role in frustrating the ambitions of the Spanish Habsburg Monarchy to recover Portugal and ultimately safeguarded Portuguese independence.

Notes

1 Alba advised at midnight on 17 June that the army was about to march; the surrender was almost certainly prompted by spies reporting these preparations. See Henry Kamen, *The Duke of Alba* (New Haven, CT: Yale University Press, 2004), 149–50; Lorraine White, "Strategic Geography and the Spanish Habsburg Monarchy's Failure to Recover Portugal, 1640–1668," *The Journal of Military History* 71 (April 2007): 407.

2 Quoted in Kamen, *Alba*, 150.

3 See Bert S. Hall, *Weapons and Warfare in Renaissance Europe: Gunpower, Technology and Tactics* (Baltimore: Johns Hopkins University Press, 1997); Bert S. Hall, "The Changing Face of Siege Warfare: Technology and Tactics in Transition," in *The Medieval City Under Siege*, ed. Ivy A. Corfis and Michael Wolfe (Woodbridge: Boydell Press, 1995), 257–75; Clifford R. Rogers, "The Military Revolutions of the Hundred Years War," in *The Military Revolution Debate: Readings on the Military Transformation of Early Modern Europe*, ed. Clifford R. Rogers (Boulder, CO: Westview Press, 1995), 64–76; Simon Pepper, and Nicolas Adams, *Firearms & Fortifications: Military Architecture and Siege Warfare in Sixteenth-Century Siena* (Chicago: University of Chicago Press, 1986), esp. chapter 1.

4 Mareia Concepción Porras Gil, *La organización defensiva española en los siglos XVI–XVII: Desde el río Eo hasta el Valle de Arán* (Valladolid: Universidad de Valladolid, 1995), 35–42. This text succinctly analyses the various schools of military architecture. See also J.P.C.M. van Hoof, "Fortifications in the Netherlands," *Revue Internationale d'Histoire Militaire* 58 (1984): 99–101; Bruce P. Lenman, "Introduction: Military Engineers from Polymath Courtiers to Specialist Troops," in *Military Engineers and the Development of the Early-Modern European State*, ed. Bruce P. Lenman (Dundee: Dundee University Press, 2013), 17.

5 See Geoffrey Parker, *The Military Revolution: Military Innovation and the Rise of the West 1500–1800*, 2nd ed. (Cambridge: Cambridge University Press, 1996), 16, 24, 26; Geoffrey Parker, "In Defense of *The Military Revolution*," in *Military Revolution*, ed. Rogers (Cambridge: Cambridge University Press, 1996), 348. For an examination of the correlation of the 1640–68 war in terms of strategy, tactics, army size, and composition, see Lorraine White, "Guerra y revolución military en la Iberia del siglo XVII," *Manuscrits* 21 (2003): 63–93.

6 See White, "Strategic Geography," 378–82.

7 For a series of contemporary drawings of castles along the border around 1509–10, see Duarte de Armas, *Livro das fortalezas* (Lisbon: Arquivo Nacional da Torre do Tombo, 1990), a facsimilie of Ms 159 in the Arquivo.

8 Luís de Meneses Conde da Ericeira, *História de Portugal Restaurado* (Lisbon, 1679–98), re-edited in 4 vols. (Porto: Livraria Civilização, 1946), 233–34; Biblioteca Nacional de Lisboa, Códice 10868, Dr. Ayres Varella, "Notícias da cidade de Elvas: Tiradas dos papeis, que escreveu pellos annos de 1654. . . ," f. 64.

9 Horácio Madureira dos Santos, *Catálogo dos decretos do extinto Conselho de Guerra*, vol. 1 (Lisbon: Gráfica Santelmo, 1957), 122; A.E. Martins Zúquete, *Nobreza de Portugal*, vol. 3 (Lisbon: Editorial Enciclopédia, 1961), 330; Ericeira, *História*, vol. 1, 245.

10 Francis A. Dutra, "Matias de Albuquerque: A Seventeenth-Century *capitão-mor* of Pernambuco and Governor-General of Brazil" (PhD diss., New York University, New York, 1968), 166; Santos, *Decretos*, vol. 1, 129; Ericeira, *História*, vol. 1, 234–36. He had been recalled in disgrace from Brazil in 1635 and subsequently imprisoned.

11 A(rquivo) N(acional da) T(orre do) T(ombo) (Lisbon), C(onselho de) G(uerra), Livro de Registo 1, f. 95-v, *Carta Patente*.

12 Rafael Valladares, *La rebelión de Portugal 1640–1680* (Valladolid: Junta de Castilla y León, 1998), 40.

13 Francisco Marques de Sousa Viterbo, *Dicionário Histórico e Documental dos Architectos, Engenheiros e Constructores Portuguezes ou a Serviço de Portugal*, vol. 3 (Lisbon: Imprensa Nacional, 1899–1922), 387, copy of *alvará*, dated 21 May 1671.

14 Ericeira, *História*, vol. 1, 245; Paulette Demerson, "Correspondance diplomatique de François Lanier resident de France à Lisbonne (1642–1644)," pt. 1 (1642), *Arquivos do Centro Cultural Calouste Gulbenkian* 33 (1994): 808.

15 Ericeira, *História*, vol. 1, 267, 277, 285.

16 Paulette Demerson, "Correspondence diplomatique de François Lanier resident de France à Lisbonne (1642–1644)," *Arquivos do Centro Cultural Calouste Gulbenkian* 32 (1993): 539.

17 Margarida Helena de la Féria Vala, "Os engenheiros militares no planeamento das cidades: entre a Restauração e D. João V, 1640–1750" (PhD diss., University of Lisbon, Lisbon, 2007), 550, http://hdl.handle.net/10451/578.

18 Demerson, "Correspondance" (1994), 741, 746, 763; Fernando Cortés Cortés, *Subsidios documentais para o estudo das fortificacões de Évora e de outras praças militares alentejanas nos inicios da Guerra da restauração* (Évora: Bolseira de Doutoramento do Programa HERITAS, 1986), 204.

19 Michèle Virol, *Vauban: de la gloire du roi au service de l'état* (Seyssel: Champ Vallon, 2003), 54; Christopher Duffy, *Siege Warfare: The Fortress in the Early Modern World, 1494–1660* (London: Routledge, 1979), 136.

20 Gastão de Mello de Matos, *Nicolau de Langres e a sua obra em Portugal* (Lisbon: Comissão de História Militar, 1941) provides a useful biography.

21 Matos, *Langres*, 25.

22 Victoria Sanger, "Vauban urbaniste: l'exemple de Brest," in *Actes du colloque 'Vauban et ses successeurs dans les ports du Ponant et du Levant,' Brest, 16–19 mai 1993 et Toulon, 8–11 mai 1997* (Paris: Association Vauban, 2000), 46; Vauban to Louvois, February 27, 1674, in Guillaume Monsaingeon, *Vauban, 1633–1707, un militaire très civil: lettres* (Paris: Scala, 2007), 260. Sainte-Colombe died in 1682 in Brest.

23 María Cruz Villalón, *Ciudades y núcleos fortificados de la frontera hispano-lusa: El territorio de Extremadura y Alentejo. Historia y patrimonio* (Cáceres: Universidad de Extremadura, 2007), 280.

24 ANTT, C.G., Decretos, 1641, maço 1, no. 255, decree dated 14 October 1641.

25 ANTT, C.G., Consultas, maço 2B, no. 84, Report of the Count of Torre and Gregório de Valcaçar dated, 6 April 1642, cited in Cortés Cortés, *Subsidios*, 203.

26 ANTT, C.G., Consultas, maço 5, no. 46, letter dated 7 June 1645.

27 Possidónio Martins Laranjo Coelho, ed., *Cartas dos governadores da província do Alentejo a El-Rei D. João IV e a El-Rei D. João VI*, 3 vols. (Lisbon: Academia Portuguesa da História, 1940), vol. 2, 202, letter dated 23 November 1650.

28 Coelho, *Cartas dos governadores*, vol. 2, 84, letter dated 7 June 1645.

29 Ibid., 202.

30 Allain Manesson-Mallet, *Les Travaux de Mars ou la fortification nouvelle tant régulière, qu'irrégulière*, 3 vols. (Paris, 1671), 93.

31 See White, "Strategic Geography," 386.

32 Manuel Lopes d'Almeida and César Pegado, eds., *Livro segundo do registo de cartas dos Governadores das Armas (1653–1657)* (Coimbra: Biblioteca da Universidade, 1940), 226, letter dated 17 July 1657. On *atalaias* during the medieval period, see João Gouveia Monteiro, *Os castelos portugueses dos finais da Idade Média* (Coimbra: Colibri, 1999), 216–22.

33 Coelho, *Cartas dos governadores*, vol. 2, 61, letter dated 1 September 1644. Not until two years later were the Portuguese reported to be marching to attack the town. Memorial Histórico de España, *Cartas de Algunos PP. de la Compañía de Jesús sobre los sucesos de la monarquía entre los años de 1634 y 1648* (Madrid, 1861–1864), XVIII, 374, letter dated 7 August 1646, Madrid.

34 Mannesson-Mallet, *Les travaux* (1671), 93.

35 Allain Manesson-Mallet, *Les Travaux de Mars ou la fortification nouvelle tant régulière* (Paris, 1684–1685), 175.

36 Ibid.

37 Ericeira, *História*, vol. 1, 434.
38 Nicolas Perrot d'Ablancourt, *Mémoires de Monsieur d'Ablancourt, envoyé de sa majesté très chrêtienne Louis XIV, en Portugal, contenant l'histoire de Portugal depuis le traité des Pyrénées de 1659 jusqu'à 1668* (Paris, 1701), 181.
39 Manesson-Mallet, *Les travaux* (1684–1685), 175.
40 Ericeira, *História*, vol. 2, 118. The recently constructed fort of San Cristóbal guarded the bridge over the Guadiana to Badajoz, on the Portuguese side of the river.
41 Demerson, "Correspondance" (1993), 542.
42 Duffy, *Siege Warfare*, 4. However, in "Introduction," 25, as Lenman points out, while the initiative was not uncommon in early modern Europe, it was seldom successful.
43 Cristovão Aires de Magalães Sepúlveda, *História orgánica e política do exército portuguez: provas*, 17 vols. (Lisbon: Imprensa Nacional, 1902–1932), vol. V, 68.
44 Ibid., 87. The school appears to have been short-lived. Teodósio died shortly after in 1653, though not before he reputedly assisted in the design of bastions in Évora and fortifications in Lisbon.
45 Ericeira, *História*, vol. 2, 225. Ericeira referred to him at this juncture as *engenheiro-mór*.
46 Ibid., 235.
47 Duffy, *Siege Warfare*, 28.
48 Sepúlveda, *História orgánica*, vol. V, 91–92.
49 Ibid., 87, copy of *álvara*.
50 Francisco Manuel de Mello, *Tacito Português*, livro V, cited in Sepúlveda, *Historia orgánica*, vol. V, 94; W.R. Shea, "Descartes in the Philosophical Haven of the Netherlands," *Canadian Journal of Netherlandic Studies* VI, no. i (Spring 1985): 61–85. Gillot was also a Huguenot.
51 Luís Serrão Pimentel, *Méthodo lusitánico de desenhar as fortificaçoens das praças regulares, & irregulares, fortes de campanha, e outras obras pertencentes a architectura militar. . .* (Lisbon, 1680), 467–68.
52 Matos, *Langres*, 44–45.
53 See Coelho, *Cartas dos governadores*, vol. 1, 357, 269–70.
54 H.J. Witkam, "Jean Gillot (1614–1657): un ingeniero de Leiden muerto en Olivenza," in *Encuentros/Encontrosl de Ajuda* 3 (Badajoz: Diputación Provincial de Badajoz, 1997), 233, cited in Cruz Villalón, *Ciudades*, 275.
55 Manuel Lopes d'Almeida, *Notícias da aclamação e de outros sucessos* (Coimbra: Biblioteca da Universidade, 1940), CLXXXIII, doc. CLX.
56 Coelho, *Cartas dos governadores*, vol. 2, 201; Viterbo, *Diccionário*, vol. 1, 365; Vala, "Engenheiros militares," 561, who notes Saint Paul's salary was raised to 36,000 *réis* in 1648.
57 As was Pellefigue when he sailed to Brazil. Viterbo, *Diciónario*, vol. 1, 143.
58 Coelho, *Cartas dos governadores*, vol. 2, 227. Gillot's appointment apparently specified the inclusion of four assistants.
59 Ibid., vol. 3, 266, letter dated 11 October 1662.
60 Ibid.
61 Vala, *Engenheiros militares*, 553–54.
62 Sepúlveda, *História orgánica*, vol. V, 92. Pimentel was sent to the main war front in 1658 and participated in the siege of Badajoz. Viterbo, *Dicionário*, vol. 2, 260.
63 Pimentel, *Methodo*, Proémio.
64 Coelho, *Cartas dos governadores*, vol. 2, 202.
65 Cruz Villalón, *Ciudades*, 277; Matos, *Langres*, 65–66; Sepúlveda, *História orgánica*, vol. V, 92.
66 Vala, "Engenheiros militares," 554.
67 For France's celebrated military engineer, Vauban, too. See Lenman, "Introduction," 28.
68 Alberto Iria, ed., *Cartas dos Governadores do Algarve (1638–1663)* (Lisbon: Academia Portuguesa da História, 1978), 403, letter dated 13 February 1661.
69 As Vauban had observed, it was difficult to build up a pool of competent engineers with adequate accumulated expertise because of the high casualty rates among their ranks. Lenman, "Introduction," 28.

70 A.N.T.T., C.G., Decretos, *maço* 16, no. 52.

71 Viterbo, *Dicionário*, vol. 2, 237.

72 He sailed in the fleet of António Telles de Meneses. Viterbo, *Dicionário*, vol. 1, 243.

73 He returned to Portugal 1653 and was sent first to the Algarve, then to Entre Douro e Minho. He was married to a Portuguese. By 1666, he had risen to the rank of *maestro de campo* and later founded the Academia de Fortificação de Viana do Castelo. He died there in 1688. Vala, "Engenheiros militares," 572; Santos, *Cartas e outros documentos*, 53.

74 He died in Brazil in 1656. Augusto Fausto de Sousa, "Fortificações no Brasil," *Revista do Instituto Histórico e Geográfico Brasileiro* XLVIII, Pt. II. (1885): 93.

75 Virgínia Robertes Rau and María Fernanda Gomes da Silva, *Os Manuscritos do Arquivo da Casa de Cadaval Respeitantes ao Brasil*, vol. 1 (Coimbra: Universidade de Coimbra, 1956–1958), 122–30. He was rewarded with an appointment as *capitão engenheiro* only during the voyage. He returned to Portugal in 1660 and was sent to Beira. Viterbo, *Dicionário*, vol. 1, 413–14.

76 Santos, *Decretos*, 204–5. Though not strictly speaking an engineer, Pinheiro was said to know the city of Bahia and was the person who fortified it. Viterbo, *Dicionário*, vol 2, 237.

77 Lenman, "Introduction," 27.

78 A.N.T.T., C.G., Consultas, Caixa 44, maço 8, Consulta dated 24 January 1648.

79 Report of his capture in Coelho, *Cartas dos governadores*, vol. 1, 182, letter dated 7 September 1647; Ericeira, *História*, vol. 2, 262–63; E. Paar, "Jan Ciermans: Een Bossche vestingbouwkundige in Portugal," *De Brabantse Leeuw, Jaargang* XLIX (2000): 210.

80 Ablancourt, "Mémoires," 169. He returned to France, to La Rochelle, in 1668. In 1674, Vauban reported that "with all of his qualities, he is on his knees, without having done anything for the six or seven years he has remained in La Rochelle." Monsaingeon, *Vauban*, 259.

81 Biblioteca de Ajuda (Lisbon), códice 51-II-15, f. 95, "Relação da batalha do Montijo."

82 Erik Swart, "'Qualifications, Knowledge and Courage': Dutch Military Engineers, c. 1550–c. 1660," in *Military Engineers*, ed. Bruce P. Lenman (Dundee: Dundee University Press, 2013), 62.

83 Santos, *Cartas e outros documentos*, 204–5, letter dated 15 May 1657.

84 Ericeira, *História*, vol. 4, 308.

85 Cited in Vala, *Engenheiros militares*, 491.

PART 2

Sizes of the armies and the rise of the fiscal state

4

ARMY SIZE, STATE EXPENDITURE, AND WARFARE CULTURE IN SIXTEENTH-CENTURY PORTUGAL

Hélder Carvalhal[1]

Introduction

This chapter examines the relation between army size, state expenditure, and warfare culture in sixteenth-century Portugal. It directly tackles one of the components of the military revolution debate, more specifically the mounting size of armies and the financial efforts that states had to develop in order to muster and maintain a large number of effectives, sometimes along several battlefronts, during the early modern period. Using sixteenth-century mainland Portugal as a case study, the chapter argues that this country did not witness the same rate of growth in army size, nor were the necessary economic, social, and political conditions met in the first place. The reasons to explain such a lack of progress go beyond economic and demographic factors. Political and cultural aspects equally determined the survival of a relative archaism into the sixteenth century and beyond.

After a brief bibliographic review, a quantitative and qualitative analysis to three interrelated topics is offered, to demonstrate this argument. The first topic explores the relationship between the evolution of the number of effectives, the demographics, and military recruitment, to determine army sizes across the aforementioned period. Additionally, the recruitment capacity as against the evolution of demography is factored in, using several benchmarks. The second topic examines the state's military expenditure. This attempts to determine whether resources were increasingly spent on warfare or whether, on the contrary, redistribution from the Portuguese Crown to the nobility continued to be privileged, affecting warfare. The third topic concerns warfare culture and its impact not only on military recruitment but also on matters of political decision-making, with obvious consequences on the main topic of this chapter. The results of this threefold analysis help clarify why, according to the point of view stated earlier, the army in sixteenth-century mainland Portugal never grew in size. Consequently, it falls short of meeting all of the traditional components for the existence of a Military Revolution. Instead, the Portuguese monarchy generally kept to a continuity which did not differ substantially from the period before. Therefore, military change was of little significance to sixteenth-century Portugal.

Debates around the Military Revolution and the case of early modern Portugal

Since Michael Roberts set down the founding concepts of military revolution in the mid twentieth century, many authors have advanced with different iterations of the conceptual underpinnings of this theory. Those included the dissemination of new tactics and technology, the increase in size of armies, and the evolution of fortification. Debates have centred on the chronology of the changes, the relevance of those changes, and even the definition of the concept.[2]

One of the major debates regards the growth of armies and its links to the rise of the early modern state.[3] Steven Gunn points out a division between historians and sociologist historians who identify war and competition between states as the key to state development, on one hand, and their counterparts who see war as but one of many other relevant factors in the emergence of the state, on the other.[4] There is no absolute consensus about the exact period when army numbers increased significantly. Geoffrey Parker advocates that a revolution started in the early sixteenth century, the structural change in fortifications being its driving force, allowing in turn for subsequent developments in tactics and the growth in the number of effectives. Other authors, such as Jeremy Black, mark out a significant increase in the size of armies as being limited to the period 1660–1720 only – that is, before the advent of bigger transformations at the end of the eighteenth century.[5]

On the other hand, costs with warfare increased considerably in the period between 1500 and 1700. Along with the improvement of fortifications, the provision of naval forces and the recruitment and upkeep of troops were the at the top of expenses.[6] To support these additional costs, states had to gradually find other sources of income, notably through a more efficient taxation system and redoubled mechanisms of credit. Over the past three decades, there has been much debate around the progressive transition of different European powers from being a "domain state" to a "tax state" and, finally, to a "fiscal state."[7] This was a long and unequal process throughout Europe. While Spain, the Netherlands, and Sweden are usually mentioned as examples where the "tax" state emerged earlier, other cases–such as England or Denmark–remained "domain" states for a longer period.

Regarding the Portuguese context, quantitative studies on army sizes are still lacking. They would help clarify the picture in the long run. In what concerns accounts of military recruitment, much remains to be done. Few scholars have dealt more profoundly with this topic – such as António M. Hespanha and Fernando Dores Costa – for the seventeenth and eighteenth centuries. The literature has often stressed that the absence of mainland episodes of war between 1476 and 1640 (with the brief exception of the Spanish invasion of Portugal in 1580) explains the durability of somehow-archaic military practices.[8] This idea is close to David Eltis's for England in the late fifteenth century up to the mid sixteenth century, where the lack of engagement with European Continental wars opened up a gap in the development warfare. Likewise, the generalized absence of Portugal from the European battlefields contrasted with multiple experiences of warfare overseas, in which naval war or a strong amphibious component during siege episodes remained much more prominent than were open field battles.[9]

This point, while certainly valid for many territories, seems to be excessively deterministic for the internal context of Portugal, in that it does not necessarily imply that the needs of recruitment in mainland Portugal were slim. On the other hand, conflicts in the North Africa–Mediterranean complex increased the defensive needs of mainland Portugal, due to the rise of Moorish piracy on the coast. Thus, this elongation of the Portuguese frontier southwards into North Africa – as the North African outposts were regarded by contemporaries – cannot be dissociated from a more efficient and enlarged basis of recruitment. This made additional workforce available to both Europe and the African continent. In fact, attempts to reform the way military recruitment and training was made –to implement a new order of battle (*ordenanças*) inspired in the Italian Wars model – had happened since the early 1520s.[10] Although it was not implemented until 1570, some of these early contingents even experienced overseas warfare in both Africa and Asia, with mixed success.[11] Despite the general acceptance of such evidence in sixteenth-century Portuguese military history, it has hardly been confronted by other relevant data, starting with the number of resources that the state would spend on war. Therefore, much empirical and comparative work still needs to be done.

The development of the state topic has been widely debated globally for the past fifty years. Portugal is not an exception. Legal historians have been highly influenced by António M. Hespanha's work, which contradicts the more traditional vision of a centralizing state in the late 1400s while advocating for the autonomy of peripheral powers and their ability to contest the political centre well into the end of the early modern period.[12] In fact, during the sixteenth century, the king and the royal family controlled only one-third of the kingdom's total area, representing 38 per cent of the population.[13] This had obvious implications for warfare, as the monarchy continuously had to foster cooperation with the most powerful stakeholders (lay lords and ecclesiastical lords).

Economic historians participating in the debate of the development of the state have examined the rise of the fiscal state and, more recently, the capacity of institutions and the state to manage the debt stock from the 1500s onwards. There has been a debate about the transition from a "domain" state to a "tax" state, following the Bonney–Ormrod model. For the late medieval period, some authors have highlighted the state appropriation of a tax (*sisa*) that was municipal in its origin and the request of extraordinary sums of money (*pedidos*) at the Portuguese parliament (*Cortes*). Whereas in the late 1300s and early 1400s, the rationale for the appropriation of those subsidies was tied to war efforts, it afterwards became clear that they were also meant to help maintain the royal family and their clientele, through the redistribution of resources. Approximately two-thirds of the state expenditure between 1473 and 1527 consisted of redistributive payments – such as subsidies to the royal family and the high nobility, annuities, household pensions, scholarships, and dowries.[14]

The sixteenth century saw the implementation of institutional reforms and changes and setbacks to the fiscal regime, mostly with the new statute of the treasury (*Regimento da Fazenda*) in 1516 and with the reconversion of the taxation model (*sisas*) in the 1560s. The impact of overseas trade on Portuguese finances must be highlighted, especially between the early sixteenth century and the mid 1530s and in the past quarter century.[15] Because of this, sixteenth-century Portugal has usually been described as a period of stagnation in fiscal innovation, where the state developed only slowly.[16] The continuity of some features of a "domain" state (after Portugal had arguably grown into becoming a "tax" state even before 1500) would delay the transition to a "fiscal" state, while the redistribution of resources among the royal clientele continued as the major current.

Stagnation did not necessarily imply a low level of "stateness" if Portugal is to be compared with its European counterparts. The new institutional economic history has recently shown that the fiscal capacity of both Portugal and Spain in 1500 was higher than England's, for instance. This remained true until the mid seventeenth century, when the Dutch Republic eventually showed a greater ability to claim from society higher fiscal resources.[17]

Lastly, we should highlight the importance of credit, as the first emissions of public debt in Portugal started in the year 1500.[18] The Portuguese Crown presented warfare as the rationale behind the first emissions, but overseas trade has been recognized as the driving force towards indebtedness. Because of the revenues from overseas trade, the Crown was able to control the debt stock until 1544. After this point, the rapid growth of accumulated debt due to the provisioning of the Indies armadas had short-term consequences, such as the closing down of the Portuguese factory (*feitoria*) in Antwerp, in 1549. Little is known about the developments from 1549 to 1560, the time when the first default happened – close in time to the defaults in Spain and France in 1557 and 1558, respectively.[19] Again, it would be helpful to understand more clearly how much of that credit was used to pay for soldiers and supplies both overseas and (if at all) on the mainland. We should be able to draw some conclusions from that.

Army size: number of effectives, demography, and military recruitment

For a correct assessment of the issues surrounding the size of armies in early modern Portugal, some aspects that existed from before, in the medieval period, must be pointed out. First, there was no "national" army, something which can even be considered artificial and which would materialize only in the modern period. The army that the king was able to gather, mostly transiently, was nothing more than the product of smaller armies combined. Thus, it was composed not only of the contingents directly under the king's command (such as the municipal militias, members of the royal demesne, or paid mercenaries) but also of the seigniorial armies.[20] According to the recruitment estimates by Francisco Pereira Pestana for c.1530, only 55 per cent to 60 per cent of the total number of troops were summoned directly by the monarch, and these included dependents of the royal household and men recruited from the royal jurisdictions. The remaining came from the military orders, the secular church, and the high nobility.[21] While these figures pose a number of issues (discussed later on), they illustrate the royal dependency on peripheral powers.

A second, connected aspect is the permanence of seigniorial recruitment until late in the early modern period. Because the right to recruit, at the local and regional levels, in many cases was in the hands of the nobility, the king always depended on the nobles to increase his recruitment capacity. Thus, the dichotomy of cooperation and (occasional) conflict between these two stakeholders was very much alive throughout all of the early modern period.[22]

Finally, there were differences between the estimated numbers of recruitment, the contingents actually mustered, and (most of the times) the number of men who actually made it to the battlefield, the latter being the most reliable to estimate army sizes.[23] After these considerations, the major question is whether the number of effectives on the battlefield increased.

In the long run – that is, from the early fifteenth century until the ending of the dynasty of Aviz (1578–80)–the most relevant military episodes clearly always involved a number of effectives between sixteen thousand and twenty thousand (Table 4.1). This remained true well into the early modern period.[24] Exceptions to this threshold of twenty thousand units seem to have been theconquests of Ksar es-Seghir (1458) and Asilah (1471), where Afonso V was able to gather, respectively, twenty-two thousand and twenty-three thousand effectives.[25] That the difference in numbers in the conquest of Ceuta (1415) and King Sebastião's in the battle of El-Ksar el-Kebir (1578) is so short seems staggering. Similarly for the battle of Alfarrobeira, the army of King Afonso V against his uncle, the regent *infante* Pedro (1449), was not radically different in size from the one that conquered Azemmour in 1513. This is especially relevant given that the king's army, at the inherent context of civil war, did not represented the sum of all Portuguese effectives.

TABLE 4.1 Number of effectives in Portuguese armies in the Iberian and North African war theatres (fifteenth and sixteenth centuries)

Setting or battle	Portuguese effectives	Year
Ceuta	18,600–19,000	1415
Alfarrobeira	16,000	1449
Toro	19,000–19,600	1476
Azemmour	20,000	1513
El-Ksar el-Kebir	c.20,000	1578

Sources: Encarnação, "A batalha de Toro," 148; Hespanha, "Introdução," 9–11; Monteiro, *A Guerra*, 90–94; Monteiro, "The evolution of the army," 228; and Sousa, "The war on land," 247–248.

TABLE 4.2 Size of European armies, 1475–1595

	Spanish Monarchy	Netherlands	France	England	Sweden	Portugal
1475	20,000	–	40,000	25,000	–	19,600
1555	150,000	–	70,000	20,000	15,000 (1559)	20,000
1595	200,000	20,000	80,000	30,000	15,000	20,000 (1578)

Sources: Table 1; Parker, "A Military Revolution," 44; Lynn, "Recalculating French Army," 125; and Lindgren, "Men, Money and Means," 130–1.

Comparisons with other European powers on Table 4.2 put this evolution into perspective. Pondering the size of armies in early modern Europe, on the basis of the number of effectives, reserve troops, and mercenaries, is complex.[26] In the case of Portugal, the number of effectives in campaign was seemingly not far from the real recruitment capacity, setting aside the issue of there being "paper soldiers."

Like elsewhere in Europe, the evidence for military recruitment available does not always corroborate the propensity to stagnation that is observable in the Portuguese number of effectives. On the contrary, it is excessively optimistic.[27] One good example is the recruitment estimates mentioned earlier from Francisco Pereira Pestana, a distinguished military officer, which were transmitted to King João III (r.1521–1557) around c.1530. The context during this period was of Moorish power being asserted in North Africa. Repercussions in Portugal took the form of a debate regarding the possible invasion of the Kingdom of Fez or the conservation of the existing Portuguese outposts.[28] Pestana, unrealistically, declared that João III would be able to gather between forty thousand and forty-five thousand effectives, consisting of 7,100 horse riders, thirty thousand infantry (ten thousand town militia and twenty thousand foot soldiers), plus mercenaries and artillery.[29] This estimate was a fallacy, not only because Pestana included troops which would be hard to muster – from garrisons in North African and Atlantic outposts to the private forces of ecclesiastics and lay lords (discussed in the segment about warfare culture) – but also because of the extraordinary costs, since the enterprise would cost an estimated 150,000 *cruzados* (or 150,000 ducats). This sum would be difficult for the monarchy to obtain, in a context of an increasing public debt and escalating financial rupture (see the state expenditure segment).

All the previous estimates on the number of effectives have to be compared against the demography of the realm, focusing on its evolution from the mid fifteenth century to the mid sixteenth century. Recent scholarship has argued that during the decades before the depression caused by the Black Death (c.1320–30), Portugal had around a million inhabitants.[30] This was lower than the first reliable numbers, dating from the *Numeramento* (1527–32) ordered by King João III, in which the overall population number (depending on the coefficient of individuals per household) falls between 1.12 million and 1.25 million.[31]

On one hand, the second half of the fifteenth century was a period of growth, both in the economy and in terms of population, the latter increasing to numbers close to pre–Black Death levels.[32] This period of growth, which became steadier as the sixteenth century drew nearer, suggests a total population close to that indicated in the *Numeramento*. On the other hand, there were factors which, other than stopping this growth, perhaps diminished its increase rate. From 1400 onwards, famine, bad crops, episodes of war, and epidemics happened all around the kingdom, making steady demographic growth difficult.[33] After 1500, there was another issue to consider: the emigration to India, from the opening of the Cape Route. Authors diverge slightly on figures and averages: both indicators vary according to period and context. Guinote, Frutuoso, and Lopes stressed that until 1524 the maximum number of people emigrating per year to India was three thousand. The figure increased to four thousand on at least two occasions: the armadas of 1528 and 1571.[34] In turn, Godinho presented slightly higher figures suggesting that more than four thousand individuals shipped to India in 1524 and in 1538 between four thousand and five thousand.[35] Despite these variations, clearly, some thousands (usually men in active age) were sent overseas per year, and many did not return, dying in shipwrecks, from diseases, and as war casualties. Other factors, such as natural disasters (the plague in 1506, 1527, and 1569 and an earthquake in 1531) and food shortages, point to making a more conservative estimate of the total population.

Table 4.3 presents the ratio of effectives per setting (as described in Table 4.1) when compared with the closest benchmark for estimating population. As can be seen, the percentages of effectives in the period covering between 1415 and 1580 were close to 2 per cent. Despite not being especially populous, Portugal's military recruitment capacity was considerable throughout this period.[36] When compared, the ratio of effectives – the percentage of population in the army – in the mid sixteenth century would be, in theory, slightly inferior to Spain's (close to 2 per cent from the second quarter of the sixteenth century), comparable to Sweden's (around 1.5 per cent in 1555), and far superior to France's (less than 0.5 per cent throughout sixteenth century).[37]

TABLE 4.3 Ratio of effectives per total population, 1415–1580

Effectives (year)	Total population estimates (year)	Ratio of effectives per total population (percentage)
18,600–19,000 (1415)	1 million (1415)	1.86%–1.90%
16,000 (1449)	900,000 (1450)	1.78%
19,000–19,600 (1476)	1 million (1500)	1.90%–1.96%
20,000 (1513)	1.12 million (c.1530)	1.79%
20,000 (1578)	1.2 million (1580)	1.67%

Sources: Table 1; Rodrigues, *História da População*, 519.

This evidence suggests that military needs on the mainland could be satisfied by the existing recruitment ratio. Major challenges would be met as overseas requirements increased, since the demand for the navy and the outposts in Africa and Asia was continuous.

State expenditure

According to the military revolution debate, conceptual thinking around the topic of the rise of army sizes has been linked to the development of the state's ability to generate financial resources. In turn, the rise of the fiscal state has been seen as a consequence of warfare needs, because the latter justified increased taxation levels. Given the context of overseas warfare and intercontinental trade throughout the sixteenth century, the Crown decided to continue with its redistributive policy towards their clientele rather than making a considerable investment in military recruitment, aiming to add to the army. State expenditure was generally assigned according to political and economic needs. Thus, it was clearly in line with the former period. This suggests a certain degree of stagnation at the level of "stateness."

There are three possible ways to explore state expenditure in military affairs: the state "budgets"; the exceptional expenses; and the growth of public debt, account for the credit amassed by the Crown since the early 1500s. During this period, state budgets dealt with estimates of expenditure and not exactly with what was being spent in the end. They are available in a limited number, and the way they were envisaged through time makes a direct comparison difficult.[38] Nevertheless, a comparison with other (similarly under developed) lists of state expenditure and revenues provides us with benchmarks for the years 1527, 1534, 1543, 1557, 1563, and 1588.

Table 4.4 shows the expenditure from 1527 to 1588 (which is the first known budget under the Habsburg composite monarchy). By adding figures for all the categories identified with the redistributive policy – that is, annuities, dowries and scholarships, subsidies to the high nobility, household pensions, and royal family subsidies –all benchmarks total 50 per cent or more, with only two exceptions (1557 and 1588, respectively, with 33.5 per cent and 28.8 per cent). This indicates that the redistributive policy remained relevant for most of sixteenth century, although it gradually lost pre-eminence as the period ended.

Two reasons explain this decrease. First and foremost, the expenses with overseas affairs, which are clear in the percentages for 1534, 1557, and 1588 (respectively, 24.8 per cent, 31.4 per cent, and 36.3 per cent). The early 1530s marked a turning point for North Africa, because of the rise of Moorish power, the debate held at the Portuguese court on whether the Portuguese outposts should be maintained or partially abandoned, and the ceaseless call for more means and men. Consequently, among these overseas expenses was the cost of the armadas and the garrisons of each outpost, namely soldiers and other military staff.

Nevertheless, it is difficult to accurately tell how much expense was dedicated solely to maintaining and/or enlarging the army. The budget for the last

TABLE 4.4 Set expenditure, 1527–88 (in percentage of the state budget)

	1527	1534	1543	1557	1563	1588
Alms and public works	5.0	1.0	0.8	1.0	1.1	2.2
Annuities (*tenças*)	26.7	29.5	33.8	24.7	33.1	22.1
Debt servicing	11.9	4.0	n/a	6.0	13.2	17.3
Dowries & scholarships	5.0	4.8	n/a	1.6	3.7	0.3
Subsidies to the high nobility	3.1	2.0	9.2	4.0	6.0	2.6
Household pensions (*moradias*)	17.9	8.6	12.8	0.6	2.5	3.8
Judicial system	2.6	3.0	2.8	1.7	3.5	7.4
North Africa and the navy	13.6	24.8	n/a	31.4	n/a	36.3
Royal chamber and/or treasury	5.5	5.5	4.7	18.8	8.1	6.0
Royal family subsidies	8.7	7.1	5.1	2.6	5.4	0.0
Exceptional expenses	n/a	9.7	12.0	7.6	12.2	2.0

Sources and criteria: Categories adapted from Henriques, *State Finance*, p. 285 (Fig.36). The category "North Africa and the navy" contained expenditure on the Atlantic outposts. "n/a" is used when the estimate was not included or was not discernible. Data per benchmark as provided by Pereira, "O Orçamento,"208–210(1527); *CSL*, vol. I, 38–42 (1534); Pinto, "Folha de receita e despesa do Reino para 1543," 161–4 (1543); *Gavetas*, vol. I, 891–5 (1557); Pinto, "Folha de receita e despesa do Reino para 1563," 169–172 (1563); and Biblioteca Nacional de Portugal (Lisbon), cód. 637, fls. 11v–34v (1588).

benchmark (1588) indicates that a little over one-third (35 per cent) of the expenditure with overseas affairs was assigned to the payment of wages and the maintenance of soldiers and military staff. This would represent 12.7 per cent of the yearly total. While relevant, this estimate is without comparison, making its evolution impossible to see. Yet it is still lower, for instance, than the estimate for annuities, which continued to be one of the top bulk expenses.

A second other reason lies perhaps in the growing tendency to obtain a more careful and considered plan of expenditure, especially given the context of public debt growth in the mid sixteenth century, as well as higher challenges in the upkeep of the overseas trade. The evolution of some of these categories supports this argument. For instance, the apparent coincidence between the benchmarks of 1534, 1543, and 1563 and the request for extraordinary subsidies in the *Cortes* (see next paragraph) should be highlighted. In turn, after 1560, more resources were being assigned to servicing the debt. This is clear from the increase in the respective percentage in 1588, although it can already be noticed in 1563. The fact that from 1534 onwards budgets started to include a category for extraordinary expenses is revealing. This can be attributed, hypothetically, to high officials of the king's treasury's awareness (*vedores da fazenda*) of the financial situation's deserving concern.[39]

Apart from the expenditure calculations by the monarchy, the exceptional expenditure should be taken into account. This came through additional requests for funding (*pedidos* or *serviços*), which were usually presented before parliament (*Cortes*). In the same way as in the late medieval period, the sixteenth-century *Cortes* under the Aviz dynasty urged parliamentary representatives to disburse the *serviços* needed, in order to cover this type of expenditure. Between 1525 and 1580, the *Cortes* met six times. In four of them (Torres Novas in 1525, Évora in 1535, Almeirim 1544, and Lisbon in 1562), the Crown was able to collect extraordinary revenues worth 550,000 *cruzados* (or 2.2 million *reais*).[40] Behind these requests was the need to pay for dowries, the expenses with armadas and overseas trade, and military costs from the North African outposts. Between 1523 and 1544, the Crown had an extraordinary expenditure of 1.092 billion *reais*, of which half (51.3 per cent) was destined to pay for dowries, more than one-quarter (29 per cent) for armadas to the Indic, and only 14.7 per cent for military expenses in North Africa.[41] This order reflected the priorities of the Crown, as redistribution and the overseas trade came first, and warfare only second, as an unplanned contingency.

An alternative way to assess state expenditure with military recruitment relies, even if only partially, on the evolution of sovereign credit through the emission of public debt during the sixteenth century. As already noticed, extraordinary expenses were high, and additional *serviços* fell short of financial necessities. Therefore, the conditions were created for the debt stock to increase. We know that the debt stock increased in this period and that this became a problem for state finances during the rule of João III, specifically from 1540 onwards. The need to finance the overseas expeditions was the main reason why public debt kept growing, because money was required not only to arm ships and buy silver – the exchange currency for spices – but also to recruit soldiers, subsidize fortification works in North Africa and the province of Algarve, and to pay for additional war-related expenses.[42]

Unfortunately, we cannot accurately discern how much of the credit generated from debt emission was allocated to funding the army alone. Out of the emissions carried out between 1500 and 1580, approximately half concerned warfare and fortifications in North Africa.[43] As other scholars have noted, these emissions were bought by nationals (often close to the king) for relatively small amounts, especially when compared with financial credit granted elsewhere in Europe.[44] Only sporadically were these emissions substantial in terms of warfare, such as the credit of 100,000 *cruzados* (40 million *reais*) that allowed King Sebastião to part fund the offensive war against Fez, in 1578.[45] While this topic remains largely unexplored and deserves further study, we suggest that credit was of little significance to military change, especially in what concerns the increase in size of armies. It certainly boosted the number of effectives momentarily in times of crisis, but no structural change happened regarding the overseas garrisons and even less in the mainland.

Warfare culture

Finally, what extent warfare culture slowed down military change remains to be evaluated. That is, what were the consequences of the well-established martial culture, personified by the chivalric ethos, to the progressive attempts of improving warfare? This question is not new: the deepening incompatibility between the service of nobles' seeking the king's patronage and the modernization of warfare in the overseas outposts has already been stressed by other authors.[46] Many nobles showed their contempt for the new tactics and order of battle (*ordenança*). The idea of having to fight unmounted, side by side with others considered to be inferior, completely overturned deeply embedded values.

Nobles were expected to serve the king whenever they were most needed, much in the same way of the *auxilium et consilium* of medieval times. Yet practice did not always support the theory. The military service in India became progressively more popular than service in North Africa, as the chances for attaining wealth were higher in India.[47] In both – just as in the mainland – requests for more men were trivial throughout the entire period. However, in times of extreme need, there were men who contested the obligation to serve overseas, especially in India –for instance, the noble firstborns (*morgados*) in their responding to the king's request for them to join the Indian armada of 1537. During the subsequent litigation (which they eventually won), the nobles said in their defence that they would fight only for what they considered to be the "border" of the kingdom (i.e., the Moroccan outposts).[48] Economic motivations were clearly at stake, because in theory the noble rank and status ensured them the means to live comfortably, not having to risk their lives abroad. Most remarkable was the open departure from the monarch's orders.

There were divergences regarding the service in Africa as well. In a critical moment of heavy Moorish attacks on the North African outposts (in 1541, by the Saadian army), King João III decided on conducting a general inquiry into every Portuguese village and town. The inquiry aimed to determine whether each royal or seigniorial officer (depending on who had jurisdiction) could enlist all able men for service to the king in battle, along with horses and arms. Unsurprisingly, there was resistance to this. Perhaps the most relevant evidence is the small number of inquiries that are known today. Out of more than eight hundred villages and towns in Portugal in 1541, only twenty to thirty inquiries were returned to the king, most of them from locations controlled by the Crown directly, by a royal family member, or by a member of the nobility close to the monarch. Therefore, many of the jurisdictional lords likely chose to ignore the action. As Romero de Magalhães put it, "the [early] modern state in Portugal took its time until manage to assemble a military organization without having nobles and jurisdictional lords as mediators."[49]

Moreover, the king was perfectly aware of the resistance that the local nobles might put up. The regiment to be followed by the royal officers ordered them to leave the (potentially problematic) nobility until last: "you will place the *fidalgos* last in the inquiry. And you will make it with so much dissimulation that it has to appear as a pure coincidence."[50] Although openly provoking the nobility was not convenient, measures had to be taken so that the nobles did not cause unnecessary complications. Also, control over them had to be increased, because noble resources would probably enable at least some of them to muster more men, mounts, and arms.

The implications of warfare culture were also considerable regarding the several attempts to implement innovative tactics through a new order of battle. Scholarship has mostly explored two situations: an early attempt of military change during the 1520s and its definite implementation in 1570, during the rule of King

Sebastião. On both occasions, resistance from different social strata was visible. From commoners to nobles, the population saw the new order of battle (*ordenanças*) as oppressive. The nobility expressed the same contempt as did their counterparts in the North African outposts. João Rodrigues de Sá e Meneses, the city governor (*alcaide-mor*) of Porto at that time, is known to have made his divergence public, having served among the commoners (*gente baixa*).[51] Nobles from other locations around the kingdom did the same.

The problem, though, was not merely the inherent hierarchical conflict enshrined in the *ordenança*. Again, the greatest challenge for the Crown was to prevent nobles from withdrawing resources, especially their own servants, from the enlarged recruitment basis. Evidence from the 1520s indicates that in Évora, after the recruitment of the vassals (*criados*) of local nobles, the latter not only refused participation but also barred those affiliated to them from participating.[52] In Tavira and Faro (in the province of Algarve), the nobles went even further, by threatening the royal officer (and the commoners) with death if he dared to proceed with the *ordenança*.[53]

Lastly, the nobility's reaction to the implementing of the *ordenanças* in 1570 should be highlighted. This time, the juridical framework was more defined, with some of the mustering powers' being attributed to the municipalities (*câmaras*). More specifically, in the absence of the governor (*alcaide*) – who was often the jurisdictional lord – the municipalities had the right to elect a captain to carry out the recruitment.[54] Facing a new attempt to constrain their military prerogatives, the nobles were quick to contest this royal intention. The high nobility, among them the Duke of Braganza and the Count of Tentúgal, protested vehemently, mentioning that taking away from them the nomination of officials responsible for recruiting troops in their jurisdictions was something they would not accept.[55] Given the moderate success of its late sixteenth-century implementation, the recruitment on behalf of the nobles continued and cooperation had to be achieved among powers. Perhaps the greatest proof of the continuous influence of the nobility in warfare lies on the origin of the bulk of militias led by King Sebastião to North Africa in 1578 (from the centre and south of the realm), as this was traditionally an area of royal influence, as opposed to the seigniorial north.

Warfare culture was clearly an obstacle to military change, both overseas and on the mainland. In Portugal, the chivalric ethos was incompatible with the recent tactics being transferred from other European warfare scenarios. The nobility openly confronted innovations in tactics and the order of battle, and it was reluctant, to say the least, to cooperate with the monarchy. Therefore, we can conclude that military change was unwelcome to large portions of the society, starting with the nobles, who were interested in conserving their martial model.

Conclusions

Despite the renowned attempts to introduce innovations in tactics and a new order of battle, military change was not significant in sixteenth-century Portugal.

There was no visible increase in the size of the Portuguese army in the long run. On the contrary, the maximum size of twenty thousand effectives, seen occasionally on the battlefront, seemingly repeated itself from the late fifteenth century until at least the end of the early modern period. Yet up until the end of sixteenth century, the Portuguese recruitment capacity kept up with the rest of Europe, including countries that were engaged in European Continental wars and that had a greater need to muster as many men as possible. Presumably, the recruitment capacity was enough to fulfil the needs of the mainland. On the contrary, military efforts overseas required a significantly more numerous workforce and were in permanent *deficit*.

Likewise, the analysis of state expenditure in its various forms – whether according to state budgets, extraordinary expenditure, or credit – tells a mixed story. On one hand, continuity regarding the late medieval period is noticeable, because royal redistribution still had a considerable weight in the calculated total expense. On the other hand, expenditure with overseas affairs increased substantially over time. Many necessities contributed to this, including the assembly of armadas for the Indic (which took the lion's share) and for the coast patrol, the fortification of outposts, and provisions and ammunition for numerous locations in the empire. The costs from soldiers were also included in the gross total, although we cannot isolate and compare them effectively. Still, we found no correlation between a hypothetical increase in resources spent overseas and the increase in recruitment and effectives in the army. Statecraft seems to be in a state of relative stagnation for most of the sixteenth century, and even if there were eventual bursts of development, they were not caused by warfare.

Warfare culture also played a role in the failure of military change. Despite the several attempts to "modernize" recruitment procedures and, consequently, to depend less on the nobility and the ecclesiastical lords, the Crown continued to redistribute resources, hoping that these stakeholders would provide military service whenever necessary. Royal attempts at military innovation were seen as an interference in the military prerogatives of local governors (*alcaides*), indirectly diminishing their authority. As these attempts continued, the Crown faced much opposition.

In spite of providing matter for discussion, the Parkerian model of the Military Revolution does not seem to hold well in this scenario. Instead, military change in sixteenth-century Portugal was not significant, it was badly received by large portions of society, and the continuities from the late medieval period were the norm.

Notes

1 CIDEHUS, University of Évora. This work was funded by national funding through the Portuguese Foundation for Science and Technology, under the project UIDB/00057/2020. The author thanks António Castro Henriques, Susana Münch Miranda, and Tiago Viúla de Faria for their bibliographical suggestions and comments about a handful of relevant topics to this piece.

2 Among the main literature that champions the concept and its applicability, see Geoffrey Parker, *The Military Revolution: Military Innovation and the Rise of the West, 1500–1800* (Cambridge: Cambridge University Press, 1996) and also David Eltis, *The Military Revolution on Sixteenth Century Europe* (London: I.B. Taurus, Academic Press, 1995). For strong criticism of the concept, its chronology, and application, see Jeremy Black, *A Military Revolution? Military Change and European Society, 1550–1800* (Basingstoke: Palgrave Macmillan, 1991), 93–96; several essays on Clifford J. Rogers, ed., *The Military Revolution Debate: Readings on the Military Transformation of Early Modern Europe* (Boulder, CO: Westview Press, 1995); David Parrott, *The Business of War: Military Enterprise and Military Revolution in Early Modern Europe* (Cambridge and New York: Cambridge University Press, 2012), 71–100; and, more recently, in Frank Jacob and Gilmar Visoni-Alonzo, *The Military Revolution in Early Modern Europe: A Revision* (London: Palgrave Macmillan, 2016), 1–14, 85–88.

3 Charles Tilly, *Coercion, Capital, and European States, AD 990–1990* (Cambridge, MA: Blackwell, 1990), 20–28, 67–95; Jan Glete, *War and State in Early Modern Europe: Spain, the Dutch Republic and Sweden as Fiscal-Military States, 1500–1660* (London and New York: Routledge, 2002), 10–41; Steven Gunn, David Grummitt, and Hans Cools, "War and the State in Early Modern Europe: Widening the Debate," *War & History* 15, no. 4 (September 2008): 371–88.

4 Steven Gunn, "War and the Emergence of the State: Western Europe, 1350–1600," in *European Warfare, 1350–1750*, ed. Frank Tallett and D.J.B. Trim (New York: Cambridge University Press, 2010), 50–73.

5 Jeremy Black, *European Warfare, 1494–1660* (London and New York: Routledge, 2002), 47–48.

6 Frank Tallett, *War and Society in Early Modern Europe, 1495–1715* (London and New York: Routledge, 1992), 168–87; Irving A.A. Thompson, "'Money, Money, and Yet More Money!' Finance, the Fiscal-State, and the Military Revolution: Spain, 1500–1650," in *The Military Revolution Debate*, edited by Clifford J. Rogers (Boulder, CO: Westview Press, 1995), 273–98.

7 See the essays on Richard Bonney, ed., *The Rise of the Fiscal State in Europe, c.1200–1815* (Oxford: Oxford University Press, 1999) and also Richard Bonney and William M. Ormrod, "Introduction: Crises, Revolutions and Self-Sustained Growth: Towards a Conceptual Model of Change in Fiscal History," in *Crises, Revolutions and Self-Sustained Growth: Essays in European Fiscal History, 1130–1830*, ed. William M. Ormrod, Margaret Bonney, and Richard Bonney (Stamford: Shaun Tyas, 1999), 1–21.

8 António M. Hespanha, "Introdução," in *Nova História Militar de Portugal*, ed. António Manuel Hespanha, vol. 2 (Lisbon: Círculo de Leitores, 2004), 9–33.

9 About these topics see: Francisco C. Domingues, "The State of Portuguese Naval Forces in the Sixteenth Century," in *War at Sea in the Middle Ages and the Renaissance*, ed. John B. Hattendorf and Richard W. Unger (Woodbridge: The Boydell Press, 2003), 187–97; José Virgílio Pissarra, "O Galeão Português e o desenvolvimento das marinhas oceânicas, 1518–1550" (PhD diss., University of Lisbon, Lisbon, 2016); and also Miguel Dantas da Cruz, "From Flanders to Pernambuco: Battleground Perceptions in the Portuguese Early Modern Atlantic World," *War in History* 26, no. 3 (July 2019): 316–41.

10 Jean Aubin, "Le capitaine Leitão: un sujet insatisfait de D. João III," in *Le Latin et L'Astrolabe: Recherches sur le Portugal de la Renaissance, Son Expansion en Asie et les Relations Internacionales*, vol. 1 (Lisbon and Paris: Centre Culturel Calouste Gulbenkian, Comissão Nacional para as Comemorações dos Descobrimentos Portugueses, 1996), 309–69; Pedro de Brito, "Knights, Squires and Foot Soldiers in Portugal During the Sixteenth-Century Military Revolution," *Mediterranean Studies* 17 (2008): 118–47 (129–45).

11 Luís Costa e Sousa, "The War on Land," in *War in the Iberian Peninsula, 700–1600*, ed. Francisco García Fitz and João Gouveia Monteiro (Abingdon and New York: Routledge, 2018), 247–48.

12 See, among other works, António M. Hespanha, *As Vésperas do Leviathan. Instituições e poder político: Portugal, século XVII* (Coimbra: Almedina, 1994).

13 Leonor Freire Costa, Pedro Lains, and Susana Münch Miranda, *An Economic History of Portugal, 1143–2010* (Cambridge: Cambridge University Press, 2016), 21–22.

14 António Castro Henriques, *State Finance, War and Redistribution in Portugal, 1249–1527* (PhD diss., University of York, York, 2008), 273–300; see as well João Cordeiro Pereira, "O Orçamento de Estado Português no Ano de 1527," in *Portugal na Era de Quinhentos: Estudos Vários* (Cascais: Patrimonia Historica, 2003), 159–210.

15 Costa et al., *An Economic History*, 97–99.

16 Álvaro Ferreira da Silva, "Finanças Públicas," in *História Económica de Portugal (1700–2000)*, ed. Pedro Lains and Álvaro Ferreira da Silva, vol. 1 (Lisbon: Imprensa de Ciências Sociais, 2005), 237–61; Bartolomé Yun-Casalilla, "Introduction: The Rise of the Fiscal State in Eurasia from a Global, Comparative and Transnational Perspective," in *The Rise of Fiscal States: A Global History, 1500–1914*, ed. Bartolomé Yun-Casalilla and Patrick K. O'Brien (Cambridge and New York: Cambridge University Press, 2012), 1–35 (4); see as well Leonor Freire Costa, "Fiscal Innovations in Early Modern States: Which War Did Really Matter in the Portuguese Case?" GHES Working Paper, No. 40 (Gabinete de História Económica e Social, Lisbon, 2009).

17 António Castro Henriques and Nuno Palma, "Comparative European Institutions and the Little Divergence, 1385–1800," EHES Working Paper No. 117 (European Historical Economics Society (EHES), Paris, 2019): appendix A1; see as well Leonor Freire Costa, António Castro Henriques, and Nuno Palma, "Portugal's Early Modern State Capacity: A Comparative Approach," unpublished manuscript.

18 See the rationale behind Manueline charter dated 20 February 1500 in José Joaquim da Costa Gomes, *Colecção de leis da dívida pública portuguesa* (Lisbon: Imprensa Nacional, 1883), 120–21.

19 António Castro Henriques, "Uma dívida oceânica," *Revista Contraste* 36 (2001): 12–16. The ongoing project "Sovereign Debt and Private Credit in Portugal (1668–1797)" (PTDC/HAR-HIS/28809/2017), coordinated by Leonor Freire Costa, will contribute to this topic.

20 João Gouveia Monteiro, *A Guerra em Portugal nos finais da Idade Média* (Lisbon: Editorial Notícias, 1998), 79–83.

21 Biblioteca da Ajuda (Lisbon), Cód. 51-V-37, fls. 407–31. Published in Otília Rodrigues Fontoura, *Portugal em Marrocos na épocade D. João III: abandono ou permanência* (Funchal: Centro de Estudos de História do Atlântico, [1966] 1998), 185–94.

22 See, among others, Hespanha, "Introdução," 9–33; Jeremy Black, *Kings, Nobles and Commoners: States and Societies in Early Modern Europe* (London: I.B. Taurus, 2004), 54.

23 This was a structural issue during the pre-modern period. See Hespanha, "Introdução," 25–26; Monteiro, *A Guerra*, 79–83.

24 On this volume, see the chapter by Fernando Dores Costa. For the late medieval period, João Gouveia Monteiro stressed that the figure of twenty thousand effectives was achievable only in ideal and sporadic conditions. See Gouveia, "The Evolution of the Army," 228.

25 Paulo Dias, "A conquista de Arzila pelos Portugueses – 1471 (MA diss., New University of Lisbon, Lisbon, 2015), 13–17.

26 John A. Lynn, "Recalculating French Army Growth During the Grand Siècle, 1610–1715," in Rogers, *The Military Revolution Debate*, edited by Clifford J. Rogers (Boulder, CO: Westview Press, 1995), 117–47 (119).

27 About the exaggeration on numbers of "paper soldiers," see Black, *A Military Revolution?*, 6–7; Lynn, "Recalculating French Army Growth. . . ," 128–32.

28 Fontoura, *Portugal em Marrocos*, 185–94. On the respective North African context, see Weston F. Cook, *The Hundred Years War of Morocco: Gunpowder and the Military Revolution in the Early Modern Muslim World* (Boulder, CO: Westview Press, 1994), 167–216.

29 Outside North African expeditions, the Portuguese monarchy rarely hired mercenaries. See José Virgílio Pissarra, "Navios de remo," in *Navios, Marinheiros e Arte e Navegar, 1500–1668*, ed. Francisco Contente Domingues (Lisbon: Academia da Marinha, 2012), 80.

30 António Castro Henriques, "Plenty of Land, Land of Plenty: The Agrarian Output of Portugal (1311–20)," *European Review of Economic History* 19, no. 2 (2015): 149–70 (168–69). Rodrigues argued that in 1340 Portugal would contain nine hundred thousand inhabitants. See Teresa Rodrigues, *História da População Portuguesa: das longas permanências à conquista da modernidade* (Porto: Afrontamento, 2008), 519.

31 Rodrigues, *História da População*, 519; Serrão, using the coefficient of 4.3 individuals per household, obtained a middle figure on 1.216 million inhabitants. See José Vicente Serrão, "População e rede urbana em Portugal nos séculos XVI–XVIII," in *História dos municípios e do poder local (dos finais da Idade Média à União Europeia)*, ed. César Oliveira (Lisbon: Círculo de Leitores, 1996), 63–77.

32 Ana Maria Rodrigues, "The Black Death and Recovery, 1348–1500," in *An Agrarian History of Portugal, 1000–2000: Economic Development on the European Frontier*, ed. Dulce Freire and Pedro Lains (Leiden and Boston: Brill, 2017), 45–68.

33 Costa et al., *An Economic History*, 24–25.

34 Paulo Guinote, Eduardo Frutuoso, and António Lopes, *Naufrágios e outras perdas da "Carreira da Índia," séculos XVI e XVII* (Lisbon: Grupo de trabalho do Ministério da Educação para as Comemorações dos Descobrimentos Portugueses, 1998), 49–50.

35 Vitorino M. Godinho, *Mito e Mercadoria. Utopia e Prática de Navegar, séculos XIII–XVIII* (Lisbon: Difel, 1990), 364–69.

36 Similar conclusions for the late medieval period can be found in Monteiro, *A Guerra*, 79–87.

37 Jan Lindgren, "Men, Money, and Means," in *War and Competition Between States*, ed. Philippe Contamine (Oxford and New York: Oxford University Press, 2000), 134, 137.

38 On this point, see Henriques, *State Finance*, 281–85; Bonney, "Introduction," in *The Rise of the Fiscal States: A Global History, 1500–1914*, ed. Bartolomé Yun-Casalilla and Patrick K. O'Brien (Cambridge and New York: Cambridge University Press, 2012), 10–11.

39 Gomes, *Colecção de leis da dívida pública portuguesa*, 114–15.

40 Frei Luís de Sousa, *Anais de D. João III* (Lisbon: Sociedade Propagadora dos Conhecimentos Úteis, 1844), 416; Joaquim Romero Magalhães, "As estruturas políticas de unificação," in *História de Portugal*, ed. Joaquim Romero Magalhães, vol. 3 (Lisbon: Círculo de Leitores, 1993), 61–114 (74).

41 Sousa, *Anais*, 415–16.

42 Henriques, "Uma dívida oceânica," 12–16.

43 Gomes, *Colecção de leis da dívida pública portuguesa*, 120–69.

44 Henriques, "Uma dívida oceânica," 12–16.

45 Gomes, *Colecção de leis da dívida pública portuguesa*, 159–60.

46 Malyn Newitt, "The Portuguese Nobility, and the Rise and Decline of Portuguese Military Power, 1400–1650," in *The Chivalric Ethos and the Development of Military Professionalism*, ed. D.J.B. Trim (Leiden: Brill, 2003), 89–115; Vasco Resende, *A Sociedade da Expansão na época de D. Manuel I: mobilidade, hierarquia e poder entre o Reino, o Norte de África e o Oriente* (Lagos: Câmara Municipal, 2006), 38, 161–69.

47 Henriques, *State Finance*, 267–72.

48 Diogo do Couto, *Da Ásia de Diogo do Couto: Dos feitos que os portugueses fizeram no descobrimento dos mares e terras do Oriente*, vol. 5 (Lisbon: Regia Officina Typografica, 1780), 271.

49 Joaquim Romero Magalhães, "As Estruturas Sociais de Enquadramento da Economia Portuguesa de Antigo Regime: os concelhos," in *Concelhos e organização municipal na época moderna: miunças 1* (Coimbra: Imprensa da Universidade de Coimbra, 2011), 11–39 (19).

50 Arquivo Nacional da Torre do Tombo (Lisbon), *Corpo Cronológico*, Part 2, mç. 235, no. 9 [Letter of João III to the royal officer (*corregedor*) in Esgueira. Lisbon, 18 May 1541].

51 For the case study of Porto, see Elaine Sanceau, "A ordenança no Porto no reinado de D. João III," *Boletim Cultural da Câmara do Porto* 29, no. 3–4 (1966): 504–44; Aubin, "Le Capitaine Leitão," 309–69; Brito, "Knights," 136–40.
52 Aubin, "Le Capitaine Leitão," 309–69.
53 Brito, "Knights," 141–42.
54 Magalhães, "As Estruturas," 20–21.
55 See Mafalda Soares da Cunha, *A Casa de Bragança, 1560–1640: Práticas senhoriais e redes clientelares* (Lisbon: Editorial Estampa, 2000), 254–56.

5

WAS THERE AN EARLY MODERN MILITARY REVOLUTION IN MAINLAND PORTUGAL?

Fernando Dores Costa

Was there an early modern military revolution (MR) in mainland Portugal? I introduce a deliberately contradictory and, hopefully, complex reply. There was such a revolution insofar as attention has always been given to European military innovations and their practical use – maritime fortifications and the fortification of terrestrial frontiers being the most significant, along with the recruitment of foreign experts and innovations in battle (albeit with some resistance), which are inherent in the process of dissemination. There was no revolution, however, in the sense that an increase in the number of men actually mobilized in times of war (apparently limited to a maximum of around twenty thousand) is not evident. Similarly, the structural association between fiscal innovations during periods of war (which in part were only temporary until 1762) and the increase in resources extracted from society by the state is also not clear.

This chapter explores four main hypotheses:

1   Portugal's peripheral location within the European system, which resulted in relatively few wars and a weak, warlike culture
2   Difficulties in recruitment because of a strong aversion to military service
3   Portugal's limited demographic capacity, resulting in a structural shortage of men for war
4   Portugal's financial constraints, since fiscal innovations in times of war were merely temporary and subsequently marginal

Some of the characteristic aspects of the MR are undeniably present in Portugal.[1] For example, military fortifications followed new construction rules, first in maritime fortresses, which were more exposed to military threats in the sixteenth century, and later on land frontiers. No strong defensive barrier was built; instead, there were three fortified areas which adopted the engineering designs of the seventeenth century: Elvas, Valença do Minho, and Almeida.[2] The recruitment of foreign engineers crystallized as a tradition, prompting the discontent of native Portuguese. Some denounced the poor quality of these foreigners, who were employed merely because they came from abroad.[3]

The dissemination of information is also evident in battle formation. Records dating back to the beginning of the sixteenth century show formations that can be identified as Swiss. In the royal charter of 15 February 1526, military exercises were introduced as substitutes for those generally engaged on Sundays and holy days, and seen as a way to render leisure time useful.[4] Resistance to this appropriation of leisure time by the royal authorities was predictable.

Furthermore, King Sebastião's 1570 *ordenanças*, which became the central "myth" of the traditional narrative on war in Portugal, were the result of pressure for men to exercise frequently in order of battle. The military capability of a population relied on its state of readiness, which also explains the king's visit to the southern provinces of the kingdom to inspect the results.[5]

There are also works about the art of war published in Portuguese, although their quantity is an inaccurate measure of the degree of dissemination of the discipline, which could be achieved in the original language.[6] Publication in Portuguese had more to do with promoting the author's military culture, as illustrated by the case of Luís Mendes de Vasconcelos.[7] This military culture was a European literary corpus whose precepts circulated among different political units. Following the acclamation of the first king of the House of Braganza in 1640, Joanne Mendes de Vasconcelos, a man with military experience, was asked to comment on a draft statute (*regimento*) of military laws consisting of an overview of the art of war, a project that ultimately was not be adopted.[8] When, in meetings of the Council of War (created by the new king in December 1640), an issue arose concerning the details of style, a suggestion was to ask how it was done in Flanders. The military system of that time was transnational or, to be more precise, trans-state. Governed by state-level decisions, the military system was, in effect, dependent on the relationship between a prince and his nobility, yet tradition and resources were not compartmentalized, allowing for constant inflows. The presence of foreign soldiers was rare in Portugal, but they became significant during the Restoration War[9] – and in the campaign of 1762, with the presence of English troops and the recruitment of two Swiss battalions. In demonstrating the international nature of war, the presence of foreign generals in periods of imminent danger increased: the Count of Schomberg between 1660 and 1668 and the Count of Lippe in 1762 (the latter formally remaining the supreme authority of the army until 1777). As crisis returned at the end of the eighteenth century, so too did foreigners, such as the Marquis of Waldeck and the Count of Goltz.

Despite the opposing tradition, having foreign combatants in his service was not a discreditable factor for the prince, nor was it Machiavellian. On the contrary, it meant that he had sufficient resources to recruit and support men at greater cost than what it would have cost to do the same for his own subjects. To the nobility, an ideal model of organization for war relied on the use of foreigners so as not to prevent the use of the native workforce in the production of noble incomes. At the same time, suspicion arose concerning the greater independence of the royal government in relation to its nobility. Yet in Portugal, this question never arose, because no extraordinary resources were available and nor was there any reason to seek them.

1 Evolution of the size of armies on Europe's periphery

During the sixteenth and eighteenth centuries, wars were rare in Portugal. There was a protracted war with the Hispanic Monarchy (which the Portuguese generally called Castile and afterwards Spain) between 1641 and 1668. Half a century later, the Portuguese participated in a Europe-wide conflict, the War of the Spanish Succession. Another half-century later, the kingdom became involved in the final stage of the Seven Years' War (1757–62). Then, almost fifty years after that, in 1795, the political turn of Godoy's Spain led to military prevention the year after and to a brief and essentially diplomatic military conflict in 1801. By this time, war was a distant catastrophe which now appeared to a generation that had no memory of it. At the time, this was used to justify the problematic lack of military preparedness, and it provides the backdrop for the following reflections.

The Hispanic Monarchy, in decline from the mid seventeenth century, paradoxically became a factor in preserving the Kingdom of Portugal. Even if the traditional image of the "decline of Spain" was unacceptable, characterized as it was by a weaker diplomatic and military capability and a multiplicity of extra-peninsular problems that preoccupied its rulers, the government of Madrid was hardly in a position to focus on Portugal. They merely did so when issues arose regarding the control of the Río de la Plata, as in 1735. The main dispute between the crowns of Lisbon and Madrid concerned the occupation of the bank opposite Buenos Aires. Moreover, the organization of any action against Portugal from the land frontier always proved difficult, because of the region's geographical and social characteristics: unsuitable transport routes and a sparse, largely rural population. The other key factor was related to England's maritime hegemony and alliance with Portugal, which rendered Portugal unassailable by the rival naval forces of France and Spain.

There were times when Portugal did enter into the calculations of the politicians of the *Respublica Christiana* (or of the European system of powers), but at others, it was of little account: the arrival of navigators in India (1498); its annexation by the Spanish Habsburg Monarchy in 1580; its successful separation from the latter, from which it emerged victorious (1640–68); and the initial stage of support for the alliance in favour of Archduke Charles of Austria (later emperor) during the crisis of the Spanish Succession (1703). Nevertheless, during the first half of the sixteenth century, Portugal likely entered into these calculations in view of its presence in the Far East, as it did throughout the eighteenth century, owing to the importance of its Brazilian possessions. The Portuguese nobility had no experience of war in Europe and was only marginally concerned about such conflicts, if at all. This explains why Portugal turned to foreign experts in its time of need.

The rarity of moments of crisis that required a significant military response resulted in few instances where an increase in the size of military forces can actually be observed. A comparison of these moments across time does not seem to suggest a substantial increase in the number of soldiers deployed during times of imminent conflict, as occurred elsewhere in Europe. This is the primary factor to consider in the complex answer mentioned earlier: the absence of an MR in Portugal.

An increase in the number of soldiers mobilized, in response to the social and economic outcome of the technical and tactical changes that led to fiscal innovations and to the creation of a state apparatus is at the core of the concept of MR. Yet the available figures for army size for Portugal provide little evidence of this. There is no series of figures resulting from administrative control that was not supposed to deceive its leaders. Yet the scarcity and poor quality of information on the actual size of armies is not particular to Portugal. The same can be seen in other European powers, including the largest states. What is surprising is the scarcity and unreliability of the figures used by historians.

In addition, the figures used should not be taken at face value; after all, they are part of war. The figures released relating to the forces mobilized by a particular power were part of its external propaganda and internal propaganda and were intended to safeguard its prestige and to attempt to influence its opponent's decision-making. Princes possessed specific statuses, and states enjoyed particular reputations. Thus, biased images of states circulated that were closely associated with their military capacity – in other words, their bravery in combat. Reputation was cultivated and condensed into the qualification of groups with the epithet "those fellows are brave," assigning them zoomorphic homogeneity and determination. In East Asia, sixteenth-century authors writing about the Portuguese mention the defence of the "Portuguese name" – that is, its reputation. Its condition was condensed into its name. Narratives of encounters, as well as the figures given, also contributed to establishing this reputation.

In earlier times, the size of armies was hugely exaggerated. The culmination is a contrast between the number of combatants and fatalities within their own armies and those of their opponents in a given conflict. Figures given for the size of armies are clearly a rhetorical device. An example can be found in the accounts of the Battle of Salado (1340). Given that the Christian army was a quarter the size of that of the Moors, the number of casualties in the reports seem unrealistic: the *Livro de Linhagens* indicated that there were 57,300 dead and captive Muslims, whereas the *Crónica* gave a figure of 450,000 dead.[10] Suspiciously, the Christian casualties numbered no more than twenty.[11]

We can still be misled by the propaganda of that time. In the nineteenth and twentieth centuries, nationalist authors who accepted the exaggerated claims of the chroniclers cherished this propaganda, and it provided them with an even wider contemporary audience through a notion of being a "chosen nation."

The size of armies has been the subject of debate among historians of warfare.[12] In Portugal, there is an example regarding the difference between what occurred on the battlefield and what was later claimed: in 1762, the government of the

Marquis of Pombal announced that in that year it had mobilized forty thousand men – as the marquis had promised. While Portugal's representative in London tried uphold that claim, the British knew this to be untrue and used this to dismiss the efforts of the Portuguese.

On the other hand, the number of men actually engaged in the army may have been considerably lower than what was reported, either through regular mustering or through the "paper soldiers" in muster rolls. The number of men recorded in musters could be inflated by the army officers themselves. Marcos da Isaba, for example, states that half the soldiers were "paper soldiers" and notes the practice of declaring men who did not exist and of substituting servants for soldiers.[13]

Forces deployed from the end of the fifteenth century to the beginning of the nineteenth century

1475: Intervention in the War of the Castilian Succession. The Castilian nobility divided into two parties and Afonso V, king of Portugal, declared his support for his niece as candidate to succeed to the Castilian crown, backing this up with military action. This involved the incursion of a Portuguese army into the neighbouring kingdom up to the most distant point from the border (Toro, where the battle took place). In contrast, incursions during the Restoration War (1641–68) were directed at nearer targets. In 1475, the army appears to have numbered 19,600 men – such as on 25 May 1475, when it left Arronches and crossed the border into Castile, there were 5,600 cavalry and 14,000 infantry.[14] In the battle of Toro (located about 90 kilometres from the Portuguese border) – on 1 March 1476 – eight thousand effectives were on each side.

1580: Often described as the expedition to "conquer Portugal," the army led by the Duke of Alba intended to consolidate the power of the new king, Philip II of Spain. However, the conflict was limited to the opposition of a number of Portuguese nobles who did not accept Philip's claim to the throne. This was manifested by their support of António, prior of Crato. Consequently, the deployment of António's army did not represent the full military capability of the kingdom. The rest of the nobility negotiated its relationship with the new ruling house. Alba's army was estimated at thirty thousand men (others claimed just twenty-six thousand). The military action of Alba's army consisted of a combination of an incursion via the land frontier and naval action near Lisbon, culminating in the Battle of Alcântara.[15]

1588: The Portuguese participated in the Invincible Armada. The armada left Lisbon on 28 May 1588 with 130 ships, eight thousand sailors, and eighteen thousand soldiers. The Portuguese participation included eleven ships, nine from 225 tons to 70 tons and two from one hundred to two thousand men recruited in several cities in a long process. At the beginning of May, there were 1,840 men.[16]

1596: When the English attacked Cádiz, there was a mobilization of soldiers in Portugal in anticipation of a possible attack. Lisbon had been attacked earlier in

1589.[17] Several ways of enlisting men were combined: through colonels, seigniorial levies, and *aventureiros* (gentlemen volunteers).[18]

1624: Bahia was recaptured. There was a naval expedition to Bahia.[19]

1641–68: The Restoration War was the longest war and should have resulted in significant structural change. In fact, the level of military activity varied widely, and in most years, warfare was limited. In the initial stages of the war (1643–6), the Portuguese tried to obtain a military advantage to influence the diplomatic negotiations that preceded the conclusion of the Treaty of Munster. But this failed and was followed by the second stage of minimal military activity (1647–56). In the third stage, the forces of the Spanish king were mobilized to exploit what was expected to be a weakening of the Lisbon government after the death of João IV and during the minority of his heir Afonso VI. In 1658, in a prolonged campaign, the Portuguese failed in their attempt to capture Badajoz and suffered heavy losses. In response, the Spanish laid siege to Elvas, but the Portuguese won their first victory in battle in January 1659. After the 1659 peace between France and Spain, the period between 1662 and 1665 saw an increase in the intensity of the Spanish offensive. See Table 5.1 for the sizes of the armies at this time.

During the Restoration War, in 1664, the year in which the greatest number of men were deployed to the Alentejo, the total of twenty-eight thousand soldiers seems to be exceptional. Nevertheless, the forces deployed by the government of

TABLE 5.1 Sizes of the armies during the Restoration War[20]

Year	Army	Infantry	Cavalry
1643	Portuguese army marching on campaign	12,000	2,000
1644	"Spanish" army under the Marquis of Torrecusa	6,000	2,500[1]
1645	"Spanish" army under the Marquis of Leganés	12,000	3,000
1657	Portuguese army coming to aid of Olivença	10,000	2,000
1657	Portuguese army besieging Mourão	9,000	2,200
1659	Portuguese army to relieve Elvas	8,000	2,900
1661	"Spanish" army under Juan de Austria	10,000	5,000
1661	Portuguese army	10,000	3,500
1662	"Spanish" army under Juan de Austria	9,000	5,000
1663	"Spanish" army marching on Évora	5,000	3,000
1663	Portuguese army under Sancho Manoel	11,000	3,000
1663	7 May muster[21]	12,582[2]	
1664	Portuguese army under the Count of Marialva	23,000[3]	5,000
1665	Portuguese army opposing the Marquis of Caracena	15,000	5,000

1 according to the author, included garrison troops and the most able civilians

2 6,105 soldiers of the *terços* (regiments) of the army of Alentejo; 1,799 soldiers of the armies of other provinces; 1,381 foreign soldiers; and 3,297 auxiliary militias from different regions

3 composed of sixteen thousand Portuguese soldiers and seven thousand foreign soldiers

Madrid to invade Portugal in 1663 and 1665 were not significantly higher than the number that the Portuguese were able to mobilize for their defence. The research currently being undertaken by Antonio José Rodríguez Hernández confirms that there were no obvious differences between the size of the armies of the Spanish monarchy and that of those of the Portuguese.[22]

We can analyse the number of soldiers lost as a result of sieges. Meneses indicated that in their battle with the Portuguese army that marched to relieve the siege of Elvas in 1659, the Spanish suffered one of their greatest-ever losses in the peninsula: after marching out with an army thirty-six thousand strong, Don Luis de Haro defended the lines on the day of the battle with just fourteen thousand infantry and thirty-five hundred cavalry. The following day, when he returned to Badajoz, there were only five thousand infantry and thirteen hundred cavalry.[23] The 1658 Portuguese siege of Badajoz must have caused a similar level of losses to the Portuguese army.

To some extent, this is supported by the idea that it was possible to gather only one army, and if that army was lost, mobilizing another would be impossible. Battle was to be avoided when it could jeopardize an army in just a few short hours and, therefore, the political consequences of the war. Another factor was the possible reaction to enforcing a limitation on military service to eight years. The Council of War reacted, stating that the Third Estate of the *Cortes*, and only that estate, had requested this for their own protection (they were accused of conspiring against their own interests, acting short-sightedly), while the nobility had always opposed this and other petitions against service. This resolution could have resulted in the total ruin of the kingdom, so the king was advised to remove the decree and order that it remain secret.[24]

1668: For the *Cortes* of 1667–8, after peace was negotiated, the Third Estate requested the disbandment of a standing army and abolition of the new taxes that supported it.

1674: In the *Cortes* of 1674, the first to be held after peace, the Crown tried to obtain a larger contribution to re-establish a standing army. The foreseen number of troops after the 1668 peace reformation was of only 4,307 infantry. The government wanted to increase 230 men in eleven *terços* and complete others, which would bring infantry to 7370 men. The expected cavalry was of fifteen companies, with a total of 750 horses. The report identified also 827 "entertained" officers (not including those paid in Lisbon), which corresponded to 15 per cent of the total expenditure. Thirty-two auxiliary *terços* with paid officers were also foreseen. The global military expense (including the innovations) was calculated at 534,232,652 *réis*.[25]

1693: In 1693, a royal order destined to increase the size of military forces was published on the basis that war engulfed all Europe. The aim was to build an army of twenty thousand infantry and four thousand cavalry. The proposal was that each of the existing *terços* would be increased to up to a thousand men. In 1698, following the final meeting of the *Cortes*, a fresh order was made to form the army, strongly indicating that the previous one had never been implemented.

1703: At the beginning of the War of the Spanish Succession, the size of the Portuguese army would have accorded with the second *Relaçam*: sixteen thousand infantry and five thousand cavalry. This corresponds to the figures given in the *Diários Bélicos* (Wartime Diaries) of Friar Conceição, who cites fifteen thousand to sixteen thousand infantry and five thousand cavalry (alongside nine thousand English and Dutch allied troops, totalling thirty thousand men).[26]

1712: A military force of about twenty-five thousand was anticipated.

1715: Approximately thirteen thousand (infantry only; in 1712, approximately twenty thousand infantry had been anticipated).

1717: Naval action resulted from the Catholic diplomacy of João V, which led to the Battle of Matapan in 1717. The Portuguese armada included seven warships, two fire ships,[27] and two auxiliary ships – with 3,840 men and 526 cannons.

1730: A foreign traveller, author of the 1730 *Descrição da cidade de Lisboa* (Description of the city of Lisbon) wrote that the standing army amounted to thirteenth thousand men – ten thousand infantry and three thousand cavalry.[28]

1735: Approximately thirty-six thousand were anticipated.[29] There was a need for 25,200 infantry, which including the artillery regiment and naval forces totalled thirty thousand infantry and a cavalry force of six thousand. The number of infantry had been decreased, though no royal order to that effect had been given.

1735: In *Instruções políticas* (Political Instructions), Luís da Cunha predicted that "without a considerable decrease in his royal coffers or a serious oppression of farmers and *artizantes* (artisans)," the king "could support 20,000 infantry and 5,000 cavalry, employing the rest of his subjects to usefully serve him in times of war, as did Victor Amadeus, King of Sardinia, while his son continued training, that is, regimenting the militia." For his part, Victor Amadeus emulated "the disposition of the Swedish government, though not entirely." However, da Cunha continued, "nothing would suffice until the king" demonstrated that he loved "I do not mean the war . . . but the troops . . . Hence [the best troops belong to the king of Prussia] for he is the most precise and most scrupulous inspector."[30]

King Pedro, "who was certainly not a warrior, demonstrated that he enjoyed watching and learning about military exercises and troop developments, and because there were few men, he employed the *terços*, known as *tabaréus*, to send everyone to the Terreiro do Paço and Junqueira. Here they were trained in the presence of the king." Among the twenty thousand soldiers, it would be advisable for "two Swiss regiments from the Catholic cantons to be included, as these men are worth twice as much."

1750: The army totalled 18,159 men.[31]

1754: The army totalled 18,067 men (including 13,311 infantry).[32]

1791: The information about the infantry in October 1791 indicates that the number of men expected came to 18,460: 15,418 men and 3,042 missing for the predicted staff. The information included the accumulated number of 12,932 deserters, a record of "lost" men that had been maintained (with some discontinuities) in each regiment since the reorganization of 1763.[33]

TABLE 5.2 Predicted and effective forces in infantry, 1797–1803[35]

	Jan. 1797	Jul. 1798	Dec. 1801	May 1803
Previewed	27,376	31,703	31,294	29,559
Missing	7,976	6,035	7,106	10,230

1793–5: A force of approximately thirty-six hundred men participated in the Rossilhão campaign as a contribution by Portugal as an ally of Spain in the war with the French Republic.[34]

1797–1803: The force expected in April 1797 was of 33,456 men in the infantry and 9,120 in the cavalry, totalling 42,576. There seems to be an increase in the dimension of the force, but this is again just the desired dimension, or a "paper army." Information about the cavalry in October 1801 indicated the lack of 1,531 of the 5,420 predicted.

2 A heightened aversion to military service?

During the sixteenth and the nineteenth centuries, the men involved in recruitment claimed that the Portuguese were greatly averse to military service. The conditions under which soldiers served were quite frequently degrading, even impossible, so their aversion to military service is not surprising. However, in addition to these conditions, the desire for "freedom" also encouraged desertion. In effect, the soldier occupied the lowest strata in society. In it, men were condemned with resorting to violence for an indefinite period of time.

But this trend towards rejection of military service which was expressed in resistance to recruitment and desertion from the ranks was not limited to just Portugal. There were similar trends in Spain, France, and Italy. In England, the absence of a standing army led to the infamous practice of impressment, in order to crew the armada. In the German territories, the presence of subsidiary military forces suggests that population surpluses were available for the market of mercenary soldiers, but their participation in the economy and with the seigniorial regime in certain regions remains little understood.

Common soldiers were not moral subjects. Similar to servants in general, they were mere instruments of those expecting obedience from them. As in the management of a household, this demand for submission was reinforced by a flagrant necessity inherent in those who, before the enemy, risked their lives. Yet even men belonging to the middle and upper strata were unable to deliberate on war and peace. Although the doctrine of the so-called just war circulated in the Christian world, it was not for subjects in general to judge the fairness of the war in which they were about to participate. Once they received an order from their ruler to participate in a war, they were required to simply obey. They were subject to the moral decisions of others. On the other hand, it relieved them of any personal responsibility: in theory, an offence committed in consequence of a higher order was the responsibility of whoever issued that order.

In Portugal, there were few signs of voluntary military service and an absence of enlistment to escape extreme deprivation. While elsewhere in Western Europe volunteering was associated with fleeing from an employer's authority, in Portugal the conditions under which soldiers served appears to have been lower than those of the day labourer. In the seventeenth century, the existence of guarantors of the cash bounty paid to newly enlisted men could indicate either the presence of men who enlisted only to receive that prize or of those who were paid by parents to substitute for their sons (known in Spain as *tornilleros*). Nevertheless, desertion could simply have been the act of coerced men who, disgusted, abandoned the army. There is evidence that pressure on guarantors could go beyond the reinstatement of the bounty: sometimes they had to replace the fugitive in the ranks, and those who were frequently the moral authors and protectors of the escape, the parents, were punished. During the Restoration War, guards were placed at the doors of the absentees' houses. Even women were imprisoned in an effort to compel their sons to return. However, there are no indications of a potential excess supply of people bringing men back to the ranks. The complaint in Portugal was always tied to the shortage of day labourers.

In the absence of an officer cadet statute – created only in 1757 – the nobility marked their initiation into the ranks as "volunteer soldiers," the diametric opposite of conscripted men. Thus, joining the army voluntarily was a socially differentiating trait.

Paradoxically, nationalist authors tried to interpret the difficulties that recruiters and commanders felt in keeping their soldiers, which necessitated the mobilization of militia forces during times of conflict, and their extraordinary, yet temporary, deployment in response to great danger, as an imagined willingness of the populace to march in defence of their king. If this had been so, a type of "nation in arms" would have existed as early as the sixteenth century. In this case, Portugal would have been a unique case in Europe and, in effect, a state without parallel, but this was clearly the triumphant image that all nationalists want to promote. The aforementioned system of *ordenanças* of 1570 was interpreted by the nationalist authors as a system of recruiting troops before the existence of a standing army – effectively suggesting that "communities" taxed themselves – when actually it was simply a system of regular training for men in battle formation. The local effects of recruiting just one man from each parish for India could disrupt the entire parish. The latitude enjoyed by recruiters produced a general fear that one – on one's sons, relatives, or servants – could be recruited. Recruiters were therefore showered with gifts, first to avoid recruitment and afterwards to release those who had been recruited.

The quality of the combatants themselves comes from habit – essential training – and not from a national peculiarity that characterizes them in the first place. However, as it is inherent to the reproduction of societies, the prolonged results of familiarity permeate the socialization of modern humans as part of their own nature and the nature of "the others." The quality of men as combatants comes from an incorporated habituation – the essential military training of men – and not from a national peculiarity that would characterize them since birth. The Portuguese are seen as being resistant to subordination and hierarchy and to the use of ordered forms of battle. But aversion to service can be found in many latitudes. It was not a question of national character, because everyone flees from this "enslavement," as it was frequently called. It was, instead, the intensity of the use of the arts of shaping body and mind.

3 A shortage of men for war?

The attempt to relate military capacity and population is a bold venture which challenges the limitations of social history. The lack of data necessarily leads to a series of conjectures. The topic of population presents the added difficulty of having been seen as the supreme expression of decadence from the sixteenth to the eighteenth century. During that period, the population was permanently decreasing, not only when compared to the figures of an imagined and distant golden age but also when compared to a closer era. According to Severim de Faria, the proof of this was a continuous decrease in the size of the Portuguese army. Referring to the conquests of Ceuta and the armies that participated in the campaign for Afonso V's succession to the Kingdom of Castile, Faria declared that Ceuta was taken by twenty thousand soldiers and that King Afonso deployed 30,000, whereas King Sebastião was unable to raise more than eleven thousand men for the expedition to Morocco.[36] Perceptions of that period can be misleading.

An exercise in comparison can be difficult, not only in view of the uncertainty surrounding population size but also in terms of the lack of age-based and social distribution data. At best, the comparison proves merely that building an army had an impact. Where army size represents 1 per cent of the population, and where this might represent a proportion capable of being supported, this could make the army seem insignificant, as it concerned only a small group of people. To assess its importance, it needs to be compared to the total number of young men of fighting age.

The population of seventeenth-century Portugal has been estimated at between 1.5 million to two million people.[37] Therefore mobilizing twenty thousand men would correspond to 1.0 or 1.33 per cent of the total population, a figure that compares favourably with the rest of Europe at that time.[38] If, as records indicate, France had a population of twenty-one million in 1650, mobilizing 1.0 per cent would correspond to a significant army size of 210,000 men. Therefore, 1 per cent was not an irrelevant effort. It was considered the "rational" proportion. Given the remarkable population growth in Portugal during the eighteenth century – the number of households rose from 578,733 to 754,390, an increase of 30 per cent,[39] which in spite of the migratory flow to Brazil expanded the total population to approximately three million by the end of the century – mobilizing the same twenty thousand men would have required far less effort.

The assessment of the social and economic effects of forming an army could be better explained if, as mentioned earlier, it were possible to compare the imagined number of men in arms that rulers wrote in the official papers with potential military effectives. That is, with the number of young men, including the group of unmarried men who did not belong to the most prominent exempt groups. In 1798, a force of 32,000 men was expected to be raised, while an effective force of almost 23,000 was actually mobilized. These figures correspond respectively to 37 per cent and 27 per cent of the effective tax base, which consisted of men aged between seventeen and thirty years old, unmarried and engaged in professions that were less protected from recruiters. The number has been estimated at only 85,700, from a total of approximately 889,000 men over sixteen years old in a population of 2.8 million. This assessment is based on an exercise to compare figures that honour the memory of pioneering statistician Marino Franzini.[40] This presents a different impression – and merely an impression – of the social impact of raising an army: gathering troops could correspond to taking more than one, in fact almost two, from every five of the most eligible young men.

Nevertheless, the "weight" of each army varied considerably among different European states. With regard to the figures analysed by Corvisier in reference to the ratio of 1.0 soldiers per head of population, the following comparison can be made:

TABLE 5.3 Recruitment capacity, eighteenth century (1.0 soldiers per head of population size)

State	Year	Number of soldiers
Prussia	1786	29
Sweden	End of eighteenth century	45
Piedmont	1738	75
Austria	1786	96
France	1789	145
Russia	1796	130
Spain	1759	160
Great Britain	1783	310

In Portugal in the sixteenth century, with a population of 1.5 million individuals (or even less: see the discussion in the chapter by Hélder Carvalhal), mobilizing twenty-thousand soldiers (even if not permanently) would mean taking one out of every seventy-five inhabitants. In contrast, at the beginning of the nineteenth century, with a population of three million, the soldier to population ratio was 1 to 150, at that time in a more permanent way. This proportion is closer to that attributed to Spain or France yet lower than that for other states, except for Great Britain. Corvisier wrote that in the *Ancien Régime*, the mobilization of a significant regular army could be achieved outside of society, England being the best example.[41] In this instance, *outside of society* meant extracted merely from its fringes.

Given a finer approach on the basis of assumptions such as the relation between the number of unmarried men aged sixteen to forty years old (the target group for recruitment) that can be inferred from the Spanish census of 1797 (8.2 per cent of the total), in the case of Prussia, the proportion would not be 194,000 soldiers to 5,700,000 inhabitants but, significantly, 194,000 of a group of 467,400 men – that is, a ratio of 1.0 soldiers to 2.4 men. A figure representing nearly half of all men in the group seems economically unsustainable if it were to discount the fact that the soldiers were also workers. The contrast between countries would thus be largely mitigated, because this would have the effect of classifying all men as soldiers. The duality of the roles of both soldier and worker is decisive.

4 Fiscal innovation justified by war

From the sixteenth century to the eighteenth century, war and only war justified fiscal innovation in European society. The political ideal was that of princes guided by love for their vassals, while expecting they be provided with the necessary support to fulfil their mission, namely with regard to defence. The strength of princes was repeatedly stated to reside in the hearts of their vassals.

Fiscal innovation was regarded with suspicion and at times provoked rebellion. Because changes to the political system of the time were seen as an inherent response to violations of the pact between princes and their subjects, authority could be reinforced only by invoking the exceptionality of conditions arising from a danger that, for a limited time, was imposed out of necessity – in other words, when the lives of the people were at risk.

Initially, the expenditure on defence was low in the general calculations of the king's spending, as there were no professional forces. In times of war, the monarchs would make requests, which required a meeting of the *Cortes*. The request was renewed when a new ruling house was installed, and thus, the first standing army was raised. Once the war was over, a resolution from the Council of State and the Council of War, sent by the Prince Regent to the *Cortes*, stated that maintaining six thousand permanent troops, a *terço* in Cascais, and six thousand cavalry, some money for fortifications and munitions would be necessary and that the taxes would remain until the army contractors had been paid.[42] But the Third Estate objected to the permanence of the taxes. Meanwhile, the Third Estate asked the Prince Regent, Pedro, to commission an inquiry into possible cases of misappropriation that could have occurred in the huge sum of 29 million *cruzados* that had been granted to the king for war.[43] If this figure is correct, the cost of the war for the Third Estate would have climbed to an average of 1,074,000 *cruzados* a year.

In 1668, a number of individuals who had chosen war as a way of life were identified, and to avoid the risk of them crossing into service in Castile, it was argued that they had to be kept in service. Extraordinary taxes were reduced when the war ended in 1668 and again in 1715, the latter following the reintroduction of war taxation during the War of the Spanish Succession. Extraordinary taxes were partly temporary up to 1762, when in this year of war, the *décima* was reinstated once more. It subsequently remained in force permanently, without a reduction.

After the 1668 peace and the measures imposed by the *Cortes* of that year (as mentioned earlier), the reimposition of taxes had to rely on danger or the need for a new war.[44] The opinion of the Marquis of Cascais on a paper that explained the relationship between war and the justification for imposing greater authority could be construed as a curious way of drawing attention to this matter.[45]

The "burden" of expenditure on military forces during the second half of the eighteenth century may seem surprisingly heavy, yet what was called the state was essentially a noble household, albeit a peculiar one: the royal household and its army. Naturally, the expenditure of the household included pensions and interest on loans – some of them remuneration for real and imaginary service – and this could include paying army officers as a type of special pensioner.

In any case, war taxes did not constitute a significant portion of the state's revenues. These taxes related primarily to international and domestic trade and to the contract for the monopolized exploitation of tobacco.[46] The *décima*, known as the "military tax," was much lower than the ecclesiastical tithe (*dízimos*). This latter tribute was closest to a dynamic tax on economic activity, capable of tracking its fluctuations and evolution in the longer term.

Royal revenues in 1681 included the 200 *contos* (i.e. 1 *conto* equal to 1 million *réis*) raised from the Three Estates – which was equivalent to the aforementioned 500,000 *cruzados* – which correspond to a mere 12 per cent of total revenues. In the seven years from 1797 to 1803, the *décima* amounted to an annual average of 647,000 *contos* – that is, 7.8 per cent of total revenues.[47] If we accept the estimate for *dízimos* of 8,000 *contos* made by the governor of the kingdom, principal Sousa, this tax would not even amount to 1 per cent of total revenues. If estimated at 150,000 *contos*, ecclesiastical tithes would equate to a little over 5 per cent of gross domestic product (GDP).[48] In a study dating from 1843, Franzini claimed that the *décima*, which was set at a figure of 1,200 *contos*, corresponded to only 1.5 per cent of an estimated total GDP of 80,000 *contos*.[49] However, we cannot associate periods of military danger with increases in the potential for fiscal innovation or structural change in the state's finances.

Conclusion

Arguably, the war effort in Portugal did not translate into a significant escalation in the mobilization of military forces or structural changes to public finances. Naturally, in the sixteenth century, soldiers were mobilized whenever necessary, only becoming a permanent standing army at a second stage, after 1640 and especially during the second half of the eighteenth century. Yet the army was not large in number and was almost always far below 1 per cent of the population. Only during the Peninsular War (1808–14) did the number of Portuguese soldiers – in effect an accidental subsidiary army of the British army of Wellington in the war of attrition against France – exceed forty thousand.

Portugal emerged as an imperfect "island" because the neighbouring power, Spain, did not exercise enough authority to enforce Portugal's reduction to a satellite state or to absorb it. The land frontier proved unfavourable to any military action – the Franco–Spanish invasion of 1762 was a disaster[50] – and in the naval sphere, the English would not allow the conquest of Lisbon. This led to the insularity of the kingdom and an overdetermination of its geographical position, since the evolution of the Hispanic Monarchy and Britain's naval hegemony – both decisive – are human, rather than natural, factors. On the eve of the War of the Spanish Succession, because of the influence of the king of France, it seemed most likely that the Portuguese court would favour the French candidate. However, because the French candidate could not ensure the protection of Portuguese navigation in the Atlantic, the British option prevailed.

Britain's military attributes, particularly its shortage of permanent infantry forces and the dependence of its overseas authority on naval power, cannot be considered the natural result of its insularity; rather, it was the result of Britain's overreliance on the outcomes of social conflicts (which were not inevitable). Despite the British's and Portuguese's different paths, the Portuguese case seems to follow that of the British.

Portugal's sui generis insularity could have changed due to its long-term integration into European alliances. Luís da Cunha suggested that the king of Portugal should adopt the military reforms of the house of Savoy. Portugal and Savoy were both medium-size states that shared certain parallels, which translated diplomatically into marriages within both houses. Quite insignificant at first, the size of the Savoyard army grew significantly between 1690 and 1713, from under nine thousand to twenty-four thousand men; further growth between 1701 and 1710 saw an increase to the highest point of around twenty-seven thousand in 1704. From 1700 to 1729, Victor Amadeus claimed to have recruited seventy thousand soldiers: fifty-five thousand native troops and fifteen thousand foreign troops. However, despite these reforms, Savoy remained a third-rate power dependent on its allies.[51]

Nevertheless, military reorganization in Portugal allowed the building of an army of enough significance to enable it to join the combined forces of its great allies following this example. A system of ten provincial militia units (as he calls them) acknowledged by Luís da Cunha was established in the domains of the house of Savoy in 1714 (and amounting to ten thousand men in 1727). The conscription of every men between the ages of eighteen and forty was obligatory – parents being held accountable – and the recruits were subjected to two annual training manoeuvres.

In 1703, to secure Portugal's inclusion in another alliance, we saw the alignment of its king with the Anglo-Dutch league in favour of the Austrian candidate to the Spanish throne. In the Methuen Treaty of 1703, the king of Portugal was expected to mobilize an additional force of thirteen thousand to join the allied armies, exceeding its regular army of fifteen thousand. The funding of Portugal's participation in the war was considered in view of an expected allowance from the allies England and the Netherlands. A revenue forecast for 1708 includes the sum of 750 *contos* paid by the allies, which can be compared with the only 400 *contos* from the *décimas*. It was, therefore, a subsidiary army. But the vicissitudes of war did not force this path.[52]

In the mid seventeenth century, Severim de Faria stressed that Portuguese expansion was directed not towards Europe but rather away from this continent. The kingdom was therefore a state engaged in the two spheres: European and extra-European. However, apart from the heritage determined by Portugal's overseas discoveries, this was a characteristic common to several European states. Its specificity lies in its disproportionate involvement in the affairs of these two spheres. In the case of Portugal, this was biased against Europe, unlike other European powers that engaged in extra-European affairs (notably Spain, France, Britain, and the Netherlands).

Notes

1 António Manuel Hespanha, ed, *Nova História Militar de Portugal*, vol. 2 (Lisbon: Círculo de Leitores, 2004).
2 On the evolution of fortifications, see the chapters in section one of this volume.
3 Cristóvão Aires M. Sepúlveda, *História orgânica e política do exército português: Provas*, vol. 17 (Coimbra: Imprensa da Universidade, 1902–32), 16, 20.
4 Elaine Sanceau, "A ordenança no Porto no reinado de D. João III," *Boletim Cultural da Câmara do Porto* 29, no. 3–4 (1966): 513.
5 The term *ordenanças* cannot be translated as "ordinances." *Ordenanças* is a polysemic term. It can be used to qualify laws and orders, but here it has another meaning. The term *order* in this case refers not to law, regulation, or even custom or tradition but to the order of combat that men must become accustomed to through training. It was a system created in 1570 that required all adult men to be organized in companies that were intended to undergo periodic training that would keep them in conditions to be used in case of need. It was mistakenly identified as a system where communities self-recruited men for the army. See Fernando Dores Costa, *Insubmissão: Aversão ao serviço militar no Portugal do século XVIII* (Lisbon: Imprensa de Ciências Sociais, 2010).
6 Loureiro published the "Relação da jornada" of the King Written by João Cascão: F. de Sales Loureiro, ed., *Uma jornada ao Alentejo e ao Algarve* (Lisbon: Horizonte, 1984).
7 Rui Bebiano, "Organização, teoria e prática da guerra," in *Nova História de Portugal*, vol. 7: *Portugal da Paz da Restauração ao ouro do Brasil*, ed. Avelino de Freitas de Meneses (Lisbon: Presença, 2001), 130–47.
8 Luís Mendes de Vasconcelos, *Arte Militar dividida em três partes. . .* (Termo de Alenquer: Por Vicente Alvarez, 1612); Costa, *Insubmissão*, 262.
9 Sepúlveda, *História orgânica e política do exército português*, vol. 3, 49–152.
10 Fernando Dores Costa, "Sobre os militares estrangeiros na Guerra da Restauração," in *Dinámica de las fronteras en periodos de conflicto. El Imperio español*, ed. M.A. Melón Jiménez et al. (Cáceres: Universidad de Extremadura, 2019), 71–86.
11 Bernardo Vasconcelos e Sousa, "O sangue, a cruz e a coroa: a memória do Salado em Portugal," *Penélope* 2 (1989): 28–29.
12 David Parrott, *Richelieu's Army: War, Government and Society in France, 1624–1642* (Cambridge: Cambridge University Press, 2001); John A. Lynn, "Food, Funds, and Fortresses: Resource Mobilization and Positional Warfare in the Campaigns of Louis XIV," in *Feeding Mars. Logistics in Western Warfare from the Middle Ages to the Present*, ed. John A. Lynn (Boulder, CO, San Francisco and Oxford: Westview Press, 1993), 137–59; John A. Lynn, "Recalculating French Army Growth During the Grand Siècle, 1610–1715," in *The Military Revolution Debate: Readings on the Military Transformation of Early Modern Europe*, ed. Clifford J. Rogers (Boulder, CO: Westview Press, 1995), 117–47; John A. Lynn, *Giant of the Grand Siècle: The French Army – 1610–1715* (Cambridge: Cambridge University Press, 1997), 32–64; Pádraig Lenihan, ed., *Conquest and Resistence: War in Seventeenth Century Ireland* (Leiden: Brill, 2001), 345–64.

13 Marcos de Isaba, *Cuerpo enfermo de la milicia española* (Madrid: Ministerio de Defensa, 1991), 79, 117–19.

14 Saul Gomes, *D. Afonso V* (Lisbon: Círculo de Leitores, 2006), 206. For further details and discussion on the fifteenth and sixteenth centuries, see the chapter of Hélder Carvalhal in this volume.

15 Rafael Valladares, *A conquista de Lisbon 1587–1583* (Lisbon: Texto Editores, 2010); Queiroz Veloso, *D. Sebastião 1554–1578* (Lisbon: Empresa Nacional de Publicidade, 1935).

16 Augusto Salgado and João Pedro Vaz, *Invencível Armada – 1588 – A participação portuguesa* (Lisbon: Tribuna da História, 2004), 50.

17 Luís Gorrochategui Santos, *The English Armada: The Greatest Naval Disaster in English History* (London: Bloomsbury Academic, 2018).

18 Costa, *Insubmissão*, 154–56.

19 Brito de Lemos, *Abecedário Militar* (Lisbon: Pedro Craesbeeck, 1631); Stuart Schwartz, *Da América Portuguesa ao Brasil* (Lisbon: Difel, 2003), 143–83.

20 D. Luís de Meneses, *História do Portugal Restaurado*, 2 vols. (Lisbon: na Officina de João Galrão, 1679–1698), 1: 378, 459, 519; 2: 27, 59, 329, 388, 514, 521, 614.

21 Fernando Dores Costa, "Formação da força militar durante a Guerra da Restauração," *Penélope* 24 (2001): 110.

22 Antonio José Rodríguez Hernández is author of *Los tambores de Marte: el reclutamiento en Castilla durante la segunda mitad del siglo XVII (1648–1710)* (Valladolid: Universidad de Valladolid-Castilla Ediciones, 2011).

23 Cláudio de Chaby, *Synopse dos decretos remetidos ao extincto Conselho de Guerra*, vol. 8 (Lisbon: Imprensa Nacional, 1892), 166.

24 Arquivo Nacional da Torre do Tombo (Lisbon), *Manuscritos da Livraria*, liv. 380, fls. 13–15v.

25 Ibid. *Entertained* means an officer who does not occupy a command, due to the downsizing of the army during peace, but who remains as a reserve corps member on the payroll.

26 *Segunda relaçam verdadeyra da marcha, e operaçoens do Exercito da Provincia de Alentejo governado pelo Marquez das Minas D. Antonio Luis de Sousa, dos Conselhos de Estado, & Guerra delRey nosso Senhor, & Governador das Armas da dita Provincia; rendimento da Praça de Alcantara, & diversaõ intentada pelo inimigo na Praça de Elvas* (Lisbon: na Officina de Antonio Pedrozo Galram, 1706); Fernando Dores Costa, "A participação portuguesa na Guerra da Sucessão de Espanha," in *O Tratado de Methuen (1703)*, ed. José Luís Cardoso et al. (Lisbon: Horizonte, 2003), 71–96.

27 A. Saturnino Monteiro, *Batalhas e Combates da Marinha Portuguesa*, vol. 7 (Lisbon: Sá da Costa, 1996). Ships were loaded with inflammable materials are deliberately set on fire and steered, without a crew, into an enemy fleet.

28 Castelo Branco Chaves, ed., *O Portugal de D. João V visto por três forasteiros*, 2nd ed. (Lisbon: Biblioteca Nacional, 1989), 73.

29 Costa, *Insubmissão*, 64.

30 Cunha, "*Instruções políticas*," 268–70.

31 Costa, *Insubmissão*, 64.

32 Ibid., 66.

33 Ibid., 71–72.

34 Ibid., 376.

35 Ibid., 71–82.

36 Manuel Severim de Faria, *Notícias de Portugal*, ed. Francisco Lourenço Vaz (Lisbon: Colibri, 2003).

37 José V. Serrão, "O quadro humano," in *História de Portugal*, ed. António Manuel Hespanha vol. 4 (Lisbon: Círculo de Leitores, 1993), 50–51.

38 Frank Tallett, *War and Society in Early-Modern Europe, 1495–1715* (London and New York: Routledge, 1992).

39 Serrão, "O quadro humano," 51.

40 Costa, *Insubmissão*, 84–85; Marino M. Franzini, *Reflexões sobre o Actual Regulamento do Exército de Portugal* (Lisbon: Imprensa Régia, 1820).

41 André Corvisier, *Armées et sociétés em Europe de 1494 à 1789* (Paris: Presses Universitaires de France, 1976), 73.

42 Biblioteca Nacional de Portugal (Lisbon), Cód. 275, fls. 19v.

43 Ibid., fl. 32v.

44 Costa, *Insubmissão*; Pedro Cardim, " 'Nem tudo se pode escrever': Correspondencia diplomática e información 'política' en el Portugal del seiscientos," *Cuadernos de Historia Moderna: Anejos* 4 (2005): 120.

45 Hespanha, *Nova História Militar*; Luís Chaves, *D. Pedro II* (Lisbon: Empresa Nacional de Publicidade, 1959), 90; Costa, *Insubmissão*, 96–97.

46 Fernando Dores Costa, "Crise financeira, dívida pública e capitalistas: 1796–1807" (MA diss., New University of Lisbon, Lisbon, 1992), 20.

47 José Luís Cardoso, "Pombal, o terramoto e a política de regulação económica," in *O Terramoto de Lisbon: Impactos Históricos*, ed. A.C. Araújo et al. (Lisbon: Horizonte, 2007), 168.

48 Marino M. Franzini, "Considerações acerca da renda total da nação portuguesa," *Revista Universal Lisbonense* 24 (2 March 1843): 293–97.

49 Costa, *Insubmissão*, 95–142.

50 Christopher Storrs, *War, Diplomacy and the Rise of Savoy, 1690–1720* (Cambridge: Cambridge University Press, 1999), 23–54.

51 Costa, "A participação portuguesa."

52 Ibid., 74.

6

"SMALL GOVERNMENT OR BIG GOVERNMENT?"

Assessing state expansion in the war for colonial Brazil[1]

Miguel Dantas da Cruz

This chapter explores the relation between war efforts in seventeenth-century colonial Brazil and the eventual expansion of the Portuguese state in the Americas, in terms of its fiscal and bureaucratic components. The chapter proposes a different interpretation or a parallel development path for one of the better-established theorizations that has arisen from the military revolution debate: the theory that associates the growth of professional armies with the growth of the modern state.

Originally hinted by Max Weber and Otto Hintze and further developed by Michael Roberts (1956), the theory that connects the dots between the revolution in military affairs and the broader transformation of the state is rather convincing: to pay for cumbersome new model armies, states were forced to obtain more resources and collect more taxes, becoming in the process more intrusive and more present in people's everyday lives. The theory is so convincing that has captivated the interest of a scholarship that goes beyond the historiographical agenda of those who are essentially concerned with the Military Revolution or with military history in general. In fact, as a topic of research, the theory is probably even more pervasive in other fields or subfields, such as economic history proper, and is probably revisited more by scholars who are interested mainly in reconstituting the "sinews of power," to use the famous expression of John Brewer (1989), or in exploring the Financial Revolution, to use the words of Dickson (1967).[2]

The transformative role of war in the birth of the fiscal state, as with any other deterministic view, is not bulletproof, though – particularly in the debate about the Military Revolution. There seems to be a problem with the timetable of the major developments, as Jeremy Black argued several years ago. There is a mismatch in the initial formulation between the growth of armies, which started in the sixteenth century, and the consolidation of monarchical power, which occurred mainly during the eighteenth century.[3] The emergence of modern states is not as straightforward as one might be led to believe and should not be understood by looking only to a country's military effectiveness, which is a usual historiographical tendency, as was recently noted.[4]

We know that the fiscal state replaced the patrimonial state in Western Europe, which meant that the majority of a country's resources were afterwards derived from taxes – normally, indirect taxes – and not from the patrimony of the royal house or from royal monopolies. However, we fail to fully appreciate the development of institutional solutions and arrangements that lie behind that transformation, as was foreseen by Charles Tilly several years ago.[5] We tend overlook how those "intermediate institutions" carried what can be described as ambiguous, if not conflicting, implications as far as the rise of the all-pervading modern state is concerned.

The growth of armies did not always lead to larger state bureaucracies and more-obedient royal agents, despite rising taxes. That was certainly the case in England but not everywhere else. In other places, the footprint of the state remained small. In fact, it was so small that we can justifiably ask whether we should use the concept of the state, since that may be misleading.[6] Until the beginning of the nineteenth century, the state continued to play an indirect role. As emphasized elsewhere,[7] but not often enough, the central state continued to depend on private agents and entrenched local powers and mostly relied on tax farming. Of all the institutions of the French *Ancien Régime*, tax farming was one of the most disparaged by the revolution[8] and its "modernizing" agenda.

This chapter builds on Tilly's preposition, and it argues that the increase in fiscal resources earmarked for war in colonial Brazil was not accompanied by royal intrusion. The war the Portuguese had with the Dutch did not produce an upsurge of royal authority. In fact, one can claim that in the initial moment, the increase in fiscal resources was achieved, or agreed on, only because a fragile imperial state withdrew itself, as I try to show. War would eventually play the role that the aforementioned theory purported it to have played in the consolidation of a more recognizable modern state, with its ample bureaucracy replacing local elites, but only in a second moment in the beginning of the eighteenth century.

This chapter first sets the stage in the first two sections by surveying the political and military history of colonial Brazil and then undertakes an exploration of the fiscal arrangements that allowed the Portuguese to wage war in their foremost colony.

Brazil: a distant afterthought

The Portuguese arrived in Brazil in 1500; despite the highly optimistic tone of the initial remarks, nothing of major significance was done. For the first few decades, Brazil was a distant afterthought at best. The colonization of Brazil would represent an unattainable endeavour for such a small country already heavily committed in North Africa and Asia. Additionally, at first glance, the territory seemed to produce only one valuable commodity: Brazilwood. This meant that exploration was relegated to private interests, associations of merchants that continuously rented the right to explore the Brazilian coast. This happened in 1502 and in 1506, for example. Merchant associations established trading posts protected by small garrisons (twenty-four men in the factory of Cabo Frio), but there was no real effort to establish structured colonial settlements. During the first three decades of the sixteenth century, there were almost no settlers, in the traditional sense of the word. There were only a few convicts, deserters, and shipwreck survivors who lived scattered among the Indigenous population.

The intrusions of other European powers, namely the French, forced a more hands-on approach, though not exactly one led by the Crown. Colonization remained a private endeavour for a few more decades, again a tell-tale sign of the geographic focus of Portuguese imperial policy. The solution used was not new. The donatary captaincies (*capitanias-donatarias*), or proprietary colonies, were an offshoot of old medieval lordships and had been successfully implemented in the Atlantic Islands since the fifteenth century. In Brazil, they ensured that the Portuguese presence would continue to expand without putting too much of a burden on the monarchy's finances. However, with a few exceptions, the donatary captains were unsuccessful. They were also unable to guarantee the defence of the territory.

Partly because of that, the Crown established a general government in 1549. This renewed interest in that distant territory did not change the symbolic status of Brazil, which continued to be viewed as a secondary battleground.[9] With the Habsburgs ruling in Portugal, Brazil acquired new strategic importance, buttressing the Spanish colonies in South America.[10] The number of military personnel involved in the defence of Brazil remained small, however. In the years that preceded the Dutch invasion of the capital of Brazil, in 1624, the governor general had fewer than two hundred professional soldiers at his disposal.[11] In Salvador da Bahia, the Dutch also faced the local militia, called *ordenanças*, a few thousand[12] unpaid, poorly trained, and highly disorganized men – subjects who could bear arms. Unsurprisingly, the invading force, a fleet thirty-three hundred soldiers strong and carrying 450 cannons, took the city with relative ease. Eventually, they were expelled by an Iberian rescue force in 1625.[13]

The rich donatary captaincy of Pernambuco, the Dutch's second target in Brazil, was even less protected. In 1629, and before the arrival of the reinforcements that Matias de Albuquerque (the brother of the donatary) brought from Europe, the territory had only 130 paid soldiers.[14] More importantly, these soldiers were apparently paid with the royal revenues directly by the Crown. There were no other participants, no other powers, and no other institutions, as would also be the case in the following decades. Even after the first Dutch invasion in Bahia, Madrid was thinking mainly of using traditional royal revenues, such as the revenues of the Bull of the Crusade (the sale of indulgences), to support the much bigger garrison left in the territory by the commander of the expeditionary force that expelled the Protestants.[15] Basically, Phillip IV used revenues that were collected and controlled by his royal officials.

There were, however, signs that things were changing. By 1626, the Salvador municipal council was already using the proceeds from municipal taxes, in particular the tax on wine, to pay that army.[16] As I try to show in the next sections, this would fundamentally change the role of municipalities in the Portuguese Atlantic Empire, altering the power dynamics between the local elites (who controlled the colonial municipalities) and the Crown. Far from making the latter more ubiquitous, war and taxation would make it retreat.

The Dutch threat and the Iberian response

The Iberian Union (1580) meant that the Portuguese were no longer spared from major European conflicts, as had been the case for several centuries. The last major conflict that they had had with other European powers was in 1475–6, when the Portuguese king, Afonso V, tried to claim the right of his niece to the Spanish throne. The Iberian unification changed all that. Although the Portuguese received many concessions from the Habsburg pretender, mainly related to the conservation of the kingdom's autonomy, they lost the ability to conduct their own foreign police. This meant that all enemies of the Habsburgs became the enemies of Portugal, and the country, especially its empire, quickly begun to suffer the effects of that partnership with Madrid.

The Portuguese Asiatic suffered more at the hands of the English and especially the Dutch, with their East India Company (VOC). In 1621, the Dutch established a charter company for the West Indies, as well, the Dutch Indian Company. Despite its inauspicious start, mainly related to a lack of funding, the WIC was able to organize three expeditions to the South Atlantic between 1623 and 1625. Two of them were sent to the coast of Africa and one to Bahia, the last of which achieved temporary success. Jacob Willekens's fleet, carrying thirty-three hundred infantry soldiers, set sail from Zuider Zee in January 1624, arriving in Bahia in mid April. Operations against the city lasted only one day, partly due to the inability of the Portuguese military leadership. The population eventually fled the city and took refugee inland. From there, the organized resistance, while awaiting metropolitan help, began a guerrilla campaign against the Dutch, attacking Dutch small military units in the cane fields and scrublands. The Portuguese tactics were particularly successful and would be used until the end of the war with the Protestants, and although there was a specific Lusophone name to describe these tactics – *Guerra Brasílica* – they certainly were not specific to colonial Brazil. The "skulking" way of war, decried by many professional European soldiers, was often considered a barbarous and unrestrained way of war that occurred on the fringes of all European empires in the "New World."[17]

Metropolitan help did come the next year (1625). Mobilizing its multiple resources, Madrid assembled in just a few months the largest naval force ever to have crossed the Atlantic: fifty-six ships, 1,185 guns, and 12,463 troops; the force was led by D. Fradique de Toledo y Osorio, one of the king's best generals. The "last great enterprise in the Iberian world in which the traditional feudal obligations and military values of the nobility were effectively mobilized by the crown," in the words of Stuart Schwartz,[18] was a multinational operation. Portuguese,

Spaniards, and Italians took part in the month-long siege of the city, which was ransacked twice in under a year, first by the protestant soldiers, then by the troops of the Habsburgs.

When D. Fradique returned to Europe, he left a large military unit behind for the defence of Bahia. What would later be called the old *tercio*, the *terço velho*, was ideally a thousand men strong and was the first major military unit in Portuguese America; the unit immediately placed a major financial burden on the empire, which certainly did not go undetected by local observers, among whom was the famous Jesuit António Vieira.[19] Changes would have to be made to accommodate the new military spending.

In the meantime, the WIC, which had never stopped its attacks on Iberian shipping, continued its attempts to secure a stronghold on the Brazilian coast. In 1630, and after several years of successful naval looting,[20] the Dutch directed their attention to the captaincy of Pernambuco, the highly successful proprietary captaincy of Albuquerque Coelho. The Dutch thought that the Habsburgs, with their armies overstretched in Europe, would not be overly eager to protect what was only a proprietary colony.

The massive expeditionary force, comprising sixty-five ships, 1,170 guns, and 7,280 men, arrived at Pernambuco on 14 February 1630, started operations on 16 February and took the capital of Olinda on that same day. The force faced much stiffer resistance at the port of Recife, the nearby village, which was defended by a few hundred men led by Matias de Albuquerque. Matias de Albuquerque was the brother of the proprietor and he was also the lieutenant governor sent by Madrid out of fear of the pending Dutch attack.[21] He was also a flexible military leader. Albuquerque's familiarity with the less-than-orthodox naval tactics used in North Africa allowed him to keep the Dutch in check in a terrain that was totally foreign to them. For a few years, the Dutch were confined to Recife and Olinda, being unable to control the countryside. That had been the pattern in Bahia in 1624–5 and would also happen in the later stages of the war in Pernambuco after the 1645 Portuguese uprising against the WIC.

The numbers and composition of Albuquerque army fluctuated over time. The local militias, more than three thousand men strong, and the Indigenous groups were gradually phased out and substituted with men brought from Europe.[22] In addition to being more in tune with some of their commanders' military preferences, these European soldiers were considered to be less prone to defecting. The further away a soldier was from home, the less likely he would be to desert.[23] The first batch of "Old World" soldiers was brought with the fleet of D. António de Oquendo, the Spanish admiral who led the first metropolitan attempt to rescue Pernambuco in 1631.

Oquendo's expeditionary force did not have the same flair as the 1625 Voyage of the Vassals, nor was it as well equipped. The twenty-seven ships, 440 guns, and approximately five thousand men[24] were not enough to reclaim the captaincy. The force was bound to fail, but in the meantime, they were able disembark approximately a thousand men at Bahia, which eventually became the new *tercio*, *terço novo*. The Iberian command feared that Bahia was also under siege – hence the reinforcement of the capital, which by now had a garrison of two thousand men. The Spanish fleet was also able to land an additional eight hundred men in Pernambuco in the aftermath of its clash with the Dutch fleet – or, to use the words of the famous historian Charles Boxer, in the aftermath of the "Homeric duel between Pater [the Dutch commander] and Oquendo."[25]

Of the eight hundred men who landed, seven hundred belonged to the *terço* of the Neapolitan Giovanni di San Felice, the count of Bagnolo. By 1632, the resistance army in Pernambuco was composed of approximately fifteen hundred men, mostly quartered in the Portuguese strongholds of Arraial Velho, Cabo de Santo Agostinho, and Sirinhaém. After a number of defeats at the hands of the Dutch, the army was reduced to approximately 780 men: 600 Iberians and 180 Neapolitans. In the meantime, a mass migration from the northern captaincies to Bahia began. Those who stayed behind in Pernambuco were hoping for metropolitan help, which was known to be in preparation.

Their hope was misplaced, however. Since France had joined the Thirty Years' War on the side of the Protestants at the beginning of 1635, Madrid was now dangerously close to reaching the limit of its military power – hence the limited ambitions entertained by the fleet of D. Lope de Hoces y Córdoba, which set sail from Lisbon in September 1635. Far from being an attempt to expel the Dutch with a single and decisive military blow, the second metropolitan rescue operation could only try to even things out, reinforcing the numbers of the resistance army. D. Lope de Hoces landed approximately sixteen hundred to seventeen hundred soldiers in the colony: seven hundred Portuguese, five hundred Castilians, and four hundred Neapolitans.

This Pernambucan army, now with twenty-one hundred men, most of whom were recruited in Europe and led by a battle-hardened commander, Luís de Rojas e Borja, was soundly routed in the Battle of Mata Redonda in 1636. This defeat, in one of the few examples of European-style battles in colonial Brazil, paved the way for pacification and appeasement between some of the settlers of Pernambuco and other northern captaincies and the new masters of territory. In the meantime, the resistance army continued to withdraw to Salvador da Bahia, where it helped the two *terços* of the city fight off the sieging forces of the WIC.

The third metropolitan attempt to dislodge the Dutch from South America was part of a broader plan to end their naval superiority. Two fleets were prepared: one bound for Brazil, composed of thirty-eight ships and carrying 5,218 infantry, and the other destined for the North Sea, where it was routed by the Dutch in the famous Battle of the Downs (31 October 1639). Fernando de Mascarenhas, the count of Torre, led the Iberian fleet to Brazil, setting sail from Lisbon in September 1638. The need to repair the ships prevented him from going straight to Pernambuco. He headed to Salvador da Bahia, putting even more pressure on the population of the capital, which now had to take care of more than five thousand men.

The expedition only set off for Pernambuco in November 1639, facing the Dutch fleet in January of the next near. The five-day battle was inconclusive but meant that the completely scattered Iberian fleet had failed in its mission to reclaim Pernambuco. The only thing that the Portuguese commander could do was land approximately twelve hundred men, the Luís Barbalho party, to cause as much damage as they could to the economy of Dutch Brazil on their way back to Salvador da Bahia. They destroyed sugar mills and burned cane fields while constantly scuffling the Dutch military detachments.

When the Portuguese declared their independence from the Habsburg Monarchy in December of 1640, the situation in Brazil was in a stalemate. It would be inconceivable for the small kingdom to attempt anything against the Dutch. Not only the Portuguese lost access to the Habsburgs' vast military reserves, they now had to face the same Habsburgs in Iberia. Politcal choices had to be made. Secure independence and reclaim Pernambuco at the same time would be suicidal. Yet things changed in the colony a few years later, in 1645. An uprising led by local Pernambucan elites dragged the kings of the new ruling house of Portugal into a war that they could hardly afford.

A more difficult situation for the new ruling house is hard to imagine, a situation that got entangled in the diplomatic front of the Portuguese secession from Spain. If Dutch Brazil was to be returned to the Portuguese Crown, it had to be through local/colonial efforts, in terms of both manpower and financial resources, which the Crown was more than relieved to have.

More manpower, less state: seventeenth-century experience

If the specialized literature mentioned in the introduction of this chapter serves us well, the power of the Crown, the power of royal authorities, and their capacity to encroach on the day-to-day affairs of the population should have increased with the war. At first glance, there are signs pointing in that direction. The crown took control of the disputed captaincy of Pernambuco not only during the war but also after it, in 1654, in part because the proprietary family was not able to defend its captaincy. Albuquerque Coelhos's fears about there being too much royal intrusion in the wake of major operations were certainly confirmed.[26] At the same time, the Crown created a council dedicated exclusively to the administration of its imperial possessions – the *Conselho Ultramarino* (Overseas Council). The Portuguese Overseas Council replicated, to some degree, the Habsburg model for colonial administration, which revolved around the *Consejo de Indias* (Council of the Indies) and was also attempted in Portugal during the Iberian Union in the form of the Portuguese Council of the Indies (1604–14).

However, the disputed captaincy of Pernambuco nominally remained a proprietary colony until 1716, when the last donatary sold his rights to the Portuguese Crown. In fact, charts of proprietary captaincies continued to be granted throughout the second half of the seventeenth century, and the total integration of those colonies in the dominions of the king was achieved only in 1753, a period marked by undisputed royal consolidation.[27] Regarding the supposedly centralized underpinnings of the new political body, the aim of the Overseas Council was not to define a consistent imperial policy, as has been well documented.[28] The Overseas Council was created for administrative reasons, to improve procedures and communications with the colonies, and to represent the colonies' interests in Lisbon, without unnecessary delay. Its members frequently sided with the settlers against what might have been considered a desired expansion of royal administration (so much for the rise of the modern state).

There are additional and more-powerful reasons to argue that the Portuguese–Dutch War, especially after the Portuguese separation from the Habsburg Monarchy (1640), was a time marked by the scaling back of the state. The best example of this process can probably be found in the way the payment and maintenance of the troops were negotiated, particularly in Bahia.

As mentioned earlier, the municipal council of Salvador increased its role immediately after the city was reclaimed by the Iberian expedition in 1625. In 1631, with the new *terço*, the expenses of the military garrison reached 33 million *reis*, equal to approximately 15 per cent of the sugar production of the captaincy. In addition to other municipal tasks, such as maintaining public works, the alderman and other municipal officials had to find ways to pay for this extensive army. As elsewhere during the seventeenth century, payment was never regular, provoking frequent military uprisings, and was normally made both in cash and in kind with rations (in Brazil, they included manioc flour and meat). The royal treasury was not able to provide for the troops because the only significant tax the king levied in the colony was the tithe (*dízimo*), and this was used to pay the clergymen and civil servants, mainly the judiciary.[29]

The initial arrangement was contentious. Diogo Luís de Oliveira, the governor general (1627–35), tried to take control of part of the tax on wine that the municipal council had started to use to pay for the army. He was, however, undercut by Casa da Suplicação, one of the premier courts in the Portuguese government. The complaints of the aldermen were carefully considered in Madrid and, after the secession of 1640, in Lisbon. There was constant concern about any sign of restlessness. Thus, unsurprisingly, the decisive agreement of 1652, signed between the governor-general, Count of Castelo Melhor (1650–4), and the general population, led by the municipal councillors of Salvador, seemed rather one-sided.

The leading elements of that society agreed to continue to pay for the army, but only under certain formal conditions. They agreed only to pay the rations of the 2,134 men enlisted at that time. The population was borderline insolent, saying that if the "infantry was ever to be increased . . . it will not be paid by us."[30] The payment would be made monthly in a process overseen by a municipal official who would check whether there was someone missing. The intervention of royal authorities was generally discarded, except when municipal officials believed that they might need protection. The agreement clearly stated that royal authorities should not play any role in the collection of taxes – that would be done by local authorities – but they should act as bodyguards: "Your Excellency [the governor-general] will provide us with sergeants necessary to the collections."[31] At the same time, the governor general ought to make sure that all military personnel show due respect to municipal authorities, even if by some change the municipal authorities failed to meet their fiscal obligations.

The local authorities demanded, in exchange for their commitment, the recognition of their role in the collection and application of several taxes, starting with the tax on wine, which remained their main source of income. The municipality demanded both the ability to control the yields of metropolitan salt, which was a royal monopoly, and the imposition of 80 *reis* over each box of sugar, which was the main colonial staple. They also wanted to take over and explore the major contract of flour produced by the three nearby villages of Camamu, Boipeba, and Cairu. Additionally, they wanted to keep for themselves the *terça dos concelhos* – a third of the municipal excises, which was normally handed to the Crown. Over time, they also took control over two other impositions on olive oil and tobacco.[32]

The municipal councillors stated, slightly condescendingly, that they did not want any royal revenues, although none of those taxes was traditionally collected by the municipalities. According to them, that would pave the way for undesired expenditures. They believed, and made their belief clear, that if the king had no royal revenues in this arrangement, he or the governor would refrain from enacting provisions related to special military expenditures or back wages.[33] This condition, far from being unselfishly motivated, was, above all, a way to keep royal authority at bay.

In the name of the king, the governor gratefully accepted the proposed conditions, which were, as it has been noted elsewhere, a blow to the royal authority of a particularly fragile dynasty.[34] The Braganzas were so anxious about their political footing in Europe that there were plans prescribing the transference of the Crown to the New World.[35] The aldermen were so sure of themselves that they even claimed that the troops, now totally dependent on the municipality, "ought to be held together complete and in propriety for any eventuality" in the city.[36] In other words, the leading members of Bahian society were making clear that they did not expect the army to be mobilized elsewhere without their authorization. The army of King João IV was, at least in their minds, a Bahian army. There was almost a transference of the sovereignty function, which could not be more at odds with pervasive literature about the general trends of the Military Revolution. Salvador was not alone. Other cities in Portuguese America, such as Olinda and Rio de Janeiro, played the same role. Even the smaller captaincies, with no more than one or two companies, made similar arrangements.[37]

If the rise of the fiscal state is solely a function of the increase of indirect taxes needed for mass military mobilization, then Brazil was no exception. However, if it also means the rise of a bureaucratic apparatus, then mid-seventeenth-century Brazil does not fit the model. There was no significant fiscal innovation or institutional transformation, as happened in the mother country with the creation of the *Junta dos Três Estados* to oversee the collection of *décima*, a universal income tax of 10 per cent, which was unparalleled in Europe at that time.[38]

That institutional innovation certainly "ticks more boxes" as far as state building is concerned. However, even then, the metropolitan municipalities were not absent from that process. In fact, these municipalities were central, going beyond the collection of taxes during the war in the Spanish border, which lasted for twenty-eight years (1640–68). The metropolitan municipalities authorized recruitment, provided armaments, assisted military governors in exercising their powers, and repaired fortresses and walls.[39] To be sure, in the mother country they were not leading the process, which was headed by the Crown via a new political body purposely built for fiscal management in times of war: Junta dos Três Estados. This type of centralized encroachment, as watered-down as might have been, did not happened in colonial Brazil, and that is the main point of this chapter: the increase in taxes in Brazil did not lead to the encroachment of royal authority. There were no new comprehensive taxes like the *décima*, there were no new political bodies to oversee tax collection, and even the army, which should guarantee the King's will, was seen with some distrust in Lisbon, their allegiance being frequently questioned.

In the mid 1670s, with the war with the Dutch long gone (which had ended in 1654), the fiscal system that put so much power in the hands of local elites and municipalities began to be re-evaluated. In the Overseas Council, amid accusations of negligence and malpractice, emerged a conspicuous anxiety: the suspicious allegiance of the army, which the councillors believed would always take the side of those who provided its means of subsistence. The Overseas Council probably still remembered the *Revolta da Cachaça* (Rio de Janeiro, 1660), a revolt, ignited by increased taxation on locally produced liquor, that the army became involved in on the side of the conspirators. Such recurrent fears led the Overseas Council to state in 1676 that "the municipalities should administer solely municipal excises; they also should not have the infantry at their orders to help them in any event [since] the infantry put itself on their side, as experience has shown."[40]

At that time, no action was taken, however. The idea that taxes were more tolerable when collected by local officials, as the 1624 *Croquant* uprisings in Quercy (France) proved, prevailed: "The People [*Povo*] will always find great complaint, with substantive grounds, when they see what they give in the hands of royal ministers," the Count of Óbidos, the second viceroy of Brazil (1663–7), had said a few years before. He too had been confronted with the possibility of handing over the collection and management of all taxes to the *provedor-mor* (the chief financial officer of the Crown), a possibility that he refused.[41]

More manpower, more state: eighteenth-century experience

The relation between warfare and the rise of the fiscal state in the Portuguese South Atlantic, which was doubtful at best in the seventeenth century, saw major developments in the beginning of the eighteenth century. After several decades of peace, Portugal entangled itself in another international conflict, this time the War of the Spanish Succession (1701–14), which had a major theatre of operations in Iberia as well as some emblematic offshoots in the Americas, where the French attacked southern Brazil in 1710 and 1711.

After failing to take the city of Rio de Janeiro in September 1710 – the French landing force fought its way into the city but was defeated by a combination of regulars, militias, and armed slaves – the French assembled a second expedition the next year:[42] this time, a much-better-prepared expedition, comprising seven ships of the line, five frigates, one galliot, and three bomb-ketches. The expedition's commander was an experienced corsair named René Duguay-Trouin, who was able to surprise the Portuguese garrison in Rio de Janeiro in September 1711, despite the warnings sent to the garrison by Lisbon.

The Portuguese's military superiority in terms of raw numbers and their stiff but inconsistent resistance were to no avail, and the city was eventually taken after being abandoned. In addition to looting the city, the French, fearing Portuguese reinforcements from Minas Gerais, demanded a large ransom. Duguay-Trouin threatened to raze the city to the ground. The population paid 244 million *reis*, a hundred boxes of sugar, and two hundred heads of cattle. Famous nineteenth-century historian Francisco Varnhagen said that the losses were in fact much larger, amounting to 12 billion *reis*.[43] The figure, if accurate, is absolutely abysmal. It corresponded, according to some contemporary estimates, to five years of Portuguese military operations in the Iberian Peninsula during the War of the Spanish Succession.[44]

When the news about the fall of Rio de Janeiro reached Lisbon at the beginning of 1712, it caused great anxiety. The country had changed sides during the war because it believed that the Bourbon block could not provide the help needed on the imperial front, which the Portuguese wanted to protect at all costs. Lisbon had been relying on the naval superiority of the Great Alliance that supported Archduke Charles of Habsburg, particularly the strength of the Netherlands and Great Britain, though such support was not stipulated in the multilateral agreements.

The French attack was compounded by a wave of contestation, revolts, and uprisings that swept through colonial Brazil. Royal authority was constantly challenged by Portuguese subjects in the Americas, and those subjects even started two civil wars. One civil war was in the rich territory of Minas Gerais, where gold had been discovered in the last years of the seventeenth century and where the famous *Paulistas* had been trying to fend off newcomers since 1707 (they failed). The other civil war, which took place between 1710 and 1711, was in Pernambuco, where an entrenched elite of sugar planters tried to do the same thing, deposing the governor in the process. There was another uprising in Bahia, in part fuelled by the catastrophic surrender of Rio de Janeiro.[45]

An increasing number of meetings were held by the Council of State and the Overseas Council.[46] The country was in a difficult situation. It needed to send military reinforcements to Brazil both to secure the territory against a hostile new invasion and to quash the internal revolts. However, this meant increasing taxes on an already-restless colonial population. This was probably the first time the empire was being conceived in a truly top-down fashion, with royal ministers voicing their concerns about the loyalty of overseas subjects. There were even cries for a revolving system of military regiments to avoid undesirable ties with the population, according to which every military unit in Brazil ought to be replaced each year by another one sent by the mother country because "in so little time the soldiers would not coalesce with the people [settlers] nor with their ways."[47] The most famous minister of the Overseas Council during this time period, António Rodrigues da Costa, even proposed the extinction of the suspicious *terço* of Pernambuco, which sided with the conspirators.[48] Such was his distrust.

Of particular concern to the royal ministers was the taxation arrangement that had been instrumental in paying for the army for the last several decades. If the settlers, represented in the municipalities, were not to be trusted, their control over the army – the very army that might take their side – had been at least an imprudent solution. The municipalities ought to be replaced by royal officials, by the state.

The opportunity finally arose, first in Bahia, when the aldermen, confronted by the increase in taxes and other changes introduced since the 1652 agreement, proposed stepping aside. There was a surprising split in the Overseas Council, where some councillors were more worried about the growth of the bureaucracy of salaried royal officials that the change would inevitably entail.[49] They feared, as did many others,[50] what we call today operational costs. The faction that wanted to end municipal autonomy in military affairs had the majority in the council, however. The already-mentioned Rodrigues da Costa said that "it is always convenient to the Royal service of Your Majesty to take these [fiscal/military] administrations away from the overseas municipalities, as well as their overall jurisdictions." Rodrigues da Costa could not have been more open about his political and institutional vision for the empire, an empire in which the state, not local elites and their municipalities, would hold sovereignty functions. In this vision, he was seconded by Francisco Monteiro de Miranda, another overseas councillor, who stated that

> when Your Majesty's grandfather gave them [the municipalities] this administration, it promised advantages to the Royal Treasury; nowadays it does not give advantages, it takes them away, as we experience with all municipal administration of royal revenues in the Conquests.[51]

A few months later, the king upheld the council's proposal. Salvador was finally stripped of its former military function, and the same was done in Rio de Janeiro and Pernambuco soon after.[52] The door was finally opened for the growth of state bureaucracy.

Closing remarks

It is difficult to argue against the role of warfare in the development of the modern state. Portugal and its empire were no different from any other early modern European power. This chapter has tried to show that the relation was not as straightforward as one would assume amid the Military Revolution. Most of the all, this chapter has tried to show that we cannot equate the rise of taxation earmarked for military expenses with the rise of the all-pervading state or with a bureaucracy of royal agents and massive overreach. The fiscal state, as opposed to the patrimonial state, did not include the suppression of concurrent powers. In fact, what colonial Brazil shows is that large-scale operations made royal authority more dependent on local powers, not less, arguably to the point that it had to share sovereignty functions. At the same time, this case also warns us against getting caught up in bewildering coeval conceptualizations of mercantilists, among others.

Cities and local governments, which were far from merely being instruments of the central government, always played some kind of role, starting with the supervision of tax-farming procedures. This chapter shows how leading municipalities in colonial Brazil used their political weight against a particularly fragile ruling house.

The War of Spanish Succession reshaped the role of these municipalities, which seems to validate Jeremy Black's assertion about the temporal discrepancy between absolutism and the growth of the armies. The Military Revolution might have happened in the Portuguese Empire, but only if we are willing to accept this chronological discrepancy. By the beginning of the eighteenth century, Lisbon was much more eager, as well as more able, to impose its policy on local elites and their municipalities, which continued to be important in the Portuguese world – but now stripped of one their distinctive powers. The attempt in Rio de Janeiro to recover the lost fiscal/military function at the end of the eighteenth century was significant but quickly rebuffed by Portuguese authorities. In the words of the minister of the navy, such a concession would be "contrary to the most instituted principles of the whole Public and Economic administration."[53]

Notes

1 This work was supported by national funds through FCT – Fundação para a Ciência e a Tecnologia, I.P. – within the framework of the contract programme prescribed by numbers 4, 5, and 6 of article 23 of the D.L. 57/2016 of August 29 and changed by Law 57/2017 of July 19. The author received additional funding from his institution's strategic project (UID/SOC/50013/2019).
2 These are just a few classic examples. For a more up-to-date discussion on the importance of taxation in the rise of the modern state, see Richard Bonney, ed., *Economic Systems and State Finance* (Oxford: Clarendon Press, 1995).
3 Jeremy Black, *A Military Revolution? Military Change and European Society, 1550–1800* (Basingstoke: Palgrave Macmillan, 1991), 5–8, 67.
4 Steven Gunn, "War and the Emergence of the State: Western Europe, 1350–1600," in *European Warfare, 1350–1750*, ed. Frank Tallett and D.J.B. Trim (New York: Cambridge University Press, 2010), 51.
5 Charles Tilly, "Reflections on the History of European State-Making," in *The Formation of Nation States in Western Europe*, ed. Charles Tilly (Princeton, NJ: Princeton University Press, 1975), 48.
6 This is an idea that has received a fair amount of attention in the Iberian and Latin American academies, with the scholarship becoming so large that it is almost impossible to discuss it here in a meaningful way. I opt, therefore, to direct the interested reader to the groundbreaking work of António Hespanha upon which the debate has been built.

See António Manuel Hespanha, *As Vésperas de Levithan – Instituições e Poder Político, Portugal – séc. XVII* (Coimbra: Almedina, 1994).

7 Paul Kennedy, *The Rise and Fall of Great Powers* (London: Unwin Hyman, 1988), 52–53; Marjolein 't Hart, "The Emergence and Consolidation of the 'Tax State.' II: The Seventeenth Century," in *Economic Systems and State Finance*, ed. Richard Bonney (Oxford: Clarendon Press, 1995), 283.

8 Eugene White, "From Privatized to Government-Administered Tax Collection: Tax Farming in Eighteenth Century France," *The Economic History Review* 57, no. 4 (November 2004), 636.

9 Miguel Dantas da Cruz, "From Flanders to Pernambuco: Battleground Perceptions in the Portuguese Early Modern Atlantic World," *War in History* 26, no. 3 (July 2019): 316–41.

10 José Manuel Santos Pérez, "Brazil and the Politics of the Spanish Habsburgs in the South Atlantic (1580–1640)," *Portuguese Literary & Cultural Studies, the South Atlantic, Past and Present* 27 (2017): 104–20.

11 "Registo da folha Geral deste Estado. . . ," *Documentos Históricos* (hereinafter *DHBN*) 15, 33–37. See also Wolfgang Lenk, *Guerra e Pacto Colonial: A Bahia contra o Brasil Holandês (1624–1654)* (São Paulo: Alameda, 2013), 37, 149.

12 There is no exact number, though estimates range, according to the sources, from sixteen hundred to three thousand men. See Lenk, *Guerra e Pacto*, 39.

13 Subsequently called the *Jornada dos Vassalos*, the Voyage of the Vassals, this was a multinational enterprise that included Portuguese soldiers, Spanish soldiers, and Italian soldiers. It was also a sign of the Habsburgs' commitment to protecting the Portuguese portion of their global empire. See Stuart Schwartz, "The Voyage of the Vassals: Royal Power, Noble Obligations, and Merchant Capital Before the Portuguese Restoration of Independence, 1624–1640," *American Historical Review* 96, no. 3 (June 1991): 735–62.

14 Evaldo Cabral de Mello, *Olinda Restaurada: Guerra e Açúcar no Nordeste, 1630–1654* (Rio de Janeiro: Topbooks, [1975] 1998), 225–26.

15 Royal decree, 11 December 1625. Arquivo Histórico Ultramarino (hereinafter AHU), Bahia, Luísa da Fonseca, Box 3, doc. 394.

16 Letter from the municipal council of Salvador to the king, 16 May 1626. AHU, Bahia, Luísa da Fonseca, Box 3, doc. 423.

17 Harold Selesky, "Colonial America," in *The Laws of War – Constraints on Warfare in the Western World*, ed. Michael Howard, G. Andreopoulos, and M. Shulman (London and New Haven, CT: Yale University Press, 1994), 59–85. The conflict in colonial Brazil was frequently seen as a slow-paced style of warfare, or *guerra lenta*, which was completely different (or so we have been led to believe) from the coeval style of European warfare that was supposedly based in offensive principles. This discussion was revisited by Rafael Valladares, "Las dos guerras de Pernambuco. La armada del conde da Torre y la crisis del Portugal hispánico (1638–1641)," in *El Desafío Holandés al Dominio Ibérico en Brasil en el Siglo XVII*, ed. José Manuel Santos Pérez and George Cabral de Souza (Salamanca: Ediciones Universidad de Salamanca, 2006), 38–39.

18 Schwartz, "The Voyage," 748.

19 Lenk, *Guerra e Pacto*, 54.

20 The capture of the Spanish silver fleet in 1628 yielded 11 million guilders for the company's shareholders. This was the heyday of the company, which also seized forty thousand boxes of sugar, an estimated value of 8 million guilders, from the Portuguese.

21 Mello, *Olinda Restaurada*, 226.

22 Ibid., 226–28.

23 Geoffrey Parker, *The Army of Flanders and the Spanish Road – 1567–1659, the Logistics of the Spanish Victory and Defeat in the Low Countries' Wars* (Cambridge: Cambridge University Press, 1972), 30.

24 Lenk, *Guerra e Pacto*, 61.

25 Charles Boxer, "The Action Between Pater and Oquendo, 12 September 1631," *The Mariner's Mirror* 45, no. 3 (1959): 179.

26 Valladares, "Las dos guerras," 40.

27 António Vasconcelos de Saldanha, *As capitanias do Brasil – Antecedentes, desenvolvimento e extinção de um fenómeno atlântico* (Lisbon: CNCDP, [1992] 2001), 401–3.

28 Edval de Souza Barros, *Negócios de Tanta importância: O Conselho Ultramarino e a disputa pela condução da guerra no Atlântico e no Índico (1643–1661)* (Lisbon: CHAM, 2008).

29 The brunt of imperial taxation was imposed in the mother country in the customhouses.

30 "Registo das condições que os oficiais da Câmara puseram sobre a aceitação da infantaria," *DHBN* 77, 359.

31 Ibid., 361.

32 Consulta (record of a discussion) of the Overseas Council 23 April 1676. *DHBN* 88, 89–95.

33 "Registo das condições. . . ," 356.

34 Miguel Dantas da Cruz, *Um império de conflitos. O Conselho Ultramarino e a defesa do Brasil* (Lisbon: ICS, 2015), 222.

35 Evaldo Cabral de Mello, *Um Imenso Portugal. História e Historiografia* (São Paulo: Editora 34, 2002), 67; Luís Reis Torgal, *Ideologia Política e Teoria do Estado na Restauração*, vol. 1 (Coimbra: Biblioteca Geral da Universidade, 1981), 321–22.

36 "Registo das condições," 356.

37 For example, in Paraíba, according to a relation provided by the Overseas Council to the king, we know that the officers were paid by the royal treasury, with the municipality's taking care of the soldiers' wages. Consulta of the Overseas Council, 7 October 1675. *DHBN* 88, 55–74.

38 See Leonor Freire Costa, Pedro Lains, and Susana Miranda, *An Economic History of Portugal, 1143–2010* (Cambridge: Cambridge University Press, 2016), 8, 116–19. See also the broader discussion on some fiscal experiences in Europe and in Portugal, in Bartolomé Yun-Casalilla and Patrick O'Brien, *The Rise of Fiscal States: A Global History, 1500–1914* (Cambridge: Cambridge University Press, 2012).

39 Joaquim Romero Magalhães, "Dinheiro para a Guerra: as Décimas da Restauração," *Hispania* LXIV–1, no. 216 (2004): 164.

40 Consulta of the Overseas Council, 23 April 1676. *DHBN* 88, 89–95.

41 Letter from Count of Óbidos to captain Lopo Curado Garro, 7 May 1664. *DHBN* 9, 168–66.

42 About these expeditions, see Maria Fernanda Bicalho, *A Cidade e o Império: o Rio de Janeiro no Século XVIII* (Rio de Janeiro: Civilização Editora, 2003).

43 Francisco Adolfo de Varnhagen, *História Geral do Brazil*, vol. II (Rio de Janeiro: Em casa de E. e H. Laemmert, [1854–1857] 1877), 815–16.

44 Military expenditure for 1708 was budgeted at 2.203 billion *reis*. Fernando Dores, "O século XVIII," *Nova História Militar de Portugal*, ed. António Manuel Hespanha, vol. 2 (Lisbon: Círculo de Leitores, 2004), 189–90.

45 Luciano Raposo Figueiredo, *Rebeliões no Brasil Colônia* (Rio de Janeiro: Zahar, 2005), 54.

46 Cruz, *Um império*, 77–82.

47 Consulta of the Overseas Council, 3 August 1712. *DHBN* 96, 53–61.

48 Consulta of the Overseas Council, 17 December 1712. *DHBN* 93, 144–45.

49 Cruz, *Um império*, 229–36.

50 Bodin, for example, expressed this concern in 1576. Bonney, *Economic Systems*, 168.

51 Consulta of the Overseas Council, 3 August 1712. *DHBN* 96, 53–61.

52 Cruz, *Um império*, 236–38.

53 Notice of Rodrigo de Sousa Coutinho, 20 August 1799. AHU, Rio de Janeiro, Avulsos, Box 180, doc. 36; Box 175, doc. 86; Box 176, doc. 45; Box 168, doc. 12.536.

PART 3

Tradition and innovation in warfare

7

TRANSFORMATION OF MILITARY TECHNOLOGY IN PORTUGAL

The impact of the Iberian Union on artillery[1]

Brice Cossart

Introduction

The historiography about the concept of military revolution has produced a huge array of studies focusing on different states and territories. Michael Roberts's work, which originated the concept, associated the main shift of early modern warfare to the crucial military innovations brought by seventeenth-century Dutch and Swedish armies.[2] One generation later, Geoffrey Parker identified the artillery train with which King Charles VIII of France invaded Italy in 1494 as the key element which sparked the transformation of early modern warfare in Europe.[3] The success of his narrative generated a long debate among military historians about the chronology and the significance of the different military innovations, but their studies remained in the same fertile crescent established by Roberts and Parker: mainly England, France, Italy, the Netherlands, and the lands of the Habsburgs.[4] More recently, the debate has shifted towards global history as some scholars have proposed focusing on military innovations in Asia and thus re-examining Parker's thesis on the "rise of the West."[5] Meanwhile, until recently, Portugal and its empire have remained on the margin of this prolific historiography. The present book pleads for a reassessment of the role of Portugal in the narratives of the military revolution, while this chapter argues more specifically that the Iberian Union (1580–1640) of Portugal with Habsburg Spain had a decisive impact on the development of Portuguese military technology.

In 1580, King Philipp II of Spain launched a vast military operation to support his dynastic rights to the vacant Portuguese throne. The following annexation of Portugal and its empire by the monarchy of the Spanish Habsburgs marked the beginning of an association between the two Iberian powers. Whereas the Portuguese monarchy has raised little interest among historians of the Military Revolution, its Spanish neighbour has been under the spotlights since Geoffrey Parker identified it as a pioneer state at the forefront of "radical military change."[6] The Kingdom of Portugal remained under Habsburg governing for six decades, until the revolt of 1640, which put an end to the union.[7] It is thus legitimate to ask the following question: to what extent did the Iberian Union impact the military technology used in Portugal ?

The purpose of this chapter is not to assert that early modern Portuguese military technology developed only under Spanish government. Several studies have shown that the Portuguese army and navy resorted to innovations such as embarked artillery, bronze cannons, and bastion fortifications long before the Iberian Union.[8] During the sixteenth century, the construction of the Portuguese Empire relied on this military technology as much as it constituted a vector of these innovations towards Asia.[9] Nevertheless, in contrast to the blossoming effervescence characterizing the decades of exploration and empire building, the period of Habsburg domination often tends to appear as a dark time in Portuguese history. This chapter aims to show that, far from this negative image, the Iberian Union gave a new impulse to the evolution of military technology in Portugal. In this regard, not only does it constitute a period worth studying for the specialists of Portugal, but it is also a particularly interesting moment for those who might be interested in the circulation of military technology.

In addition, the question of the Spanish connection with Portuguese military affairs during the Iberian Union remains unsettled. On one hand, the dominant paradigm of the "composite monarchy," coined by John Elliott to describe the political organization of the Spanish monarchy, emphasizes the political, juridical, and fiscal fragmentations.[10] The political entity under the Habsburgs' authority is thus considered a mere association of smaller states bound together by the fact that they shared the same sovereign. This vision is exemplified by the agreement taken by King Philip II at the *Cortes* of Tomar (1581) to respect the independence of the Portuguese Crown.[11] On the other hand, the rising scale of warfare required common military efforts beyond the fragmented nature of this composite monarchy. In this perspective, some historians have shown that when it came to military matters, Castilian-dominated institutions (the Council of State and the Council of War, the *juntas de guerra*) were often involved in the government of military affairs regarding Portugal and its empire.[12] While the historiography has focused mostly on the tensions generated inside the composite monarchy by the use of fiscal and military resources from one state to another, my aim is to shed light on one aspect which stemmed from this shared use of military resources but which has been little studied: the transfer of military technology through key individuals.

The chapter proposes to tackle this issue only from the point of view of artillery. Despite the apparent narrowness of the topic, artillery is a particularly relevant element to grasp the transformations at the core of the elastic concept of military revolution. In Parker's narrative, bronze cannons brought fundamental changes in fortification and in naval combat, and they constituted an important lever for the growth of armies.[13] Instead of participating in the debate on which innovations were the most significant to induce a radical change in warfare, the chosen method follows the experts who served the artillery in Portugal as officers, gunmakers, engineers, or simple gunners. Therefore, the purpose is to prove that under the Iberian Union, Portugal was a key territory for the circulation of European military expertise, and as a result, it cannot be separated from the wider movement of transformation of warfare which affected most of Western Europe in that time.

First, the chapter shows how the Council of War, in Madrid, took over the control of artillery in Portugal. Second, it sheds light on the dynamic circulation of experts which was generated as Portugal became a strategic territory in the wide network of the Habsburg Monarchy. Third, it reveals the emergence of some institutional innovations by focusing on the new schools which opened in Lisbon in order to provide formal training for gunners. Finally, it tackles the circulation of military expertise in both Spanish colonial structures and Portuguese colonial structures.

I The Castilian lead over Portuguese artillery

By the time of the conquest of Portugal, the management of artillery had become one of the most centralized administrative branches of the Spanish monarchy. All the weaponry of the realms of Castile and Aragon – including Sardinia, the Balearic islands, and the Spanish African *presidios* – was placed under the authority of one individual, the captain general of artillery.[14] This position was a highly political one as it came with a seat at the king's Council of War, in charge of governing all military matters.[15] The captain general of artillery was the head of a vast administration which had gained a certain independence from the rest of the military apparatus and included its own account managers, officers, and troops.[16] Similar structures were put under direct supervision of the viceroys and governors in the various Habsburg states in Italy and Flanders.[17] In other words, in all territories, the monarchy of the Spanish Habsburgs tended to keep artillery under close reach of the executive powers and in tight connection with the central government.

Portugal was no exception. The management of artillery was given to the captain general of artillery, as his authority already extended to all other territories of the Iberian Peninsula.[18] After the royal court left from Portugal in 1583, two lieutenancies of artillery were created, one in Lisbon and the other one in the Azores.[19] Like in Burgos, Barcelona, Malaga, Pamplona, and Majorca, the lieutenants of artillery were locally in charge of the daily management of artillery and kept a constant communication with the captain general of artillery and the Council of War in Madrid.[20] They were always chosen among Castilian captains who had proven their loyalty to the members of the Habsburg government through years, or even decades, of service. In 1583, the lieutenancy in Lisbon was given to Alonso de Céspedes, a seasoned soldier who had worked for Philipp II for eighteen years in Italy and Flanders, rising from the ranks of simple infantry to the high status of *sargento mayor*, the second in command of a three-thousand-person *tercio*.[21] After his death in 1589, he was replaced by Hernando de Acosta, a man who had already been in the same office in Cartagena for several years.[22] In 1595, his successor was

Alonso Alfaro de Narvaez, an infantry captain who had served the king for thirty years in Italy, Spain, and Portugal.[23]

Thus, Philippe II's government decided to build its own structure for the management of artillery in Portugal and put it under the control of trustworthy Castilian captains. The will to ensure the authority over this strategic weaponry also appears in the choice of individuals in charge of other key positions, such as the accountancy of artillery. The holder of this office had important financial responsibilities: he had to keep count of all cannons, cannonballs, and gunpowder stocks in Portugal and of every expense for the production of artillery and payment of artillery employees. In 1587, the office was given to a Castilian veteran, Francisco Sánchez de Moya, who had served as infantry soldier in Naples for several years, before becoming the chief gunner of Pamplona.[24] One source identified him as *criado* of the captain general of artillery, which meant that these two men were bound by patronage.[25]

From the point of view of the Spanish Habsburgs, this reliable Castilian structure for the management of artillery was all the more necessary given that Portugal soon became one of the most strategic military spaces in the empire. The Portuguese squadron of galleons inherited from the Aviz dynasty was administratively integrated into the Armada del Mar Océano, the main naval force of Castile, while a small group of Spanish galleys was attached to Lisbon to patrol along the coast of Portugal.[26] More importantly, the harbour of Lisbon was turned into the main platform for the preparation of huge naval operations like the armada of 1588 against England. The size of this fleet, which gathered 130 ships, 2,431 cannons, and 123,790 cannonballs, required a convergence of war material from all Iberian, Italian, and Flemish territories of King Philipp II.[27] Eight years later, in 1596, a comparable fleet was again assembled in Lisbon under the command of Martín de Padilla, to invade Ireland.[28] The artillery staff of Portugal was thus regularly involved in the large-scale deployment of firepower. The mobilization and coordination of such a massive amount of weaponry was hardly compatible with the respect of Portuguese independence from the Castilian government. In this sense, having one structure at the scale of the whole Iberian Peninsula, piloted by one person, the captain general of artillery, was an efficient way to ensure the transversal power necessary to bridge over the political fragmentation of the monarchy. This organization supposed that multiple circulations of material and staff occurred between the different states of the Spanish Habsburgs and Portugal.

II New dynamics for the circulation of experts

The presence of the Spanish monarchy in various areas of Europe, especially in Italy and Flanders, facilitated the recruitment of international military experts who were attracted by a career under the patronage of the king of Spain. Therefore, many specialists of artillery and fortification who served the Spanish Habsburgs moved to Portugal through the cross-border network of the captain general of artillery.

The new design of fortification, called *trace italienne*, which is at the core of Parker's concept of military revolution, was implemented by a handful of specialists, among which the most renowned were Italian engineers. Before the Iberian Union, King Sebastião of Portugal hired such an Italian expert, Filippo Terzi, who later passed to the service of the Spanish Habsburgs.[29] However, after 1580, the circulation of Italian engineers in Portugal was enhanced by the fact that many of them were already on the Spanish artillery payrolls and just moved inside the Iberian Peninsula through the authority of the captain general of artillery.[30] Thus, after a long experience in designing fortresses for the Spanish Habsburgs in Milan, Pamplona, Sardinia, the Balearic islands, and Alicante, Italian engineer Giovan Giacomo Paleari Fratino (called *El Fratin* by the Spaniards) and his brother Giorgio, supervised the fortification of Porto Viana do Castelo, São Julião da Barra (near Lisbon), and Setúbal.[31] In the early 1590s, a Florentine artist and engineer, Brother Giovanni Vincenzo Casale, worked on the forts protecting the entrance of the Tagus river in front of Lisbon.[32] In 1590, he realized firing tests with heavy artillery in order to check the defence of the bay of Lisbon. He did so with the lieutenant of artillery and Tiburzio Spannocchi, a Sienese engineer who was considered by the Council of War the best reference in fortification after he designed fortresses in many territories including Sicily, the Basque country, Cadiz and Galicia.[33] After the death of Casale in 1593, his works were completed by Leonardo Torriani, an engineer from Lombardy who had fortified the Canary Islands and some Spanish citadels in North Africa before making a long career in the fortifications of Portugal.[34]

Similar dynamics happened in the manufacturing of cannons. Gun-manufacturing facilities already existed in Lisbon before the Iberian Union, but they became especially productive when the demand for large bronze cannons rose as a result of the organization of huge armadas.[35] Thus, in 1587, four Spanish master gun founders were transferred from Castile to Lisbon to participate in the production of cannons for the armada against England.[36] There they worked together with Luis Cesar, a local master gun founder, and Bartolomeo Sommariva, an Italian master who had been serving King Philipp II for a decade.[37] The supervision and control of this production was assigned to Diego de Prado, a Castilian officer who later wrote two manuscripts on gunnery and cannon-making techniques.[38] In 1589, a German gun founder from Aachen, Jan Vantrier, was hired by the Duke of Parma in the Low Countries under orders to join Lisbon, where he produced cannons until his death, in 1603.[39] In other words, Lisbon converted into a point of encounter for gun founders coming from various areas of Europe, and this situation certainly stimulated the exchange of knowledge and techniques from different manufacturing traditions.

From the beginning of sixteenth century, gunners, who were specialists in the use of cannons, were traditionally either Portuguese or recruited by Portuguese agents in Flanders and Germany.[40] After 1580, this recruitment was reshaped by the international networks of the Spanish Habsburgs. A document of the Portuguese squadron of the Armada del Mar Océano in 1602 shows only a small proportion of Portuguese among a crew of forty-five gunners (Figure 7.1).[41] Flemish artillerists

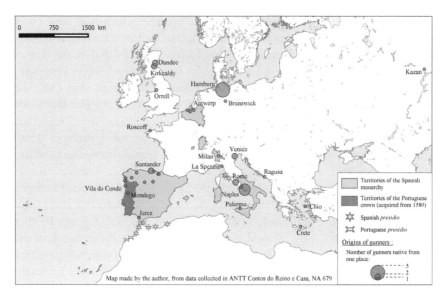

FIGURE 7.1   Origins of forty-five gunners from the Portuguese squadron of the Armada del Mar Océano (1602).

were still present, coming essentially from the lands loyal to the Habsburgs, while Germans came predominantly from Hamburg, certainly because of the strong diplomatic and commercial ties this Hanseatic city kept with Spain.[42] Spaniards amounted to only about 25 per cent of this group of gunners and were in majority from northern Spain. However, the most striking characteristic is the massive presence of Italian gunners, who constituted almost one-third of the group. Most of them were subjects of the Spanish Habsburgs from Lombardy, Sicily, and especially Naples, but some had also been recruited in the neighbouring territories such as Venice, the Papal States, and Genoa. The Mediterranean emphasis on the recruitment was perceptible in the presence of one Ragusan, two Greeks, and even one man from Kazan, identified as a Turk. This international crew was completed by a French person and a handful of Scots who might have been Catholics seeking the protection of the Spanish Habsburgs.

This gathering of technicians who had learnt their art in so many places and who must have had as many different work experiences was undoubtedly favourable to the circulation of the most up-to-date knowledge and techniques. In addition, the Spanish monarchy fostered the exchange of technical knowledge by creating new teaching institutions.

III New institutions for the teaching of gunnery

During the second half of the sixteenth century, the Spanish monarchy experienced a huge increase in its needs for gunners to handle a fast-growing number of cannons.[43] This led to the emergence of a new type of institutions. In the 1560s, a first school of gunners opened in Milan, following the model of the Venetian neighbour.[44] In the next decade, similar schools were created in Sicily and Andalusia.[45] The abundant documentation about the school created in Seville in 1576 shows that the teaching included a practical component on a shooting ground and a more theoretical component in the form of lectures given by a mathematician.[46] The training was validated by a formal examination through questions which were asked of the apprentice by veteran gunners in front of royal officers. Such an institution represented an important innovation in a society where the vast majority of technical knowledge was transmitted informally, from the master's hands to the apprentice's.[47] Compared to the traditional system of apprenticeship, where one master trained a handful of apprentices over his whole career, the schools of gunners multiplied the transfer of skills, enabling one master gunner to teach his art to dozens of individuals per year.[48] Because they massively supplied the state with skilled labour necessary for the large-scale deployment of artillery, these new institutions directly strengthened the transformations at the core of Parker's concept of military revolution.[49]

After the losses of the Invincible Armada in 1588, the Council of War launched a programme to reinforce the teaching of gunnery in the Iberian Peninsula. By the end of the century, the Spanish monarchy boasted a vast network of schools of gunnery in places such as Burgos, Hondarribia, San Sebastian, Pamplona, Cartagena, Malaga, Cadiz, Ferrol, A Coruña, and Barcelona.[50] Portugal was not left aside. In August 1588, right after the departure of the Invincible Armada from Lisbon, the Council of War asked a certain Bartolomé de Andrada "to teach in school" in the castle of São Jorge.[51] Andrada had served the king as a master gunner in Sicily, where he was teaching his art in one of the four schools on the island.[52] He had come all the way to Portugal to join the armada against England but eventually did not embark, because he fell sick just before departure. After his recovery some weeks later, the Council of War decided to make fruitful use of his special teaching skills and his ability to speak several languages - particularly relevant given the fact that gunners converged on Lisbon from all over Europe - and thus opened the first school of gunners in Portugal. Several years later, the same role was performed by Juan Carlos, a veteran soldier whom the Council of War considered "the best expert in gunnery, artificial fires, explosive mines and night shots."[53]

By that time, the teaching of gunnery had increased in Portugal. In 1590, the captain general of artillery, don Juan de Acuña Vela, claimed that several master gunners were in charge of teaching their art in the castles of São Jorge and São Julião in Lisbon and in the fort of San Felipe in Setúbal.[54] According to his words, their lectures were public and intended for anyone who might be interested in learning how to use cannons.[55] Nevertheless, this allegation did not mean that attendance to the lessons was not filtered. Exactly the same set of vocabulary was used to describe the lectures in the Seville school, but only subjects of the Spanish Habsburgs were allowed to sign up for the lessons, and foreigners with even decades of residence in Spain had to struggle with the royal administration to be admitted.[56] What the captain general of artillery probably meant by "public" lectures was mostly that they were free of charge for students, the cost being covered by the monarchy.

Besides these schools created in the fortresses of Lisbon and Setúbal, lectures on artillery were also implemented in naval settings. In 1589, Lazaro de la Isla, chief gunner of the royal squadron of galleys stationed in Portugal, started his own school of gunners.[57] A year after, his personal initiative received the official approval of the Council of War "to teach the art of gunnery, geometry and artificial fires."[58] Being the son of a gunner and having fought in the battle of Lepanto (1571), the capture of Tunis (1573), and the conquest of the Azores (1583), Lazaro de la Isla was undoubtedly an expert in artillery.[59] In 1595, he published a famous artillery treatise in Madrid, later re-edited in Valladolid (1603) and Lisbon (1609).[60] After several years of artillery lectures on board the galleys, he pursued his teaching career in the schools of gunners in Burgos (1597) and Cadiz (1604).[61] The trajectory of this expert from one training centre of the Iberian Peninsula to another strengthened the idea that the teaching of gunnery implemented in Portugal was fully inserted into the wider network of schools which was built by the government of the Habsburgs in the last decades of the sixteenth century.

IV Cross-imperial circulation of military technicians

This chapter has so far focused on phenomena circumscribed to the Iberian Peninsula. The main argument has been that the transversal structure under the authority of the captain general of artillery fostered the cross-border circulation of military experts and institutional models between Portugal and the European territories of the Spanish Habsburgs. However, the authority of the captain general of artillery did not reach further than Madeira and the Azores. Given the importance of overseas territories for both Spain and Portugal, the chapter looks into the extent to which these circulations expanded to the Iberian colonial territories. This question involves the rising interest of historians in the study of the connections and entanglements between the Spanish and Portuguese empires during the Iberian Union.[62] The topic deserves thorough archival work, but this chapter wishes only to superficially remark on the cross-imperial circulations of military experts between the two Iberian empires.

The first remark is that the artillery of the *Estado da Índia* and of the annual convoys travelling through the Cape route to Portuguese India (*Carreira da India*) stood aside the authority of the Council of War. This administrative divide appears clearly in 1608, when almost two hundred cannons were sold by the Council of War to "the Portuguese Crown, in order to equip the galleons going to the Eastern Indies."[63] Throughout the Iberian Union, the armament of these ships remained essentially a topic of local government which was discussed and negotiated by the Council of Finance and the Council of State in Lisbon, in connection with the royal Council of Portugal in Madrid.[64] These Portuguese-dominated institutions proved to be quite reluctant to hire individuals belonging to the patronage network of the captain general of artillery; for instance, in 1593, when the galleons San Simon and San Pablo, initially part of the Armada del Mar Océano - under the management of the Council of War - were sold to the Crown of Portugal, several veteran gunners were dismissed and had to beg for new positions under the protection of the captain general of artillery.[65] From a military point of view, such dismissals were counterproductive, insofar as Portuguese ships and fortresses in India suffered from a chronic dearth of gunners.[66] They can only be understood as a resentful reaction to Castilian involvement in Portuguese military affairs, which was perceived as a violation of the formal administrative separation agreed in Tomar in 1581.

In the overseas territories, Portuguese colonial authorities were unwilling to resort to Castilian support, because they feared it might lead Castilians to make claims to Portuguese possessions.[67] This, however, did not totally prevent the cross-imperial circulation of military experts. After many years at the service of the Spanish monarchy, the Milanese engineer Giovanni Battista Cairati finished his career in Portuguese Africa and India, building bastion fortresses in Mombasa, Bassein, and Daman in the 1590s.[68] In 1629, two Spanish veterans of the wars in Flanders accompanied the Count of Linhares when he was sent as viceroy in Goa with a strong agenda for military reforms, in order to face the rising Dutch threat in Asia.[69] Nevertheless, another example highlights the kind of tensions that could result from the direct involvement of Spanish military experts in Portuguese colonial territories. In its first years of activity, the gun foundry in Portuguese Macao resorted to two Spanish gun founders hired in Manila.[70] Their replacement by the Portuguese gun founder Manuel Tavares Bocarro in 1626, under the pretext of their lack of abilities, was seemingly motivated by political reasons, given that some Portuguese sources called them "the Spanish enemies who came from Manila."[71] Although more research is needed on this issue, these few elements show that the circulation of military experts from the Spanish colonial empire to the Portuguese colonial empire was less fluid than from Spain to Portugal.

The circulation operated slightly better in the opposite way, from Portugal to the Spanish Empire. Certainly, the grasp of the Council of War over the artillery of Portugal limited the opportunities for Portuguese military experts to find jobs in their home country insofar as they suffered from the concurrence of many foreigners who were often better inserted into the administrative structure and patronage network of the court in Madrid. For these individuals, one strong option must have been to work for the Portuguese colonial administration, because it tended to favour its own compatriots. Another one was to join the Spanish colonial administration, which was in constant need of artillery specialists. Statistics on the origins of crewmembers on board transatlantic ships (Spanish *Carrera de Indias*) reveal that about 5 per cent of gunners came from Portugal.[72] The records of examinations passed in the Seville school of gunners in the years 1600–6 registered eight Portuguese candidates.[73] Even though these were small contingents, they nonetheless demonstrate that the Iberian Union offered new career prospects to a few Portuguese military technicians willing to get involved in the Spanish colonial structures.

The dynamics underlying the involvement of Portuguese technicians in the Spanish colonial administration can be better understood from an example. In the last decades of the sixteenth century, the multiple attacks of English corsairs on the American settlements of the Spanish monarchy increased the necessity to provide them with heavy weaponry.[74] Among the various projects to create gun foundries in colonial settings, one proposition aimed to take advantage of the discovery, in Cuba, of copper pits and build a manufacture of bronze guns next to this source of metal supply.[75] The man chosen to lead this project was Francisco Sánchez de Moya, previously mentioned in this text as a Castilian gunner who had become account manager of the artillery in Portugal.[76] As said before, this officer had strong ties with Juan de Acuña Vela, the Spanish captain general of artillery, and he successfully turned the gun foundry project of Cuba into a reality.[77]

The composition of the team that he was asked to gather for this project gives some insights on the bonds this officer had created with other military technicians during his stay in Lisbon, between 1587 and 1597. As for the gun founders, Sánchez de Moya chose Hernando and Francisco Ballesteros.[78] Originally from Ubeda in Andalusia, these two brothers worked for several years as assistants of the German master Jan Vantrier, in the gun foundry of Lisbon.[79] With them came four gun founder assistants, among whom three were Castilians and one, called Ambrosio Golbin, was from Lisbon.[80] Besides this nucleus of gun founders dominated by Castilians, the team sent to Cuba included mostly Portuguese technicians: a master blacksmith called Pedro Alvares, from Guimarães; a master carpenter (to make gun carriages) called Gonzalo de la Rocha, from Braga; and a cannonball maker, Salvador Gonzales, and his son, both from Lisbon.[81] Apparently, for this expertise on cannonball making, the first choice of Sánchez de Moya had fallen upon a mulatto named Acosta who finally preferred to stay in Lisbon for a higher salary.[82]

All the Portuguese technicians chosen by Sánchez de Moya to accompany him to the new gun manufacture in Cuba must have been previously working for the artillery of Portugal. In this sense, the circulation of military experts fostered by the transnational networks of the Spanish Habsburgs generated new daily contacts between Portuguese technicians and individuals such as the German founder Vantrier and his Castilian disciples, the Ballesteros brothers. These interactions undoubtedly favoured the circulation of technical knowledge. They also allowed some Portuguese technicians to develop personal bonds with Spanish officers (e.g., Sánchez de Moya), who through their connections with the highest spheres of the Habsburg military apparatus had the capacity to turn those personal ties into new career opportunities. In other words, this example confirms that military knowledge circulated in the Iberian empires through an articulation between state structures and informal networks.[83]

Conclusion

This collective volume addresses the key question of whether Portugal and its empire experienced a military revolution in the early modern period. Naturally, the main problem is that there is no consensus among historians on what the Military Revolution actually was or on if it even ever happened. To overcome this difficulty, this chapter has focused on the circulation of military technicians to prove that at least under the Iberian Union, if not before, Portugal was a significant node attracting gunners, gun founders, engineers, and other military technicians from various places in Europe, including Italy, Germany, the Low Countries, Spain, Greece, Great Britain, and France. These multiple movements of individuals constituted as many channels for the circulation of military knowledge and technology. Therefore, it seems unconceivable to accept the idea that Portugal might have remained on the margin of the major transformations in warfare which occurred in other parts of Europe.

This chapter also argues that the association of Portugal with the Spanish Habsburgs between 1580 and 1640 was beneficial from the point of view of the circulation of military technology. The dispersion of the Habsburg territories in Europe and the attractiveness of Spanish patronage favoured the hiring of artillery experts coming from all over the continent. In addition, in spite of the formal political separation between Castile and Portugal which was agreed in Tomar in 1581, the circulation of this international pool of experts was permitted by the implementation of a cross-border administrative structure under the authority of the captain general of artillery and the royal Council of War. In this period, the area of Lisbon became a particularly important military hub, frequented by many technicians who brought together their knowledge and experience of warfare. To facilitate the transfer of skills, the Council of War implemented in Portugal an institutional model, the school of gunners, already operational in other territories ruled by the Habsburgs. These teaching centres were resolutely a modern feature of armies, in a time when England boasted only one of such schools, in London, while France only acquired them under the reign of Louis XIV (1643–1715).[84]

This structural organization generated new personal bonds among military experts which, in some cases, produced movements of Portuguese technicians outside Portugal, through the military apparatus of the Spanish Empire. In contrast, foreign experts belonging to the patronage network of the royal court in Madrid experienced more difficulties in penetrating Portuguese imperial structures. Paradoxically, these structures were the most in need of military expertise because they were in charge of defending the territories which most suffered from the growing concurrence of other European powers. Such impediments probably resulted from the rising tensions between Lisbon and Madrid, as a consequence of structural issues stemming from the divergent interests of Portuguese elites and the Habsburg government regarding the use of shared resources inside the composite monarchy.[85]

In this regard, the relatively fluid movement of war material and military experts between Castile and Portugal came at a cost. The cross-border administrative network implemented by the Council of War threatened the principle of the composite monarchy which presided over the association between the two Iberian powers: the independence of Portugal vis-à-vis Castilian government. It certainly contributed to the rising Portuguese resentment against Habsburg rule which culminated in the Portuguese revolt of 1640 and the end of the Iberian Union.[86] Despite this outcome, the impact of the Habsburg government on the transformation of Portuguese military technology should not be neglected. During six decades, as this chapter has shown, Portuguese military technicians had many opportunities to collaborate with the experts of the Spanish Habsburgs and learn from their different knowledge and experience. When the two monarchies took separate paths, this stock of skills and competence must have been of some value to Portugal in its struggle for independence.

Notes

1 This chapter presents research that was carried out at two institutions. Part of it is based on my doctoral research on gunners which took place at the European University Institute in Florence, Italy. But it displays also some preliminary results of my current research project "GLOBALGUNS" implemented at the University Pablo de Olavide, Seville, Spain. This project has received funding from the European Union's Horizon 2020 research and innovation programme under the Marie Skłodowska-Curie grant agreement No. 845675, which is titled "Guns for a Global Empire: Deployment of Artillery Technology in the Iberian Colonial Space (1580–1640)." I am therefore grateful to these institutions for providing me with a fruitful environment to develop this research. Also, I thank Professor Bartolome Yun-Casalilla for his comments and suggestions. Any mistakes in this chapter are my responsibility.
2 Michael Roberts, *The Military Revolution, 1560–1660: An Inaugural Lecture Delivered Before the Queen's University of Belfast* (Belfast: M. Boyd, 1956).
3 Geoffrey Parker, *The Military Revolution: Military Innovation and the Rise of the West, 1500–1800* (Cambridge: Cambridge University Press, 1988).
4 Clifford J. Rogers, ed., *The Military Revolution Debate: Readings on the Military Transformation of Early Modern Europe* (Boulder, CO: Westview Press, 1995).
5 Tonio Andrade, *The Gunpowder Age: China, Military Innovation, and the Rise of the West in World History* (Princeton, NJ and Oxford: Princeton University Press, 2016); Gábor Agoston, "Firearms and Military Adaptation: The Ottomans and the European Military Revolution, 1450–1800," *Journal of World History* 25, no.1 (2014): 85–124; Tonio Andrade, Hyeok Hweon Kang, and Kirsten Cooper, "A Korean Military Revolution? Parallel Military Innovations in East Asia and Europe," *Journal of World History* 25, no. 1 (2014): 51–84. Richard Eaton and Philip B. Wagoner, "Warfare on the Deccan Plateau, 1450–1600: A Military Revolution in Early Modern India?," *Journal of World History* 25, no. 1 (2014): 5–50; Matthew Stavros, "Military Revolution in Early Modern Japan," *Japanese Studies* 33, no. 3 (2013): 243–61.
6 Parker, *Military Revolution*, 24.
7 John H. Elliott, "The Spanish Monarchy and the Kingdom of Portugal, 1580–1640," in *Conquest and Coalescence*, ed. Mark Greengrass (London: Edward Arnold, 1991), 48–67.
8 António Manuel Hespanha, ed., *Nova História militar de Portugal*, vol. 2 (Lisbon: Circulo de Leitores, 2003); Tiago Machado de Castro, "Bombardeiros na Índia: Os homens a as artes da artilharia portuguesa (1498–1557)" (MA diss., University of Lisbon, Lisbon, 2011); Roger Lee de Jesus, "Abastecer a Guerra noutro Oceano: o Armazém das Armas de Goa em 1545–1546," in *Nos 600 da conquista de Ceuta: Portugal e a criação do primeiro sistema mundial*, ed. Francisco Contente Domingues and Jorge Silva Rocha (Lisbon: Comissão Portuguesa de História Militar, 2015), 169–220; Charles R. Boxer, *The Portuguese Seaborne Empire, 1415–1825* (London: Hutchinson, 1969); Francisco Bethencourt and Kirti Chaudhuri, *História da Expansão Portuguesa, vol. 1: A Formação do império (1415–1570)* (Lisbon: Temas e Debates, 1998).

9 Geoffrey Parker, "The Artillery Fortress as an Engine of European Overseas Expansion, 1480–1750," in *City Walls: The Urban Enceinte in Global Perspective*, ed. James D. Tracy (Cambridge: Cambridge University Press, 2000), 386–416; Andrade, *The Gunpowder Age*, 199–201; Vitor Luis Gaspar Rodrigues, "Mestres-fundidores portugueses na China," in *Portugal – China: 500 anos*, ed. Miguel Castelo Branco (Lisbon: Babel, 2014), 158–63.

10 John H. Elliott, "A Europe of Composite Monarchies," *Past and Present* 137 (1992): 48–71.

11 Elliott, "The Spanish Monarchy"; John H. Elliott, *Imperial Spain, 1469–1716* (London: Penguin Books, 2002), 274.

12 Jean-Frédéric Schaub, *Le Portugal au temps du Comte-Duc d'Olivares (1621–1640): Le conflit de juridictions comme exercice de la politique* (Madrid: Casa de Velázquez, 2001); Bartolomé Yun-Casalilla, *Iberian World Empires and the Globalization of Europe 1415–1668* (Basingstoke: Palgrave Macmillan, 2019).

13 Parker, *Military Revolution*.

14 See the instructions given to captain general Francés de Álava: Archivo General de Simancas (AGS) Guerra y Marina (GYM), leg. 76/133 (17 May 1572).

15 Juan Carlos Domínguez Nafría, *El Real y Supremo Consejo de Guerra (siglos XVI–XVIII)* (Madrid: Centro de Estudios Políticos y Constitucionales, 2001).

16 Brice Cossart, "Les artilleurs et la Monarchie Catholique: Fondements technologiques et scientifiques d'un empire transocéanique (1560–1610)" (PhD diss., European University Institute, Florence, 2016).

17 Ibid.

18 See the instructions given to captain general Juan de Acuña Vela, AGS GYM lib. 43, fol. 22v-35r (30 August 1586).

19 AGS GYM leg 148/320 (year 1583) and leg. 209/139 (26 August 1587).

20 AGS GYM leg. 88/250 (17 August 1578), leg. 174/82 (3 July 1576), and leg. 364/152 (20 July 1592); Andreu Seguí Beltrán, "La administración de la artillería del Reíno de Mallorca en el siglo XVI," *Bolletí de la Societat Arqueològica* 69 (2013): 143–57.

21 AGS GYM leg. 209/139 (26 August 1587). On the charge of *sargento mayor*, see Fernando González de León, *The Road to Rocroi: Class, Culture and Command in the Spanish Army of Flanders, 1567–1659* (Leiden and Boston: Brill, 2009), 22.

22 AGS GYM leg. 364/152 (20 July 1592).

23 AGS GYM leg. 437/120 (13 March 1595), lib. 70, fol. 129v (2 April 1595) and leg. 604/214 (24 March 1603). The accounts of his infantry company in Lisbon: Arquivo Nacional da Torre do Tombo (Lisbon), *Contos do Reino a Casa*, NA. 676.

24 AGS GYM leg. 209/172 (1587). See the biography written by his widow in Archivo General de Indias (AGI) SANTO DOMINGO, leg. 20/8 (1621).

25 AGS GYM leg. 215/121 to 123 (1587).

26 David C. Goodman, *Spanish Naval Power, 1589–1665: Reconstruction and Defeat* (Cambridge and New York: Cambridge University Press, 1997). On the squadron of 4 to 8 Spanish galleys in Lisbon, see: AGS GYM leg. 175/7 & 8 (1583) and leg. 364/3 (15 January 1592).

27 Colin Martin and Geoffrey Parker, *The Spanish Armada: Revised Edition* (Manchester: Manchester University Press, 1999), 26.

28 Richard B. Wernham, *The Return of the Armadas: The Last Years of the Elizabethan War Against Spain, 1595–1603* (Oxford: Oxford University Press, 1994); Edward Tenace, "A Strategy of Reaction: The Armadas of 1596 and 1597 and the Spanish Struggle for European Hegemony," *The English Historical Review* 118, no. 478 (2003): 855–82.

29 Miguel Soromenho and Lucas Branco Ricardo, "The Architectural career of Filippo Terzi in Portugal (1577–1597)," in *Da Bologna all'Europa: Artisti bolognesi in Portogallo (secoli XVI–XIX)*, ed. Sabine Frommel and Micaela Antonucci (Bologna: Bologna University Press, 2017), 101–23.

30 See the accounts of artillery for 1570–80: AGS Contaduria Mayor de Cuentas (CMC), 2ª época leg. 414.
31 Viganò Marino, "El Fratin mi ynginiero," in *I Paleari Fratino da Morcote, ingegneri militari ticinesi in Spagna (XVI–XVII secolo)* (Bellinzona: Casagrande, 2004); A. Pirinu, "La traça del fratin: il progetto dei fratelli Paleario Fratino per il forte di S. Filippo a Setúbal e per la collina di S. Giuliano ad Alghero," *Archeologia medievale* XXXVI (2009): 195–210.
32 Eugenio Battisti and Mazzino Fossi, "Casali Giovanni Vincenzo," *Dizionario Biografico degli Italiani* 21 (1978).
33 AGS GYM leg. 281/176 (17 February 1590). For a biography of Spannochi, Alicia Cámara Muñoz, "El ingeniero cortesano: Tiburzio Spannocchi de Siena a Madrid," in *"Libros, caminos y días": el viaje del ingeniero*, ed. Alicia Cámara Muñoz and Bernardo Revuelta Pol, 11–42 (Madrid: Fundación Juanelo Turriano, 2016).
34 Alicia Cámara Muñoz, Rafael de Faria Moreira, and Marino Viganò, *Leonardo Turriano: ingeniero del rey* (Madrid: Fundación Juanelo Turriano, 2010).
35 Rafael Valladares, *La conquista de Lisboa: Violencia militar y comunidad política en Portugal, 1578–1583* (Madrid: Marcial Pons, 2008), 211; David C. Goodman, *Power and Penury: Government, Technology and Science in Philip II's Spain* (Cambridge: Cambridge University Press, 1988), 109.
36 AGS GYM leg. 213/195 (1587).
37 AGS GYM leg. 203/34 (28 November 1587) and leg. 222/55 (25 March 1588). Sumariba was on the payroll of Spanish artillery since 1577: AGS CMC 2ª epoca leg. 414.
38 AGS GYM leg. 209/189 (4 September 1587) and leg. 284/265 (9 May 1590). His manuscripts: Diego de Prado, "La obra manual y pláctica de artillería" (1591), Biblioteca Nacional de Madrid, mss 9024. Diego de Prado y Tovar, "Encyclopaedia de fundición de artillería y su plática manual" (1603), Cambridge University Library.
39 AGS GYM leg. 365/129 (25 May 1589), 131 (1 April 1589), and leg. 604/400 (17 December 1603).
40 Castro, "Bombardeiros," 32–43.
41 Arquivo Nacional da Torre do Tombo (Lisbon), Contos do Reino e Casa, NA 679 (1602).
42 Carlos Gómez-Centurión Jiménez, *Felipe II, la empresa de Inglaterra y el comercio septentrional (1566–1609)* (Madrid and España: Editorial Naval, 1988).
43 Brice Cossart, "Los artilleros a escala de la Monarquía Hispánica: el salto cuantitativo de las armadas atlánticas," in *Estudios sobre Guerra y Sociedad en la Monarquía Hispánica. Guerra marítima, estrategia, organización y cultura militar (1500–1700)*, ed. Enrique García Hernán and Davide Maffi, 205–23 (Valencia: Albatros, 2017).
44 AGS Estado (EST) leg. 1260/115, 116, and 117. For the Venetian schools of gunners, see Michael E. Mallett and John R. Hale, *The Military Organisation of a Renaissance State: Venice c.1400 to 1617* (Cambridge: Cambridge University Press, 2006), 403–7.
45 Cossart, "Les artilleurs."
46 Brice Cossart, "Producing Skills for an Empire: The Seville School of Gunners During the Golden Age of the Carrera de Indias," *Technology and Culture* 57 (2017): 459–86.
47 Stephan R. Epstein, "Craft Guilds, Apprenticeship and Technological Change in Pre-industrial Europe," *The Journal of Economic History* 58, no. 3 (1998): 684–713; Bert De Munck, *Technologies of Learning: Apprenticeship in Antwerp Guilds from the 15th Century to the End of the Ancien Régime* (Turnhout: Brepols, 2007); Bert De Munck, Steven L. Kaplan, and Hugo Soly, eds., *Learning on the Shop Floor: Historical Perspectives on Apprenticeship* (Oxford and New York: Berghahn Books, 2007).
48 Brice Cossart, "Un nouveau paradigme de l'apprentissage technique: Les écoles d'artilleurs de Philippe II d'Espagne," in *Mobilités d'ingénieurs en Europe, XVe–XVIIIe siècle: Mélanges en l'honneur d'Hélène Vérin*, ed. Stéphane Blond, Liliane Hilaire-Pérez, and Michèle Virol (Rennes: Presses Universitaires de Rennes, 2017), 185–98.
49 Parker, *Military Revolution.*

50 AGS GYM leg. 246/191 (20 February 1589), leg. 254/221 (22 December 1589), leg. 280/228 (6 February 1590), leg. 281/32 (7 February 1590), leg. 398/291 (19 February 1594), leg. 627/126 (16 June 1604), leg. 688/57 (14 March 1605).
51 AGS GYM lib. 45, fol. 62r (24 August 1588).
52 Ibid. On the four Sicilian schools: AGS EST leg. 1157/103 (30 May 1591).
53 AGS GYM lib. 70, fol. 58r (28 September 1594).
54 AGS GYM leg. 280/255 (18 February 1590).
55 Ibid.
56 Cossart, "Les artilleurs," 283–86.
57 AGS GYM leg. 271/37 (5 December 1589).
58 AGS GYM leg. 316/117 (1590).
59 He appears among the most renowned captains in the report of the invasion of Terceira: AGS GYM leg. 148/311 (1583). For other biographical details, see AGS GYM leg. 271/37 (5 December 1587) and the preface of his book: Lazaro de la Isla, *Breve tratado de artillería, geometría y artificios de fuegos* (Madrid: Viuda de Pedro Madrigal, 1595).
60 Isla, *Breve tratado*.
61 AGS GYM lib. 77 fol. 139v (29 March 1597), leg. 627/126 (16 June 1604).
62 Serge Gruzinski, *Les quatre parties du monde: Histoire d'une mondialisation* (Turin: Éditions de La Martinière, 2004); Sanjay Subrahmanyam, "Holding the World in Balance: The Connected Histories of the Iberian Overseas Empires, 1500–1640," *American Historical Review* 112, no. 5 (2007): 1359–85; Helge Wendt, ed., *The Globalization of Knowledge in the Iberian Colonial World* (Berlin: Edition Open Access, 2016); Bartolomé Yun-Casalilla, *Iberian World*.
63 AGS GYM leg. 688/34 (7 June 1608).
64 Schaub, *Le Portugal*, 150–53, 271.
65 AGS GYM leg. 397/96 (5 February 1593), 124 (16 March1593) and leg. 389/212 (1 April 1593), 238 (27 May 1593), 253 (9 May 1593).
66 Vitor Luis Gaspar Rodrigues, "Reajustamentos da Estratégia militar naval do 'Estado da India' na viragem do século XVI para o XVII," in *O Estado da India e os Desafios Europeus: Actas do XII Seminario Internacional de História Indo-Portuguesa*, ed. João Paulo Oliveira e Costa and Vitor Luis Gaspar Rodrigues (Lisbon: Centro de História de Além-Mar, 2010), 443–56; André Murteira, "A Carreira da India e as incursões neerlandesas no índico occidental e em águas ibéricas de 1604–1608," in *O Estado da India e os Desafios Europeus: Actas do XII Seminario Internacional de História Indo-Portuguesa*, ed. João Paulo Oliveira e Costa and Vitor Luis Gaspar Rodrigues (Lisbon: Centro de História de Além-Mar, 2010), 457–501.
67 Yun-Casalilla, *Iberian World*, 351; Subrahmanyam, "Holding."
68 Parker, "The Artillery Fortress," 395.
69 Domingo Centenero de Arce, "Soldados portugueses en la Monarquía católica, soldados castellanos en la India Lusa," in *Portugal na Monarquia Hispânica: Dinâmicas de integração e de conflito*, ed. Cardim Leonor Freire Costa Pedro and Mafalda Soares da Cunha (Lisbon: Centro de História de Além-Mar, 2013), 47–72.
70 Rodrigues, "Mestres-fundidores," 161.
71 Ibid., 161–62.
72 Cossart, "Producing Skills," 465.
73 AGI Contratación (CT) leg. 4871.
74 Keneth R. Andrews, *Elizabethan Privateering: 1585–1603* (Cambridge: Cambridge University Press, 1966); Richard B. Wernham, *After the Armada: Elizabethan England and the Struggle for Western Europe, 1588–1595* (Oxford: Oxford University Press, 1984). Wernham, *The Return of the Armadas*.
75 AGI CT leg. 5254/2(1) (1597).
76 AGI SANTO DOMINGO, leg. 20/8 (1621).
77 Ibid.
78 AGI CT leg. 5254/2(1) (1597).

79 AGI CT leg. 5254/2(3) (1597). See also Pedro Mora Piris, *La Real fundición de bronces de Sevilla, siglos XVI a XVIII* (Seville: Escuela superior de ingenieros, 1994), 33.
80 AGI CT leg. 5254/2(8), (10), (11), and (17) (1597).
81 AGI CT leg. 5254/2(5), (14), and (16) (1597).
82 AGI CT leg. 5254/2(1) and (14) (1597).
83 Bartolomé Yun-Casalilla, "Social Networks and the Circulation of Technology and Knowledge in the Global Spanish Empire," in *Global History and New Polycentric Approaches: Europe, Asia and the America in a World Network System*, ed. Manuel Pérez García and Lucio De Sousa (Basingstoke: Palgrave Macmillan, 2018), 275–291; Yun-Casalilla, *Iberian World*, 332.
84 Steven A. Walton, "The Art of Gunnery in Renaissance England" (PhD diss., University of Toronto, Toronto, 1999), 294; Pierre Lemau de la Jaisse, *Carte générale de la monarchie françoise* (Paris: Author, 1733), section "artillerie du Roy, au 15 février 1730."
85 Yun-Casalilla, *Iberian World*, 399–401.
86 Schaub, *Le Portugal*, 20–21, 284.

8

PORTUGUESE MILITARY EXPEDITIONS TO SOUTHEAST ASIA, 1597–1606

André Murteira

This chapter approaches the beginning of the seventeenth-century Portuguese–Dutch War in Asia in light of the discussion on the military revolution. More specifically, it focuses on the much-debated issue of whether a military revolution in Europe produced a European military exceptionalism that made Europeans militarily superior to non-Europeans in the early modern period. For this purpose, the chapter examines case studies of three great but unsuccessful Portuguese expeditions against the Dutch dispatched to Southeast Asia between 1597 and 1606. An important historiographical tradition has assumed that Asian military influence on the Portuguese in Asia during the sixteenth century made the Portuguese militarily inferior to their European enemies such as the Dutch in the seventeenth century.[1] In accordance with this view, this group of expeditions has been described in what might be called rather Dutch-centric terms, where the setbacks that the Portuguese suffered at the hands of the Dutch occupy a place of honour in the accounts. I believe, however, that this "classic" Eurocentric narrative improves when it is supplemented by the neglected account of the defeats inflicted on the Portuguese exclusively by Asian allies of the Dutch. I argue that these defeats contradict the idea that the expeditions failed because the Portuguese were only too well adjusted to an Asian military context and therefore ill prepared to face the European novelty represented by the Dutch.

The motive for approaching the old subject of the war between the Portuguese and the Dutch in this way lies in turning it into a potentially useful case study to assess a larger question: was there a military revolution that conferred on Europeans a decisive military superiority over the rest of the world? This has been a much-debated question in global military historiography in the past two decades.[2] Geoffrey Parker, as is well known, promoted the role of the military revolution in European military successes outside of Europe after the sixteenth century.[3] If we are indeed able to conclude that the Dutch defeated the Portuguese in the East because the latter, after their initial successes, had missed the train of military innovation by confining themselves to wars outside of Europe, then that reinforces the classic Parker thesis. If, on the other hand, we find this to be an oversimplification, we shall have to look for other explanations.

In 1596, Cornelis de Houtman's pioneering expedition reached Banten in Java after a long voyage from Europe via the Cape of Good Hope route. It was the first Dutch fleet to do so, but many followed in its wake. As a result, in 1602, the famous Dutch East India Company (*Verenigde Oost-Indische Compagnie*, or VOC) was formed. The only European powers present in Asia at the time were the Spanish in the Philippines and the Portuguese, who controlled a network of ports that stretched from Mozambique to China. The Portuguese domains in the East were called the *Estado da Índia*, and most of the Portuguese positions lay on the western coast of India. As a result of the Iberian Union of 1580–1640, both the Spanish and the Portuguese were subjects of the so-called Spanish Monarchy of Philip III, although their overseas empires remained formally autonomous entities. The Spanish Monarchy was then at war in Europe with its former Dutch subjects of the United Provinces, who, from 1568 to 1648, carried out a successful war of independence against their former masters. Once the ships of Dutch merchants had reached Asia, the war in Europe was bound to spread East, as in fact it quickly did.

Between 1597 and 1606, three great Portuguese expeditions to Southeast Asia were dispatched from Goa (the *Estado da Índia*'s capital, in western India). This

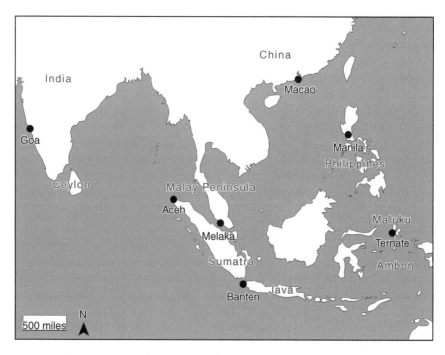

MAP 8.1 Portuguese expeditions to Southeast Asia, 1597–1606 – area of operations

group of expeditions formed the most important series of offensive initiatives of the *Estado* against the Dutch at a time when the Portuguese could still pose a serious threat to their still-precarious position. Their mission was to expel the Dutch from Asia altogether. Arguably, if the Portuguese had found more success, they might have achieved that goal. The expeditions all ended unsuccessfully, however, and the last of them, in 1606, resulted in a great loss of men and ships. The extent of the losses effectively made the resumption of these expeditions impossible. From then on, the *Estado da Índia* was never again in a position to threaten the existence of the VOC, whose strength grew continuously over the following decades.

The expeditions were all fitted out in reaction to the first appearances of the Dutch in Asia, which took place mainly in the Malay-Indonesian archipelago.[4] Most of the much-desired Asian spices could be found in the region: Banten in Java was the harbour most visited by the Dutch from the beginning. The main alternatives to this Javanese city port were Aceh, in Northern Sumatra, and the so-called Spice Islands archipelagos in today's Eastern Indonesia: Ambon, Maluku, and Banda. The Johor sultanate, at the southern tip of the Malay Peninsula, was also visited. Relations with the Portuguese differed from region to region. In Ambon and Maluku, there was a situation of open warfare between the fortified positions of the *Estado da Índia* in Ambon and Tidore and a coalition led by the neighbouring Sultanate of Ternate.[5] This granted the Dutch a fine welcome by Ternate, whose sultan promptly invited them to take up arms against the Portuguese. Banten and Aceh, on the other hand, were at peace with the Portuguese at the time, which may have contributed to the serious incidents that plagued the first visits of the Dutch to the two ports.[6] Johor had a more ambivalent position, with anti-Portuguese and pro-Portuguese factions competing for the attention of the sultan. The former factions had the upper hand for a while, making Johor an important ally of the VOC during the first years of the company's existence.[7]

The Lourenço de Brito expedition (1597–8)

As soon as Viceroy D. Francisco da Gama learnt in Goa of the first Dutch visit to Banten in 1596, he fitted out a war fleet commanded by Lourenço de Brito to punish the Javanese kingdom for having received the northern Europeans.[8] The fleet left India in September 1597 carrying approximately five hundred troops; it was composed of two galleons, two large galleys (one more joined the fleet in Melaka), and approximately ten smaller vessels (*fustas* or *galeotas* – i.e. galliots).

When they arrived in Banten, some Portuguese, unbeknown to their commander, captured and sacked one or two Chinese ships and committed some abuses on land, provoking a reaction from the locals. A Dutch source adds that there were also differences regarding an earlier payment made by the Portuguese to the Banten authorities to dissuade them from favouring Houtman in 1596 (a bribe circumspectly ignored by Portuguese sources).[9]

Whatever the case may have been, the three majestic Portuguese galleys suffered a surprise attack from an armada of Javanese rowing ships. With part of their crews on land and the space on board still cluttered by the booty taken from the Chinese ships, they were unable to use their artillery to defend themselves, and they were all taken by boarding. A portion of the crews – between seventy and 150 men – was massacred and the other portion imprisoned. The galleons and other remaining vessels could not come to their aid, held back by a combination of strong winds and tides. Without attempting to retaliate, Lourenço de Brito decided to return to Melaka, where he arrived in July 1598. His mission remained unaccomplished, and the result was precisely the opposite of what was first intended. The aim of the expedition had been to intimidate Banten into not welcoming the Dutch again. It succeeded, however, only in precipitating a reconciliation between the two sides as a means of guarding against further attacks from Goa or Melaka.

The few sources on this expedition are frustratingly short on details. Nevertheless, the inability of the Portuguese galleons to come to the galleys' aid and their subsequent incapacity to carry out any kind of retaliation seems to confirm the limitations that could hamper European full-rigged ships when operating near the coast. Naval warfare on coastal and fluvial waters was crucial in Southeast Asia in general and in the Malay-Indonesian archipelago in particular. The superiority of European galleons on the open sea did not extend to areas with shallow waters and narrow passages, which were more suitable for light, shallow-draft oared vessels.[10]

The André Furtado de Mendonça expedition (1601–3)

In 1598, a carrack was prepared to travel directly from Lisbon to Melaka to assist in the *Estado da Índia*'s war against the many Dutch ships sent that year to the East.[11] However, the English blockade of Lisbon in 1598 prevented the departure of any ship to Asia that year. The project to send reinforcements from Europe directly to Southeast Asia did not resume until 1605. The relief dispatched to Asia was sent to India instead. In 1601, an armada of six galleons was dispatched to Goa alongside the regular fleet. These were not Portuguese ships but Spanish or Castilian ships. They were part of a group of twelve galleons commissioned in Biscay and Guipúzcoa in 1598–9. By the end of 1599, King Philip III ordered the transfer of six of them to the forces of the Kingdom of Portugal to serve in the *Carreira da Índia* – that is, the Portuguese route to India.[12] The order was fulfilled only in 1601. It was the answer to an August 1599 request by the governors of Portugal, who had asked for aid from Castile to fit out a relief expedition to Asia.[13]

Initially, all six vessels were meant to remain in the East. None of them, however, succeeded in doing so. In the king's letter informing the viceroy in Goa of having sent the armada, he stressed that only three of the galleons could stay in Asia.[14] The others would have to return with the three carracks of the regular fleet because six ships were needed to return with cargo, and it was not possible to fit out more than three carracks for the purpose. The situation became even worse after the voyage to India, which went badly for both fleets. The three carracks of the regular fleet and the six galleons of the relief fleet all left Lisbon on risky late dates: five of the galleons departed on 10 April, two of the ships on 20 April and a galleon and a carrack on 27 April. Due to these late departure dates, five of the ships had to return to Portugal, and only four of the galleons that had left earlier succeeded in passing the Cape of Good Hope. One of them was later shipwrecked on the island of Socotra in the Western Indian Ocean. Thus, only three galleons arrived in India – that is, half of the relief fleet – and they were unaccompanied by any of the carracks of the regular fleet.[15] The small number of ships that managed to reach India that year made it impossible for any of them to remain there, given the need to dispatch as much cargo as possible to Portugal.

The complete failure of this plan to supply the *Estado da Índia* with naval reinforcements from Europe had its origin, therefore, in the lack of means to ensure the regular traffic of the *Carreira da Índia* and in the high number of failed voyages on the route. These were not one-off problems but rather pre-existing structural problems of the *Carreira* that would continue to be present in the following decades. If they already made it hard to ensure the *Carreira*'s proper functioning in regular times, they made it even more difficult to deal with the additional effort required to supply the Portuguese domains in Asia with large-scale naval relief.

Thus, none of the six galleons "taken" from the Kingdom of Castile – which was certainly done despite strong Castilian resistance – to reinforce the Portuguese fleets in Asia ultimately fulfilled their objective. The galleons, however, were only reinforcements for an expedition that the Crown had previously ordered Goa to send to Southeast Asia and was eventually carried out without them. Aires de Saldanha, appointed viceroy in 1600, had as his main mission to organize a great punitive expedition to Southeast Asia against the Dutch and whoever welcomed them in the region.[16] Philip III intended the viceroy to command it himself, and perhaps the fact that Aires de Saldanha had earlier served as captain of Melaka contributed to his appointment. In Asia, however, the viceroy preferred to delegate the task to André Furtado de Mendonça, a famous commander who had previously distinguished himself in the war against the Mappila Muslims from Calicut (southwestern India).[17]

The second expedition set out from India in April or May 1601 with André Furtado de Mendonça in command.[18] The fleet had more full-rigged ships – six – and fewer galleys – only one – than the first expedition, along with approximately twenty light vessels. Most of the latter were lost along the way in a storm near Ceylon. Two more galleons joined the fleet in Melaka, and the expedition, carrying supplies for eight months, numbered approximately thirty-three hundred men between the troops and crews.

The first stop was Melaka, where some of the light ships lost in Ceylon rejoined the fleet, alongside some new ships of the same type found in the harbour. There was a plan to use the expedition to unlock by force the long-standing negotiations with Aceh on the concession of a fortress to the Portuguese in the northern Sumatra sultanate. Nevertheless, the first chosen target of the armada was Banten in Java.[19]

A set of instructions for the expedition, sent from Portugal too late, warned that the fleet should not count on the possibility of resupplying in Melaka, which always lacked supplies.[20] The warning proved to be right, and some of the supplies brought from India were spoiled during the voyage as well. Thus, André Furtado, after leaving Melaka in September 1601, had to call at Palembang in Sumatra to acquire more provisions. Here, in addition to seeking supplies, he attempted unsuccessfully to negotiate an alliance against Banten. Although he failed in that goal, he did manage to establish contact with a few potential allies in Banten. For the attack on the city, defended by thirty thousand men, he agreed to collude with a faction that aspired to take power in the kingdom.[21] However, in the last days of December, when the attack was being prepared, five Dutch ships from Europe appeared in the Javanese port.

In Banten, Furtado faced a Dutch fleet with only five full-rigged ships, but these ships had higher mobility and greater firepower than the Portuguese naval forces, which helped the Dutch render the Portuguese attacks largely inconsequential. After his naval skirmishes with the Dutch, Furtado cancelled the assault on Banten. Whether the cancellation was due to fear of the Dutch or because during the fighting the fleet had been dragged beyond the point of return to the port was unclear.[22] In any case, the result was that contrary to the original plan, he decided to proceed to Ambon in the Spice Islands to face the Dutch there.

A retaliatory expedition to Java was thus aborted and turned instead into a relief expedition to the Portuguese positions in the eastern part of the Malay-Indonesian archipelago. These positions had been requesting such an effort since at least the fall of the fort of Ternate in 1575. The problem was that the expedition had already left Melaka poorly supplied. This shortage of provisions was partially compensated for by the purchase of supplies at Palembang and then on the island of Sumbawa during the trip to Ambon, where the fleet arrived in February 1602. Nevertheless, extending operations in this way to a remote region dependent on supplies from abroad also dangerously extended the expedition's supply lines.

These lines were even more extended when, from Ambon, it was later decided to go to Maluku, also in eastern Indonesia. By that time, André Furtado had spent months busily repressing, with great violence, the local enemies of the Portuguese and of the Christian communities they supported. With the journey to Maluku, he intended, on the one hand, to find Dutch ships to attack, since he had not met any in Ambon (the only ones passing through had fled the armada). On the other hand, he intended to retake the former Portuguese fort of Ternate, which had fallen to the Sultanate of Ternate in 1575.[23] Arriving in Tidore in September 1602, Furtado did not succeed in either of the two objectives, largely due to the logistical difficulties that had been afflicting the expedition since the beginning, which did not let him remain in the region for the length of time needed. While in Ambon, lacking provisions, he dispatched requests for reinforcements to Melaka and Manila in the Philippines. The latter was more helpful, sending Furtado supplies and a troop contingent of two hundred men. With these reinforcements and his men, he set up an eight-month siege of Ternate. He eventually gave it up, pleading lack of necessary ammunition to stay longer in Maluku, which he left around May 1603.[24]

André Furtado returned to Melaka with his armada, where he remained for the next few years. This was what he had been instructed to do when he left Goa, but with the understanding that Melaka would serve as a base for his galleon fleet to operate against the Dutch and their allies, which never happened. After the double failure of his expedition in Banten and Ternate, the only offensive operations that Furtado carried out when he was in Melaka were expeditions against Johor with fleets of light ships.

The Jesuit missionaries in Maluku and Ambon clearly realized that André Furtado's failure in the region could hardly be repaired. Luís Fernandes, the superior of the Society of Jesus in Ambon, wrote in a letter to Rome that he was considering evacuating the mission.[25] Later events proved his instinct right: the *Estado da Índia* did nothing more for Ambon, and in 1605, the Portuguese fortress in the archipelago fell easily to the VOC. The Portuguese never tried to recover it. Their fort at Tidore in Maluku was also taken by the VOC in the same year. It did not suffer the same fate, because the Spanish from the Philippines intervened shortly afterwards, reconquering it for themselves and establishing a position in Maluku, where they managed to maintain an official Iberian presence for a few more decades. In doing so, they proved right an Italian Jesuit of the mission of Ambon, Lorenzo Masonio, who in 1600 had argued that any military expedition to the region should be made from Manila and not from Goa. The reason he gave was simply that it took a month to get there from Manila and a whole year to do it from Goa.[26] Thus, launching the operation from Manila would facilitate not only the expedition itself but also its resupplying. That the only significant support for André Furtado arrived from the Philippines shows the accuracy of Masonio's remark. The history of previous Iberian military initiatives in the area since 1580 already pointed in this direction: almost all of these operations were launched from Manila, not Goa or Melaka.[27]

One last consequence of the expedition worthy of mention was the impression that it made on the Sultanate of Aceh. Although André Furtado did not end up calling at Aceh, the sultan was correctly informed that he had orders to force the concession of a fortress there. This brought the sultan instantly closer to the Dutch, with whom he had been at odds since their first visit – exactly as had previously happened in Banten after Lourenço de Brito's expedition.

The Dutch contribution to the ultimate failure of André Furtado's expedition was doubtless important, but this should not make us overlook the equally significant role played by the local allies of the Dutch. Dutch ships diverted the expedition from Banten, but subsequently, the Portuguese had to deal with only non-European opponents. Logistical difficulties on the one hand and Ternate's resilience on the other dictated the fiasco of Furtado's Maluku incursion. Similarly, in 1597, Lourenço de Brito was defeated only by non-Europeans, namely by the Banten Javanese. Ternate's ability to withstand a siege by European troops also shows the importance that siege warfare could assume in Southeast Asia. Attacked populations did not always choose to withdraw to a safe place, leaving their positions to the enemy, as traditional historiography has sometimes assumed.[28] They could and often did choose to resist and fight. According to Portuguese and Spanish sources, logistical problems were still the main reason for the failure of Ternate's siege. However, the history of the following expedition offers an unequivocal example of successful resistance to a large-scale European attack.

The D. Martim Afonso de Castro expedition (1606)

The third and largest expedition took place in 1606, commanded in person by a viceroy, D. Martim Afonso de Castro.[29] Despite being the largest of the three expeditions, it turned out to be the one most limited in range – it never got past Melaka – and the one that suffered the most at the hands of the Dutch – it lost no fewer than nine carracks and galleons in two series of combat in Melaka with a VOC fleet led by Cornelis de Matelieff (the highest number of Portuguese naval casualties ever recorded in their clashes with the VOC). However, on the way to Melaka, D. Martim suffered a no less important setback at Aceh.

The decision to send a viceroy to Southeast Asia to solve the "Dutch problem" of the *Estado da Índia* in person was made directly at court. It was not the first time that such a decision had been made. As mentioned earlier, in 1601, the king unsuccessfully ordered the previous viceroy, Aires de Saldanha, to lead the expedition that was eventually headed by André Furtado de Mendonça. Moreover, in some respects, the orders issued to D. Martim Afonso de Castro in 1605 merely reiterated the instructions to Aires de Saldanha in 1601 in more detail.[30] The viceroy was again told to depart for Melaka from Goa in April. He should proceed as soon as possible to Java to attack the Dutch and their local allies there (Banten, in the first place). The only important addition was that while waiting for the proper monsoon to sail from Melaka to Java, the armada should take the opportunity to punish Johor for its connections to the VOC. Melaka's other traditional enemy in the region, Aceh, should also be compelled, by force if necessary, to grant the concession of a fortress to the Portuguese. However, this had already been conveyed in André Furtado de Mendonça's previous orders.

As in 1601, reinforcements from Europe were promised to supplement the military means mobilized by the *Estado da Índia*. This time, however, the promise was duly kept: three galleons departed for Asia alongside the regular fleet that left for India in 1605. The former were supposed to sail directly from Europe to Melaka, where they would remain to await the arrival of the viceroy's armada from Goa. They were also supposed to inaugurate a regular link between Lisbon and Melaka, through which two ships would annually supply the latter with people and whatever else was needed.

This attempt to reinforce the *Estado*'s naval forces from Europe went better than the preceding 1598 and 1601 efforts, in that the three galleons all reached Asia and remained there. However, they sailed not directly to Melaka as planned but rather to Goa. They arrived in bad condition, vindicating previous warnings that without an early departure in January or early February, they risked not reaching their planned destination (they departed in March).[31] As for the attempt to set up an annual Lisbon–Melaka voyage, it was not resumed after this failure, which was not the first of its kind.[32]

Nevertheless, the galleons were able, despite everything, to join the armada of D. Martim Afonso de Castro, as planned. This fleet was by far the most important Portuguese naval force deployed in Asia in the seventeenth century. D. Martim's instructions were to outfit eight full-rigged ships in Goa, which were to be joined by the three galleons dispatched directly from Lisbon to Melaka.[33] In the end, an armada of fifteen or sixteen full-rigged ships left India and were joined by two merchant carracks bound for Macao.[34] A caravel, four galleys, and between twenty-one and twenty-three light ships (*fustas* and galleots) followed alongside the large full-rigged ships. The bulk of the at least three thousand men transported by the armada were soldiers.

These figures are enough to give an idea of the expedition's magnitude. To compare this expedition with André Furtado de Mendonça's 1601 armada, the new armada grew from eight full-rigged ships to fifteen or sixteen and from one galley to four (the number of light ships was similar). Furtado's expedition already represented a considerable escalation in relation to the Lourenço de Brito armada. Before the viceroy's departure to Melaka, Goa's city council estimated the expedition's total cost at 800,000 *cruzados*, almost four times what André Furtado's expedition was claimed to have cost (more than 200,000 *cruzados*).[35] We have more reliable estimates in the form of a list of the armada's expenses, which arrive at a total figure of 452.9 *contos* (1,132,250 *cruzados*).[36] According to António Manuel Hespanha, this would correspond to about one-quarter of the total revenue of the Kingdom of Portugal around that time.

As had happened with André Furtado's expedition, departing from India at the recommended time was not possible. D. Martim's instructions were to leave Goa in mid April, expressly mentioning the previous damage suffered by Furtado's light ships due to his late departure.[37] The viceroy, however, managed to depart only on April 22. Afterwards, he had a long stop at Cochin, in southwestern India, which he left only on May 19.[38] When the armada called at the Nicobar Islands in June, a number of rowing vessels had already been lost, as had – more importantly – two full-rigged ships: one of the two merchant carracks and a galleon.[39] The best time to sail the Straits of Melaka had already passed, which may explain the decision to stop at Aceh, where the armada appeared at the end of June.[40]

As we have just seen, in 1601 Aceh already feared – with good reason – that André Furtado intended to take a fortress in the sultanate. This was indeed part of the Portuguese plan, although Furtado never actually attempted it. Five years later, however, D. Martim called at the sultanate's capital and demanded the concession of a fortress. The Acehnese feigned interest in negotiating for a while, to better strengthen their harbour's fortifications. Once they had finished, they proceeded to bomb the armada. D. Martim replied by launching an amphibious assault, but as a result of the last-minute fortification works, the Portuguese could no longer land at the bar of the harbour and had to land along the "open coast, with great risk and delays."[41] They still managed to gain a precarious position on land, but at the cost of enormous losses (two hundred of their best soldiers, according to one source).[42] The strong resistance they met, along with the fresh news that Matelieff had laid siege to Melaka, led them to withdraw the landed force and instead proceed to Melaka with the entire fleet.

Historical precedents

This group of expeditions has been given its due importance by historians but in what might be called rather Dutch-centric terms, with the naval setbacks that André Furtado and D. Martim suffered at the hands of the Dutch in Banten and Melaka, respectively, occupying a place of honour in the accounts. However, this brief summary is sufficient to illustrate that this "classic" Eurocentric narrative gains from being supplemented with the neglected account of the defeats inflicted on the Portuguese exclusively by non-Europeans: Lourenço de Brito's galleys were taken in 1597 by a Javanese fleet at Banten, André Furtado had to abandon the siege he laid to Ternate in 1603, and the Acehnese repelled D. Martim's amphibious attack in 1606.

The Dutch contributed nothing to these three setbacks. They were all defeats inflicted on the Portuguese exclusively by non-Europeans, contradicting the idea that the expeditions failed because the *Estado da Índia* was too well adjusted to local military contexts and therefore ill prepared to face the European novelty represented by the Dutch. While the latter idea may have been true, the fact remains that the Portuguese military apparatus also failed against the non-European opponents that it was supposedly well prepared to face. Moreover, regardless of the particulars of each of the episodes, these expeditions can also be said to indicate a pattern, in that they gave continuity to what was a sixteenth-century tradition of Portuguese military failures in the region.

There were indeed sixteenth-century precedents for all three episodes. The rise of the Sultanate of Aceh in Sumatra had already led to the expulsion of the Portuguese from Pasai in the 1520s, the only position they ever held in Sumatra. Around the same time, the only Portuguese attempt to secure a position on the neighbouring island of Java, at Banten, also met with an inglorious end. The *Estado da Índia* succeeded only in establishing a stronghold in remote Ternate (1522) in Maluku, which for decades was the only fortified Portuguese position east of Melaka.[43] The stronghold's inherent vulnerability led to its eventual fall in 1575, after a long siege, during which it insistently asked for help from Goa and Melaka but to no avail.[44] Arguably, when André Furtado failed to retake Ternate almost thirty years later, he was repeating an earlier defeat, as were Lourenço de Brito when he was beaten in Banten and D. Martim when he failed to take Aceh.

In other words, not only unpreparedness for a European-type war but also an old vulnerability of the *Estado da Índia* – its persistent difficulty in projecting its power into Southeast Asia – led to the failure of the expeditions of 1597–1606. The main reason behind this difficulty seems to have been the competing demands of the Western Indian Ocean, especially of the western coast of India, where the Portuguese concentrated most of their fortresses, personnel, and naval forces. The Portuguese presence in other areas, especially east of Ceylon, was much more demilitarized.[45]

This scant military presence beyond Ceylon did not mean, however, that the region was unimportant to the *Estado da Índia*. The spice trade with the Malay-Indonesian archipelago (especially with Ambon and Maluku) and the trade with China and Japan via Macao were vital for the finances of the *Estado*. A good part of the revenue of Portuguese customhouses on the western India coast came from trade with these distant regions. The scant official Portuguese presence in the area was compensated for by the existence of dynamic groups of private merchants and missionaries. Militarily, these groups could not, however, replace the official forces of the *Estado*. Because of this, the military imbalance between the western and eastern parts of the Portuguese domains in Asia was always seen as a problem, especially given the economic importance of the unprotected eastern part.

The intention to correct this imbalance was part of an ambitious attempt to reorganize the *Estado da Índia* in 1571.[46] Finally, for Lisbon, the *Estado* had become too great and widespread for its own good. The viceroy in Goa should thus permanently relinquish his power over the eastern and westernmost areas of the *Estado* to two governors. The governor in the west would rule over all Portuguese positions in East Africa and was charged with promoting territorial expansion in the interior in the fabled gold-producing region of Munamatapa. His counterpart in the east had jurisdiction over all Portuguese positions in Southeast Asia and Far East Asia, which he should rule from Melaka. Just as the creation of the governorship in East Africa was meant to be a base for the conquest of Munamatapa, the East Asia governorship was meant to facilitate the conquest of Aceh, a long-standing Portuguese ambition (which would be attempted, however, only by D. Martim Afonso de Castro in 1606, with the poor results already described).

The project was a victim of the problem it tried to solve. By autonomizing Melaka and its dependencies (and East Africa) from Goa, the king intended to make these areas more militarily self-sufficient. To do that, however, he needed to request significant initial military support from Goa. The status quo in Goa made sure that support was never forthcoming, thereby dictating the failure of the initiative. In 1623, the plan was briefly revived, but without any palpable results. Melaka therefore continued to be dependent on the irregular support that Goa was able or willing to send to it (we saw earlier how difficult it was to supply Melaka with reinforcements directly from Europe).

Conclusion

The *Estado da Índia*'s difficulty in projecting power east of Ceylon may not have had serious effects in the sixteenth century, but it certainly proved to be of lasting consequence at the beginning of the seventeenth century. The combined actions of the newly arrived Dutch and their local allies showed the military vulnerability of

Portuguese positions in the region. Understanding the extent of the contributions of different Southeast Asian allies of the Dutch to the military setbacks of the Portuguese in 1597–1606 is obviously important for answering the question whether there was a European military exceptionalism in the early modern period. If we conclude that non-European actors and local circumstances played a large part in Portuguese defeats, then the argument that explains the victories of the Dutch mainly on the basis of their superior experience in European warfare seems to lose strength. We can therefore say that the findings presented earlier fit well with the more recent historiography questioning the existence of a significant military divide between Europeans and non-Europeans.

However, reasons remain for us to believe in some form of European military exceptionalism in fields such as fortification architecture and, especially, naval warfare on the open sea. The VOC fleets of cannon-armed, full-rigged ships were certainly more dangerous foes than the naval enemies the Portuguese had to face in Asia in the sixteenth century. We thus have good reasons to argue that in this specific field, unfamiliarity with certain types of European warfare was a disadvantage. Nevertheless, Portuguese ships faced similar difficulties when confronting Dutch ships in European waters and in the Atlantic in general, where, unlike in Asia, the Portuguese had long experiences of facing other Europeans. This suggests that the poor naval performance of the *Estado da Índia* fleets against their Dutch enemies had reasons beyond unfamiliarity with European naval warfare.[47]

Notes

1 António Manuel Hespanha, "Introdução," in *Nova história militar de Portugal*, ed. António Manuel Hespanha, vol. 2 (Lisbon: Círculo de Leitores, 2004), 9–33; António Manuel Hespanha, "Conclusão: guerra e sistema de poder," in ibid., 359–66; Fernando Dores Costa, "Recrutamento," in ibid., 68–93; Fernando Dores Costa, "O estatuto social dos militares," in ibid., 93–101; Vítor Luís Gaspar Rodrigues, "A guerra na Índia," in ibid., 198–223.
2 Geoffrey Parker, *The Military Revolution: Military Innovation and the Rise of the West, 1500–1800*, 2nd ed. (Cambridge: Cambridge University Press, 1996); Geoffrey Parker and Sanjay Subrahmanyam, "Arms and the Asian: Revisiting European Firearms and Their Place in Early Modern Asia," *Revista de Cultura-Review of Culture* 26 (2008): 12–48; Jeremy Black, *European Warfare, 1494–1660* (London: Routledge, 2002); Jeremy Black, *Beyond the Military Revolution: War in the Seventeenth Century World* (London: Palgrave Macmillan, 2011); Peter Lorge, *The Asian Military Revolution: From Gunpowder to the Bomb* (Cambridge: Cambridge University Press, 2008); Tonio Andrade, *Lost Colony: The Untold Story of China's First Great Victory Over the West* (Princeton, NJ: Princeton University Press, 2011); Tonio Andrade, *The Gunpowder Age: China, Military Innovation, and the Rise of the West in World History* (Princeton, NJ: Princeton University Press, 2016); Frank Jacob and Gilmar Visoni-Alonzo, *The Military Revolution in Early Modern Europe: A Revision* (London: Palgrave Macmillan, 2016); J.C. Sharman, *Empires of the Weak: The Real Story of European Expansion and the Creation of the New World Order* (Princeton, NJ: Princeton University Press, 2019).
3 Parker, *The Military Revolution*, 82–114.
4 For overviews of the first years of the Dutch in Asia, see Victor Enthoven, *Zeeland en de opkomst van de Republiek: handel en strijd in de Scheldedelta, c. 1550–1621* (Leiden: Luctor

et Victor, 1996), 192–211; Ernst van Veen, *Decay or Defeat? An Inquiry into the Portuguese Decline in Asia, 1580–1645* (Leiden: Research School of Asian, African and Amerindian Studies, Universiteit Leiden, 2000); Gerrit Knaap, Henk den Heijer, and Michiel de Jong, *Oorlogen overzee: militair optreden door compagnie en staat buiten Europa, 1595–1814* (Amsterdam: Boom, 2015), 19–84.

5 Leonard Andaya, *The World of Maluku: Eastern Indonesia in the Early Modern Period* (Honolulu: University of Hawai Press, 1993), 132–44; Manuel Lobato, *Política e comércio dos portugueses na Insulíndia: Malaca e as Molucas de 1575 a 1605* (Macao: Instituto Português do Oriente, 1999), 91–164, 291–332.

6 On the relations between Aceh and the Portuguese in the sixteenth century, see Paulo Jorge de Sousa Pinto, *Portugueses e malaios: Malaca e os sultanatos de Johor e Achém, 1575–1619* (Lisbon: Sociedade Histórica da Independência de Portugal, 1997), 95–119, 167–78; Lobato, *Política e comércio*, 62, 65–66, 71–73, 206–11; Jorge Manuel dos Santos Alves, *O domínio do norte de Samatra: A história dos sultanatos de Samudera-Pacém e de Achém, e das suas relações com os Portugueses, 1500–1580* (Lisbon: Sociedade Histórica da Independência de Portugal, 1999), 153–72; Jorge Manuel dos Santos Alves, "Samatra," in *História dos portugueses no Extremo Oriente*, ed. A.H. de Oliveira Marques, vol. 1, bk. 2 (Lisbon: Fundação Oriente, 2000), 95–104. On Banten see Claude Guillot, "Les Portugais et Banten (1511–1682)," *Revista de Cultura* 13–14 (1991): 80–91.

7 Peter Borschberg, *The Singapore and Melaka Straits: Violence, Security and Diplomacy in the 17th Century* (Leiden: KITLV Press, 2010), 60–156.

8 For the main primary sources on the history of Lourenço de Brito's expedition, see city council of Goa to the king, Goa, 1597, in J.H. da Cunha Rivara, ed., *Archivo portuguez oriental*, vol. 1, bk. 2 (Nova Goa, 1876), 50–51; Diogo do Couto, *Da Ásia de Diogo do Couto: Dos feitos que os portugueses fizeram no descobrimento dos mares e terras do Oriente*, vol. 12 (Lisbon: Regia Officina Typografica, 1788), 47–58, 89–93; "Historische Beschrijvinghe de seer wijt veroemde Coopstadt Amsterdam," in G.P. Rouffaer and J.W. Ijzerman, eds., *De eerste schipvaart der Nederlanders naar Oost-Indië onder Cornelis de Houtman, 1595–1597: journalen, documenten en andere bescheiden*, vol. 3 (The Hague: Martinus Nijhoff, 1929), 45–46; "Reisverhaal van Jacob Cornelisz. van Neck van de tweede schipvaart naar Oost-Indie onder zijn beleid gedaan, 1598–1599," in J. Keuning, ed., *De tweede schipvaart der Nederlanders naar Oost-Indië onder Jacob Cornelisz. van Neck en Wybrant Warwijck, 1598–1600*, (The Hague: Martinus Nijhoff, 1938–1951), vol. 1: 40–42; "A true report of the gainfull, prosperous, and speedy voiage to Iava in the East Indies, performed by a fleet of 8 ships of Amsterdam," in ibid., vol. 2: 37–38; "Het journaal van Heyndrick Dirrecksen Jolinck," in ibid., vol. 5, bk. 1, 92.

9 Another passage suggests that the Portuguese proposed the establishment of a fortress in Banten, while another says that there were suspicions that they planned to take over the city. Rouffaer and Ijzerman, *De eerste schipvaart*, vol. 1, note on back of map IV; vol. 3, 45–46; Keuning, *De tweede schipvaart*, vol. 2, 37–38.

10 Michael W. Charney, *Southeast Asian Warfare, 1300–1900* (Leiden: Brill, 2004), 128–30.

11 Instructions to Cosme de Lafeta, Lisbon, 17 March 1598, in Maria Manuela Sobral Blanco, "Os holandeses e o império português do Oriente," vol. 2 (BA diss., University of Lisbon, Lisbon, 1974), 39–41.

12 C.R. Boxer, "The Papers of Martin de Bertendona, a Basque Admiral of Spain's Golden Age, 1586–1604," *The Indiana University Bookman* 10 (1969): 15–16.

13 Governors of Portugal to the king, August 1599, in Blanco, "Os holandeses e o império português do Oriente," vol. 2, 43.

14 King to Aires de Saldanha, viceroy of India, Madrid, 14 March 1601, in ibid., vol. 2, 62–66.

15 "Tratado das batalhas do galeão Santiago no ano de 1602," in Bernardo Gomes de Brito, ed., *História Trágico-Marítima*, vol. 2 (Lisbon: Edições Afrodite, 1972), 738.

16 King to Aires de Saldanha, viceroy of India, Madrid, 14 March 1601, in Blanco, "Os holandeses e o império português do Oriente," vol. 2, 62–66.

17 On André Furtado, see C.R. Boxer and J.A. Frazão de Vasconcelos, *André Furtado de Mendonça, 1558–1610* (Lisbon: Agência Geral do Ultramar, 1955).

18 For the main primary sources on the history of André Furtado's expedition, see André Furtado de Mendonça to Father Nicolau Pimenta, Ambon, 10 May 1602, in ibid., 117–22; Philip III, Lisbon, 15 February 1603, in ibid., 165–71; André Furtado Mendonça to governor of Philippines, Ambon, 1 May 1602, in Francisco Colín, *Labor evangélica de los obreros de la Compañía de Jesús en las Islas Filipinas*, ed. Pablo Pastells (Barcelona: Imprenta y Litografía de Henrich y Compañia, 1904), 344n1; António Brito Fogaça to governor of Philippines, Cavite, 14 October 1602, in ibid., 345n1; André Furtado Mendonça to governor of Philippines, Ternate, 25 March 1603, in ibid., 348–49n1; Gallinato to governor of Philippines, Tidore, 24 May 1603, in ibid., 349–53n1; Father Brício Fernandes to viceroy of India, Ambon, 1 May 1602, in Hubert Jacobs, ed., *Documenta Malucensia*, vol. 2 (Rome: Jesuit Historical Institute, 1980), 551–71; "Het journaal van de Gelderland," in Perry Moree, ed., *Dodo's en galjoenen: de reis van het schip Gelderland naar Oost-Indie, 1601–1603* (Zutphen: Walburg Pers, 2001), 91–95; "Kopie-brief, vermoedelijk van Willem Cornelisz Schouten," in ibid., 148–52; Cornelis van der Geyn, 21 September 1606, in ibid., 153–56; Hans Bouwer, 27 September 1604, in ibid., 157–67.

19 Archbishop of Goa to the king, Goa, 6 April 1603, in Pinto, *Portugueses e malaios*, 285–86; royal letter, Lisbon, 20 February 1603, in Boxer and Vasconcelos, *André Furtado de Mendonça*, 158–60; Father Nicolau Pimenta to Father Claudio Acquaviva, Margão, 1 December 1601, in Jacobs, *Documenta Malucensia*, vol. 2, 529–31.

20 King to Aires de Saldanha, viceroy of India, Madrid, 14 March 1601, in Blanco, "Os holandeses e o império português do Oriente," vol. 2, 62.

21 André Furtado de Mendonça to Father Nicolau Pimenta, Ambon, 10 May 1602, in Boxer and Vasconcelos, *André Furtado de Mendonça*, 117–18.

22 Ibid.; Father Brício Fernandes to Aires de Saldanha, viceroy of India, Ambon, 1 May 1602, in Jacobs, *Documenta Malucensia*, vol. 2, 560–61.

23 André Furtado de Mendonça to Father Nicolau Pimenta, Ambon, 10 May 1602, in Boxer and Vasconcelos, *André Furtado de Mendonça*, 120; André Furtado Mendonça to D. Pedro de Acuña, governor of Philippines, Ambon, 1 May 1602, in Colín, *Labor Evangélica*, 344n1; Father Brício Fernandes to Aires de Saldanha, viceroy of India, Ambon, 1 May 1602, in Jacobs, *Documenta Malucensia*, vol. 2, 570–71.

24 André Furtado Mendonça to D. Pedro de Acuña, governor of Philippines, Ternate, 25 March 1603, in Colín, *Labor Evangélica*, 348–49n1; Gallinato to D. Pedro de Acuña, governor of Philippines, Tidore, 24 May 1603, in ibid., 349–53n1.

25 Father Luís Fernandes to Father Claudio Acquaviva, Ambon, 17 July 1603, in Jacobs, *Documenta Malucensia*, vol. 2, 626–29.

26 Father Lorenzo Masonio to Father Claudio Acquaviva, Ambon, 30 April 1600, in ibid., vol. 2, 490–91.

27 Ibid., vol. 2, 7★–8★.

28 This traditional view was criticized by Michael Charney in *Southeast Asian Warfare*, 73–78.

29 For the main primary sources on the history of D. Martim's expedition, see "Rol dos capitães da armada de D. Martim Afonso de Castro," in Boxer and Vasconcelos, *André Furtado de Mendonça*, 131–34; Diogo do Couto to D. Francisco da Gama, Goa, 27 December 1607, in ibid., 137–40; "Derrota que fez a armada de Dom Martim Af. de Castro Vizorrey de Cochim para p.ª o Sul," in ibid., 141–42; Father Braz Nunes, Melaka, 10 October 1607, in ibid., 143–45; "Discurso sobre o progresso dos Olandeses," in ibid., 147–52; "Relação do sucesso que teve a armada do viso-rei Dom Martim Afonso," in Pinto, *Portugueses e malaios*, 293–97; city council of Goa to the king, Goa, 1606, in Rivara, *Archivo portuguez oriental*, vol. 1, bk. 2, 171–72; city council of Goa to king, Goa, 1607, in ibid., vol. 1, bk. 2, 193–95, 199–200; François Pyrard, *Voyage de de Laval aux Indes orientales (1601–1611)*, ed. Xavier de Castro, vol. 2 (Paris: Chandeigne, 1998), 663–68; "Extract uyt het journael van den heer Cornelis Matelief de Jonge,"

in *Machtsstrijd om Malakka: De reis van VOC admiraal Cornelis Cornelisz. Matelief naar Oost-Aziê, 1605–1608*, ed. Leo Akveld (Zutphen: Walburg Pers, 2013), 114–60; "Twee brieven van Jacques L'Hermite de Jonge," in ibid., 332–60; Lucas Jansen, Dirck van Leeuwen, and Lodewick Issaacks Eyllofs, Masulipatnam, 15 February 1608, in J.K.J. de Jonge, ed., *De opkomst van het Nederlandsch gezag in Oost-Indië (1595–1610): verzameling van onuitgegeven stukken uit het Oud-koloniaal archief*, vol. 3 (The Hague, 1865), 218–21.

30 King to D. Martim Afonso de Castro, viceroy of India, Valhadolid, 5 March 1605, in Blanco, "Os holandeses e o império português do Oriente," vol. 2, 101–13.

31 King to viceroy of Portugal, Valhadolid, 27 December 1604, in Pinto, *Portugueses e malaios*, 287–89.

32 Lobato, *Política e comércio*, 282–90.

33 King to D. Martim Afonso de Castro, viceroy of India, Valhadolid, 5 March 1605, in Blanco, "Os holandeses e o império português do Oriente," vol. 2, 102–3.

34 "Rol dos capitães da armada de D. Martim Afonso de Castro," in Boxer and Vasconcelos, *André Furtado de Mendonça*, 131–34; "Extract uyt het journael van den heer Cornelis Matelief de Jonge," in Akveld, *Machtsstrijd om Malakka*, 140–42.

35 City council of Goa to the king, 1605, in Rivara, *Archivo portuguez oriental*, vol. 1, bk. 2, 146.

36 António Manuel Hespanha, "As finanças da guerra," in Hespanha, *Nova história militar de Portugal*, 185–86.

37 King to D. Martim Afonso de Castro, viceroy of India, Valhadolid, 5 March 1605, in Blanco, "Os holandeses e o império português do Oriente," vol. 2, 103.

38 "Discurso sobre o progresso dos Olandeses," in Boxer and Vasconcelos, *André Furtado de Mendonça*, 148.

39 "Relação do sucesso que teve a armada do viso-rei Dom Martim Afonso," in Pinto, *Portugueses e malaios*, 293.

40 "Derrota que fez a armada de Dom Martim Af. de Castro," in Boxer and Vasconcelos, *André Furtado de Mendonça*, 141–42; "Relação do sucesso que teve a armada do viso-rei Dom Martim Afonso," in Pinto, *Portugueses e malaios*, 293–94.

41 "Relação do sucesso que teve a armada do viso-rei Dom Martim Afonso," in Pinto, *Portugueses e malaios*, 293–94.

42 Boxer and Vasconcelos, *André Furtado de Mendonça*, 148–49.

43 Alves, *O domínio do norte de Samatra*, 110–11; Luís Filipe F.R. Thomaz, "O malogrado estabelecimento oficial dos portugueses em Sunda e a islamização da Java," in *Aquém e além da Taprobana: Estudos luso-orientais à memória de Jean Aubin e Denys Lombard*, ed. Luís Filipe F.R. Thomaz (Lisbon: CHAM, 2002), 381–607; Lobato, *Política e comércio*, 97–104.

44 Lobato, *Política e comércio*, 114–21.

45 Luís Filipe F.R. Thomaz, "Os portugueses nos mares da Insulíndia no século XVI," in *De Ceuta a Timor* (Lisbon: Difel, 1994), 567.

46 Pinto, *Portugueses e malaios*, 82–85; Lobato, *Política e comércio*, 74–76; Nuno Vila-Santa, "Revisitando o Estado da Índia nos Anos de 1571 a 1577," *Revista de Cultura – International Edition* 36 (2010): 88–112.

47 I argued this point extensively in André Murteira, "The Military Revolution and European Wars Outside of Europe: The Portuguese-Dutch War in Asia in the First Quarter of the Seventeenth Century," *The Journal of Military History* 84 (April 2020): 511–35.

9

REASSESSING PORTUGUESE MILITARY SUPERIORITY IN ASIA IN THE SIXTEENTH CENTURY – THE CASE OF LAND WARFARE[1]

Roger Lee de Jesus

The arrival of Vasco da Gama's armada to India in 1498 opened the Asian markets to European forces and accelerated the development of artillery in this region of the world. Equipped with superior technology, the Portuguese imposed their presence, combining trade and warfare. Most studies on the Military Revolution assess Portuguese forces in Asia to have been superior, usually focusing on naval warfare and the efficient use of broadside gunnery, which ignores or devalues land-based warfare.

This chapter therefore aims to reassess and debate the existence of Portuguese superiority in land warfare in the *Estado da Índia* (the name formally given to the Portuguese Empire in Asia). This assessment is conducted in the context of the European force's having to resist several military land operations, starting as far back as their settlement in the region, because the use of gunpowder was not limited exclusively to the Portuguese and guns were used similarly by both sides. This chapter therefore broadly evaluates the impact of Portuguese warfare in Asia. It argues that both Portuguese and local landlords adapted to new ways of waging war and that the Europeans experienced a partial loss of superiority after the first decades of the sixteenth century. To reach this conclusion, first the idea of Portuguese military superiority is challenged, and then a number of battles and sieges are analysed by using both Portuguese and Asian sources, emphasizing the context of India. A map of the Portuguese presence in the Indian subcontinent can be found at the end of this chapter.

The Military Revolution and the Portuguese Empire

This debate is directly connected to the concept of military revolution, as coined by Geoffrey Parker, which refers to the military developments beginning during the Italian Wars that had a deep impact not only on how war was waged but also from political, social, and financial points of view, promoting the rise of the West.[2] The long debate fuelled by Parker's book still resonates today, because the academic community continues to discuss the implications of such a deterministic theory.[3] The participation of the Portuguese Kingdom in this *revolution* was connected mainly with the dissemination of new military developments to the country's overseas empire and especially to a newly discovered and developed naval firepower, along with the "artillery fortress as an engine of European overseas expansion" (to quote one of Parker's well-known studies). Given that the Portuguese had few resources with which to provide an effective military presence in Asian lands, the *Estado da Índia* relied on a network of coastal fortresses and factories (a *Venetian model*, according to William R. Thompson),[4] which attempted to control commercial networks and routes, resorting to local allies to intervene in, or instigate, internal wars.[5] To a certain extent, the introduction of violence and warfare to Asian mercantile routes by the Portuguese gave the latter some level of leadership as part of the complex commercial game that extended from the eastern coast of Africa to the Far East.[6]

The Portuguese had effective firepower, which, allied with the speed of their ships, gave them significant naval superiority on the Indian Ocean. Artillery was successfully used on board, allowing for the use of broadside gunnery in a line-ahead formation, as evidenced in Portuguese sources dating back to the beginning of the sixteenth century. The pioneering naval development led by the kingdom was responsible for a certain European military hegemony in Asia at the beginning of the century.[7] This seemingly superior nature contributed to some coastal cities' (e.g. Cochin and Cannanur) entering into alliances with the Portuguese.[8]

Decades ago, P.J. Marshall asserted that during the sixteenth century the Portuguese presence "had begun to be absorbed into Asia, participating in its trade and politics but not dominating them."[9] This idea is somehow linked to the so-called easternization of the Portuguese armadas in this century, which can be explained as the gradual transition towards the regular use of small rowboats rather than high-board ships, the former of which were better suited to wars waged in the coastal areas of the Indian Ocean.[10] This process was also connected to the idea of the consequent decadence of the Portuguese military and administrative structures, justifying, to some extent, the Portuguese defeat during Dutch expansion in Asia. Despite these circumstances, André Murteira recently showed that this process does not entirely explain the reasons for the defeat, reassessing the idea of a military revolution in the *Estado da Índia* at the beginning of the seventeenth century. According to Murteira, the inability of the Portuguese to reinforce their fleet through the India Run was parallel to the Portuguese defeat in the Atlantic Ocean and should be seen as a complex process that needs to be further compared in the future.[11] Despite this recent effort, the idea of a military revolution and its application to the Portuguese case in the sixteenth century has rarely been discussed in historiography.[12]

Military superiority?

Portuguese military superiority is commonly associated with naval power and the destructive effects of Portuguese armadas, high sea scouting, defending fortresses, and attacking strategic cities. This idea is related to what some research has described as the ability of the Portuguese to maintain a technological gap, therefore also maintaining their technological superiority, especially where firepower was concerned.[13]

However, this is also related to a general idea that European warfare was superior to Asian practices while at war, in both material and tactical terms. A Eurocentric (or Westernized) view, it devalues, or simply ignores, any Asian military ability, as demonstrated by Jeremy Black and, more recently, J.C. Sharman.[14] Furthermore, this idea is based on an almost homogenizing view of the Indo-West Pacific world as a united reality, which ignores a considerable amount of diversity. In the same debate, the old idea that the arrival of the Portuguese in Asia started some kind of a military revolution has been largely proved to have been a product of misinformation, since gunpowder and guns were already known and used.[15] However, from a technical perspective, Portuguese artillery was highly desired in India, an example being wrought iron pieces that were not as developed in the region.[16] In China, the breech-loader system and the size of the pieces caught the eye of military officers, as Tonio Andrade recently defended.[17] The military gap between Europe and Asia was therefore not as considerable as imagined.[18]

As stated previously, the major area in which the Portuguese were considered superior was in naval warfare, where ships where built to sustain the explosive power of gunpowder and used for broadside gunnery. A good example of their superiority is the 1509 naval battle of Diu, when the Portuguese fleet, commanded by Viceroy Francisco de Almeida, obtained a remarkable victory against a Mamluk fleet through the judicious use of broadside guns, sinking a galley with this use of artillery.[19]

Portuguese sources from the sixteenth century tend to emphasize this supposed technological gap between the Portuguese and local forces, especially disregarding the Indian potentates. Governor Afonso de Albuquerque was severely criticized by Afonso Real because his victories were against "naked little black men without weapons."[20] This description is often used as a literary topos in sources from this period and can be found in several chronicles, such as the one written by Gaspar Correia.[21] Racial prejudice was then transposed to military evaluation.[22] These kinds of comments were based mostly on the lack of defensive armour, especially in southern India, where the Portuguese fought at the beginning of the sixteenth century. Standing in stark contrast to heavy European armour, which was made up of various pieces of iron plate, local soldiers preferred lighter protection that thus left them more vulnerable, such as cotton jackets.[23]

On the same note, no Asian state had a naval force (with few exceptions, such as China, which had a different system), unlike European states, which had been developing theirs since medieval times.[24] Portugal's opponents were therefore often merchants who would defend themselves or try to intervene in order to either share or regain their position in Asian trade. From a materialistic perspective, some Asian sail ships did not even use iron nails, which weakened them and made them vulnerable to Portuguese guns.[25]

On a political note, Michael Pearson argued that, in the case of the Sultanate of Gujarat, sultans and nobles were not interested in commercial and maritime trade, since their concept of power was based on land tenure and strength in land warfare.[26] Geneviève Bouchon also showed how in South India, maritime trade was handled and developed by merchant communities instead of the local authorities.[27] Confucianism and Brahmanical orthodoxy could also explain this lack of interest, given that such religious views saw the "just" sovereign as exempt from meddling in commerce.[28] Despite this idea, recent studies show that these reasons are too simplistic to explain the complexity of sixteenth-century Asian states, where migrations of elites from diverse backgrounds created an extensive network of cultural and political interpenetration, where merchants were welcomed and cared for by local sultans.[29]

These situations did not prevent fierce resistance to the Portuguese attempt to control commercial networks, of which three examples will be recalled.[30] The first is opposition to the Kannur's Mappillas (local Muslim converts of the Malabar coast) in the 1520s and 1530s, where waging war with small sailing and rowing ships put the *Estado da Índia* under great pressure, from Malabar through the Cape Comorin and to the island of Ceylon.[31] The second is related to the first contacts with China and to the resounding defeat of Martim Afonso de Melo's fleet in 1522, at the hands of the Celestial Empire's fleet, which was composed of robust junk ships.[32] The latter brings us to the long conflict between the Sultanate of Aceh (Sumatra) and Portuguese Melaka; from the 1530s onwards, the local potentate established a strong and successful Ottoman liaison, which enabled the revival of the locally produced pepper trade, receiving state-of-the-art armaments to fight against the Portuguese.[33]

In addition to this ability to resist Portuguese expansion, most Asian potentates also demonstrated their skill when it came to learning and replicating the techniques and technologies brought by the Portuguese. This knowledge could be transmitted in an official way (e.g. through local workers in Portuguese dockyards) or informally (by Portuguese mercenaries[34]). Let us also recall, for instance, various episodes in which the Portuguese supported local landlords, where Portuguese soldiers would fight alongside local soldiers, thus allowing for a better understanding of their modus operandi. Such was the case of Cristóvão da Gama's small army in Ethiopia in 1541–2 and Martim Afonso de Sousa's support of Bahadur Shah of Gujarat in 1535.[35] As for weaponry, the Portuguese also taught the locals how to make arms, as in Sri Lanka, where the Portuguese started to buy arms in the seventeenth century to supply the *Estado da Índia*.[36]

In one way or another, Portuguese technology spread along the Asian seas. China, for instance, seized several Portuguese artillery pieces and replicated them with some success, later using them in the 1522 confrontation.[37] In 1546, a Portuguese official complained to the governor that many artillery pieces were being smuggled to the local kingdoms around Cochin, identifying more than 130 cannons in those states, all recognized for bearing the heraldic device of the Portuguese kingdom.[38] The case of the Battle of Raichur, in 1520, is critical due to its political context and because it involved twenty hired Portuguese arquebusiers, as recently studied by Richard Eaton and Phillip Wagoner.[39] The wars of the Decan Plateau in India, in which the sultanates of Bijapur and Ahmadnagar opposed the Hindu Empire of Vijayanagar, are an interesting case study of the reception and development of the new firepower brought by Portuguese and other external agents, as was Ottoman influence.

From what has been said, the central idea is that Portuguese military superiority in the mid sixteenth century has not been proven. The first decades of Portuguese presence may have been marked by some military superiority, which mainly translated into the imposition of naval control. Resistance and setbacks from the 1520s onwards show that multiple adversaries of the *Estado da Índia* were scattered throughout Asia, developing firepower in their own way. Witnessing this proliferation of firearms, Francisco de Lima wrote disappointedly to the Portuguese king in 1548 that, at that time, "the entire world is full of firearms."[40]

Waging war in Asia: some case studies

The first case to be analysed is the Portuguese defence of Cochin, in 1504, by captain Duarte Pacheco Pereira. At the time, the Samudri Raja of Calicut, supported by Muslim merchants (most of them Gujarati people), was the main adversary of Portuguese trade in the region. To remove them, he prepared an attack on Cochin, where the Portuguese had built their new fortress. Some Portuguese chroniclers speak of eighty thousand men against as little as a hundred Portuguese soldiers, numbers that were, of course, heavily exaggerated. A more critical look reveals around five thousand men from Calicut at most, attacking approximately 130 Portuguese, supported by the small army of Cochin.[41] Several attacks between March and May were launched in an attempt to approach the city. However, the defenders had an important factor working in their favour: the physical conditions of the land. As we know, the island of Cochin is found in a lagoon, with many rivers, streams, and even swamps. Because the Samudri men travelled by land, the Portuguese took advantage of their position to force them to fight outside the city, in the area of the river. Trapped in this area, they could gain access only through small openings, narrowing the size of the battlefield. This allowed the Portuguese to use their firearms and even artillery, reducing the disproportionate number of men. They held their position not only on land but also in small boats, using the rivers to travel quickly from one position to another, preventing the enemy from advancing. At the time, European weapons were clearly superior to the local forces, whose body armour was unsuited to this kind of attack. The Calicut force lost hundreds of men during the attacks and many more subsequently, when an epidemic worsened their circumstances. The defence of Cochin was one of the first land operations where Portuguese superiority was clear – not only thanks to their weaponry but mostly thanks to their knowledge and use of the physical space.

The other case study involves campaigns launched by Governor Afonso de Albuquerque (1509–15). Albuquerque is known as one of the most important Portuguese governors of the sixteenth century, creating a strong network of fortresses across the Indian Ocean that, ultimately, led to the formation of what came to be known as the *Estado da Índia*. The conquest of Goa (1510), Melaka (1511), and Hormuz (1515), and even the failed attempt to take Aden (1513), were all amphibious operations, which features a remarkable use of firepower and visionary military organization that did not require significant land operations.[42] In actual fact, the defeat of Albuquerque in Aden clearly shows a diminished Portuguese superiority when naval power was not involved, in which a strong chain of command was unable to oversee and control the operation.[43] However, the defence of Goa in 1512 should also be considered.[44] Upon the governor's return from Melaka, he found that an important fort (Passo de Benasterim) near the city of Goa, on the same island, had been taken by the Sultan of Bijapur's local forces. He expected to successfully retake the castle by using broadside guns, but they proved to be ineffective against the structure. His opponents also used cannons to defend themselves. The sea attack having proved unsuccessful, the governor then started to make preparations for a siege but was forced to engage in battle in the fields around the fort. The use of an ordinance system should be highlighted at this point: it consisted of mixed formations of pike wielders and arquebusiers, with a strongly enforced hierarchy that underwent frequent training. Albuquerque began using this structure some years before, having been influenced by Portuguese veterans from the Italian Wars. Deployed in the field, the ordinance corps used formations known as *caracol* (snail) and *galé* (galley), tactics which had been successful when used in Europe. The advance of these men, followed by some light Portuguese cavalry, was enough to force the enemy to retreat and therefore surrender the castle. Their military superiority was then showcased in their use of strictly organized combined arms, against an enemy that already had strong firepower.

Dozens of military operations would take place in the following decades, but none with a strong land force. This would be true up until the time of Governor João de Castro (1545–8), who not only tried to enhance how the military was organized (redeploying the ordinance system, which had been abolished after the death of Afonso de Albuquerque, in 1515), but also led a few interesting campaigns that provide an insight into Portuguese warfare in this period. It was a delicate time, because the *Estado da Índia* was at war on two fronts: in Goa, against the Sultanate of Bijapur, and in the North, against the Sultanate of Gujarat.

The conflict with Bijapur centred on the possession of the lands surrounding Goa, Bardez, and Salcete (known in Portuguese sources as *Terras Firmes*), which this sultanate handed over to the *Estado da Índia* in 1543. The various campaigns undertaken under the orders of Sultan Ibrahim Adil Shah I sought to destabilize Bardez and Salcete and force their reintegration into the sultanate. The pitched battles that took place in 1547 (in September, leading to the destruction of the Pondá fort, 15 kilometres south of Goa, and in Salcete in December) were fought against relatively small forces. The sultan did not intervene. In this case, the *Estado da Índia* often resorted to maritime blockades at the Bijapur port of Dabul or the destruction of several port cities, to pressure the sultanate to end hostilities.[45] At the same time, João de Castro was aware that the sultanate was dependent on Portuguese imports of sulphur and horses from the Persian Gulf for it to wage its own internal wars against neighbouring kingdoms, so he used trade as leverage to negotiate peace.[46] Despite several victories when recapturing outposts in the *Terras Firmes*, the Portuguese administration managed to provide a swift answer to the military threat and retake the lands around Goa.

The war in the north bears significantly more relevance for this case study because it shows that the Sultanate of Gujarat had a military capacity that rivalled that of the Portuguese. At the time, the sultanate had one of the strongest Asian economies[47] and a well-organized military structure, as demonstrated by several clashes against the *Estado da Índia*.[48] One of them was at the end of the second Gujarati siege of Diu, in 1546. The siege itself is relevant because the fortress was in a precarious situation for almost eight months. The captain of Diu said to Castro, "I was expecting an attack from the Gujarati, and they besieged me like the French."[49] The Portuguese naval forces coming from Goa managed to launch a surprise attack on the besiegers, charging them from the fortress when they were expecting them to land in the Gujarati camp directly. The diversion had a massive impact, allowing the Portuguese to gain an incredible victory in November 1546. Although this siege was conducted under the supervision of Khwaja Safar, lord of Surat and captain of the sultan, he was given the freedom to recruit and organize the operation by using any means available.[50] As well as the mobilized troops themselves, the potential of the weapons used during the siege can be gauged (as thirty-six bronze guns were taken at the end of the siege), and proof has been found that serpentine gunpowder was produced in the camp built in front of the fortress.[51]

One year later, João de Castro organized a new operation to the north, retaliating after the Siege of Diu but also reaffirming the presence of the Portuguese in the region, preventing a Gujarati fleet from being built in the local ports.[52] Sailing to the Portuguese fort of Bassein, he learnt that Sultan Mahmud Shah III was in the region, near Broach. He prepared his men and sailed there with 120 small vessels made up of approximately eighteen hundred men. The governor was then ready for a direct confrontation with the sultan of Gujarat, who had around five thousand men, including cavalry, field artillery, and war elephants. Again, the Portuguese were deployed in mixed formations, advancing slowly in the field. However, the Gujarati forces started to retreat, the Portuguese forces chasing them but stopping promptly when it dawned on João de Castro that they were falling into a calculated ruse. The Gujarati aimed to separate Portuguese soldiers from their vessels in an attempt to catch them in the open field with no means with which to retreat. He immediately ordered the soldiers to return to the landing area, waiting for the Gujarati forces to engage again. The latter never attacked, wanting to avoid engaging in combat close to the river. In this case, Portuguese superiority quickly disappeared when the troops were distanced from their naval power. The sultan knew this, and the governor knew it too.

The military operations during Castro's period show that during this time, so-called Portuguese superiority was not as easily proven as it had been previously. The Gujarati forces, which had strong connections to Ottoman military developments, were on the same level as the Portuguese, as manifest in the siege of Diu, in the battle of Broach, and even in the menacing idea of the construction of a fleet. The technological gap was not a true advantage, because it was almost nonexistent on land. Given that the governor was well aware of the delicate circumstances the *Estado da Índia* found itself in, he forced multiple amphibious attacks that sought to spread terror and devastate coastal settlements, thus retaining the image of commanding a destructive power that could launch a quick attack on any location. Surrounded by enemies, João de Castro resorted to alternative methods, those that had been used previously and that had been proven to be effective, to overcome these problems: he established lines of strategic diplomacy, allying himself with common enemies (Ahmadnagar and Vijayanagar against Bijapur, and the Sur Empire against Gujarati), fomented internal wars, and sought to take advantage of the naval superiority of the Portuguese to gain a logistical advantage. In the case of the sieges of Diu (1538 and 1546), it was this ability to maintain a supply line of the fortress that ensured the capacity to resist the operation.

More than twenty years after João de Castro, Viceroy Luís de Ataíde managed to hold off one of the greatest menaces to the Portuguese presence in Asia in the sixteenth century. Between 1570 and 1571, the sultanates of Bijapur, Ahmadnagar and other small realms in southern India were plotting to attack several fortresses at the same time. Goa, Chaul, Honnavar, and Chaliyam were besieged during those years, events that ended unfavourably for the local kingdoms.[53] The case of Chaul is the most famous and most relevant for the case made herein. The operation was led by the sultan of Ahmadnagar, Murtaza Nizam Shah I, at the head of a great army that had significant artillery. Some Portuguese sources have exaggerated the numbers, stating them to have been between fifty thousand and a hundred thousand men. As in the sieges of Diu, the main advantage of the Portuguese consisted in their naval power, which allowed small reinforcements to arrive during the operation. Meanwhile, they were immediately involved in diplomatic negotiations, trying to get help from other enemies of the besiegers and using other questionable means. Some Indian chronicles even refer to bribery as being the main force leading to the Ahmadnagar retreat in Chaul.[54] Despite the considerable investment and deep destruction of the Portuguese fort, the Sultan ordered the operation to retreat and abandon the project.

As evidenced, Portuguese superiority was not always clear. Victory was mostly unplanned and, in fact, less predictable than might be expected, mostly having been achieved by using a combination of several elements. One of them was the effective use of naval resources, which contributed to fruitful amphibious attacks. These operations, which combined naval potential with swift landings and attacks, had been used since the dawn of the Portuguese presence in Asia.[55] They sought to impose a climate of terror on coastal populations not only as pre-emptive strikes but also as part of a deterrence strategy. Examples of this strategy can be seen on the attack on Dabul in 1509, when Viceroy Francisco de Almeida, heading for Diu, partially destroyed the city of Bijapur;[56] Afonso de Albuquerque's campaigns on the Arabian coast in 1507;[57] and even the multiple attacks on the Gujarati coast during and after the second siege of Diu.[58] Aside from this aspect, we find the use of diplomacy (especially among common enemies) and the thorough knowledge of geography and the physical space – both elements of a supposed Portuguese military superiority during the sixteenth century.

Conclusions

As has been argued herein, it cannot be proven that Portuguese military superiority in Asia in the sixteenth century was linked to a gap in technological or tactical development. Any attempt to understand Portuguese victories and Portuguese presence in that part of the globe must be explained, as previously stated, through a combination of several factors. The capacity of the Portuguese to successfully adapt to the local military environment allowed for this external force (of European origin), to construct the *Estado da Índia*, which, though external, had the size and impact of a local potentate. The first two decades of the sixteenth century may, to some extent, have been the period of greatest innovation and mutual learning, which was then followed by fast development of the Asian states, competing with the *Estado da Índia*, as seen in the various rebellions and resistance against the *Estado* from the 1520s onwards.

However, this does not invalidate that there was, though only occasionally, a certain degree of technical or tactical superiority. For instance, the case of the defence of Goa in 1512 was carried out by using an ordinance system inspired by European tactical advances. These cases, however, did not constitute the majority of Portuguese military operations in Asia and cannot be deduced as examples of their military presence in the continent. As Jeremy Black stated, warfare was waged by European countries across the world "quite effectively and decisively without reference to Western methods, technology and politics."[59]

In this sense, the idea of a military revolution, as seen by Geoffrey Parker, poorly applies to the Portuguese case. Although the development of artillery and shipbuilding enabled the Portuguese Kingdom to have unprecedented firepower on board, the other arguments contained in this concept have no full applicability either in the kingdom or in the construction and consolidation of the *Estado da Índia*. On an architectural note, Portuguese forts in Asia gradually integrated the innovations developed in Europe: not until 1546–7 was the first bastion front (in Diu) built, followed by the bastion layout of the fortress of São Sebastião of Mozambique. The number of Portuguese soldiers also grew slightly over the course of the sixteenth century, though the size and capacity of recruitment did not increase during this period. The development of a bureaucratic apparatus was therefore unconnected to the expansion of military needs, and the Crown could not effectively control its subjects, given that part of them took on an informal presence in Asia outside the royal domain, in what is known as the Shadow/Informal Empire.[60]

Nevertheless, some governors, such as Afonso de Albuquerque and João de Castro, provided examples of how European combat tactics were applied, through use of an ordinance system, thus partially contradicting J.C. Sharman's idea that "the way Westerners fought in the wider world in the early modern period was almost entirely different from the way they fought wars in Europe."[61] As noted, the occasional use of ordinances in various military campaigns, with Albuquerque, Castro, and later Viceroy Ataíde, demonstrates their interest in taking advantage of a successful model to wage war in another context and environment, thus highlighting the idea contained in Parker's thesis.

In the current historiographical debate, Jeremy Black's vision has been found to be the most accurate, drawing attention to the warfare potential and resilience of the Asian powers and to the need that arises to analyse Portuguese military conflicts in Asia on an individual basis, according to the opponents and their contexts. This approach opposes the idea of conducting an analysis on Portuguese conflicts as a whole, the result of which seems to produce the effects of a European military revolution.[62]

Despite its European origins, the *Estado da Índia* presented itself as another player in Asia's complex military game of chess. The similarities with other states in this region of the world are visible, its having behaved like a local state that needed to find its own space in order to reinforce its presence and ensure profit.[63] Thus, the role of the Portuguese cannot be regarded as merely "marginal" or "insignificant"[64] but rather as a political and military entity of some relevance – one that was taken into consideration by the other local powers and that did not always bend to their political pressure.[65]

Finally, the *Estado da Índia* was aware of its limitations and its scope. It rarely launched campaigns into the hinterland or even considered directly confronting any Indian sultanate, as the Portuguese troop's military potential was mainly found in their naval forces.[66] In turn, the capacity for land warfare among great potentates, such as Mughal, was not comparable to the scarce Portuguese resources, given that it matched other European powers in the early modern period.[67] In this case, a comparison with the Spanish reality in the "New World" is of little value, since the environment in which the conquistadores' campaigns took place bears little resemblance to the Portuguese experience in Asia during the same period. The men employed and led by Cortés and Pizarro were taken mostly on private expeditions, seeking to meet particular interests in an expansion that the Spanish Crown failed to complete at the time.[68] From a technological perspective, the use of firearms and guns (which were completely foreign to the New World) was of little relevance to the whole process, which led John F. Guilmartin to claim that "the Spanish could probably have overthrown the Incas without gunpowder."[69]

In conclusion, an attempt to explain Portuguese military expansion in Asia by invoking a military revolution and presenting a unified reading of the complex phenomenon of war is too simplistic. Any interpretation must always take into

account the role of diplomacy, the local political context, the local support provided, and one's knowledge of the geographical reality.[70] In this sense, J.C. Sharman's statement that the Portuguese were successful in "capturing and defending
coastal strong points in an environment of political fragmentation" deserves the
most credit.[71]

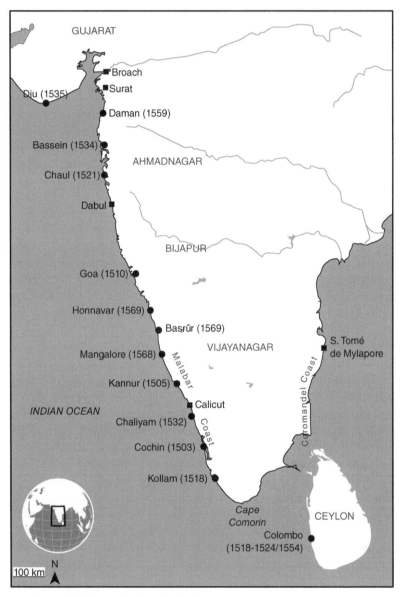

GUJARAT

Broach
Surat
Diu (1535)
Daman (1559)
Bassein (1534)
AHMADNAGAR
Chaul (1521)
Dabul
BIJAPUR
Goa (1510)
Honnavar (1569)
Basrūr (1569)
S. Tomé
de Mylapore
Mangalore (1568)
VIJAYANAGAR
Kannur (1505)
Calicut
INDIAN OCEAN
Chaliyam (1532)
Cochin (1503)
Kollam (1518)
Malabar Coast
Coromandel Coast
Cape
Comorin
CEYLON
Colombo
(1518-1524/1554)
100 km
N

● Portuguese fortress ■ Major local port

MAP 9.1   Portuguese presence in the Indian subcontinent in the sixteenth century

Notes

1 This chapter had the support of CHAM (NOVA FCSH / UAc), through the strategic project sponsored by FCT (UIDB/04666/2020).
2 Geoffrey Parker, *The Military Revolution. Military Innovation and the Rise of the West, 1500–1800*, 2nd ed. (Cambridge: Cambridge University Press, 1996). On the debate, see Clifford J. Rogers, ed., *The Military Revolution Debate. Readings on the Military Transformation of Early Modern Europe* (Boulder, CO: Westview Press, 1995); a recent and critical approach is Frank Jacob and Gilmar Visoni-Alonzo, *The Military Revolution in Early Modern Europe: A Revision* (London: Palgrave Macmillan, 2016).
3 For a critical view of the concept, see Jeremy Black, *War: A Short History* (London: Continuum, 2009), 64–69.
4 William R. Thompson, "The Military Superiority Thesis and the Ascendancy of Western Eurasia in the World System," *Journal of World History* 10, no. 1 (Spring 1999): 153–59.
5 On the use of internal wars to disrupt the local political context in the Portuguese Empire, see João Marinho dos Santos, *A Guerra e as Guerras na Expansão Portuguesa (séculos XV e XVI)* (Lisbon: GTMECDP, 1998), 289–92.
6 On the Portuguese's introducing violence in Asian trade, see Ashan Jan Qaisa, *Indian Response to European Technology and Culture, AD 1498–1700* (New Delhi: Oxford University Press, 1988), 14–17; to a more recent approach on the issue: Philippe Beaujard, *The Worlds of the Indian Ocean. A Global History*, vol. 2 (Cambridge: Cambridge University Press, 2019), 605–6.
7 John F. Guilmartin, "The Military Revolution: Origins and First Tests Abroad," in *The Military Revolution Debate: Readings on the Military Transformation of Early Modern Europe*, ed. Clifford J. Rogers (Boulder, CO: Westview Press, 1995), 315–18; José Virgílio Pissarra, "O Galeão Português e o desenvolvimento das marinhas oceânicas: 1518–1550" (PhD diss., University of Lisbon, Lisbon, 2016), 239–40; George Raudzens drew attention to this naval development, which he considered more important than the military one: "Military Revolution or maritime evolution? Military superiorities or transportation advantages as main causes of European colonial conquests to 1788," *Journal of Military History* 63 (July 1999): 631–42.
8 Philip T. Hoffman, *Why Did Europe Conquer the World?* (Princeton, NJ and Oxford: Princeton University Press, 2015), 96.
9 P.J. Marshall, "Western Arms in Maritime Asia in the Early Phases of Expansion," *Modern Asian Studies* 14, no. 1 (February 1980): 19.
10 Vitor Luís Gaspar Rodrigues, "The 'Easternisation' of the Portuguese Fleets in the Asian Seas During the 16th Century: Causes and Consequences," in *Gujarat and the Sea*, ed. Lotika Varadarajan (Vadodara: Darshak Itihas Nidhi, 2011), 221–50.
11 André Murteira, "The Military Revolution and European Wars Outside Europe: The Dutch-Portuguese War in Asia in the First Quarter of the Seventeenth Century," *Journal of Military History* 84, no. 2 (April 2020): 511–35; and his chapter in this volume.
12 The only Portuguese researcher to have seriously debated this idea is António Manuel Hespanha: see António Manuel Hespanha, "Introdução," in *Nova História Militar de Portugal*, ed. António Manuel Hespanha, vol. 2 (Lisbon: Círculo de Leitores, 2004), 9–17.
13 Santos, *A Guerra*, 255–58; Roger Lee de Jesus, "Gunpowder, Firepower and the Portuguese in the Indian Ocean (Sixteenth Century)," in *India, the Portuguese and Maritime Interactions*, ed. Pius Malekandathil, Lotika Varadarajan, and Amar Farooqui, vol. 1 (New Delhi: Primus Books, 2019), 220–31.
14 Jeremy Black, *Rethinking Military History* (London and New York: Routledge, 2004), 66–103; on the Eurocentric view: J.C. Sharman, *Empires of the Weak* (Princeton, NJ and Oxford: Princeton University Press, 2019), 124–29.
15 On the use of artillery in Asia before the arrival of the Portuguese, see the following recent works: Iqtidar Alam Khan, *Gunpowder and Firearms: Warfare in Medieval India* (New Delhi: Oxford University Press, 2004); R. Balasubramaniam, *The Saga of Indian*

Cannons (New Delhi: Aryan Books International, 2008), 17–44, and especially the debate in Peter Lorge, *The Asian Military Revolution: From Gunpowder to the Bomb* (Cambridge: Cambridge University Press, 2008), 112–14.

16 Khan, *Gunpowder and Firearms*, 59–61.

17 Tonio Andrade, *The Gunpowder Age: China, Military Innovation, and the Rise of the West in World History* (Princeton, NJ: Princeton University Press, 2016), 128–31, 135–42; and Barend Noordam's chapter in this volume.

18 For instance, see Sharman, *Empires of the Weak*, 63.

19 José Virgílio Pissarra, *Chaul e Diu – 1508 e 1509 – O domínio do Índico* (Lisbon: Tribuna da História, 2002), 80–92; according to this author, this was the first time that a gunshot sank a ship of European origin: Pissarra, *O Galeão*, p. 239.

20 The original is "negrinhos nus e sem armas": Arquivo Nacional da Torre do Tombo (Lisbon), *Feitos da Coroa*, Inquirições Particular – 3, Inquirição – 489, fl. 5r.

21 Gaspar Correia, *Lendas da Índia*, ed. Manuel Lopes de Almeida, vol. 4 (Porto: Lello e Irmão, 1975), 2: 16, 734, 3: 407.

22 On this prejudice, see Rui Loureiro, "O encontro de Portugal com a Ásia no século XVI," in *O confronto do olhar: O encontro dos povos na época das navegações portuguesas, séculos XV e XVI: Portugal, África, Ásia, América*, ed. António Luís Ferronha (Lisbon: Caminho, 1991), 207; Vasco Resende, "L'Orient islamique dans la culture portugaise de l'époque moderne, du voyage de Vasco de Gama à la chute d'Ormuz (1498–1622)" (PhD diss., École Pratique des Hautes études, Paris, 2011), 358–68.

23 Jagadish Narayan Sarkar, *The Art of War in Medieval India* (New Delhi: Munshiram Manoharlal, 1984), 125; Vitor Luís Gaspar Rodrigues, "Armas e Equipamentos de Guerra Portugueses no Oriente nas Primeiras Décadas de Quinhentos," *Revista de Cultura (Macau)* 26 (2008): 50–51.

24 Kaushik Roy, *Military Transition in Early Modern Asia, 1400–1750* (London: Bloomsbury, 2014), 127; Sharman, *Empires of the Weak*, 60.

25 On the Asian ships, José Virgílio Pissarra, "Navios orientais," in *História da Marinha Portuguesa: Navios, Marinheiros e Arte de Navegar, 1500–1168*, ed. Francisco Contente Domingues (Lisbon: Academia de Marinha, 2012), 133–34; K.S. Mathew, *Shipbuilding, Navigation and the Portuguese in Pre-Modern India* (London: Routledge, 2018), 113–16.

26 M.N. Pearson, *Merchants and Rulers in Gujarat: The Response to the Portuguese in the Sixteenth Century* (New Delhi: Nunshiram Manoharlal, 1976), 90–91, 132, 153–54.

27 Geneviève Bouchon, "Les Musulmans du Kerala à l'époque de la Découverte Portugaise," in *Inde Découverte, Inde Retrouvée, 1498–1630: Études d'histoire indo-portugaise* (Lisbon and Paris: CCCG, CNCDP, 1999), 56–75.

28 Roy, *Military*, 127–28.

29 Sanjay Subrahmanyam, *The Portuguese Empire in Asia, 1500–1700: A Political and Economic History*, 2nd ed. (Oxford: Wiley-Blackwell, 2012), 20–21; Samira Sheikh, *Forging a Region: Sultans, Traders, and Pilgrims in Gujarat, 1200–1500* (Oxford: Oxford University Press, 2009), 89–94.

30 On this resistance, see Jeremy Black, *European Warfare, 1494–1660* (London and New York: Routledge, 2002), 61.

31 For a synthetic view of this resistance, see Subrahmanyam, *The Portuguese Empire*, 98–99.

32 Andrade, *The Gunpowder Age*, 124–31.

33 Charles R. Boxer, "A Note on Portuguese Reactions to the Revival of the Red Sea Spice Trade and the Rise of Atjeh, 1540–1600," *Journal of Southeast Asian History* 10, no. 3 (1969): 415–28; Anthony Reid, "Sixteenth Century Turkish Influence in Western Indonesia," *Journal of Southeast Asian History* 10, no. 3 (1969): 395–414; Jorge dos Santos Alves, *O domínio do Norte de Samatra* (Lisbon: SHIP, 1999), 160–69.

34 Maria Augusta Lima Cruz, "Exiles and Renegades in Early Sixteenth Century Portuguese India," *Indian Economic and Social History Review* 23, no. 3 (1986): 249–62; António Manuel Hespanha, *Filhos da Terra: Identidades mestiças nos confins da expansão portuguesa* (Lisbon: Tinta da China, 2019), 233–35.

35 For these examples, see Luís Costa e Sousa, *Campanha de Etiópia, 1541–1543. 400 Portugueses em socorro do Preste João* (Lisbon: Tribuna da História, 2008); Alexandra Pelúcia, *Martim Afonso de Sousa e a sua linhagem* (Lisbon: CHAM, 2009), 164–65.
36 Cenan Pirani, "The Military Economy of Seventeenth Century Sri Lanka: Rhetoric and Authority in a Time of Conquest" (PhD diss., University of California, Berkeley, 2016), 42, 81–87.
37 Andrade, *The Gunpowder Age*, 135–43.
38 Letter from Gaspar Luís de Veiga to João de Castro (5 September 1546), *Colecção de São Lourenço*, ed. Elaine Sanceau, vol. 2 (Lisbon: CEHU, JICU, 1975), 309.
39 Richard M. Eaton and Phillip B. Wagoner, *Power, Memory, Architecture: Contested Sites on India's Deccan Plateau, 1300–1600* (Oxford and New Delhi: Oxford University Press, 2014), 241–87.
40 "Todo mundo he cheo d'espimgardas": letter dated 12 November 1548, Arquivo Nacional da Torre do Tombo (Lisbon), *Corpo Cronológico*, 2-241-88, fl. 1r.
41 Jean Aubin, "L'apprentissage de l'Inde: Cochin 1503–1504," in *Le Latin et l'Astrobe: Recherches sur le Portugal de la Renaissance, Son Expansion en Asie et les Relations internationales* (Lisbon and Paris: CCCB, CNCDP, 1996), 84–100.
42 The military campaigns of Albuquerque were recently overviewed in Alexandra Pelúcia, *Afonso de Albuquerque: Corte, Cruzada e Império* (Lisbon: Temas e Debates, 2016), 203–58; José Manuel Garcia, *O Terrível: A Grande Biografia de Afonso de Albuquerque* (Lisbon: Esfera dos Livros, 2017), 185–544.
43 On the failed attack on Aden, see Roger Lee de Jesus, "Afonso de Albuquerque e a primeira expedição portuguesa ao Mar Vermelho (1513)," *Fragmenta Historica – História, Paleografia e Diplomática* 1 (2013): 121–41.
44 João Paulo Oliveira Costa and Vitor Luís Gaspar Rodrigues, *Conquista de Goa – 1510–1512: Campanhas de Afonso de Albuquerque* (Lisbon: Tribuna da História, 2008), 77–87.
45 For the strategy of blocking Bijapur's ports, see P.M. Joshi, "Relations Between the Adilshahi Kingdom of Bijapur and the Portuguese at Goa During the Sixteenth Century," *New Indian Antiquary* II (1939–1940): 365.
46 On Bijapur's internal wars, see M.A. Nayeem, *External Relations of the Bijapur Kingdoms (1489–1686 A.D.) (A Study in Diplomatic History)* (Hyderabad: Sayeedia Research Institute, Bright Publishers, 1974), 77–131, and by the same author *The Heritage of the Adil Shahis of Bijapur* (Hyderabad: Hyderabad Publishers, 2008), 28–30.
47 Geneviève Bouchon, "Un monde qui Change," in *Histoire de l'Inde Moderne, 1480–1950*, ed. Claude Markovitz (Paris: Fayard, 1994), 26. On Gujarat's comercial dimension see Lotika Varadarajan, "Positioning Gujarat as a Medieval Mercantile Centre: Contours and Context," in *Port Towns of Gujarat*, ed. Sara Keller and Michael Pearson (New Delhi: Primus Books, 2015), 9–17.
48 Sheikh, *State and Society*, 176–80.
49 Letter from João de Mascarenhas to João de Castro (2 July 1546), published in António Baião, *História quinhentista (inédita) do Segundo Cêrco de Dio* (Coimbra: Imprensa da Universidade, 1927), 155. Translations are mine.
50 On the second siege of Diu, see Roger Lee de Jesus, "O Segundo Cerco de Diu (1546): Estudo de História Política e Militar" (MA diss., University of Coimbra, Coimbra, 2012), 54–55.
51 Leonardo Nunes, *Crónica de Dom João de Castro*, ed. J.D.M. Ford (Cambridge, MA: Harvard University Press, 1936), 131; Baião, *História*, 91.
52 A letter from Diogo Lopes de Aguião to the governor, from 27 August 1547, warned him that ships were being built in Gujarati ports: *Colecção de São Lourenço*, ed. Maria de Lourdes Lalande, vol. 2 (Lisbon: IICT, 1983), 285–86; a local chronicle also confirms this information: *Zafar ul Walih bi Muzaffar wa Alhi – An Arabic History of Gujarat by Hajji ad-Dabir*, trans. M.F. Lokhandwala, vol. 1 (Baroda: Oriental Institute, 1970), 238.
53 For a deep analysis of Ataíde's government, see Nuno Vila-Santa, *Entre o Reino e o Império: A Carreira político-militar de D. Luís de Ataíde 1516–1581* (Lisbon: ICS, 2015),

142–94; on the siege of Chaul, R.O.W. Goertz, "Attack and Defense Techniques in the Siege of Chaul, 1570–1571," in *II Seminário Internacional de História Indo – Portuguesa: Actas*, ed. Luís de Albuquerque and Inácio Guerreiro (Lisbon: IICT, 1985), 265–92.

54 Burhan-i-Massir, "History of the Nizam Shahi Kings of Ahmadnagar by Ali-Ibn 'Azizullah Tabataba," trans. T. Wolseley Haig, *The Indian Antiquary* L (August 1921): 233–34.

55 On these operations, see Malyn Newitt, "Portuguese Amphibious Warfare in the East in the Sixteenth Century (1500–1520)," in *Amphibious Warfare 1000–1700: Commerce, State Formation and European Expansion*, ed. D.J.B. Trim and Mark Charles Fissel (Leiden and Boston: Brill, 2011), 103–21.

56 Pissarra, *Chaul e Diu*, 71–74.

57 Garcia, *O Terrível*, 135–43.

58 Jesus, *O Segundo Cerco*, 131.

59 Jeremy Black, "Patterns of Warfare, 1400–1800," in *The Cambridge World History, vol. 6, The Construction of a Global World, 1400–1800 CE, Part 2, Patterns of Change*, ed. Jerry H. Bentley, Sanjay Subrahmanyam, and Merry E. Wiesner-Hanks (Cambridge: Cambridge University Press, 2015), 47.

60 J.C. Sharman is critical of the development of the bureaucratic state connected to a military revolution, as seen in "Myths of Military Revolution: European Expansion and Eurocentrism," *European Journal of International Relations* 24, no. 3 (2018): 499–500.

61 Sharman, *The Empires*, 34.

62 Black, *European Warfare*, 53–54, 59–61, 67–68.

63 João Paulo Oliveira e Costa already sketched this interpretation: see "O Império Português em Meados do século XVI," in *Mare Nostrum: Em busca de Honra e Riqueza nos séculos XV e XVI* (Lisbon: Temas e Debates, 2013), 184; George D. Winius also analysed the Portuguese Empire as part of an Asian context: "Portuguese as Players on a South Asian Stage," in *Portugal, the Pathfinder: Journeys from the Medieval Toward the Modern World 1300–ca.1600*, ed. George D. Winius (Madison: Hispanic Seminary of Medieval Studies, 1995), 195–96.

64 These qualifiers were taken from Sharman, *The Empires*, 35; Jack Goldstone, *Why Europe? The Rise of the West in World History, 1500–1850* (New York: McGraw-Hill, 2009), 56.

65 This idea goes against one of Sharman's general statements: "Europeans were almost always deferential toward local great powers," in *The Empires*, 64.

66 Marshall, "Western Arms," 18, claiming that all Portuguese victories were naval.

67 This was how Andrew de la Garza put it in his book *The Mughal Empire at War: Babur, Akbar and the Indian Military Revolution, 1500–1605* (London and New York: Routledge, 2016), 13–14.

68 Sharman, *The Empires*, 39–43; on the Spanish expansion to the New World during the reign of Charles V, see Geoffrey Parker, *Emperor: A New Life of Charles V* (New Haven, CT and London: Yale University Press, 2019), 342–75.

69 Guilmartin, "The Military Revolution," 312.

70 This idea was also outlined by Jeremy Black, "Patterns of Warfare," 29.

71 Sharman, *The Empires*, 62.

PART 4

Cultural exchange and circulation of military knowledge

10

THE PORTUGUESE CONQUEST OF ANGOLA IN THE SIXTEENTH AND SEVENTEENTH CENTURIES (1575–1641)

A military revolution in West Central Africa?

Miguel Geraldes Rodrigues

Over the past couple of decades, the literature surrounding the field of military history has traced a series of military transformations in Western Europe between the fifteenth century and the eighteenth century, and it described how they radically changed the landscape of warfare during the early modern era. Often assembled under the rubric of the Military Revolution, this literature depicts how a structured sequence of several key technological innovations and organizational reforms revolutionized not only the nature of military conflicts in Europe but its sociopolitical development as well. Beginning with the introduction of gunpowder technologies in siegecraft and open battlefields, the advent and spread of new artillery weapons and firearms brought fundamental changes to traditional European warfare, prompting the development of new military tactics, improvements in the military architecture, dramatic increases in the size of military contingents, and the emergence of professional national armies. The combination of those reforms triggered, in turn, broader structural changes in Western European societies outside the military realm, including rampant taxation for its populations, the centralization of administrative powers, and the emergence of modern absolutist monarchies. While the original accounts of the Military Revolution framed this process strictly within Western European borders, military historians gradually expanded the concept to the non-Western world, linking the military revolution concept to larger narratives of European expansion and Western imperialism.[1]

Although the debates surrounding the Military Revolution have captivated numerous scholars over the years, the historiography of the Portuguese Empire has, puzzlingly, greatly overlooked and ignored most of its discussions, especially given Portugal's pioneering role in the European oceanic expansion. The Portuguese overseas empire presents specific cases regarding key topics of the Military Revolution, such as the primacy in transoceanic navigation and naval warfare; a wide range of contacts (and conflicts) across different military realities in Asia, Africa, and the

Americas; and a unique experience associated with the logistics of administering and financing a large and heterogenous empire across the world. Portuguese oceanic expansion also spilled into the period that military historians commonly identify as the core of the revolution. What, then, can Portuguese imperial history add to the debates in the context of the Military Revolution? How does its military experience compare to other European realities? Were any of the key elements that comprised the Military Revolution reflected in the Portuguese overseas expansion? Did any of the military, tactical, or technological innovations witnessed in European warfare play a decisive role in overpowering foreign military powers encountered by the Portuguese across the world?

This chapter addresses the history of the Portuguese overseas empire in the international debates over the Military Revolution and attempts to assess through its themes the global diffusion and impact of Western military innovations in European colonial expansion. Portuguese imperial history can offer a valuable contribution to broader military historiographical discussions, particularly to narratives of Western imperialism and European military supremacy during the early modern period, because its study presents several instances of European warfare waged across distinct geographical and cultural contexts. To explore those topics, the chapter will focus on a generally overlooked region in the debates of European imperial conquest and colonialism before the Industrial Revolution, namely West Central Africa. Here the Portuguese directed a conquest in Angola during the sixteenth and seventeenth centuries, with mixed results, presenting a distinct case study on cross-cultural warfare and on the limits of European military expansion during the early modern era. By looking at the military encounters between Europeans and West Central African polities like the kingdoms of Kongo and Ndongo, this chapter illustrates how the technological and tactical innovations carried out by the Portuguese from the Military Revolution fared on an extra-European stage. It explores different instances of political negotiation, intercultural exchange, and military acculturation in Angola and shows how those processes ultimately led to the emergence of a unique style of hybridized warfare shared by both Portuguese and West Central Africans armies, offering a non-Eurocentric perspective of this conflict. Lastly, the conquest of Angola is placed within broader narratives of the Military Revolution, to evaluate whether the Portuguese conflict in West Central supports or dismisses the arguments behind this thesis.

The Military Revolution and European expansion

Before the beginning of the Portuguese and Spanish transoceanic expansion, a series of technological and organizational changes linked to military affairs took place in Western Europe, which are now viewed as the root of the Military Revolution. This concept was originally introduced by Michael Roberts during the 1950s to define a broad scheme of military reforms that radically transformed European warfare from the sixteenth century onwards. Those military innovations, however, carried major social, economic, and political repercussions for European states, and they swiftly changed the continent's geopolitical landscape, splitting "medieval society from the modern world."[2] The core argument of Roberts's theory is rooted in the tactical innovations introduced by the Dutch and the Swedish between 1560 and 1660, which exploited the full potential of the gunpowder technologies through volley fire tactics.[3] Those tactical reforms required larger numbers of well-trained troops to be effective, which pushed the professionalization and growth of the size of European armies. The need to finance gargantuan armies in turn drove European rulers to extend the limits of their authority over their respective societies through onerous taxation and the centralization of governmental capacities, which led to the emergence of the early modern sovereign state.[4]

The main contribution of Roberts's thesis was its ability to link transformations in military affairs to deeper structural changes in European societies to explain the origins of the modern state. This concept was later expanded by Geoffrey Parker, who agreed with the core claim of the thesis but challenged some of its elements. For Parker, technology, not tactical reforms, was primarily the catalyst of the Military Revolution, highlighting the scientific advances in artillery and fortification. The crucial innovation of Parker's Military Revolution, however, was the expansion of the concept beyond European borders and its application on a global scale. The emphasis on the technological factors turned Parker's attention to naval warfare, where the innovations in navigation, combined with the military changes in land artillery, resulted in the creation of large gunships capable of oceanic navigation by the beginning of the sixteenth century. Parker linked those crucial developments to the origins of European colonial expansion and presented the Military Revolution as the "key to the Westerners' success in creating the first truly global empires between 1500 and 1750," with the artillery fortress, the gunship, and infantry firepower as "the three vital innovations of the Military Revolution. . . [that] allowed the West to expand . . . to global dominance." The rise of Western imperialism was therefore explained by the "military exceptionalism" of Europe, since the continent's competitive geopolitics drove the development of superior gunpowder weapons, warships, professional armies, and financial bureaucracies able to support distant colonial enterprises from the mid seventeenth century onwards.[5]

Parker's adaptation and revision of the military revolution concept encouraged a surge in the historiographical production of this topic, with several revisions of, adjustments to, and criticisms of the thesis following its publication.[6] The theory that linked the Military Revolution to European dominance across the globe since the age of gunpowder, however, continues to spark a considerable debate to this day, as several historians keep exploring the possible diffusions and repercussions of this process on a global scale.[7] Scholars who followed Parker's ideas to understand how Europe conquered large areas of the world often point to the Spanish conquests of the Aztec and Incan empires or to English and Dutch in India and Southeast Asia as examples of small Western forces capitalizing on superior military technology to overcome their opponents abroad.[8] This position has since been criticized for its excessive emphasis on a supposed technological gap between Europe and the non-Western world during the early modern period. The development of area studies and new world history narratives has pushed a great revisionism of European imperial expansion and helped dispel many of the myths surrounding the Military Revolution and European technological supremacy before the Industrial Revolution.[9] New approaches to world history have also contested some of the previous assumptions of European technological determinism, showing that early Spanish conquests in the Americas were not absolute examples of European military triumphalism rooted in technological advantages, as previously believed.[10] The same applies to the European presence in Asia during the same period.[11] Scholars such as Jeremy Black and Jason Sharman are particularly critical of the Military Revolution narratives that blindly assume that the Western military tactics and technology were optimal across the globe, because such a view oversimplifies complex cross-cultural historical processes and displays a deep Eurocentric bias. They call for the need to highlight different examples of European warfare abroad during the early modern era, because several of Europe's military failures in Southeast Asia, North Africa, and sub-Saharan Africa are often clouded by the image of Western successes in the nineteenth century.[12]

In this revisionist trend concerning the global dimension of the Military Revolution, the Portuguese overseas empire can offer a valuable contribution, especially to historiographical discussions on European military superiority in the sixteenth and seventeenth centuries. Although there are some studies on the Portuguese military expansion within the scope of Military Revolution, this scope focuses almost exclusively on naval warfare and the Portuguese Empire in Asia, leaving its experiences in Africa overlooked. The main collective monograph dedicated to the military history of the Portuguese Empire has just one author addressing warfare in Africa and is presented as part of a wider European conflict in the Atlantic with the Dutch.[13] European violent encounters in Africa have been largely ignored by military history before the end of the eighteenth century, even in the Portuguese context, barring some exceptions.[14] The most notable contributions to its study come from Africanist scholars, where the work of John Thornton on African warfare and its connection to Portuguese imperial history needs to be highlighted.[15] The extreme focus of international military historiography on the Spanish, English, and Dutch empires in the Americas and South East Asia, therefore, make the Portuguese Empire and its expansion in Africa a valuable addition to explore in the global impact that the Military Revolution had. It presents an interesting exercise to assess the extent to which the technological breakthroughs recorded in Europe gave the Portuguese a concrete military edge over West Central African polities before the Industrial Revolution.

The Portuguese in Atlantic Africa

The Portuguese "overseas expansion" began with the conquest and occupation of the Moroccan city of Ceuta in 1415. Motivated by the search for better supplies of gold from trans-Saharan trade routes, among other economic (and political) factors, the Portuguese directed several voyages of exploration along the Atlantic

Coast of Africa during the fifteenth century.[16] While trade was the main purpose of the Portuguese when dealing with powerful sub-Saharan polities (such as the Jolof or the Mali Empire), early expeditions would sometimes result in violent encounters against smaller villages on the coast of Senegal, and its inhabitants were taken captive and sold in Portugal as slaves. Plundering expeditions in Senegambia were short-lived, however: not only were the Portuguese unable to establish an actual foothold and venture far inland, but the resistance and organization of local African communities on West African shores proved to be major obstacles as well. Those populations rapidly organized themselves to fight against foreign threats on land and at times even managed to repel the Portuguese ships from their shores.[17] Gomes Eanes de Zurara, the official chronicler of the court of Portuguese King Afonso V (1438–81), retells the expedition led by Rodrigo Annes and Diogo Dinis to the isle of Gorée around 1445 and reports their failed attempt at capturing slaves, a failure that was due to its inhabitants being "not easy to enslave" because they were "strong foes, competent in battle who use arrows bathed with a dangerous herb [poison]."[18] The local populations along the Senegambia and Upper Guinea also used small vessels to outmanoeuvre the large ships of the Portuguese, and these populations drove the Portuguese away by using poisoned arrows, which rendered the armour of the Portuguese useless. The massacres at the hands of the raiders from the Gorée or the Bissagos Islands, were but a few of the episodes which forced the small Portuguese exploratory crews to abandon their military ambitions and instead focus on establishing peaceful and commercial relations with the authorities on the coast.[19]

Despite some attempts by the Portuguese to negotiate military alliances in Atlantic Africa during the fifteenth century, such as the embassy of João Bemoim from Senegal or the mercenary support to the *Obas* of Benin, only after Diogo Cão arrived to the Kingdom of Kongo in 1483 did the Portuguese successfully establish an official alliance with an African authority.[20] The ancient Kingdom of Kongo, which stretched roughly from the Congo River in the north to the Kwanza in the south and from the Atlantic inland towards the Kwango River, was a semi-centralized political entity led by a ruler called *Manikongo*, which means 'lord' of Kongo. Upon the arrival of Cão's expedition, the *Manikongo* Nzinga-a-Nkuwu accepted establishing commercial relations with the Portuguese, sealing the agreement with an exchange of hostages. Following a decade of productive exchanges, Kongo requested a formal alliance with the Portuguese; the royal family accepted being converted to Christianity; and the *Manikongo* was baptized as João I.[21] As part of this alliance, Portugal agreed to officially provide military support to Kongo against local enemies and rebels, sending initially some small contingents of cross-bow archers and pike wielders.[22] The alliance established between the Portuguese and the *Manikongo*, and the consequent military help lent to Kongo's expansion during the reign of Mvemba-a-Nzinga (baptized Afonso I, 1506–43), resulted in a stable partnership between both parties: the *Manikongo* would pay the Portuguese mercenaries with slaves for their support, who were instructed to not take any independent action that disturbed the authority of the Kongo kings.[23]

Assessing the impact and extent of the Portuguese military aid during Kongo's expansion is difficult, especially because of political turmoil that followed Afonso's death in 1543. But the Portuguese were obviously regarded as a valuable ally, as shown when the *Manikongo* Mpangu-a-Nimi Lukeni lua Mvemba (1568–74, Álvaro I) called on Portuguese King Sebastião for military aid against an invasion of several nomadic *Jaga* groups who plundered most of Kongo around 1568–78.[24] King Sebastião ordered his then governor of São Tomé, Francisco de Gouveia Sottomaior, to relieve Kongo with a force of six hundred Portuguese soldiers in 1571. Sottomaior's army gathered at the *Manikongo*'s location along the Congo River and, equipped with muskets, fought the invaders off with success and restored Álvaro to the throne, but not without obtaining some compensation from the *Manikongo*.[25] A Portuguese settlement on the island of Luanda (under Kongo's authority), as well as logistical support for the establishment of a Portuguese foothold, were among the concessions requested in exchange for Portuguese aid. Other clauses were included, albeit less known, such as mining rights over the territory and whether Kongo had pledged vassalage to the king of Portugal. Those events were the catalyst for the gradual escalation of a Portuguese military presence in West Central Africa.[26]

The island of Luanda was located further south of Kongo and west of another political force in West Central Africa, the Kingdom of Ndongo and land of the Mbundu. The Portuguese drew the name for this territory from the name of its ruler, who was called *Ngola*, naming it the Kingdom of Angola.[27] Accurately mapping Ndongo is difficult because it was not a centralized state like Kongo was but rather an aggregation of fragmented territories called *murindas*, each ruled by a *Soba* (African warlord) who paid tribute to the *Ngola*.[28] The main regions that encompassed Ndongo (Ilamba, Kisama, Libolo, Museke, Hare, and Dongo) stretched inland along the Kwanza River and included the highlands along the Bengo River and the Lukala River. The Dande River served as a natural frontier with the Kingdom of Kongo in the north, a kingdom that had previously exerted its authority over Ndongo.[29] The Portuguese had established informal contacts with the Mbundu since the beginning of the sixteenth century, mostly through slave merchants from São Tomé looking for alternative markets south of Kongo. Following the economic growth spurred by this trade, the Portuguese Crown sent an official embassy in 1558 at the request of the *Ngola* Ndambi (1556–62). However, Ndambi died soon after the arrival of the embassy led by Paulo Dias de Novais, and his immediate successor, Ngola Kiluanje kia Ndambi (c. 1565–75), did not share his predecessors' diplomatic or religious interests.[30] The embassy ended up as a failure, and some of the Portuguese representatives were held hostage in Ndongo for many years, including Paulo Dias de Novais. Novais was able to return to Portugal only in 1565, when he began searching for political and financial support to conduct a "campaign against the rebel" of the Kingdom of Angola. After securing the assistance of the Kingdom of Kongo, thanks to the support offered against the *Jaga*, the Portuguese Crown granted a charter to Paulo Dias de Novais in 1571, with instructions for the military conquest of an African region. It was the first time that such a decree was issued since the beginning of the Portuguese overseas ventures in 1415, thus signalling a change in strategy of the Portuguese regarding their settlement and military ambitions in Atlantic Africa.[31]

Luso-African warfare and the conquest of Angola

Paulo Dias de Novais arrived to Luanda in February of 1575, accompanied by a force of seven hundred men, which would be reinforced by the troops of Sottomaior and some Kongolese nobles.[32] Despite the conquering nature of his mission, Novais's previous experience in Angola made him aware of the true extent of Ndongo's military power. As a result, his strategy was to first cement the Portuguese military foothold in Luanda and only afterwards attempt an assault against the *Ngola*. Novais masked his arrival to Luanda as a "mercenary company" and offered military support to the *Ngola* against some rebel *sobas* in the regional exchange for slaves. This tenuous agreement, however, quickly escalated to an all-out war between both parties, when Njinga Ngola Kilombia kia Kasenda (1575–92) was eventually informed by a Portuguese dissident on the true nature of Novais's mission. The *Ngola* took action against the growing military contingent of the Portuguese in his territory, launching a surprise attack in 1579 and slaughtering a Portuguese force of forty men who were trading in Ndongo, thus marking the beginning of the Angolan wars.[33] According to a contemporary report from Angola, Novais moved with sixty Portuguese soldiers and two hundred "Black Christians" to the newly built fort in Nzele (Anzele) along the Kwanza River, where he was besieged by an alleged force of twelve thousand Mbundu soldiers. The siege lasted five months, before reinforcements led by Diogo Rodrigues arrived in Luanda and sailed the Kwanza to lift the siege.[34]

The description of the first years of the campaigns in West Central Africa illustrate both the harsh conditions presented by the Angolan highlands and jungle and the Portuguese lack of preparation to face them. A missionary who accompanied Novais's company of three hundred men reported on the massive death toll caused by Africa's tropical environment, describing that more than two-thirds of the Portuguese soldiers stationed with Novais in Mocumbe perished from fevers in under two years. To complicate matters for Novais and his men, the riverside navigation on the Kwanza was not a simple task, and one of his ships capsized, losing all the supplies and gunpowder. Similarly, Kongo's own forces failed to relieve the Portuguese during Ndongo's assault because they failed to cross the Bengo River, and its troops were defeated, leaving the Portuguese isolated in the territory.[35] The military recruitment to a distant, deadly, and non-prestigious territory was equally an issue for the Portuguese. While Novais secured extensive loans to attract some mercenary troops and adventurers, the majority of the recruits were poor settlers or banished individuals sent from the kingdom for religious motives or crimes without any military training, which exacerbated the death toll.[36] The epidemiological barrier and the violent encounters and guerrilla warfare in Angola together resulted in the deaths of 3,180 out of the 3,400

Portuguese soldiers who arrived in Angola between 1575 and 1594, a death rate of over 90 per cent.[37]

Thus, the Portuguese acknowledged from an early stage that their small numbers, already plagued by large death tolls and poor recruitment, were incapable of defeating Ndongo's forces by themselves. Inspired perhaps by previous experiences in the Americas of exploiting local rivalries, Dias de Novais followed the Spanish lesson and quickly began to search for possible dissident *sobas* unhappy with the rule of the *Ngola* along the Kwanza's margins. The first ally recruited by Novais was the *soba* Songa Muxima Quitagonge in 1582, followed by the *sobas* Quicunguela and Taladongo. Those local warlords negotiated favourable privileges and rights over rival territories loyal to the *Ngola* in exchange for military assistance from the Portuguese and conversion to Christianity.[38] The Portuguese began to gradually exploit local rivalries among the *sobas* in Angola, and combining their armies with small Kongolese elite contingents to support their forces, the Portuguese achieved several victories in Muxima, Kisama, and the Ilamba. By 1585, Novais gathered already more than thirty-four allied *sobas* and had built a new fort in Massangano.[39] Those victories encouraged the Portuguese to finally attempt an ill-fated attack to the heartland of Ndongo. Captain Luis Serrão, Novais's second in command, led "the most powerful force that Portugal had assembled in Angola, some 15,000 African archers supported by 128 Portuguese musketeers" against the royal residence of the Ngola. Serrão would, however, suffer a crushing defeat at Angolme-Akitombo, close to the Lukala River in 1590, which left the Portuguese forces in shambles, in that many *sobas* left their alliance following this setback, and Portuguese ships were even attacked along the Kwanza during their retreat.[40]

The death of Dias de Novais in 1589 and the defeat of Serrão in the following year marked the end of the first stage of warfare between Portugal and Ndongo. During those campaigns, Portuguese forces and African forces fought several times, both as allies and as enemies, and overtime, they began to gradually adapt elements from each other's cultures into their own militaries, eventually to develop what John Thornton described as a "unique art of war" that was exclusive to this region.[41] One eyewitness noted that the armies of Ndongo, rather than chaotically charging the battlefield, were orderly divided into three regiments (left, right, and centre) called *embalos*.[42] Those armies were led by local *sobas*, who were responsible for recruiting their troops from their own regions and were commonly equipped with bows, battle axes, and javelins (*azagaias*). In larger battles, they often joined forces with other *sobas* forces and answered to a war captain personally appointed by the *Ngola*, called *chiambole*. The *chiambole* usually took the centre regiment of the *embalo*, composed of the "bravest of troops" (*gunzes*), who relied on shock tactics by marching against enemy formations in a frontal assault. The Portuguese adapted to this style by employing African auxiliary forces (commonly described as *guerra preta*) and slave armies in similar formations but placed the Portuguese armoured forces supported by musketeers in square formations at the rear, to deter any chaos or retreat of their allies if the frontline was breached. One of the first descriptions of Luso-African clashes was the battle of Kasikola in eastern Ilamba in

1585, where the company of Portuguese Captain André Ferreira Pereira – made up of 130 soldiers, supported by a force eight thousand to ten thousand archers (called *chorimbares* or *quimbares*), supplied by allied *sobas*, and led by a respective military commander (called *tendala*) – clashed with the force of Ngola Kilongela, a former Portuguese ally who counted with a small company of forty musketeers in his own ranks. The Portuguese achieved a massive victory, which was described as a "great miracle" by contemporary sources, since many of Ndongo's nobility (*a flor de Angola*) were defeated during this battle.[43]

Despite the Portuguese military successes, the subsequent defeats of Serrão in 1590 and later of many of Angola's governors and captains against powerful *sobas* like Kafuxi ka Mbare, Kakulu Kahenda, Angola Kalunga, and Axila Mbanza displayed local African's own adaptations to the Portuguese style of warfare. During a surprise attack led by the company of Captain Juan Castaño Véllez in Museke in 1585, the forces of the *soba* Kalunga abandoned their baggage train (called *kikumba*) and escaped into the jungle to calmly regroup. Taking advantage of the fact that the Portuguese were busy looting the provisions left behind, Kalunga ambushed the company in the following day and killed the 120 Portuguese soldiers and their captain.[44] Another *soba*, called Kafuxi ka Mbare, was particularly infamous in Portuguese accounts, because he amassed several victories over the Portuguese in the Kisama region. The Portuguese sources painstakingly retold of how Kafuxi defeated a powerful company of 130 Portuguese soldiers equipped with firearms and employing cavalry. Ka Mbari ordered his forces to feign retreat from the battlefield into the jungle, where he ambushed the horse riders with pitfall traps and minimized the effectiveness of the musketeers. Only five Portuguese escaped the massacre, and two important captains (Gaspar Veloso and António Costa) perished in this battle alone.[45]

Following the military campaigns of Furtado de Mendonça (1594–1600), João Rodrigues Coutinho (1601–3) assembled the "biggest force ever gathered in Angola," and supported by Kongo nobles, he attempted to conquer the rumoured silver mines located in Cambambe. Despite his premature death, his captain Cerveira Pereira defeated the feared *sobas* Axila Mbanza and Kafuxe and conquered Cambambe in 1603, but no mines were found, and the conquest of Angola reached a military deadlock.[46] As a result, the Crown instructed its governors to enforce peace and focus on Angola's commercial opportunities instead, particularly on the by-product of the wars, the slave trade. Portuguese governors, however, were little interested in the king's proposed peace and would often lead small raiding expeditions towards Angola's hinterland to capture as many slaves as possible for personal gain and outside the Crown's jurisdiction.[47] Those small expeditions, initially masked as "defensive wars," gradually escalated into large-scale campaigns in the late 1610s, restarting an all-out war with Ndongo after the Portuguese allied with a new force of independent African armies, the *Imbangala*. A nomad cast of warriors and raiders, the *Imbangala* were described as violent marauders and cannibals, highly militarized and specialized in capturing slaves. The recruitment of those mercenary groups gave the Portuguese the needed local military support to achieve what the Kingdom of Kongo previously failed to accomplish: the destruction of Ndongo.[48] Bento Banha Cardoso (1611–14) was the first governor to employ the help of the *Imbangala* against *Soba* Xilonga, but it was the arrival of Governor Luís Mendes de Vasconcelos (1617–21) that unleashed a new phase of Portuguese war-mongering enterprise in Angola.[49]

Vasconcelos began his governorship by proposing an ambitious project to the Crown, requesting "a permanent army . . . of 1,000 soldiers and 200 horses" and several hundred weight of musket gunpowder in order to conquer the Kingdom of Angola.[50] As a former captain-major of the armadas of India, a skilled veteran of the wars in the Flanders, and the author of a military treatise (*Arte Militar*, 1613), Vasconcelos attempted to implement his own military ideas, fostered on European battlegrounds, in a different environment.[51] However, his project was ignored by the Crown, and his tactical plans for Portuguese warfare in Angola proved disastrous and almost cost his life. The absence of a significant cavalry force in Africa due to the environmental constraints (horses had under a two-year lifespan in Angola's climate) meant that African armies could fight and manoeuvre in open formations without being overrun by cavalry. This gave plenty of space for Mbundu soldiers to perform a special movement called *sanguar* (from the ritual dance *nsanga*) and leap across the battlefield to dodge arrows and melee blows.[52] Vasconcelos initial insistence on deploying his troops in tight Western European formations resulted in heavy casualties from arrow and javelin fire, according to the recount of the events by António Cadornega, and the governor had to be saved from the battlefield by Pedro de Sousa Coelho, a veteran captain of the Angolan wars.[53]

After this setback, Vasconcelos acknowledged the need to adapt to the realities of Luso-African warfare and saw the value of the *Imbangala*, since his forces alone could not orchestrate significant military incursions into Angola. Vasconcelos formalized an alliance with several *Imbangala* and launched a massive offensive on Ndongo in 1618, capitalizing on the fact that Ndongo had a new and unproved ruler, Ngola Mbandi.[54] This use of the internal turmoil that came with the dynastic succession was heavily reminiscent of the Spanish use of the Tlaxcala against the Aztecs or the exploitation of the Inca civil war between Huáscar and Atahualpa, showcasing a clear trend in European forces' reliance on exploiting local alliances and internal strife, both in Africa and in the Americas.[55] Along with his son Joane Mendes and Captain Francisco Antunes da Silva and with the support of the *Imbangala* and some of the Mbundu elites who opposed the new ruler, including a relative of the *Ngola*, called Mubanga, Vasconcelos feigned an attack against the territory of one of the *Ngola*'s *sobas* and launched a surprise attack on Ndongo's royal residence (Kabasa) instead, destroying the city. After decades of conflicts, the Portuguese forces led by Luís Mendes de Vasconcelos managed to finally ransack Ndongo, setting fire to Kabasa and forcing the *Ngola* into exile on the Quindonga Islands, prompting a state of war, chaos, and pillage in the region. The level of devastation and violence was such that even the Portuguese bishop of Kongo criticized the procedure of the governor.[56] The number of war captives taken as slaves during this conflict is directly related to the biggest surge in the volume of the transatlantic slave trade during the entirety of the seventeenth century.[57]

After the end of Vasconcelos term, the wars in West Africa were continued by João Correia de Sousa (1621–3), whose warmongering spirit earned him the nickname Portuguese Attila.[58] Due to the turmoil in Ndongo, Correia de Sousa turned his attention to Kongo's civil war, and backed by the *Imbangala*, he launched a treacherous attack on Kasanze. He continued his slave acquisition campaigns by invading the lands under Kongo's influence in the south until the Kongolese army of the "duke" of Mbamba and the "marquis" of Pemba met the Portuguese in battle. The battle of Mbundi in 1622 marked the first conflict between Portuguese and Kongolese forces and displayed the effectiveness of Portuguese musket fire (*espingardaria*) against Kongo's heavy infantry, who, unlike Ndongo's armies, were professional elite soldiers (from noble families) equipped with large shields (called *adargueiros*) and swords, the "finest troops of the land." However, the *Imbangala*'s numbers secured the victory for the Portuguese, as the Jesuit eyewitnesses reported with horror how the allied *Imbangala* (described as barbarians) massacred and ate several of the Kongolese Christian nobles, including *Mani* Mbamba.[59] The new *manikongo*, Nkanga a Mvika (Pedro II, 1622–24), immediately avenged this offence, and after gathering most of Kongo's army, he crushed the Portuguese in the following year at the battle of Mbanda Kasi, forcing Correia de Sousa to flee from Angola.[60]

The Portuguese attacks and slave raiding expeditions in Kongo's southern regions encouraged the *Manikongo* to negotiate a secret agreement with the Dutch West India Company (WIC), who had been increasingly visiting his coasts since the beginning of the seventeenth century. Through *Mani* Nsoyo, Pedro II offered land support to WIC ships attacking Luanda, and this alliance resulted in two failed assaults on Luanda in 1624, the first led by Filips van Zuyle and the second by Piet Heyn.[61] The previous Dutch takeover of Bahia in the same year, however, allowed the Portuguese to strengthen the defences of Luanda, and the premature death of Pedro II prompted his immediate successor, Mvemba a Nkanga (Garcia I, 1624–26), to negotiate peace with the Portuguese. Those attacks, however, were a prelude for the subsequent struggle for the supremacy in the Atlantic in the following decade, with the Dutch takeover of Northeast Brazil in 1630 and the renewal of Kongo's alliance through diplomatic missions with Maurits's court in Olinda, which would lead to the eventual Dutch occupation of Angola in 1641.[62] Meanwhile in Ndongo, the Portuguese had attempted to support a rival lineage after death of the *ngola*, and despite driving his sister Njinga (1624–63) east after a series of campaigns (1626–9), in 1631 her forces conquered Matamba and turned it into her base. After gathering several *Imbangala* allies, Njinga's forces took advantage of the Dutch attacks and negotiated an alliance against the Portuguese, even receiving some firearms in return, and began harassing Portuguese positions from the east.[63] Those events, along with the escalation of the conflict in the Atlantic in the 1630s and 1640s, brought about a new era for Euro-African warfare, involving Kongo, Ndongo, Matamba, the Dutch, and the Portuguese.

The irrelevance of the Military Revolution in the Portuguese conquest in Angola

The evolution of the conflict in Angola was considerably different than traditional warfare in Europe. West Central African armies, tactics, and technology are often regarded as backwards or "primitive" by Eurocentric accounts when compared to Western military power at the onset of the Military Revolution. However, as previously shown, military success needs to be evaluated in regard to its effectiveness in its respective environment and not by how it should conform to or deviate from one specific model that assumed global primacy by the nineteenth century.[64] The Portuguese conflict in Angola provides an interesting perspective on how the European military technologies fared against non-Western armies and outside of an European context in the early modern age. Looking at the first fifty years of the Portuguese conquest in Angola (1575–1625), it was hardly spectacular and brought few returns, especially when compared to other examples of European expansion. The several setbacks imposed by African armies on the Portuguese, combined with the constant need to negotiate with local polities and adapt to different military realities in West Central Africa, clearly show that the key elements that support the military revolution theory were simply absent from the Portuguese enterprise in Angola. Similar to recent revisionisms to the Spanish conquest in the Americas, the technological advantages granted by firearms to the Portuguese were not as decisive as initially believed.[65] While in Europe they were used mainly by infantry to penetrate heavily armoured enemies, in Angola almost no native forces wore any sort of armour, save for Kongo's heavy shield infantry. Although firearms offered great range, they had a slow rate of fire, and the tactical employment of volley fire tactics required large armies of musketeers, which was simply not possible for the small Portuguese contigents in Angola. Despite its initial psychological impact, capable of inflicting fear in the African troops, by 1594 local witnesses claimed that African infantry fearlessly rushed musketeers and attempted to snatch their weapons from their hands.[66] The employment of firearms by the Kongolese and Njinga's armies, as well as other *sobas* also show that this technology was not unique to the Portuguese and not a revolutionary element for the occupation. Therefore, the military technology of the Portuguese, which was heavily employed across European battlefields at the time, was ill-guided when fighting dispersed enemies and in guerrilla warfare.[67]

Other technological advantages, such as cavalry forces, heavy armour troops or ocean-sailing gunships were not determinant enough for the Portuguese in Angola. Contrary to Thornton's claim that cavalry was not used in Angola, due to the tropical environment, its existence is documented across several sources. However, its numbers were simply not enough to provide any significant military edge. According to an inventory on the number of Portuguese troops in Angola in 1603, the interim governor had only thirty-five horses among his forces, which were reduced to seven by 1606.[68] By 1630, according to reports, no more than sixteen horses supported the Portuguese forces in Angola, showing that cavalry was used in Angola, but employed mostly for communication with the *guerra preta* and reconnaissance rather than used to charge enemy troops. African warlords like Kafuxi Ka Mbari also showed great ability in handling cavalry units, and there are countless reports of Portuguese cavalry's being swarmed by enemies, who without fear attacked cavalry.[69] Portuguese heavily armoured infantry, though offering an important advantage as an anchor around which Indigenous allies organized their formations, was not always well suited to fighting in the Angolan jungle and highlands. Like the Spanish in the Americas, Portuguese troops had to shed some of their armour, due to the heat and to improve manoeuvrability. The use of poison arrows also countered Portuguese armour, because a single wound could prove fatal, as described by a Jesuit who noted the significant casualties in the Battle of Mbata (1623), resulting from arrows imbued with a deadly poison, called *banzo* or *cabanzo*.[70] Naval dominance and riverine navigation, though valuable for securing shipping lines along the Kwanza for Portuguese fortresses, did not offer much else and could not support Portuguese efforts further than the Quindonga Islands, which limited the supposed revolutionary trait of the gunship.

Another crucial argument of the military revolution thesis, the rise of professional large armies, is once again an absent element from Portuguese colonial expansion. The small number of the Portuguese contingents in Africa, even with a technological edge, could never match the military power of the kingdoms of Kongo or Ndongo or that of other local territories ruled by powerful *sobas* along the Kwanza River and in the Central Highlands. The massive death toll from the tropical diseases and complicated recruitment hindered the establishment of anything resembling the large professional armies of Europe. Another characteristic of the Portuguese military conquest in Angola was its essential private nature. Like Spanish ventures in Mexico and Peru, the enterprise of Novais was self-financed, to the point that he was bankrupt by the time of his death, in 1589. Cortés, Pizarro, and Dias de Novais took on the financial and military responsibilities of their enterprises in the name of the Crown, and in exchange for shouldering the financial burden of their missions, they were rewarded by the allocation of lands, the exploitation of Indigenous populations, and economic privileges in the new territories.[71] Rather than a state-sponsored enterprise driving imperial conquest in the Americas and Angola, its private nature meant that Iberian monarchs did not assume any costs of migrating troops to its colonial settings. Even after the integrations of those conquests to the Portuguese Crown's domain, the governors had to bring their own troops. As a result, both the Portuguese forces and the Spanish forces had to rely heavily on Indigenous forces for the fulfilment of their military expeditions.

Lastly, perhaps the clearest example displaying how the innovations carried by the Military Revolution lacked a decisive role in Angola's conquest can be seen in the emergence of a hybrid style of warfare, developed over several years of shared conflicts between Africans and Europeans, as the "proper way to wage war" in that specific geographical and cultural context. European military tactics proved disastrous in the Angolan highlands and jungles, and an optimal employment of its technological tools could never be replicated in that environment, due to the absence of the conditions enjoyed by Western European armies. Instead, Portuguese own military largely adapted African formations and could survive only through the recruitment of several Indigenous allies. The conquest of Angola, rather than conforming to Parkers's outdated claim that infantry firepower, capital gunships, and artillery fortress carried European imperialism, fits much better with the recent revisions made by scholars like Sharman or Lee, who highlight the vital role of local Indigenous forces and paint the European position as one of deference to non-Western powers during the sixteenth-century and seventeenth-century expansions. As shown through previous examples, this was clearly the picture of the Portuguese conquest in Angola.

Notes

1 Clifford J. Rogers, "The Military Revolution in History and Historiography," in *The Military Revolution Debate: Readings on the Military Transformations of Early Modern Europe,* ed. Clifford J. Rogers (Boulder, CO: Westview Press, 1995), 1–10.
2 Michael Roberts, "The Military Revolution, 1560–1660," in *The Military Revolution Debate: Readings on the Military Transformations of Early Modern Europe,* ed. Clifford J. Rogers (Boulder, CO: Westview Press, 1995), 13–35.
3 Tonio Andrade, *The Gunpowder Age: China, Military Innovation, and the Rise of the West in World History* (Princeton, NJ: Princeton University Press, 2016), 144–46, 178.
4 Roberts, "Military Revolution," 18–21.
5 Geoffrey Parker, *The Military Revolution: Military Innovation and the Rise of the West, 1500–1800,* 2nd ed. (New York: Cambridge University Press, 1996), 3–5, 176; Daniel Headrick, *The Tools of Empire: Technology and European Imperialism in the Nineteenth Century* (Oxford: Oxford University Press, 1981).
6 David Parrott, *The Business of War: Military Enterprise and Military Revolution in Early Modern Europe* (New York: Cambridge University Press, 2012); Jeremy Black, *A Military Revolution? Military Change and European Society, 1500–1800* (Atlantic Highlands, NJ: Humanities Press, 1991); Andrew Ayton, J.L. Price, eds., *The Medieval Military Revolution: State, Society and Military Change in Medieval and Early Modern Europe* (London: I.B. Tauris Publishers, 1995).
7 Wayne Lee, ed., *Empires and Indigenes: Intercultural Alliance, Imperial Expansion, and Warfare in the Early Modern World* (New York: New York University Press, 2011); Peter Lorge, *The Asian Military Revolution: From Gunpowder to the Bomb* (Cambridge: Cambridge University Press, 2012); Andrade, *The Gunpowder Age.*
8 Philip Hoffman, *Why Did Europe Conquer the World?* (Princeton, NJ: Princeton University Press, 2015); Kenneth Chase, *Firearms: A Global History to 1700* (Cambridge: Cambridge University Press, 2003).
9 Jason Sharman, *Empires of the Weak: The Real Story of European Expansion and the Creation of the New World Order* (Princeton, NJ: Princeton University Press, 2019).
10 Matthew Restall, *Seven Myths of the Spanish Conquest* (Oxford: Oxford University Press, 2003); Wayne Lee, "Projecting Power in the Early Modern World: The Spanish Model?" in *Empires and Indigenes: Intercultural Alliance, Imperial Expansion, and Warfare in the Early Modern World* (New York: New York University Press, 2011), 1–16.
11 Adam Clulow, *The Company and the Shogun: The Dutch Encounter with Tokugawa Japan* (New York: Columbia University Press, 2014; Douglas Peers, "Revolution, Evolution, or Devolution: The Military Making of Colonial India," in *Empires and Indigenes: Intercultural Alliance, Imperial Expansion, and Warfare in the Early Modern World* (New York: New York University Press, 2011), 81–106.

12 Jeremy Black, *Beyond the Military Revolution* (New York: Palgrave Macmillan, 2011), 106–33; Sharman, *Empires of the Weak*, 1–33.

13 Pedro Puntoni, "As guerras no Atlântico Sul: A restauração (1644–1654)," in *Nova História Militar de Portugal*, ed. António Hespanha, vol. 2 (Lisbon: Círculo de Leitores, 2004), 282–91.

14 Roquinaldo Ferreira, "O Brasil e a arte da guerra em Angola (sécs. XVII e XVIII)," *Estudos Históricos* 39 (2007): 3–23; Catarina Madeira Santos, Vítor Rodrigues, "Fazer a guerra nos Trópicos: aprendizagens e apropriações. Estado da Índia e Angola, séculos XVI e XVIII," in *Jornadas Setecentistas* (São Paulo: Minas Gerais, 2005), 57–66.

15 John K. Thornton, *Warfare in Atlantic Africa, 1500–1800* (London: University College London Press, 1999); John K. Thornton, "Firearms, Diplomacy, and Conquest in Angola: Cooperation and Alliance in West Central Africa, 1491–1671," in *Empires and Indigenes: Intercultural Alliance, Imperial Expansion, and Warfare in the Early Modern World* (New York: New York University Press, 2011), 167–91; John K. Thornton, "The Art of War in Angola, 1575–1680," *Comparative Studies in Society and History* 30, no. 2 (1988): 360–78.

16 Anthony Russell-Wood, *The Portuguese Empire 1415–1800: A World on the Move* (Baltimore: John Hopkins University Press, 1998).

17 Toby Green, *The Rise of the Trans-Atlantic Slave Trade in Western Africa, 1300–1589* (Cambridge: Cambridge UniversityPress, 2012), 70–72.

18 Gomes Eanes de Zurara, *Chronica do descobrimento e conquista de Guiné* (Paris: OfficinaTypographica de Fain e Thunot, 1841), 342–46.

19 John Thornton, *Warfare*, 44–51.

20 Malyn Newitt, *A History of Portuguese Overseas Expansion 1400–1668* (New York: Routledge, 2005), 49–50.

21 Ilidio do Amaral, *O reino do Congo, os mbundu (ou Ambundos), o reino dos Ngola (ou de Angola) e a presença portuguesa de finais do seculo XV a meados do seculo XVI* (Lisbon, 1996), 21–26.

22 "Armada de Gonçalo Roiz" (1509), in António Brásio, ed., *Monumenta Missionária Africana África Ocidental*, vol. 15 (Lisbon: Agência Geral do Ultramar, 1952–1958), 60–62 (Henceforth MMA).

23 David Birmingham, *Portugal and Africa* (Lisbon: Documenta histórica, 2003), 81–93.

24 The origins of the *Jagas* is still a great mystery and source of debate. See Joseph C. Miller, "Requiem for the Jaga," *Cahiers d'Études Africaines* XIII (1973): 121–49; Beatrix Heintze and Katja Rieck, "The Extraordinary Journey of the Jaga Through the Centuries: Critical Approaches to Precolonial Angolan Historical Sources," *History in Africa* 34 (2007) 67–101; Anne Hilton, "The Jaga Reconsidered," *The Journal of African History* 22, no. 2 (1981): 191–202.

25 "Carta do Padre Garcia Simões" (7 November 1576), Brásio, *MMA*, vol. 3, 145–47.

26 Ilídio do Amaral, *O consulado de Paulo Dias de Novais: Angola no último quartel do século XVI e primeiro do século XVII* (Lisbon: Instituto de Investigação científica e tropical, 2000).

27 Joseph Miller, *Kings and Kinsmen: Early Mbundu States in Angola* (Oxford: Clarendon Press, 1976), 82.

28 "Carta do padre Garcia Simões para o Provincial" (20 October 1575), Brásio, *MMA*, vol. 3, 129–42.

29 Amaral, *Reino do Congo*, 176–77.

30 "Carta do irmão António Mendes ao Padre Geral," Brásio, *MMA*, vol. 2, 509–51.

31 "Carta da doação a Paulo Dias de Novais" (19 September 1571), Brásio, *MMA*, vol. 3, 36–51.

32 "Carta Garcia Simões," 129–42.

33 Amaral, *O consulado*, 208–10; "História da Residência dos padres da companhia de Jesus em Angola, e cousas tocantes ao Reino, e conquista" (1 May 1594), Brásio, *MMA*, vol. 4, 546–81.

34 "Carta do Padre Frutuoso Ribeiro para o Padre Francisco Martins" (4 March 1580), Brásio, *MMA*, vol. 3, 187–90.
35 "Carta do padre Baltazar Barreira para o padre Sebastiao de morais (31 January 1582)," Brásio, *MMA*, vol. 3, 208–11.
36 Ferreira, "O Brasil," 5–6.
37 José Antonio Martínez Torres, "Politics and Colonial Discourse in the Spanish Empire: The African Atlantic Possessions, 1575–1630," in *Jahrbuch für Geschichte Lateinamerikas 51* (Köln: Böhlau Verlag, 2014), 113–48, 126.
38 Amaral, *O Consulado*, 132–37.
39 "Carta do padre Baltazar Afonso" (4 July 1581), Brásio, *MMA*, vol. 3, 198–207.
40 Linda Heywood and John Thornton, *Central Africans, Atlantic Creoles, and the Foundation of the Americas, 1585–1660* (Cambridge: Cambridge University Press, 2007), 82–92.
41 Thornton, "Firearms," 178.
42 "Carta do Padre Baltazar Barreira para o Provincial" (27 August 1585), Brásio, *MMA*, vol. 3, 323–25.
43 "História da Residência," 559–77.
44 "Carta do Padre Diogo da Costa" (31 May 1585), Brásio, *MMA*, vol. 3, 332; "História da Residência," 573–74.
45 "Carta do padre Baltazar," 323–25; "História da Residência," 564–77.
46 Heywood and Thornton, *Central Africans*, 91–93.
47 Beatrix Heintze, *Angola nos séculos XVI e XVII: Estudos sobre Fontes, Métodos e História* (Luanda: Kilombelombe, 2007), 280–81.
48 Miller, *Kings and Kinsmen*, 224–64.
49 Arquivo Nacional da Torre do Tombo (Lisbon), *Chancelaria de Filipe II*, Doações, liv. 36, fl. 115.
50 Arquivo Histórico Ultramarino (Lisbon), *Angola*, Caixa 1, doc. 53 "Requerimento de Luís Mendes Vasconcelos" (1616).
51 *Dicionário bibliográfico Português. Estudos de Inocêncio Francisco da Silva aplicáveis a Portugal e ao Brasil. Continuados e ampliados por P.V. Brito Aranha. Revistos por Gomes de Brito e Alvaro Neves*, 1 vol. (Lisbon: Imprensa Nacional., 1858–1923), 276.
52 "História da Residência," 563.
53 António de Oliveira Cadornega, *História das Guerras Angolanas*, vol. 1 (Lisbon: Agência Geral das Colónias, 1940–1942), 88–90.
54 Miller, *Kings and Kinsmen*, 200.
55 Thornton, "Firearms," 167–92.
56 Arquivo Histórico Ultramarino (Lisbon), *Angola*, Caixa 1, doc. 112, "Carta do Bispo do Congo e Angola Frei Manuel Baptista" (7 September 1619).
57 Miguel Geraldes Rodrigues, "Between West Africa and America: The Angolan Slave Trade in the Portuguese and Spanish Atlantic Empires (1560–1641)" (PhD diss., European University Institute, Florence, 2019).
58 "Carta de Brás Correia" (10 December 1623), Brásio, *MMA*, vol. 7, 166–70.
59 "Relação para o senhor colector," Brásio, *MMA*, 15, 508–29; "Carta de Baltasar Afonso," Brásio, *MMA*, vol. 3, 157.
60 John Thornton and Andrea Mosterman, "A Re-interpretation of the Kongo-Portuguese War of 1622 According to New Documentary Evidence," *The Journal of African History* 51, no. 2 (2010): 235–48.
61 Mark Meuwese, *Brothers in Arms, Partners in Trade: Dutch-Indigenous Alliances in the Atlantic World 1595–1674* (Boston: Brill, 2012), 145–47; Heywood and Thornton, *Central Africans*, 145–52.
62 Mariana Françozo, "Global Connections: Johan Maurits of Nassau-Siegen's Collection of Curiosities," in *The Dutch in Brazil*, ed. M. Van Groesen (New York: Cambridge University Press, 2014), 105–23.
63 Heintze, *Angola*, 352–61.
64 Thornton, *Warfare*, 6–12.

65 Charles Haecker, "'Dirty Little Wars' in Northern Mexico and the American Southwest," in *Partisans, Guerillas, and Irregulars: Historical Archaeology of Asymmetric Warfare*, ed. Steven Smith and Clarence Geier (Tuscaloosa: The University of Alabama Press, 2019), 140–58.

66 "História da Residência," 563.

67 Thornton, "Art of War," 361–62.

68 Biblioteca Nacional de Portugal (Lisbon), *Reservados, Colecção Pombalina*, cód. 526, fl. 294; "Caderno do Governador de Angola" (26 March 1607), Brásio, *MMA*, vol. 5, 223–29.

69 Cardonega, *História Geral*, vol. 1, 134–36, 365, 387–89.

70 "Relação do Alevamentamento de D. Affonso" (24 January 1622), Brásio, *MMA*, vol. 15, 530–37.

71 Heintze, *Angola*, 249–50.

11

SUPPLIERS, KNOWLEDGE BROKERS, AND BROTHERS IN ARMS

Portuguese aspects of military innovation in Makassar

Tristan Mostert

The early seventeenth century saw the attempts of the Dutch East India Company (VOC) to become the sole European power with access to the Moluccas and to the clove and nutmeg originating there. Makassar, a trade entrepôt on South Sulawesi and the capital of the Sultanate of Gowa, increasingly became the centre of resistance against the Dutch monopolistic policies.[1] Over the course of the seventeenth century, it became a harbour where European and Asian traders alike would come to buy their spices and trade other high-value goods. While Makassar was on the one hand a proud *bandar*, or free harbour, it also participated in the political and military scramble for the Moluccas, expanding its political influence there and thus preserving its continued access to these spices. This made Makassar both a trading port of choice and a valuable ally to other powers in the region, both Asian and European, which gave it a strong impetus and the necessary channels for rapid military innovation. It was able to use its position as an international port with extensive economic and diplomatic contacts to procure military technology and expertise.

This chapter explores the Portuguese role in Makassar's military development, focusing on three aspects. It looks into Makassar's fort-building practices, which have long been recognized as extraordinary for archipelagic Southeast Asia and have often been qualified as inspired and actively supported by the Portuguese. It then explores the role of Portuguese intermediaries in access to European weapons and military expertise in general. Finally, it investigates the Portuguese community of Borrobos that developed on the north side of Makassar from the 1640s onwards and that was ultimately allowed its own defences within Makassar in the face of imminent Dutch threat.

Background: European rivalries in Makassar at the start of the seventeenth century

In the first years of contact between the VOC and Makassar, relations were friendly, but in the second decade of the seventeenth century, they increasingly soured as the VOC developed its monopolistic policies, forcing other traders out of the spice-producing regions of the Eastern Archipelago. The subsequent conflict between Makassar and the VOC has often been explained in economic terms. Anthony Reid's works on Southeast Asia, for example, often feature Makassar as an example of the kind of cosmopolitan trading port that for him defined what he termed the "age of commerce" in Southeast Asia. In his monumental work *Southeast Asia in the Age of Commerce*, as well as several subsequent studies, Makassar is presented mainly as a *bandar*, an open and cosmopolitan port town, and he contends that it was this open character that caused conflict with the VOC.[2]

However, the conflict also had strong political dimensions, which have received less scholarly attention. Makassar was the capital of a powerful state, the dual kingdom of Gowa-Tallo, which stood at the head of a federation of principalities that were loyal or subservient to them. This state encompassed large parts of South Sulawesi by the early seventeenth century. As it rose to become a powerful state, it also steadily expanded its diplomatic relationships. In the late sixteenth century, the *karaeng* of Gowa had made active efforts to build up diplomatic ties in the Moluccas and Timor and with Mataram, Banjarmassin, and Johor. In 1605, the Makasar nobility and, in the following years, the entire state converted to Islam, giving further impetus to Makassar's diplomatic contacts and its rise as an international trading port.[3] In the early seventeenth century, it was expanding its political influence and power overseas beyond South Sulawesi, for instance to the island sultanate of Buton (near Southeast Sulawesi) and the Moluccas. Here it became a rival to the interests of the North Moluccan sultanate of Ternate and its new European ally, the VOC, in terms of both political power and control of the spice trade, which the Dutch sought to monopolize. The initial cordial relations between the VOC and Makassar broke down in 1615.[4]

For the English East India Company (EIC) and the Portuguese, this conflict between the Dutch and Gowa-Tallo provided an opportunity. The Portuguese were forced out of the Moluccas in the first few years of the seventeenth century; the English completely withdrew in 1623. They instead started buying their spices in Makassar. The Malay and Makassar traders using Makassar as their base successfully continued their trade in cloves and even markedly expanded it as cloves started selling at a premium because of the Dutch attempts at monopoly.

"Strong castles and many fortresses"

By the mid seventeenth century, Makassar boasted a great number of forts, which were based largely on the same principles as European artillery fortresses. Drawings of fort Sombaopu in Makassar, which housed the Gowa royal palace, show it to have bulwarks and bastions, particularly on the sea and river sides, providing some in-depth defence in a way similar to sixteenth-century European artillery fortresses (Figure 11.1). Field work by archaeologist David Bulbeck confirmed the presence of round bulwarks and other features which would have provided defence in depth. Many of the walls found in the Makassar fortresses were made of stamped

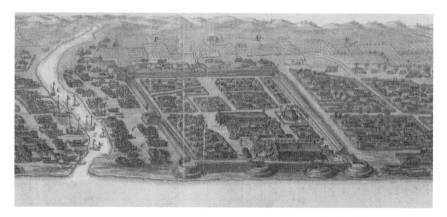

FIGURE 11.1   Sombaopu as depicted on a bird's-eye view of Makassar by Johannes Vingboons, c. 1665, showing bulwarks on the sea side and rectangular bastions
on the river side. The image is generally held to depict the situation of the
late 1630s. Collection Nationaal Archief, inv. nr. 4.VEL 619.96.

earth covered with a layer of bricks, just like European ones; Sombaopu contained
loopholes for guns.[5] All in all, as one Dutch observer remarked in 1660, Makassar
was considered to be an "unbreakable power," not least because of its "strong castles
and many fortresses," which put it in a position to look down upon the Dutch "like
a kind of Goliath."[6]

European fortress design was a central part of Geoffrey Parker's original military revolution thesis, presumed to be one of the uniquely European military
innovations that gave Europeans an edge in military confrontations overseas in
the early modern period. Whereas Parker's original thesis has now made way for
a more detailed picture of various military traditions worldwide and their mutual
influence, the artillery fortress is still widely considered to have been a specifically
European military technology that provided a marked military advantage in Asia,
although it also crossed the cultural divide easily.[7]

In *The Military Revolution*, Parker considered Sombaopu and the other Makasar
defences to be part of an ultimately fruitless seventeenth-century reaction of various Southeast Asian states to the emergence of European forts in the area.[8] He
also suggested that the forts have a clear European signature, owing much to the
strong Portuguese presence in Makassar. This assessment requires some qualification. The archaeological record and Makasar sources show that the tradition of
Makasar fortress building markedly predates the seventeenth century. Monumental
building in brick was not new to maritime Southeast Asia in general,[9] and Gowa
and Tallo were building brick fortifications well before we could reasonably expect
any European assistance. The chronicles of the Kingdom of Gowa record how the
martial ruler Karaeng Tunipalangga (r. 1546–65), who was credited with many
military exploits and innovations, was the first to build "encircling fortifications"
and mount them with "great cannons in a row."[10] The fortification history as it

can be grasped from the Gowa and Tallo chronicles is borne out by Bulbeck's archaeological research, which dates many of the brick fortifications to the six-teenth century and shows that the brickwork was made in a non-European way.[11] This military innovation, like the many others that the chronicles mention in the course of the sixteenth and early seventeenth century, occurred before Portuguese influence in Makassar became significant and before Europeans became a threat to Makassar.

From the 1610s onwards, the escalating conflict with the Dutch does seem to have motivated further extension of the Makassar fortifications, now clearly aimed at protecting the coast and the entrepôt from seaborne attack. In June 1615, just two months after the armed conflict between the Dutch and Makassars had first erupted, the English factor in Makassar, George Cockayne, wrote to his superi-ors how "the whole land is making . . . bricks for two castles this summer to be finished," in addition to stockpiling great amounts of weapons and food, in order to "entertain the Flemings."[12] In a VOC report of a military encounter before the Makassar roads in 1621, Company officials first noted a recently finished "closed fort" guarding the Makassar roads, which gave heavy fire as the Dutch tried to take a small Portuguese junk moored underneath its walls.[13] In July 1625, an Italian free trader described Makassar's defences to the Dutch governor-general as, by then, consisting of "five strong points on the seaside, with 8, 9 or 10 guns, both large and small, on each of those points."[14] In the 1630s, in response to a renewed Dutch threat, the walls of Sombaopu were further reinforced to the form we know from Dutch drawings, such as that in Figure 11.1.[15]

While several Dutch contemporary sources claim that the Makasar defences of the 1630s were built with Portuguese support, we must note that as early as the 1620s, when Portuguese influence was still much more limited in Makassar, coastal defences with bastions were being built there and that the Makasars drew on at least half a century of local experience in building brick fortifications defended by artillery. Makasar fortress building thus eludes the simple definition as a Western innovation brought to Makassar by Europeans and adopted in response to a Euro-pean threat. Although the appearance of Portuguese forts in Southeast Asia would have inspired innovations in Makassar fortification, Makassar initially incorporated these on its own terms and for its own purposes. This changed in the seventeenth century, when forts certainly *were* built in response to European threats and possibly with direct European help.

Makassar's fortifications have received comparatively generous attention from scholars.[16] Although these were among the most impressive and effective non-European fortifications in the eastern archipelago, the limited research on indig-enous fortifications elsewhere and the lingering perception that fortifications were not generally central to Southeast Asian warfare have created the impression of Makasar fortifications as extraordinary. This has obscured how Makassar, rather than being unique, seems to have been an important representative of, and vital link in, wider developments in fortress building throughout the eastern archipelago in the first decades of the seventeenth century.

The Sultanate of Buton, in the southeast of Sulawesi, might serve to illustrate this. A bone of contention between Ternate and Gowa-Tallo in the first half of the seventeenth century, its capital became increasingly heavily fortified over the course of this period, its *kraton* enclosed in impressive fortifications by the 1630s. When the sultanate stood under Makasar influence and became an enemy of the Dutch, the fortifications were attacked by VOC forces in 1637 and 1638, but these found the place too "well-fortified, with many cannon, falconets, swivel guns and firearms, and situated on an inaccessibly steep ridge" to be able to conquer it.[17] Interestingly, the history of what is still the largest fort in Indonesia remains largely to be written. Today, the fort, with its bastions of various shapes at regular intervals, still looks much as it does in a 1651 drawing by Pierre du Bois (Figure 11.2), although the fort was heavily restored in the 1980s.[18] Even though the Dutch were allied to Buton through the 1610s, 1620s, and early 1630s, there is no evidence they had any role in the fortification of the *kraton*, and the principles on which it is based seem to have been adopted locally, without direct European involvement.

Further east still, in the Moluccas, a fortification spree also took place in the first decades of the seventeenth century, which research has barely scratched the surface of. Most of the extant literature gives the impression that forts in this region didn't amount to much – the leading researcher in the field, Gerrit Knaap, contends that villages in the Central Moluccas (Ambon, Seram, and the surrounding islands) were not typically fortified in any way in the seventeenth century, with the exception of only the most powerful political centres in the region.[19]

Even locally, interest in indigenous forts has been limited. Only recently have they garnered attention from archaeologists in the Moluccas: since 2018, Muhammad Al Mujabuddawat has been surveying some of them.[20] For the wider region,

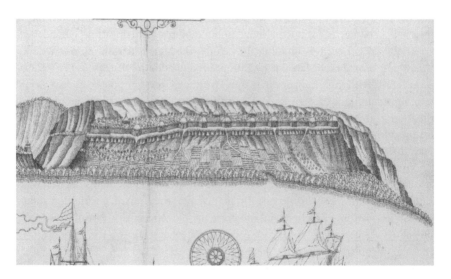

FIGURE 11.2   A bird's-eye view of the town of Buton, c. 1651. Pen drawing by Pierre du Bois, collection Nationaal Archief, The Hague, inv. nr. 4.VEL 1310.

especially Sulawesi and the South Moluccas, various recent publications have pointed to a fortification spree taking place from the 16th century onwards, and look for its cause in the emerging rivalries over access to the region both by Europeans and emerging local powers, including Makassar and Ternate, and the proliferation of gunpowder weapons.[21] Antoinette Schäpper specifically points to the VOC's bloody conquest of the Banda islands as a possible cause for part of this spree of fortifications.[22] Going by Knaap's earlier assessment of fort building in the Central Moluccas, however, she surmises that the South Moluccas followed a pattern distinct from the region as a whole.[23] I contend, on the other hand, that Knaap's assessment needs revision. Contemporary evidence in the form of Dutch campaign journals, some of them illustrated, shows widespread use of fortifications in the region by the early seventeenth century, with almost every village fortified. Rather than being distinct from the pattern Schäpper discerns, the Central Moluccas fit it in almost every respect.

The forts built in this period did not all have features that we would associate with the Military Revolution. Even without bastions or any ordnance heavier than swivel guns, however, these forts could be remarkably resilient to European siege or attack, because they made use of the features of the capricious landscape of the region. One of the more impressive of such forts was the town of Ihamahu, on the island of Saparua. Perched on top of an inaccessible coral platform, its 18-foot-high walls effectively resisted a VOC siege in 1632 (see Figure 11.3). The VOC forces resorted to scorched earth tactics instead, destroying the various gardens and groves

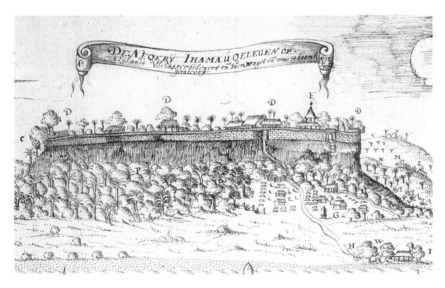

FIGURE 11.3 An anonymous pen drawing of the fortified town of Ihamahu on the island of Saparua during a siege by VOC forces and their local allies; from the private archive of governor Gijsels, Badische Landesbibliothek, Karlsruhe, inv. nr. K476, fol 27.

in the wider area, as would increasingly become the staple of their strategy in subsequent years. (They would, for instance, do the same at Buton seven years later).[24]

The inhabitants of the Moluccas were also incorporating new insights into their fortress design. In some cases, such innovations were directly introduced into the region from Makassar. From the 1620s onwards, Makasar "spice hunters," as the VOC tended to call them, created coastal defences along the shoreline, both to temporarily protect their own trade for a season and as part of open wars with the Dutch in which the Makassars allied themselves with the inhabitants of the region.[25] We see such Makasar coastal fortifications depicted in Figure 11.4, showing the final Dutch conquest of Asaudi in 1655. Such innovations were also adopted locally. Figure 11.5, a depiction of the 1649 conquest of the east Seram village of Rarakit, is one of the clearer instances, showing us a system of interlinking secondary fortifications around a primary fortification with bastions.[26] We should be careful not to rely on such images as primary evidence, but they do fit the general pattern emerging from the sources: VOC officials often showed themselves impressed with the many indigenous fortresses they encountered and described them in European terms, as having ramparts, demilunes, bastions, and redoubts.[27]

Thus, seen in a wider regional perspective, a different picture of Makassar's fortifications emerges. On the one hand, its assessment as a reaction to a

FIGURE 11.4   VOC attack at Asaudi: two makeshift Dutch palisades on the coast (C and D) are visible among the larger Makassar-built coastal fortifications defended by artillery (B) and another two fortifications on the hill to the right. While this pen drawing was probably made in the Netherlands on the basis of a now-lost original and should not be taken at face value, the general picture it sketches comports with what we know of the nature of warfare in the Ambon Islands at the time. Detail from a pen drawing in a manuscript version of Livinus Bor, Amboinse Oorlogen, in the Royal Library in Brussel (KBR), Ms. 17982.

FIGURE 11.5 Dutch forces attacking indigenous forts at Rarakit, eastern Seram, 1649. The drawing, made in Batavia by Johan van Nessel, shows a system of secondary fortifications around a primary fort with bastions. Detail from a pen drawing in a manuscript version of Livinus Bor, Amboinse Oorlogen, in the Koninklijke Bibliotheek, The Hague, inv. nr. 75 D 23.

European threat relying on Portuguese support is too simple in light of both written sources and archaeological evidence. Rather, Makassar, as an upcoming trade entrepôt with a wide network of contacts throughout the wider region, was early in adopting innovations in fortress building into an existing building tradition, inspired by European forts appearing in the region, but not necessarily with European help or in response to any kind of European threat. Neither was Makassar the end of the line: its fortification efforts appear to have been both representative of, and instrumental in, a wider wave of fortification efforts in the eastern archipelago as a whole. Expertise in effective fortifications, probably partly drawn from Portuguese examples, became increasingly valuable as gunpowder weapons were introduced into the region and the influence of the European presence was increasingly felt over the course of the late sixteenth century and early seventeenth century. Such knowledge quickly diffused through the wider region. These forts, while not usually living up to our ideal types of *trace italienne* forts with their geometric designs and angled bastions, quickly developed to a level where they were no longer the weakest link in local defensive efforts. Working from the challenge-and-response logic of the military revolution thesis, why should we expect anything more? The more significant observation is that throughout the eastern archipelago, local powers were able to formulate an effective defensive answer to gunpowder weapons in general, and those wielded by Europeans in particular, remarkably quickly.

Supplies, intermediaries, and military innovation

The guns defending such indigenous forts are a different matter. Locally cast guns in Southeast Asia were usually no heavier than swivel guns, and this is what the Dutch mostly found themselves faced with in their wars in the Moluccas. The bulwarks of Sombaopu and other Makassar forts were, by contrast, mounted with heavy guns; although Makassar also founded its own artillery, some of it quite heavy,[28] many of the guns defending the walls of Makassar in the 1630s were Danish, English, or Portuguese in origin. At the time, moreover, these guns were managed by a European: the constable-major in charge of the sultan's artillery was a renegade Englishman who had converted to Islam.[29] The rulers of the trade entrepôt of Makassar, to a much greater degree than polities further east, could capitalize on their wide range of economic and diplomatic contacts to get hold of foreign weapons technology and knowledge.

This flow of European weapons to Makassar is best documented in the archives of another European competitor of the Dutch: the English. In the years after 1615, the English were the only European company allowed a factory in Makassar. The Portuguese sailed to and fro from Malakka but were not allowed an official settlement at this time. The rulers of Gowa and Tallo were keen on receiving European gifts, requesting specific items, firearms being prominently among those. The supply of weapons to the rulers of Makassar was made official in the first treaty between the rulers of Gowa and Tallo and the EIC, concluded in 1624: every ship arriving from England had to present "great ordnance" to the rulers; a ship revisiting should provide muskets and gunpowder.[30] Weapons were not only presented to the rulers as gifts but also sold in the open market: the Makasar and Malay spice hunters sailing for Ambon every year to procure the cloves there often had to defend their trade by force, and the English were aware that without a steady flow of lead and gunpowder, "the trade [could not] subsist."[31]

The Portuguese role comes into focus more clearly over the course of subsequent decades, when the Portuguese community in Makassar grew in size and influence. By the end of the 1620s, it had perhaps grown to several hundred people.[32] In the 1640s, it subsequently swelled to unprecedented numbers after the VOC–Johor conquest of Portuguese Melaka. Many of the latter's Portuguese inhabitants opted to move to Makassar – drawn by the Sultan's reputation of "protect[ing] the Portuguese with the greatest firmness,"[33] his impressive military power, and his peace treaty with the VOC, which had been concluded a few years earlier in 1637, putting the Portuguese living there beyond the reach of the Dutch. Their numbers quickly swelled to some two thousand to three thousand.[34] The *Restauração*, the revolt in Portugal ousting the Spanish king from the Portuguese throne in December 1640, and in its wake the peace negotiations between Portugal and the Dutch Republic, would subsequently lead to peace between the *Estado* and the VOC in Asia as well, although the VOC, at the time heavily invested in a strategy of militarily ousting the Portuguese from many of their posts in Asia altogether, found excuses to keep on campaigning against the Portuguese in Asia until November 1644.

The *Restauração*, specifically, made at least one Portuguese decide to move to Makassar: Francisco Vieira de Figueiredo, a Portuguese of relatively low birth who had been making a career in Asia and who was employed by the Spanish governor of the Philippines when news of the *Restauração* reached him in 1642. At the time, he was in Cambodia on an errand for his Spanish employer. News of the revolt in Europe made him re-evaluate his loyalties, and instead of returning to Manila, he decided to sail for Makassar, bringing a small elephant which he had obtained in Cambodia for the governor but which he now felt would be better-spent on the sultan.[35]

At the time, Gowa was ruled by Sultan Malikussaid and his chancellor, Karaeng Pattingalloang, who was a member of the royal house of Tallo. In addition to being the Gowan chancellor, Pattingalloang would also become the ruler of Tallo from 1641 onwards. Pattingalloang is invariably praised in European sources as a sensible and prudent ruler and is the Makassar official we know best from the European sources, because he was fluent in several languages and had a particularly active role in government and foreign policy.[36] The manner in which the cosmopolitan character of the city of Makassar translated into knowledge and technology for its rulers in the preceding decades reached new heights in this period.

Pattingalloang was an ardent collector of books and scientific instruments, which he procured through his international contacts, in which trade, diplomacy, and knowledge exchange were inextricably intertwined.[37] Francisco Vieira soon managed to make himself indispensable to him: not only did he often serve as an official representative of the Gowan court, but he was also a knowledge broker in a quite literal sense. His name repeatedly comes up in relation to various orders that Pattingalloang placed with the VOC in the 1640s, when Pattingalloang ordered, among other things, an extraordinarily large pair of globes; a large world map in Spanish, Portuguese, or Latin; an atlas in one of those languages, telescopes, magnifying glasses, prisms, ephemeris books, a Latin–Arabic dictionary; glasses; a viewer with which to look into the sun; and a compass "of the best and largest kind."[38]

For Pattingalloang and his like-minded contemporaries, intellectual curiosity went hand in hand with a keen awareness of the practical applications of such knowledge and innovation. In Europe itself, of course, mathematics had become exceedingly important in warfare in the early modern period. Some of the fruits of the new quantified approach to warfare also made their way to Makassar, in the form of foreign military handbooks. A compendium of such handbooks, translated into Makasar, has survived in a later Bugis version.[39] The first of these, according to its introduction, was written by "Andaréa de Monyona," and has turned out to be a translation of the handbook on the use of artillery by Andres Muñoz el Bueno, chief artillerist of the king of Castile, which was first published in 1563.[40] The book, rich in tables and charts, contains information on how to gauge the calibre of a gun, how to ascertain the amount of gunpowder needed, how to aim for a certain distance, and the different types of cannons and how to use them. That book is followed by several other, shorter military "lessons" about, for instance, aiming a handheld weapon or preparing gunpowder. While one of these handbooks seems to be a Makasar Malay original,[41] many of them are ascribed to foreign weapons experts from the Islamic world, such as Pamahalajun Ahmad "from the west" and Haji Bektash "from Istanbul," attesting that Makassar was also part of Islamic networks of knowledge. Some of the other names suggest more Iberians.[42]

If we can take chancellor Pattingalloang at his word, such handbooks played a vital role in the innovations in Gowan warfare and not just to defend against Europeans. A Jesuit report from the Philippines mentions a Father Cebrián, who, when passing through Makassar, met with Pattingalloang and discussed, among other things, a recent uprising of Bone, a tributary state to Gowa-Tallo. The latter

> told the Padre several times that he had undoubtedly lost that war, had it not been for a book by a Castilian, which he carried with him, and which explained about forming squadrons and the ways of war, which he found very valuable.[43]

Apparently, these European handbooks were revolutionizing indigenous warfare in South Sulawesi as well.

Brothers in arms: the VOC attack of 1660

Originally, the Portuguese quarter was in Makassar proper, but this increasingly led to conflict with the Islamic population of the city. In the 1640s, unrest and various attempts at arson led to the resettling of the Portuguese to a newly established quarter to the immediate north of the city, called Borrobos. It became a home to several thousand Catholics, of Portuguese, Eurasian, and Asian backgrounds, with various catholic orders running schools, hospitals, and churches.[44]

Even though the wars between Portugal and the Dutch Republic and as a consequence, those between the Portuguese and the VOC, had resumed in 1651, with Portugal definitively losing many of its Asian outposts in the period, the Portuguese community in Borrobos was, for now, safe from the Dutch, mostly thanks to the impressive military power that Gowa-Tallo represented. Although the latter was a consequential party to the Great Amboina War of 1651–6, that war was fought mostly in Amboina, and the Dutch limited their efforts at Makassar to periodically mounting a naval blockade.

The subsequent peace treaty of 1656, however, ultimately did little to resolve the tensions between Makassar and the VOC.[45] When Makassar basically asserted political sovereignty over large parts of the Amboina islands and over some other areas claimed by the VOC, during negotiations in April 1659, the Dutch governor-general and his council decided to once again confront Makassar militarily.[46] On 12 May 1660, a fleet of thirty-one vessels (including smaller boats), carrying twelve hundred European soldiers, a thousand sailors, and four hundred Ambonese set sail from the Bay of Ambon. The subsequent attack is worth revisiting here[47] not only because it illustrates the formidable challenge that the Makassar fortifications continued to represent to a European aggressor but also because it gives us some insight into the defences put up by the Portuguese in Borrobos.

Aware that they would be unable to attack Makassar head on, the governor-general and council decided to employ a subterfuge: the bulk of the fleet had to sail along the coast of Makassar, firing at the defences as it went, until it reached Sombaopu. The goal was to create the impression that a large attack was going to take place there, to lure away the troops from the other strongholds. A flotilla of smaller vessels carrying the bulk of the soldiers would then take the fort of Panakukang, on the south side of Makassar, in a surprise attack. The VOC's being in possession of a fort right in the heartland of Makasar power would hopefully reverse the tables in the negotiations that were to follow.

In spite of the impressive strength of the army, most of the soldiers on board wouldn't have guessed that the goal of the expedition was Makassar. The VOC's Ambonese allies, who had ample experience in fighting the Makasars over the course of the Great Ambon War of 1651–6, were dismayed when they learnt where the fleet was going. Wouter Schouten, the ship's surgeon of one of the vessels, later recalled how "[t]he Ambonese soldiers who had gone along, brave heroes of war, had acted very courageously when we left Ambon . . . Now that they saw that we were going to Makassar to give battle there, they had suddenly become very frightened."[48]

The fleet came to a halt at Selayar, to the south of Makassar, on 5 June 1660. First, the three employees still staffing the Dutch lodge needed to be evacuated, and Van Dam went ahead with two ships to get them. Because the Dutch had been trading in Makassar over previous years, this would, he hoped, not arouse suspicion. The rest of the fleet was to slowly advance in the meantime.[49]

When the two Dutch ships arrived before Makassar, they spotted six Portuguese ships and a small Portuguese junk there, four of which were lying deep in the water and were presumably loaded with valuable cargo. Although Van Dam had only two ships at his disposal, one of these was the well-armed flagship of his fleet, and after evacuating the Dutch lodge, he decided to take a risk and attacked. Clearly, the Portuguese had been on the alert, as fire was immediately returned. The fleets seemed evenly matched for a while, until one of the Dutch ships, which was in close combat with the Portuguese lead ship, hit its powder chamber and thus destroyed the vessel. Two other Portuguese ships caught fire soon after, and two more were manoeuvred onto the beach. The sixth vessel was boarded and taken. Its crew was released to Makassar, and because the Makassar defences now also opened fire on the VOC vessels, the ships, now three in number, headed back to the fleet.[50]

The full force arrived a few days later. In the morning of 12 June 1660, half a mile south of Makassar, the eleven largest and best-armed vessels transferred their soldiers to the other ships and started their run along the coast, firing on the various fortifications. They halted at Sombaopu. Many barges and small ships lying on the beach were destroyed by the bombardment. The Makasars, meanwhile, returned fire. Wouter Schouten, first having described how the massive bombardment from the ships wreaked havoc on Makassar, then goes on to describe the impressive return fire:

> the Makassarese and Portuguese had rushed from their quarters to the aid of the king and started firing at us, rather more intensely than from Panaku-kang. Their heavy cannonballs struck the heart of our fleet, which was bat-tered badly by this. On our ship, the mainstay was shot in two, by which our mainmast was wrenched quite loose. We also got some direct hits on and below the waterline, but the holes were fixed by our carpenters immediately. Thus the enemy cannonballs of twelve, eighteen and twenty-four pounds did a lot of damage to masts, rope and sail, which brought our ships into quite some trouble.[51]

All the same, the subterfuge was working. Some four thousand Makasars defending Panakukang, under the impression that that the main attack was on Sombaopu, rushed away to defend it. Only a small force remained behind. The VOC force then landed at the beach near Panakukang with its siege equipment and managed to storm into the fort just as the remaining defenders were opening the gate to abandon the fort. After fighting off a Makasar counterattack launched from Sombaopu, the Dutch pursued the retreating soldiers up to the Garassi River, which separated Panakukang from Sombaopu, putting the area south of the river to the torch as it went.[52] The eleven ships before Sambaopu, meanwhile, had spotted the Dutch flag raised over Panakukang and headed further north, to bombard the northern parts of the city, including Borrobos, the Portuguese quarter.

The rulers had always been careful not to allow the Portuguese, or any other Europeans for that matter, to construct any kind of structure that might serve as a fortification. In 1658, the visiting Jesuit André Ferrão remarked that the rulers of Makassar

> do not allow the Portuguese to place one stone upon another. Even Fran-cisco Vieira, who is probably the richest man in all of the Indies, lives in some shacks, for this is all that houses made of bamboo amount to.[53]

In 1659, after the breakdown of negotiations, the rulers of Makassar had already started preparing for a Dutch attack by fortifying the entire coastline, but they did not yet allow the Portuguese to do so.[54] When the company employees were evacuated by Van Dam, however, they reported that over the past two weeks, the Portuguese had also started fortifying Borrobos.[55]

Consequently, when the VOC's ships sailed past Borrobos on 12 June 1660, Vieira's residence made a rather different impression from the one it had made on Ferrão two years earlier: "Along the beautiful coastline and in front of the nice buildings of their chief, Francisco de Figueiredo, they had thrown up many strong batteries and low esconcements," from which they started "firing at us vehe-mently, hitting our fleet with large iron bar shot and cannonballs."[56] Passing by

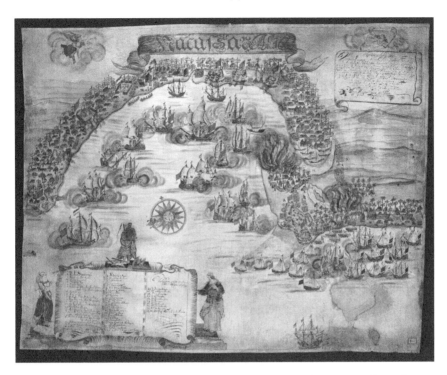

FIGURE 11.6   A drawing of the attack of 1660 by Fred Woldemar. To the right, we see the flotilla of smaller ships, the attack on Panakukang, and parts of the city being ablaze. In the top centre, we see Sombaopu (note that the shape here of the defences is slightly different from that of the Vingboons image): to its left, the English and Dutch lodges, and to its left, the Portuguese quarter, with the largest building (possibly Vieira's residence or a church) shown with a palisade and gun loopholes. Collection Bibliothèque Nationale de France, Département Société de Géographie, SGE SGY 832 RES.

the Portuguese quarter again on the way back to Panakukang, the ship on which Wouter Schouten was sailing got stuck in the rigging of the sunk Portuguese lead ship, which had exploded and sunk there four days ago, and the Portuguese tried to hit it on the waterline in order to sink it. The ship, however, eventually came loose and managed to get away.

The active Portuguese participation in the defence of Makassar was a breach of a century of Makassar's being a neutral harbour free of any outside military power, and we should perhaps consider it a measure of last resort, indicative of the increasing pressure that the VOC was exerting on it. On the other hand, the VOC's attack is also indicative of the power that Makassar continued to represent: the fleet that the Dutch brought to bear on it was formidable by VOC standards, and its only goal was to do some military muscle flexing and the temporary occupation of one outlying fort to improve the VOC's bargaining position in subsequent negotiations.

Nonetheless, the attack was, in this case, successful, and it heralded the end of the Portuguese community in Borrobos. In the negotiations after the 1660 attack, the VOC demanded that all Portuguese be expulsed from Makassar. Hasanuddin was under enough pressure at the time to agree to this condition in the resulting treaty and make initial steps to carry it out. Aware that the departure of the Portuguese would be detrimental to the city's economy, many in the Makasar upper class soon had second thoughts about this policy, but all the same, the better part of the Portuguese community soon packed up and left, heading for such places as Ayutthaya in Siam, with only a limited number of Portuguese, including Francisco Vieira, lingering on.[57] The VOC's attack thus heralded the end of Borrobos.

The Dutch attack did, however, spur Sultan Hassanudin to bring his already-impressive coastal defences to a whole new level still – in addition to repairing and reinforcing existing fortifications, he embarked on a project to build a coastal wall along the entire coast of Makassar, which would prevent another surprise landing. Ironically, however, these efforts also played a crucial role in the ultimate fall of Gowa-Tallo. Large fortification programmes are costly, and the corvée labour duties with which the post-1660 fortifications were realized were an important factor in bringing the already increasingly strained relations with Gowa-Tallo's tributary states to the breaking point.[58] Labourers from Bone, led by a noble called Arung Palakka, rose in rebellion when working to repair the damaged fortifications. Arung Palakka later sought refuge with the VOC and would become crucial as an ally to the VOC in a new round of conflict with Gowa-Tallo during 1666–9, as many of the latter's local tributaries responded to Arung Palakka's leadership and switched their allegiance, unravelling the state of Gowa-Tallo and definitively ending its reign as one of the main powers in the eastern archipelago.[59]

Conclusion

Over the century preceding the dissolution of Borrobos and the subsequent fall of Makassar, the Portuguese played various roles in the military development of Gowa-Tallo, some of which this article has sought to assess and qualify. With regard to its fortification practices, I have aimed to show that although innovations in fortress design the Portuguese brought to Southeast Asia did apparently feed into local fort-building practices, the Makasars seem to have been perfectly able to adopt such innovations without direct European support, and there has, perhaps, been too little eye for the wider Southeast Asian context of the developments in Makassar. Although Gowa-Tallo, as an economic and political power of consequence, was able to apply innovations most impressively and successfully, we see new fort-building practices finding their way to non-European fortifications in the eastern archipelago at large, and we therefore should not overemphasize Makassar's uniqueness in this regard. Rather, it was representative of, and in some cases an important link in, wider regional developments.

The Portuguese had a much more direct influence on other matters: not only did they, along with the Danes and English, directly supply the Makasar rulers with gunpowder weapons and ammunition, but they also played an important role as knowledge brokers for the courts of Gowa and Tallo, as is best illustrated by the way Karaeng Pattingalloang used his contacts to procure knowledge and expertise. Although Pattingalloang's networks were most certainly not exclusively European, as evidenced by, for instance, the Ottoman military manuals that he obtained, his active acquisition of foreign objects, books, and knowledge is best documented in the activities of his Portuguese go-between, Francisco Vieira, which were actively monitored and recorded by the VOC.

Although the rulers of Makassar successfully managed to avoid foreign powers establishing any kind of military presence on its shores up until 1660, they allowed the Portuguese to erect defensive works in anticipation of a Dutch attack in that year, in what must have been a measure of last resort by the rulers. When the attack took place in 1660, the Dutch ships were heavily fired on from various batteries in Borrobos. This Portuguese show of military force in Makassar would remain a one-off, however, because during the attack, the VOC forces managed to establish a military foothold of their own in Makassar for the first time and used it as leverage to demand the expulsion of the Portuguese from Makassar.

Notes

1 The spelling of South Sulawesi place names that I employ follows established practice among students of the region: the city of Makassar, the Makasar and Bugis people, the Makasars, the Bugis.
2 Anthony Reid, *Southeast Asia in the Age of Commerce, 1450–1680. Vol. 2: Expansion and Crisis* (New Haven, CT: Yale University Press, 1993) and, most recently, Anthony Reid, "Early Modernity as Cosmopolis: Some Suggestions from Southeast Asia," in *Delimiting Modernities: Conceptual Challenges and Regional Responses*, ed. Sven Trakulhun and Ralph Weber (London: Lexington Books, 2015), 123–42.
3 See, e.g., Leonard Andaya, *The Heritage of ArungPalakka: A History of South Sulawesi (Celebes) in the Seventeenth Century, Verhandelingen van het Koninklijk Instituut voor Taal-, Land- en Volkenkunde*, vol. 91 (The Hague: Nijhoff, 1981), 34.
4 For the evolution of the VOC–Makassar conflict and the role of Ternate, see Tristan Mostert, "Scramble for the Spices: Makassar's Role in European and Asian Competition in the Eastern Archipelago Up to 1616," in *The Dutch and English East India Companies: Diplomacy, Trade and Violence in Early Modern Asia*, ed. Adam Clulow and Tristan Mostert (Amsterdam: Amsterdam University Press, 2018), 25–54.
5 David Bulbeck, "Construction History and Significance of the Makassar Fortifications," in *Living Through Histories: Culture, History and Social Life in South Sulawesi*, ed. Kathryn Robinson and Mukhlis Paeni (Canberra: Australian National University; Jakarta: National Archives of Indonesia), 67–106.
6 Wouter Schouten, *De Oost-Indische Voyagie Van Wouter Schouten*, ed. Michael Breet and Marijke Barend-van Haeften (Zutphen: Walburg Pers, 2003), 92.
7 E.g. Tonio Andrade, *Lost Colony: The Untold Story of China's First Great Victory Over the West* (Princeton, NJ: Princeton University Press, 2011), 152–64, 316–29; Tonio Andrade, *The Gunpowder Age: China, Military Innovation, and the Rise of the West in World History* (Princeton, NJ and Oxford: Princeton University Press, 2016), 211–34.

8 Geoffrey Parker, *The Military Revolution: Military Innovation and the Rise of the West, 1500–1800* (Cambridge: Cambridge University Press, 1988), 122–23; Geoffrey Parker, "The Artillery Fortress as an Engine of European Overseas Expansion, 1480–1750," in *Success Is Never Final: Empire, War and Faith in Early Modern Europe* (New York: Perseus Books Group, 2002), 192–221. In the latter, he specifically addresses the Makasar fortifications and the VOC's conquest of them in a more nuanced way, although he does accidentally conflate the 1660 expedition with the outbreak of the Makassar War in 1666.

9 See Anthony Reid, *Southeast Asia in the Age of Commerce, 1450–1680. Vol. 1: The Land Below the Winds* (New Haven, CT: Yale University Press, 1988), 62–73, for a quick survey of Southeast Asian building traditions.

10 I quote from the critical translation by William Cummings, *A Chain of Kings: The Makassarese Chronicles of Gowa and Talloq*, Bibliotheca Indonesica, vol. 33 (Leiden: KITLV Press, 2007), 34. Bulbeck uses an earlier Indonesian translation of a different copy of the Gowa Chronicles, which in his English translation is much more elaborate and specific: "He was also the king who built brick walls around the communities of Gowa and Sombaopu; King Tumpa'risi' Kallona had built his walls only of earth." Quoted in Bulbeck, "Construction History," 77.

11 Bulbeck, "Construction History," esp. 96–98.

12 William Foster, *Letters Received by the East India Company from Its Servants in the East, Transcribed from the 'Original Correspondence' Series of the India Office Records, 1615*, vol. 3 (London: Sampson Low, Marston & Company, 1899), 151–52. For more details on the outbreak of hostilities, see Mostert, "Scramble for the Spices," esp. 44; Bulbeck, "Construction History," 79. The latter surmises that these might have been Kale Gowa, far inland, and Benteng Tallo, quite a bit to the north of Sombaopu, for reasons of chronology of the archaeological record, but the circumstances make it equally plausible that the defences that Cockayne refers to were in and around Makassar, to defend it against Dutch attack.

13 H.T. Colenbrander, ed., *Jan Pietersz. Coen: Bescheiden Omtrent Zijn Bedrijf in Indië*, vol. 1 ('s-Gravenhage: Nijhoff, 1919), 458.

14 'vijf stercke punten t'seewaart leggende [and] op yder punct omtrent 8, 9 a 10 stukken geschuts so groot als cleyn," Dagh-register Batavia, 24 July 1625, in: Ministerie Van Koloniën, Bataviaasch Genootschap Van Kunsten En Wetenschappen, and Nederlandsch-Indische Regeering, *Dagh-register Gehouden Int Casteel Batavia Vant Passerende Daer Ter Plaetse Als over Geheel Nederlandts-India, Vol. 1, 1624–1629* ('s-Gravenhage: Nijhoff; Batavia: Landsdrukkerij, 1887), 180.

15 Bulbeck, "Construction History," 80–82. Van Rechteren, who was in Makassar in 1631, describes the seaside wall, and holds that it was built with Portuguese help. His travelogue in: Isaac Commelin, *Begin Ende Voortgangh, Van De Vereenighde Nederlantsche Geoctroyeerde Oost-Indische Compagnie etc* (Amsterdam: Johannes Janssonius, 1646), 20th journey, 40.

16 This is in addition to the works cited above, e.g. Anthony Reid, "The Rise of Makassar," in *Charting the Shape of Early Modern Southeast Asia*, ed. Anthony Reid (Singapore: Institute of Southeast Asian Studies, 2000), 100–25.

17 Quoted in Pim Schoorl, "Het 'eeuwige' verbond tussen Buton en de VOC, 1613–1669," in *Excursies in Celebes: Een Bundel Bijdragen Bij Het Afscheid Van J. Noorduyn Als Directeur-secretaris Van Het Koninklijk Instituut Voor Taal, Land- En Volkenkunde*, ed. Harry A. Poeze and Pim Schoorl (Leiden: KITLV Uitgeverij, 1991), 21–61, esp. p. 36.

18 Hasanuddin, "Forts on Buton Island: Centres of settlement, government and security in Southeast Sulawesi," in *Forts and Fortification in Wallacea: Archaeological and Ethnohistoric Investigations*, ed. Sue O'Connor, Andrew McWilliam, and Sally Brockwell (Acton: ANU Press, 2020), 187–210; Laporan penelitian ekskavasi Situs Tirtatayasa, Banten & Benteng Wolio, Buton. NPO Association of Asian Cultural Properties Cooperation / Pusat Penelitian dan Pengembangan Arkeologi Nasional, Indonesia, March 2007, esp.

pp. 89–103. (Japanese and Indonesian, with English summary.) I thank Nadia Rinandi of the Pusat Dokumentasi Arsitektur (PDA) Jakarta for making this report available to me.

19 See e.g. Gerrit Knaap, "Headhunting, Carnage and Armed Peace in Amboina, 1500–1700," *Journal of the Economic and Social History of the Orient* 46, no. 2 (2003): 165–92, esp. 178.

20 I met Mujab, as he is colloquially called, in February 2019 in the Balai Arkeologi Maluku, and we were both amazed that we had grown fascinated by the same topic at the same time, each in our separate ways. Mujab was kind enough to share his pre-liminary research report about the surveys he conducted at seven of these forts, from which I thankfully draw in this section. M. Mujabuddawat, *Laporan Penelitian Arkeologi Menelusuri Jejak Benteng Tradisional di Pulau Seramdan Kepulauan Ambon Lease* (Ambon: Balai Arkeologi Maluku, 2018), unpublished.

21 Sue O'Connor, Andrew McWilliam, and Sally Brockwell, eds., *Forts and Fortification in Wallacea: Archaeological and Ethnohistoric Investigations* (Acton: ANU Press, 2020), esp. Chs. 1, 6–10, and 12. This volume came out when this chapter was already on its way to publication, and it was no longer possible to fully integrate its contents into my own chapter. The pattern that it discerned for South Maluku and Sulawesi, however, cor-responds remarkably well with the one I present here for the Ambon region.

22 Antoinette Schäpper, "Build the Wall: Village Fortification, Its Timing and Triggers in Southern Maluku, Indonesia," *Indonesia and the Malay World* 47, no. 138 (2019): 220–51

23 Ibid., 240.

24 For a summary description of the siege of Ihamahu, see Governor Gijsels to Governor-General Specx, 23 May 1632, partially printed I: P.A. Tiele and J.E. Heeres, *Bouwstoffen Voor De Geschiedenis Der Nederlanders in Den Maleischen Archipel: De Opkomst Van Het Nederlandsch Gezag in Oost-Indie*, 2e Reeks, Buitenbezittingen, vol. 2 ('s-Gravenhage: Martinus Nijhoff, 1886), 199. For Buton: Schoorl, "Het 'Eeuwige verbond," 36.

25 For an early example of the VOC's being stymied by a makeshift Makasar fortification on the island of Kelang, see Tiele-Heeres, *Bouwstoffen*, vol. II, 48–74. A brief overview of the role of the Makasars and their forts in the Hitu Wars: Ridjali, *Historie Van Hitu: Een Ambonse Geschiedenis Uit De Zeventiende Eeuw*, eds. Hans Straver, Chris van Fraas-sen, and Jan van der Putten (Utrecht: Landelijk Steunpunt Educatie Molukkers, 2004), passim.

26 The only surviving description of the attack and the fortifications is in a letter from the governor of Ambon to the governor-general, dated 21 April 1650, in VOC-archive 1179B, fol. 453v. Although it does not mention the shape of the primary fortification, it confirms the general layout of the interlinking fortifications on a precipice, connected by "strijkweeren" (parapets).

27 In addition to Bor, *Amboinse Oorlogen*, the private papers of Governor Artus Gijsels, the governor of Ambon from 1631 to 1634, contain a wealth of campaign reports with observations on indigenous forts. "Journal van Gedaene Tochten" in Badische Landes-bibliothek Karlsruhe, collection Artus Gijsels, K. 476.

28 K.C. Crucq, "De Geschiedenis van het Heilige kanon van Makassar," *Tijdschrift van het Bataviaasch Genootschap* 81 (1941): 74–95; Cummings, *Chain of Kings*, 88–89.

29 Seygers van Rechteren, in: Commelin, *Begin ende Voortgangh*, 20th journey, vol. 2, 40, mentions the Englishman in his description of Makassar dating to 1631. Van Diemen remarks about his recent death, in *Dagh-register Batavia*, 1637, 280–84.

30 British Library, India Office Records (IOR) G/10, 35.

31 IOR G/10, 71.

32 Maria do Carmo Mira Borges, *Os Portugueses e o Sultanato de Macaçar no Século XVII* (Cascais: Câmara Municipal de Cascais, 2005), 175 estimates the total Portuguese popu-lation to be five hundred people in the 1620s. A Dutch description from 1621 comes with rather more modest number: only fifty Portuguese at that time and the usual Por-tuguese population of some twenty to thirty households. J. IJzerman, "Het Schip 'De Eendracht' Voor Makasser in December 1616: Journaal Van Jan Steijns," *Bijdragen Tot De Taal-, Land- En Volkenkunde Van Nederlandsch Indië* 78 (1922): 371–72.

33 The viceroy in Goa in 1638, quoted in Steven Halikowski Smith, "No Obvious Home: The Flight of the Portuguese 'Tribe' from Makassar to Ayutthaya and Cambodia During the 1660s," *International Journal of Asian Studies* 7, no. 1 (2010): 3.

34 Two thousand was given by Frederik Willem Stapel: *Het Bongaais Verdrag* (Groningen: Wolters, 1922), 68. Three thousand was estimated by Smith: "No Obvious Home," 2.

35 Charles Boxer, *Francisco Vieira De Figueiredo: A Portuguese Merchant-Adventurer in South East Asia, 1624–1667*, Verhandelingen Van Het Koninklijk Instituut Voor Taal-, Land- En Volkenkunde, 52. ('s-Gravenhage: Nijhoff, 1967), 2, mentions how Vieira brought two elephants from Cambodia, but apparently, only one was offered to the sultan.

36 Anthony Reid, "A Great Seventeenth Century Indonesian Family: Matoaya and Pat- tingalloang of Makasar," in *Charting the Shape of Early Modern Southeast Asia*, ed. Anthony Reid (Singapore: Institute of Southeast Asian Studies, 2000), 147; Andaya, *Heritage*, 39, states that Pattingalloang was also fluent in English, French, and Arabic.

37 Reid, "A Great Seventeenth Century Indonesian Family," 147, provides a brief overview of some of the objects and books that Pattingalloang had in his collection.

38 For more on the globe, see Tristan Mostert, " 'Ick vertrouwe dat de werelt hem naer dien op twee polen keert': De VOC, de rijksbestuurder van Makassar en een uitzonderlijk grote globe," in *Aan de overkant: ontmoetingen in dienst van VOC en WIC (1600–1800)*, ed. Lodewijk Wagenaar (Leiden: Sidestone Press, 2015), 77–96.

39 The copy used for this article is in the Leiden University special collections under inv. nr. NBG Boeg 151. I was able to work with these manuals thanks to the translation efforts of Basiah Hamma Ali of Hasanuddin University (Makassar), who provided me with an Indonesian translation of the manuscript. Another copy of the same work is in the British Library Oriental Manuscript collection, Add. 12358. Another, apparently different copy is Add. 12365. Also see Reid, "A Great Seventeenth Century Indonesian Family," 149–50; Merle Ricklefs and P. Voorhoeve, *Indonesian Manuscripts in Great Brit- ain: A Catalogue of Manuscripts in Indonesian Languages in British Public Collections* (Oxford: Oxford University Press, 1977).

40 Andres Muñoz el Bueno, *Instruccion y regiminiento con que los Marineros sepan usar del Artil- leria* etc., c. 1563.

41 One of the military lessons is introduced as "an explanation from Ance Latif to his son Datoq Maharaja Laila Marala about shooting techniques" (NBG Boeg 151, p. 82). The title *ance/ince* was used to refer to Makassar Malays, and Datuk Maharaja Lela possibly refers to the leader of the Malays in Makassar from 1632 onwards, under whose leader- ship the Makassar Malays became a significant force in the Makassar War of 1666–9 or a later namesake. See Entji Amin, *Sja'irPerang Mengkasar: The Rhymed Chronicle of the Macassar War*, ed. C. Skinner, Verhandelingen Van Het Koninklijk Instituut Voor Taal-, Land- En Volkenkunde, vol. 40 ('s-Gravenhage: Nijhoff, 1963).

42 The other authors mentioned are Abransu Farguru from the country of Salanggirwaisi, whose father was from Hauri and whose mother was from Lisabewa (Lisbon); Pamahala- juna Ahmad, a world famous shooter 'from the West'; Haji Bangkatasi (almost certainly a rendering of the name Haji Bektash, the name of the Sufi Persian founder of the phi- losophy also adhered to by the Ottoman Janissaries, although the military manual that follows is certainly from a later date); and Juan di Moya, the teacher of Simau Mubalairu.

43 Printed in Hubert Jacobs, *The Jesuit Makasar Documents (1615–1682)*, Monumenta His- torica Societatis Jesu, 134 (Rome: Jesuit Historical Institute, 1988), 51. If this refers to the handbook by Andres Muñoz, the description of its being about "forming squadrons and the ways of war" would not be accurate, because this manual is a rather technical one about handling cannons. Therefore, Pattingalloang might be referring to another Spanish manual.

44 Borges, *Os Portugueses*, 175–79.

45 For an extensive analysis of this treaty and its effects, see Carl Frederik Feddersen, "Prin- cipled Pragmatism: VOC Interaction with Makassar 1637–68, and the Nature of Com- pany Diplomacy" (PhD diss., Leiden University, Leiden, 2016), 325–447.

46 Stapel, *Bongaais Verdrag*, 61–63.

47 For earlier descriptions, see e.g. W.E. van Dam van Isselt, "Mr. Johan van Dam en zijne tuchtiging van Makassar in 1660," *Bijdragen tot de Taal- Land- en Volkenkunde van Nederlands-Indië* 60, no. 1 (1908): 9–10.

48 Schouten, *Oost-Indische Voyagie*, 94. Translation by author.

49 Van Dam van Isselt, "Tuchtiging Makassar," 15–17.

50 Ibid., 16–18.

51 Schouten, *Oost-Indische Voyagie*, 99. Interestingly, Schouten mentions Portuguese taking part in the defence of Sombaopu itself, but as it is not confirmed in other sources, it seems possible that he is making an assumption.

52 Schouten, *Oost-Indische Voyagie*, 101–2.

53 This translation from Boxer, *Francisco Vieira*, 30–31, with one correction, as the original Portuguese calls Vieira the richest man in "toda a India," which Boxer translated as "the entire island." The original Portuguese in Jacobs, *The Jesuit Makasar Documents*, 155.

54 *Dagh-Register Batavia*, 1659, 226, briefly mentions the fortification efforts; letters spanning the period April 1659 to 27 May 1660 in VOC 1229, fol. 754–846 and VOC 1233, fol. 362–83, describe it rather more extensively.

55 Van Dam's expedition log, 7 June 1660. VOC 1232, fol. 289r.

56 Schouten, *Oost-Indische Voyagie*, 102.

57 Stapel, *Bongaais Verdrag*, 68; Halikowski Smith, "No Obvious Home," 3–4. Boxer, *Francisco Vieira*, 29.

58 Bulbeck, "Construction History," 84.

59 Andaya, *Heritage of Arung Palakka*, 52. This is vaguely reminiscent of European cases where the need for modern fortifications drained the means of the state (albeit in capital rather than corvée labour and goodwill) to such a degree that it could not mount a proper defence when the attack came, like Siena in the 1550s. Parker, *Military Revolution*, 12.

12

MILITARY INNOVATION AND INTRASTATE WARFARE

Portuguese artillery and sieges during the Wokou raids of the mid-sixteenth century[1]

Barend Noordam

Geoffrey Parker's iteration of the military revolution theory, which was mostly responsible for kickstarting and perpetuating the debate, accorded a central role to wall-smashing cannons in the context of European siege warfare. The nature and usage of this particular kind of artillery set in motion a train of technological innovations and institutional developments that would eventually lead to global European military dominance by the nineteenth century.[2] Historians of China have recently contributed to this debate by applying Parker's theory to the Chinese historical experience. Peter Lorge, for example, asserts that China had already had its military revolution in the twelfth and thirteenth centuries, leading to gunpowder-based weaponry, larger and more-expensive standing armies serviced by a bureaucratized state, and siege warfare around cities with long, thick, sloped walls. All this happened without the intercession of cannons.[3] Tonio Andrade, furthermore, shows that when cannons came into play during siege warfare during the early Ming dynasty, they remained relatively small and were used against enemy personnel for the most part. Chinese walls were generally already designed with such massive thickness and other features that developing heavier cannons to breach them made no sense. A second contention by Andrade is that the lack of warfare between c. 1450 and c. 1550 generally retarded the development of cannons and other military innovations in China. Lorge and Andrade seem to agree that mainly a protracted period of interstate warfare was responsible for the earlier rapid military innovation during the twelfth and thirteenth centuries and that cannons played no part in it.[4]

According to Andrade, Chinese cannon technology started developing again when the Portuguese reached Asia in the sixteenth century and their military technology started disseminating. Foremost among these designs was the breech-loading *berço*, which was named the *folangji*, or "Frankish machine," by the Chinese after the people they copied it from.[5] A second weapon with a probable Portuguese pedigree that was appropriated by the Chinese was the so-called *fagong*, which likely referred to the *falcão* bronze muzzle-loading cannon.[6]

The Chinese quickly appropriated Portuguese cannons, developed hybrid designs, and produced both in different sizes and weight classes. The rapid appropriation of the often-heavier Portuguese artillery pieces does raise the question what their inherent attractiveness was to the Chinese of the sixteenth century, because, according to Andrade, indigenous designs had remained light-weight and were mostly intended for the anti-personnel role. To answer this question, I turn to the reception of these weapons in Chinese military manuals of the 1550s to the 1570s – especially the role they were intended to play in siege warfare, according to these writings. This period witnessed a destructive conflict unfolding in the southeastern provinces of the empire involving the Wokou, organized bands of maritime raiders and pirates. This conflict generated a rich tradition of new military writings, which contained much information about the deployment of the Portuguese-derived weapons in the Chinese context, including siege warfare.

I rely on these writings to argue that despite the nigh-unbreachable walls in China, Portuguese ordnance was still used in a role beyond killing and injuring enemy personnel. Instead, they also targeted enemy weapons, siege equipment, and secondary fortifications in the field and on the walls. Thus, they started to replace older siege artillery, like catapults and large crossbows, although these older types did not entirely disappear.

I argue in this chapter that an incentive to develop larger and heavier cannon existed, despite the existence of the daunting walls. In relation to this, I argue that Chinese cannons did independently evolve into a heavier and larger design before the arrival of the Portuguese. Finally, I add nuance to the importance of interstate warfare for military innovation, by positing that this indigenous design probably evolved in the context of internal upheavals and that the Wokou conflict, which saw the use of the new Portuguese-style cannons, can also best be considered as an incidence of intrastate conflict.

Portuguese cannon and mid-sixteenth-century military treatises

The middle of the sixteenth century saw a new efflorescence in the production and publication of military manuals. This phenomenon can to a large extent be explained by the simultaneous military pressure exerted by the Mongols in the north and the Wokou pirates in the southeast during the 1550s and 1560s. This created an audience for military self-help books for beleaguered civil officials, who in many cases had to improvise defensive measures on behalf of the empire they served. Tang Shunzhi's *Wu bian* was a prime example of this tendency. Tang was a civil official serving under Supreme Commander Hu Zongxian (1512–65), who was the leader of the anti-Wokou effort until 1562. The *Wu bian* was compiled by Tang to comprehensively prepare him for his role in overseeing military affairs.[7] Tang died in 1560, but it seems that he kept his *Wu bian* updated until the end of his life, given that it contains many references to the weapons and tactics used against the Wokou in the 1550s. Included are his descriptions of the use of the *folangji* cannon during defensive sieges against Wokou assaults, which is, ostensibly, based on his own experiences.

> The men on the battlements stay to defend. If the cunning bandits gather together day and night and attack, then such people are not allowed to succeed and we must defeat them with military force. Military technologies: primary are the large *folangji*; secondary are the bird beak guns [a type of harquebus]; and next are bows and arrows. If matters become urgent, everyone is able to raise and use them without exhausting them, unlike bricks and stones. They must be accumulated and prepared in great numbers, and be able to give support one after the other.[8]

Clearly, for Tang Shunzhi, the *folangji* cannon had become the premier weapon to defend a city against assaults. But did the usage of these weapons prove that guns were becoming part of a challenge-and-response dynamic against enemy equipment, weapons, and secondary fortifications, beyond merely targeting enemy personnel?[9] Other descriptions from the *Wu bian* in the context of siege warfare show that this seems to have been the case: "For the *bianchong* is only able to strike enemies unprotected by shields, and enemies who have cover and have shields cannot be overpowered without *langji*."[10] *Langji* here is simply an abbreviation of *folangji*, or simply the result of an unintentional omission of the first vowel. The characters that represent each vowel of *langji* are similar to those normally used for *folangji*. The *bianchong*, which can be translated as "frontier gun," seems to have been a traditional Chinese handheld firearm, going by an illustration in a seventeenth-century Chinese military manual.[11] It was clearly not powerful enough to penetrate the shields that the Wokou were protecting themselves with, but the *folangji* could neutralize these defences.[12] In addition, the cannon was deemed by Tang Shunzhi to be effective against enemy equipment: "If a pirate ship moors below the wall, borrow nearby big *folangji* and combine forces to attack it. It must make them leave the walls and afterwards cease."[13] What the Chinese text means by "cease" is ambiguous, but this likely indicated that Tang expected the enemy vessel to at least be incapacitated enough by the *folangji* to cease being able to carry out its operations.

Other military treatises dating from this period, written by people connected to the anti-Wokou campaign, further support that the *folangji* was a great defensive weapon. Zheng Ruozeng (1505–80) was a friend of Tang Shunzhi and served Hu Zongxian as a private staff member. He was trained as a geographer, and he was in charge of editing and compiling the *Chou hai tu bian* (*Illustrated Compendium of Maritime Preparedness*), which eventually became a massive encyclopaedic and geographic overview of the anti-Wokou campaign.[14]

> Each piece is approximately 200 catties [120 kilograms] heavy; they use three extractable guns and each one is approximately 30 catties [18 kilograms] heavy. It uses one lead bullet and it is approximately ten liang [600 grams]

heavy. The machine's movement can be downwards, upwards, to the left, and to the right. Thus, it is that which can be used on top of city walls and is a weapon which defends military camps.[15]

Zheng Ruozeng emphasizes the flexibility in movement as a key factor in the cannon's suitability for defence. This would strongly suggest that it was mounted on a swivel, like the Portuguese *berço*. The "extractable gun" no doubt refers to the removable chamber, which could be preloaded with gunpowder and a cannonball before insertion into the cannon. Ming military commander Qi Jiguang (1528– 88), who also served under Hu Zongxian, concurred with the assessment that the *folangji* was a useful defensive weapon. In his manual *Ji xiao xinshu* (*New Book of Discipline and Efficacy*), a treatise that was based on his experiences in fighting the Wokou and that was published in the early 1560s, he advocated for installing *folangji* in strategic places in the city. They should be distributed evenly so that they could cover every section of the city wall.[16] Chinese historian Feng Zhenyu posits that another important reason for the *folangji*'s popularity in Ming China was its breech- loading mechanism, which allowed the preparation of charges and ammunition in advance. The correct amount of gunpowder was already added, and the removable chambers absorbed most of the heat of the explosion. Therefore a high rate of fire was possible without overheating the cannon as a whole.[17]

Whereas the *folangji* was lauded for its defensive qualities, its fellow Portuguese derivative, the *fagong*, was praised in the *Chou hai tu bian* for its offensive qualities:

Each piece weighs approximately 500 catties [around 300 kilograms] and uses one hundred cannonballs, each one weighing approximately four cat- ties [around 2.4 kg]. This is a beneficial weapon for attacking cities. When several tens of thousands of formidable enemies gather together, you also use it to attack cities. Their stone balls are like a small *dou* [a grain measure of about ten litres] and a big rock. That which is hit and struck is not able to endure. A wall encounters it and is at once penetrated; a building encounters it and is at once destroyed; a tree encounters it and is at once snapped; people and animals encounter it and at once become rivers of blood; a mountain encounters it and is at once penetrated several *chi* [a *chi* is around one-third of a metre]. Not only stone is not able to brave it and that's all. Ordinarily, those things which are hit by the stones move towards each other and hit [the other] things, and are without exception destroyed. Even the limbs, body, blood and flesh of humans are splattered, and also wounded and harmed. Moreover, not only the stones are devastating and that's all. The gunpowder, after being ignited, its vapour is able to lethally poison humans; its wind blasts are able to lethally inflame humans; its sound is able to shake humans to death. Therefore, if you desire to fire a *fagong*, you must dig an earthen pit and order the ignition company to hide themselves after lighting the fuse. The fire, vapour, and sound merely rush upwards, and it is possible to avoid death. You must select many intrepid men who guard and defend on behalf of it, to avoid the disaster of enemies grabbing the *fagong*. If there is no danger of [the enemy] storming the defences and being taken by force, you do not need to resort to this. Perhaps you ask if it is possible to use it during naval warfare? I say: "Just when the enemy puts the ships into formation, you can also use the small ones. But the moment you fire, the firepower is directed forwards, the boat shakes and recoils backwards, it without exception rips open and sinks. In addition, using wooden rafts to carry and use it, this is possible." You say: "Can it be used on the city walls?" I say: "It cannot." The *fagong* is suitable to attack heights, and unsuitable to attack things below [it].[18]

The *fagong* is described as both much heavier and more powerful than the *folangji*. In the context of siege warfare, it was deemed powerful enough to penetrate walls. Which kind of walls was not specified, and therefore we can construe that it possibly refers to secondary fortifications on top of city walls. In the event, it does prove that the *fagong* could have played a part in a challenge-and-response dynamic driving innovation in Chinese siege warfare. The *folangji* and the *fagong* formed a complementary pair: the former was suitable for defence, and the latter was suitable for offensive purposes.

There is descriptive evidence that they were indeed used in these roles. In 1548, Vietnamese forces attacked two Chinese cities near the border, which were defended by *folangji*. During the resulting sieges, the cannons were able to repulse attacks on the cities from siege ladders, ships in the moat, and attackers protected by cowhides.[19] In 1556, government forces attacked a Wokou pirate leader, who had taken refuge in a walled residence. *Fagong* were used to bombard the walls, battlements, and gates.[20] This latter incident should also serve to make us aware that not every siege in China had to revolve around big cities with metres-thick walls. The *Chou hai tu bian* does cast doubt on the Portuguese provenance of the *fagong*. According to this source, the *fagong* was an enlarged *folangji*, which the Chinese themselves designed. The *Chou hai tu bian*'s description of the *fagong*, however, contains a few inconsistencies. First of all, the accompanying picture shows a muzzle-loading cannon on a European-style wheeled gun carriage, not a breech-loading design.[21] Second, the description of the *fagong* does not mention a removable chamber for the ammunition and gunpowder. Finally, the celebration of the extreme penetration power of the weapon suggests it to be a muzzle-loading cannon, because they were cast in one piece. This made them more resistant to bursting and thus allowed the projectile to be fired with more force than a breech-loading cannon could.[22] Chinese historian Zheng Cheng advances a plausible theory that the *fagong* was actually based on *falcãos*, which were captured from a Portuguese armed merchant ship in 1549 near Dongshan Island, before the coast of Fujian. They were described by a Chinese civil official as *folangji datongchong*, or "Frankish large bronze guns." Zheng Cheng speculates that they were bow guns, described as large bombards by Chinese military officials involved in the encounter. Moreover, *falcão* cannons were carried by Portuguese ships in the sixteenth century, and they were roughly similar in size and weight to the *fagong* described in the *Chou hai tu bian*.[23] This would also explain the naming confusion with the *folangji*, as it was a name probably liable to be attached to any cannon with a Portuguese origin at this point in time. The strongest argument that Zheng Cheng advances that the *fagong* was based on the *falcão* is the similarity between the two names. Both vowels of *fagong* were at this time still represented by different characters, suggesting that the transliteration of the word was more important than its meaning.[24] Further compounding the confusion is the fact that the Chinese indeed enlarged the *folangji*, but these received different names. The confusing entry from the *Chou hai tu bian* was later partly copied in another military manual from 1606, titled *Bing lu*, or *Military Record*. This was written and compiled by the military officer He Rubin (fl. 1606), contributing to perpetuating the notion that the *fagong* is an enlarged *folangji*.[25]

Structural limitations inherent in the breech-loading mechanism probably prevented the *folangji* from becoming longer than around 2 metres in length. Larger examples have not been found thus far. Chinese historian Zhao Fengxian argues that lengthening the barrel beyond 2 metres meant that the likelihood of the cannonball's following a crooked trajectory, after being fired from its removable chamber, became too large. This would lead to damage to the inside of the barrel or would even cause the cannonball to get stuck and destroy the *folangji*. This quest to make larger cannon suggests that there was certainly a continuing incentive to develop heavier and more-powerful cannons, and this was realized when in the seventeenth century the *hongyipao*, or "red barbarian cannon," was appropriated from the Dutch and the English. These heavy muzzle-loading cannons seem to have rapidly replaced the heavier *folangji*.[26]

This apparent desire for bigger cannons raises the question why there was no indigenous development of larger pieces before 1550? Certainly, there seems to have been a potential challenge-and-response dynamic possible in the context of siege warfare. In fact, there is evidence that the Chinese indeed developed their own heavier ordnance independently of Portuguese influence, which will be dealt with in more detail later on. One important reason that has probably led modern scholars to mostly ignore this development is the fact that only a few military manuals appeared in the period up to 1550. When a big boom in printing press activity in China around that time likely facilitated the appearance of a dearth of new manuals in the mid sixteenth century, Portuguese cannons were already well known and had already been integrated into military theory and praxis.[27] Furthermore, modern scholarship has focused almost exclusively on the transfer processes of European weapons to China, often ignoring indigenous dynamics.

Siege warfare and the efflorescence of indigenous Chinese cannon designs

Chinese historian Wang Zhaochun identified a new large design that emerged before the middle of the sixteenth century. This was the *jiangjunpao* ("general cannon"), an example of which was unearthed near present-day Runan, in the south of Henan Province. The unearthed example weighs 348 kilograms and was probably meant for city defence. Runan cannot exactly be considered to be located in the southern part of the empire, but it was certainly not directly at the northern frontier, bordering the steppe, either. A case can be made that this cannon was meant to defend the city against internal rebellions, not external enemies. The piece dates from the Zhengde emperor's reign (r. 1505–21), a time when this area was indeed ravaged by the northern rebellion (1509–12) of the outlaw brothers Liu Liu and Liu Qi (both ?–1512). Wang Zhaochun cites He Rubin's *Bing lu*'s mentioning that three hundred of these heavier artillery pieces were manufactured in 1465, although Wang Zhaochun doesn't specify for what purpose they should be used. He Rubin mentions this information in the context of an entry about the *dajiangjunchong*, or "great general gun," indicating that Wang Zhaochun considers this larger later weapon a further development of the late-fifteenth-century *jiangjunpao*, which, given the similarity in names, is not an unreasonable assumption. *Chong* and *pao* could still be used interchangeably at this time to indicate a cannon.[28]

The *jiangjunpao* grew in size and became the *dajiangjunpao*, or "great general cannon." In both He Rubin's manual and a manual from 1632, it was depicted as a much longer version of the excavated *jiangjunpao*: a muzzle-loading cannon with several hoops around the barrel, presumably for added security against heat ruptures.[29] According to Wang Zhaochun, it could weigh up to 600 kilograms, significantly heavier than its likely predecessor.[30] When this larger weapon first entered service is hard to ascertain. An entry in a Chinese online encyclopaedia mentions 1530 as the year production started, but unfortunately, it does not provide a source for the information.[31] The weapon is mentioned in Qi Jiguang's military manual *Ji xiao xinshu*, dating from 1560, suggesting the possibility the *daijiangjunpao* could have emerged during the first half of the sixteenth century. Significantly, the cannon is mentioned in Qi's manual in the context of city defence.[32] The manual from 1632 mentions that the gun could be as heavy as 500 to 600 catties (300 to 360 kilograms) but claims that by the time the manual was written, it weighed in the range of only 250 to 260 catties (approximately 155 kilograms). It could be both installed on city gates and installed on a cart for usage in the field.[33]

Joseph Needham describes it as a heavier iron cannon with several hoops along the barrel. He extensively quotes He Rubin's entry on the *dajiangjunchong*, but as we shall see, He Rubin's information and Needham's translation confuse several issues related to the design of the *dajiangjunpao*. However, clearing up these issues reveals interesting details about the interaction of Chinese and Portuguese cannon design philosophies:

> Among the large firearms there is none that is greater than the "great general gun." Its barrel (used to) weigh 150 catties [90 kilograms], and was attached to a stand made of bronze weighing 1000 catties [600 kilograms]. It looked rather like the *fo-lang-chi* [*folangji*] cannon. Yeh Mêng-Hsiung [Ye Mengxiong] changed the weight of the gun to 250 catties [150 kilograms] and doubled its length to 6 feet [1.82 metres], but eliminated the stand, and now it is placed on a carriage with wheels. When fired it has a range of 800 paces

[around 1200 metres]. A large lead shell weighing 7 catties [4.2 kilograms] is called a "grandfather shell" (*kung*) [*gong*] and the next shell of medium size weighing 3 catties [1.8 kilograms] is a "son shell" (*tzu*) [*zi*], while a smaller shell weighing 1 catty [around 600 grams] is a "grandson shell" (*sun*). . . . If thousands, or tens of thousands, of (this weapon) were placed in position along the frontiers, and every one of them manned by soldiers well trained to use them, then (we should be) invincible. This weapon is indeed the ulti-mate among all firearms. At first its heavy weight caused some doubt as to whether or not it was too cumbersome; but if it is transported on its carriage then it is suitable, irrespective of height, distance or difficulty of terrain. . . . During the 1st year of the Chhêng-Hua [Chenghua] reign-period (+ 1465) 300 different "great general (guns)" were manufactured and 500 carriages for cannon were made.[34]

First of all, He Rubin describes a rather lighter cannon than would be expected on the basis of Wang Zhaochun's figures and on the basis of the information from the 1632 military manual, especially because He Rubin explicitly assigns the cannon to the same lineage as the pieces manufactured in 1465. According to Wang Zhao-chun, during the early sixteenth century, the smaller ancestors of these weapons could already weigh in excess of 300 kilograms. That He Rubin would consider a comparatively light cannon of around 90 to 150 kilograms to be the "ultimate among all firearms" seems strange. He Rubin seems to be mixing different cannon designs in his description. There is also the issue of the cannon's being described as looking like a *folangji*. Going by the accompanying illustration in He Rubin's manual, the muzzle-loading *dajiangjunchong* with multiple hoops looks easily distin-guishable from the breech-loading *folangji* with its smooth barrel. Finally, a cannon of 90 kilograms requiring a bronze stand of over 600 kilograms seems excessive and wasteful. Bronze was more expensive than iron, and surely cheaper means of installing a cannon that size could have been devised. According to the source text, Needham clearly made a few translation mistakes, ones that further muddle He Rubin's already-confusing account. The character that Needham translates as "stand" can be translated as "mother." The breech-loading *folangji* and its remov-able chamber were in Chinese sources of the time often designated as "mother" and "child," respectively. Although the chamber is not denoted as "child" here, but rather as a body (*shen*), He Rubin seems to be instead describing a breech-loading cannon here. This suspicion is further confirmed when, upon closer examina-tion, He Rubin does not claim that the cannon "looked" like the *folangji*. A more exact translation would be that the cannon was *zhuang fa*, "loaded and fired," like a *folangji*.[35]

Here He Rubin is most likely describing the *wudidajiangjunpao*, or "invincible great general cannon." A description of this weapon turns up in one of Qi Jiguang's later manuals, the *Lianbing shi ji* (*Practical Record of Training Soldiers*), published in 1571. This manual was based on his experience in fighting nomad Mongols along the northern frontier. Qi Jiguang narrates in his manual that in the past heavy and long pieces of around 1,000 catties/600 kilograms, like the *dajiangjunpao* and the *fagong*, were too unwieldy in battle against the swift-moving Mongols. They needed at least ten men to move into position. In urgent situations, preparing the cannon for a sufficiently powerful discharge was difficult, and the soldiers did not dare add gunpowder directly to the warm cannon after it was fired. At the same time, the killing power of handheld firearms to hold off Mongol-mounted assaults was deemed too slight. The solution was the *wudidajiangjunpao*, a hybrid design converting the *dajiangjunpao* into a breech loader. It was installed on a carriage, which could be handled by three to four men, and it came with three chambers. These could, of course, be loaded correctly in all tranquillity before battle commenced. They could be loaded with cannonballs, able to penetrate walls, or shrapnel could be loaded for use against concentrated enemies. An even later manual by Qi Jiguang, cited by historian Feng Zhenyu, states that the weight of the cannon was 1050 catties (630 kilograms), which corresponds closely with He Rubin's description of the weapon's altogether weighing 1150 catties (690 kilograms). Feng Zhenyu also claims that Qi Jiguang was responsible for the innovation, but in the military commander's writings, he does not seem to claim the weapon to be his brainchild.[36] This episode shows that the Portuguese weapons did not automatically supplant Chinese designs but were instead appropriated and combined in creative ways.[37]

This interpretation of He Rubin's description is further corroborated when we connect it with the information that civil official Ye Mengxiong (1531–97) modified the "child" and dispensed with the "mother," to make the chamber a standalone cannon.[38] Thanks to an informative blogpost about Ye Mengxiong's contribution to cannon designs on the weblog *Great Ming Military*, I was directed to yet another Chinese military treatise, the *Deng tan bi jiu* (*Necessary Investigations for Ascending the Platform*).[39] This was written by military officer Wang Minghe (fl. 1584) and published in 1599.[40] In this manual, Wang Minghe narrates the story of Ye Mengxiong's modifying a breech-loading *dajiangjun* by discarding the "mother" barrel and enlarging the chamber to fire the three kinds of ammunition that He Rubin described. The new cannon was named *shenchong*, or "divine gun." The descriptions of the weights of the cannons also completely match He Rubin's account. The performance characteristics and the positive evaluation of the cannon as the ultimate artillery against barbarians seem to also have been copied in full from Wang Minghe's account.[41] He Rubin had conflated all the information pertaining to the *dajiangjun* cannon lineage in one entry, hence leading to the confusion. This leaves the issue of the enlarged chamber of the 150-kilogram *wudidajiangjunpao's* receiving such a positive evaluation. Unfortunately, the manual does not provide more information that could explain why this alteration by Ye Mengxiong created such a powerful cannon, despite dispensing with a "mother" barrel.

There are thus strong indications that the Chinese were already moving towards heavier ordnance independent of Portuguese influence and that the initial driver of this innovation was siege warfare in the context of inland armed conflicts. Can we discern a similar pattern of intrastate warfare's driving the appropriation of

Portuguese cannons, and could they have had a revolutionary impact on Chinese siege warfare, hitherto unnoticed?

Intrastate warfare as a driver of military innovation

That the *berço* and the *falcão* were initially probably copied to deal with the Portuguese maritime threat would not raise many eyebrows. Soon after the *berço* was appropriated as the *folangji*, civil official Wang Hong (1466–1535) championed it as a weapon to be deployed against the Mongols along the northern frontier.[42] The *folangji* and *fagong* would also later be advocated to be used as ship-board ordnance by anti-Wokou generals Qi Jiguang and Yu Dayou (1503–79).[43] The high rate of fire that the *folangji* was able to sustain no doubt made it a useful addition in defending the empire against highly mobile nomad enemies. The *fagong*, as we have seen, was considered to be too powerful to be easily adapted to seaborne service. Nevertheless, the two military treatises of Tang Shunzhi and his erstwhile fellow student and friend Zheng Ruozeng surprisingly dwell extensively on the cannons' advantages during sieges, a type of warfare that the Mongols usually did not engage in.[44] Furthermore, Chinese officials would be hard-pressed to find a Mongol wall to breach with their recently acquired *fagong*. These two types of cannon were, seemingly, praised for their qualities in the context of land-based warfare in the southeastern reaches of the Ming Empire. Can we draw a tentative conclusion from these, admittedly small, snippets of information that the conditions of warfare in this part of the empire had somehow changed to favour renewed innovation in the art of siege warfare?

As a tentative answer, I propose that the traditional maritime lens through which historians have viewed the Wokou raids of the mid-sixteenth century still often obscures the significant connections between the maritime disturbances and incidences of inland armed uprisings. As alluded to earlier, the Wokou crisis of the 1550s and 1560s was not just a maritime frontier conflict. It had a significant inland component as well, and many of the resulting military confrontations were land-based, including sieges. The Wokou were a multi-ethnic group of Japanese, Chinese, Ryukyuan, and even Portuguese traders-cum-pirates. However, their main component seems to have consisted of coastal Chinese, who were dependent on maritime trade. They had been deprived by Ming court-ordered prohibitions on maritime trade from legally tending to their livelihoods. These had been issued in the 1520s in response to unruly Japanese and Portuguese traders but were consistently enforced only in the 1550s, in effect criminalizing important sections of the coastal population and giving them an incentive to turn to piracy, smuggling, and inland raiding.[45]

During these raids, Wokou bands would sometimes resort to laying siege to cities by using advanced weaponry. In 1556, for example, Ming civil official Ruan E (1509–67) and his troops were besieged in Tongxiang, Zhejiang, and the Wokou unsuccessfully attacked the city walls with *folangji* cannons and other Portuguese firearms.[46] On another occasion, in 1561, Wokou bandits even moved as far inland as the southern landlocked province of Jiangxi.[47] That the Wokou crisis was also closely entangled with other societal upheavals with less-obvious ties to maritime trade is showcased by the organized armed groups operating on both sides of the conflict. For example, incidences of Wokou incursions often occurred simultaneously with uprisings of so-called *shankou*, or "mountain bandits." They were prevalent in Fujian in the late 1550s, before eventually being put down by Qi Jiguang.[48] As for Qi Jiguang, he commanded militia forces whom he recruited in Zhejiang from among a group of miners in Yiwu County. This militia actually predated Qi Jiguang's recruitment drive, as it was originally formed on local initiative to defend the community's mines against a rival group of miners who wanted to wrest control of them away from Yiwu County.[49]

The land-based dynamic of warfare probably led to many incidences of siege warfare. Although exact statistics of the number of sieges are lacking, the contents of the *Chou hai tu bian* underlines the importance of this type of armed confrontation. The manual was a huge collaborative project of the civil and military elites involved in the anti-Wokou campaign and included their opinions on a variety of military affairs. The chapter on city defence is by far the largest and most comprehensive in size and content.

The use of Portuguese-derived cannons almost certainly played into this dynamic. Take, for example, the potential of the larger cannon in changing the parameters of the way sieges were conducted on both the offensive and defensive. As in Europe, cannons could have increased the size of besieging armies, because their longer ranges, in comparison with earlier catapults and crossbows, necessitated siege lines further away from the city walls. This increased the dimensions of the killing field that an attacker had to cross to reach the city walls. On the other hand, the attackers now also had weapons with which they could bombard secondary defensive fortifications from farther away.[50] The cannon could have set off a round in the evolution of secondary fortifications and armour design, a topic that awaits further exploration. The evidence from the military manuals does suggest that larger cannons were by the mid-sixteenth century finally replacing catapults and large crossbows as the main weapon for destroying enemy siege equipment and secondary fortifications. However, the new cannons presumably did not impact the size and length of the city walls already in place. Besieging armies already needed to be quite large in the Chinese context, even before the discovery of gunpowder, because the existence of large walled cities similarly predated the chemical mixture.

In fact, a case can be made that armies could have been reduced in size, because of the use of firearms. Catapults and big crossbows required crowds of men and their muscle power to operate during sieges, but a cannon needed at most a crew of ten and even less when the weapon did not need repositioning during battle. These weapons were thus huge labour-saving devices that could have led to the reduction in size of armies or the assignment of people to other roles during sieges. Moreover, more cannons could be deployed than catapults and with the same available workforce, increasing firepower significantly. This could have had an impact on cost as well: these cannons would have been much cheaper to operate.

On the other hand, they were presumably more expensive to manufacture than big crossbows and catapults, and the consumption of gunpowder needs to be factored in as well. Unfortunately, at present, we lack the statistical analyses and price comparisons to assess the impact of the new cannons on Chinese siege warfare, but they theoretically had a significant effect on the financial cost and human labour involved in sieges.

For several technical reasons, therefore, the introduction of larger cannons could have led to significant changes in Chinese siege warfare, perhaps even earning the label "revolutionary." Arguably, intrastate competition could be an important driver of military innovation in China, and the pre-eminence of the interstate competition model should be reconsidered. After all, the *dajiangjunpao* apparently arose in the context of internal rebellions, and the Portuguese-derived cannons were greatly appreciated during the Wokou incursions.

However, addressing Andrade's argument that a lack of warfare of any kind stunted the growth of Chinese cannons from 1450 to 1550 is more complicated. This century saw fewer armed conflicts, but those that occurred were mostly internal in nature. However, if we simultaneously push the boundaries of this period slightly back into the past to 1448 and forward almost two decades to 1568, another dynamic comes into focus. In 1448, a big peasant rebellion led by Deng Miaoqi (d. 1449) broke out in the southern province of Fujian, and 1568 more or less coincided with the end of the Wokou threat.[51] Within this expanded timeframe, we can observe a long-term shift of the main military challenge to the empire towards internal armed conflicts, especially in the southern, more urbanized, half of the empire. Therefore, the Wokou crisis certainly seems to have been a continuation of a pre-existing trend towards the emergence of sustained inland campaigns and sieges, relying on infantry and artillery.[52]

As Andrade notes, warfare in the south tended to resemble European patterns more closely.[53] These conditions can help explain the enthusiastic adoption of Portuguese cannons, the simultaneous innovations in indigenous cannon designs, and their use during siege warfare. However, the political conditions in the southeast of the empire also provide ample grounds for positing potential limits on the impact of Portuguese cannons on Chinese siege warfare.

The first was the eventual winding down of the violence in the south at the end of the 1560s. The main ringleaders of the Wokou were defeated, the maritime trade prohibitions were relaxed, and tranquillity returned for more than half a century. During this time, it is doubtful there was much incentive to develop siege artillery, city defences, and the armour protection of both the attacking and defending forces.

A second reason is related to the costs of military innovation and the extent of state intervention to finance it. A main contention of Parker's iteration of the Military Revolution is that new siege artillery and responses in fortification designs drove up the costs of warfare for the state and stimulated the latter's expansion. In the case of the Ming Empire's response to internal rebellions, however, the state seems to have relied on the localities to furnish the necessary funds and resources for city defence. The available research on this topic is too scant to make detailed comparisons to early modern European states, but seemingly, the Ming generally invested in military defences only in cases of national emergencies. These emergencies were recognized as such generally only if they occurred at the northern frontier. Even in the case of the Wokou crisis, most of the funding and the logistics were left to local governmental and voluntary societal initiatives.[54] In contrast, a European polity like the Dutch Republic invested heavily in defensive military infrastructure after 1600, although in this case, local governing bodies and associations of citizens were asked to contribute as well.[55]

In the case of Ming China, the internal political context of rebellions would probably have acted as a brake on military innovations in comparison with the interstate competition dynamic of early modern Europe. Any incidence of interstate war would have counted as a national emergency for the involved polities, whereas for Ming China, these emergencies occurred mostly along the northern frontier where incidences of siege warfare were mostly absent. Moreover, the reliance on local initiatives might explain the continued depiction of the catapult as a viable weapon system beyond antiquarian curiosity in the military treatises dating from the mid-sixteenth century. The Ming Empire generally tried to keep the knowledge of firearms secret and their production restricted to the managerial oversight of its officials. This included newer Portuguese-derived weapons like the *folangji*.[56] On the other hand, Kenneth Chase argues that the proliferation of military treatises describing these weapons in detail probably meant that this policy became increasingly a dead letter in the course of the sixteenth century.[57] Nevertheless, the highly fluid and unpredictable flow of the Wokou raids and the ad hoc local military preparations necessary to counter them probably impeded the quick and consistent manufacture of relatively complicated artillery designs.

Wooden catapults, on the other hand, had been a staple of Chinese siege warfare for centuries, did not require complex metallurgical skills, and could therefore be more easily improvised by financially hamstrung local officials. Moreover, as Thomas Allsen stated, "the technology of siege machines made use of the relatively 'mobile' skills of the carpenter, while that of cannon required those of the far more stationary forger or founder."[58] Catapults would also be easier to use for untrained local peasant militia, who would be recruited ad hoc as city defenders.[59] Perhaps for this reason and the added advantage of economizing on gunpowder, eminently practical-minded General Qi Jiguang included a description of a simplified catapult design for city defence in his *Ji xiao xinshu*.[60] Indeed, a military manual describing a siege in as late as 1640 mentioned the use of wooden catapults by the defenders of Neijiang in Sichuan Province.[61] Finally, catapults could sometimes reach targets that *folangji*, *fagong*, and *dajiangjunpao* could not, because the former lobbed their projectiles in an arch-like trajectory. As such, larger cannon were a more suitable replacement for the large crossbows than they were for the catapults.

Conclusion

As so often is the case in the still-understudied field of Chinese military history, we lack key research and statistical surveys of available primary sources to establish the changing nature of military logistics and upkeep, resource extraction, weapon production in relation to the impact of cannon development in the context of sieges. This chapter attempts to draw some tentative conclusions about this impact on the basis of military theoretical writings, though they are writings by men who were known to be involved in the practical side of the military business as well. These writings offer the first extensive glimpse into the usage of cannons since the beginning of the Ming dynasty and offer insight into the nature of the integration of Portuguese-derived ordnance into Chinese warfare in the mid-sixteenth century. In the context of siege warfare, the Portuguese weapons did not focus on enemy combatants exclusively anymore, as had been the case earlier with their Chinese predecessors. Instead, they were used also to destroy armoured and unarmoured enemy equipment and secondary fortifications. Consequently, the existence of massive walls did not have to be an impediment to the development of cannon artillery in the Chinese context. This is underlined by the fact that Chinese cannons were indeed getting bigger and heavier long before the Portuguese technology reached Asia, as can be seen from the existence of the *dajiangjunpao*-lineage of iron cannons. By the mid-sixteenth century, both Chinese and Portuguese designs, as well as their hybrid offspring, had become central to siege warfare as the heaviest weapons involved and had mostly replaced older forms of heavy siege artillery. The Portuguese weapons, however, did not kickstart the trend towards heavier cannons; they rather seem to have accelerated existing indigenous developments and provided a solution for a pre-existing Chinese need for more powerful cannons. There are tantalizing clues that this need arose in a context of intrastate warfare, not interstate war, which is seen by many scholars as the major driver of European military innovation. The *dajiangjunpao* probably found use as a city defence weapon in the context of internal rebellions of the early sixteenth century, and the Portuguese weapons were praised – albeit not exclusively – in the context of siege warfare against the Wokou. They were, in effect, segments of the economically disenfranchised Chinese coastal population's rebelling against the central government. Siege warfare was an important aspect of the conflict with the Wokou.

Could we then perhaps consider intrastate warfare as a driver of military innovation in the case of China? With respect to sieges and the weaponry involved, we can argue that internal conflicts drove military innovations. However, institutional factors probably held these innovations back from becoming revolutionary in character. Internal conflicts never received the same kind of central government attention and support as the northern frontier bordering the steppes did. Instead, ad hoc local initiatives and improvisation were key ingredients of the military response to internal uprisings, contributing to the survival of older, simpler weapons like the catapult. They also led to interesting innovations, including Qi Jiguang's infantry training regime and tactics, but their staying power and institutional continuity after the Wokou threat had subsided was probably subject to severe restrictions. Furthermore, we know little about how the local government response to internal conflicts was funded or whether these financial measures stayed in place afterwards. A lack of government institutional continuity also characterized the opposition.

The Wokou were loosely organized in several bands, and individually, they did not last longer than a decade at most. Consequently, they offered only limited institutional stability and continuity in which military innovations could take place and be perpetuated. European states were more durable and provided a more stable resource base. Nevertheless, as drivers of Chinese military innovation, intrastate wars need to be taken more seriously and should help nuance the Eurocentric focus on interstate conflicts.

Notes

1 This article was conceived and partly written when the author was a recipient of the Freie Universität Berlin–Hebrew University of Jerusalem joint postdoctoral fellowship. At present, the author is a member of the European Research Council's Horizon 2020 project "Aftermath of the East Asian War of 1592–1598," based at the Universitat Autònoma de Barcelona.
2 Geoffrey Parker, *The Military Revolution: Military Innovation and the Rise of the West, 1500–1800* (Cambridge: Cambridge University Press, 1995), 6–44.
3 Peter A. Lorge, *The Asian Military Revolution: From Gunpowder to the Bomb* (Cambridge: Cambridge University Press, 2007), 1–2.
4 Tonio Andrade, *The Gunpowder Age: China, Military Innovation, and the Rise of the West in World History* (Princeton, NJ: Princeton University Press, 2016), 15–28, 64–72, 96–102, 107–14, 135–43, 298; Lorge, *The Asian Military Revolution*, 1–2.
5 Andrade, *The Gunpowder Age*, 135–43; Kenneth Chase, *Firearms: A Global History to 1700* (Cambridge: Cambridge University Press, 2003), 142–43; Herbert Franke, "Siege and Defense of Towns in Medieval China," in *Chinese Ways in Warfare*, ed. Frank A. Kierman (Cambridge, MA: Harvard University Press, 1974), 172.
6 Zheng Cheng 郑诚, "Fagong kao – 16 shiji chuan Hua de Oushi qianzhuang huopao jiqi yanbian" [发熕考 – 16 世纪传华的欧式前装火炮及其演变], *Ziran kexueshi yanjiu* [自然科学史研究] 32, no. 4 (2013): 507–8.
7 Xu Baolin 许保林, *Zhongguo bingshu tonglan* [中国兵书通览] (北京: 解放军出版社, 1990), 399–402.
8 Tang Shunzhi 唐顺之, "Wu bian (Before 1560)" 武编 (Before 1560), in *Chuangshi cangshu – ziku – bingshu* [传世藏书-子库-兵书], ed. Zhang Xinqi 张新奇 (海南: 海南国际新闻出版中心, 1995), 1243.
9 By *secondary fortification*, I mean any kind of defensive architecture besides the primary city or town wall, including the improvised field fortifications of besieging forces. These could also be mounted on top of the primary wall.
10 Tang, "Wu bian (Before 1560)," 1243.
11 Cheng Ziyi 程子颐, "Wubei yao lüe shisi juan (1632)" [武備要畧十四卷 (1632)], in *Siku jin hui shu congkan: Zibu; di ershiba ce muci* [四庫禁燬書叢刊. 子部; 第二十八册目次] (北京: 北京出版社, 2000), 33.
12 Feng Zhenyu 冯震宇, "Lun folangji zai Mingdai de bentuhua" [论佛郎机在明代的本土化], *Ziran bianzhengfa tongxun* [自然辨证法通讯] 34, no. 3 (2012): 58–59.
13 Tang, "Wu bian (Before 1560)," 1243.
14 Kai Filipiak, *Krieg, Staat und Militär in der Ming-Zeit (1368–1644): Auswirkungen militärischer und bewaffneter Konflikte auf Machtpolitik und Herrschaftsapparat der Ming-Dynastie* (Wiesbaden: Harrassowitz Verlag, 2008), 256–57.
15 Zheng Ruozeng 鄭若曾, *Chou hai tu bian (1562)* [籌海圖編 (1562)], ed. Li Zhizhong 李致忠 (北京: 中華書局, 2007), 901.
16 Qi Jiguang 戚继光, "Ji xiao xinshu (1560)" [纪效新书 (1560)], in *Chuangshi cangshu – ziku – bingshu* [传世藏书-子库-兵书], ed. Zhang Xinqi 张新奇 (海南: 海南国际新闻出版中心, 1995), 1083.

17 Feng, "Lun folangji zai Mingdai de bentuhua," 58.

18 Zheng, *Chou hai tu bian (1562)*, 899–900.

19 Zhou Weiqiang 周维强, *Folangjichong zai Zhongguo* [佛朗机铳在中国] (北京: 社会科学文献出版社, 2013), 86.

20 Zheng, "Fagong kao – 16 shiji chuan Hua de Oushi qianzhuang huopao jiqi yanbian," 509.

21 Zheng, *Chou haitubian (1562)*, 899–903.

22 Chase, *Firearms*, 143.

23 Vitor Luís Gaspar Rodrigues, "Armas e Equipamentos de Guerra Portugueses no Oriente nas Primeiras Décadas de Quinhentos," *Revista de Cultura* 26 (2008): 43–49; Zheng, "Fagong kao – 16 shiji chuan Hua de Oushi qianzhuang huopao jiqi yanbian," 507–8.

24 Zheng, "Fagong kao – 16 shiji chuan Hua de Oushi qianzhuang huopao jiqi yanbian," 507–8.

25 He Rubin 何汝賓, "Bing lu (1606)" [兵錄 (1606)], in *Siku jin hui shu congkan: Zibu; di jiu ce muci* [四庫禁燬書叢刊. 子部; 第九冊目次] (北京: 北京出版社, 2000), 660; See, for example Zhao Fengxiang 赵凤翔, "Mingdai folangjichong hexin jishu tezheng jiqi zhuanbian yanjiu" [明代佛郎机铳核心技术特征及其转变研究], *Ziran bianzhengfa tongxun* [自然辩证法通讯] 39, no. 3 (2017): 32.

26 Andrade, *The Gunpowder Age*, 197–98; Zhao, "Mingdai folangjichong hexin jishu tezheng jiqi zhuanbian yanjiu," 36–37.

27 Timothy Robert Clifford, "The Rules of Prose in Sixteenth-Century China: Tang Shunzhi (1507–1560) as an Anthologist," *East Asian Publishing and Society* 8, no. 2 (2018): 153.

28 John W. Dardess, *Ming China, 1368–1644: A Concise History of a Resilient Empire* (Lanham: Rowman & Littlefield Publishers, Inc., 2012), 120–23; Wang Zhaochun 王兆春, *Zhongguo huoqi shi* [中国火器史] (北京: 军事科学出版社, 1991), 99–100.

29 Cheng, "Wubei yao lüe shisi juan (1632)," 30; He, "Bing lu (1606)," 662.

30 Wang, *Zhongguo huoqi shi*, 163–64.

31 Anonymous, "Dajiangjunpao" [大将军炮, Encyclopaedia], *Baike Baidu* (blog), 2019, https://baike.baidu.com/item/%E5%A4%A7%E5%B0%86%E5%86%9B%E7%82%AE.

32 Qi, "Ji xiao xinshu (1560)," 1086.

33 Cheng, "Wubei yao lüe shisi juan (1632)," 30.

34 Joseph Needham et al., *Science and Civilization in China. Volume 5: Chemistry and Chemical Technology. Part 7: Military Technology: The Gunpowder Epic* (Cambridge: Cambridge University Press, 1986), 330–37.

35 He, "Bing lu (1606)," 662.

36 Feng, "Lun folangji zai Mingdai de bentuhua," 60–61; Qi Jiguang 戚继光, "Lianbing shi ji (1571)" [练兵实纪 (1571)], in *Chuangshi cangshu – ziku – bingshu* [传世藏书-子库-兵书], ed. Zhang Xinqi 张新奇 (海南: 海南国际新闻出版中心, 1995), 1191–92.

37 Chase, *Firearms*, 145.

38 Ye Mengxiong was a civil official with an interest in military affairs; see Kathleen Ryor, "Wen and Wu in Elite Cultural Practices During the Late Ming," in *Military Culture in Imperial China*, ed. Nicola Di Cosmo (Cambridge, MA: Harvard University Press, 2009), 224, 367.

39 Chunqiu Zhanguo 春秋戰國, "Ye Meng Xiong's Cannons," *Great Ming Military* (blog), 17 April 2015, http://greatmingmilitary.blogspot.com/2015/04/ye-meng-xiongs-cannons.html.

40 Wang Minghe 王鸣鹤, "Deng tan bi jiu (1599)" [登坛必究 (1599)], in *Zhongguo bingshu jicheng* [中国兵书集成], vol. 20–24 (北京: 解放军出版社, 1990), 361–68.

41 Ibid., 3907–8.

42 Andrade, *The Gunpowder Age*, 124–25.

43 Feng, "Lun folangji zai Mingdai de bentuhua," 61; Zheng, "Fagongkao – 16 shiji chuan Hua de Oushi qianzhuang huopao jiqi yanbian," 510; Zhou, *Folangjichong zai Zhongguo*, 102.

44 Chase, *Firearms*, 161.

45 For a recent summary and reassessment of the debate surrounding the Wokou, see Ivy Maria Lim, "From Haijin to Kaihai: The Jiajing Court's Search for a Modus Operandi Along the South-Eastern Coast (1522–1567)," *Journal of the British Association for Chinese Studies* 2 (2013): 1–26.

46 Ivy Maria Lim, *Lineage Society on the Southeastern Coast of China: The Impact of Japanese Piracy in the Sixteenth Century* (Amherst: Cambria Press, 2010), 87.

47 James Ferguson Millinger, "Ch'i Chi-Kuang Chinese Military Official: A Study of Civil-Military Roles and Relations in the Career of a Sixteenth Century Warrior, Reformer, and Hero" (PhD diss., Yale University, New Haven, CT, 1968), 46–47.

48 Yonghua Liu, "The World of Rituals: Masters of Ceremonies (Lisheng), Ancestral Cults, Community Compacts, and Local Temples in Late Imperial Sibao, Fujian" (PhD diss., McGill University, Montreal, 2003), 48.

49 Thomas G. Nimick, "Ch'i Chi-Kuang and I-Wu County," *Ming Studies* 1 (1995): 17–19.

50 Herbert Franke speculates that battle tactics during siege warfare had to be adapted to the much longer range of the new cannons; see Franke, "Siege and Defense of Towns in Medieval China," 172. He states that *folangji* could have an effective range of up to 1 *li*, or around 600 metres.

51 See Kai Filipiak, "Der Bauernaufstand des Deng Maoqi 1448/1449 als Audrück einer Zäsur in der Geschichte der Ming-Dynastie," *Monumenta Serica* 54 (2006): 119–48.

52 Kai Filipiak, "'Saving Lives' – Lü Kun's Manual on City Defense," *Journal of Chinese Military History* 1 (2012): 139–40; James W. Tong, *Disorder under Heaven: Collective Violence in the Ming Dynasty* (Stanford, CA: Stanford University Press, 1991), 50, 52, 63.

53 Andrade, *The Gunpowder Age*, 112.

54 For a detailed analysis of the responsibilities of local civil officials for organizing the defence of cities in the late sixteenth century, see Filipiak, "'Saving Lives'"; Kenneth M. Swope, "Clearing the Fields and Strengthening the Walls: Defending Small Cities in Late Ming China," in *Secondary Cities and Urban Networking in the Indian Ocean Realm, c. 1400–1800*, ed. Kenneth R. Hall (Lanham: Lexington Books, 2008), 129–30, 132–33.

55 Mahinder S. Kingra, "The Trace Italienne and the Military Revolution During the Eighty Years' War, 1567–1648," *The Journal of Military History* 57, no. 3 (1993): 440–41; Geoffrey Parker, "In Defense of the Military Revolution," in *The Military Revolution Debate: Readings on the Military Transformation of Early Modern Europe*, ed. Clifford J. Rogers (Boulder, CO: Westview Press, 1995), 352–53.

56 Zhou, *Folangjichong zai Zhongguo*, 91.

57 Chase, *Firearms*, 151–53.

58 Thomas T. Allsen, "The Circulation of Military Technology in the Mongolian Empire," in *Warfare in Inner Asian History (500–1800)*, ed. Nicola Di Cosmo (Leiden: Brill, 2002), 272.

59 Swope, "Clearing the Fields and Strengthening the Walls," 134–35.

60 Qi, "Ji xiao xinshu (1560)," 1059–60.

61 Swope, "Clearing the Fields and Strengthening the Walls," 142–43.

13

THE MILITARY REVOLUTION IN GLOBAL HISTORY

East Asian perspectives

Tonio Andrade

Introduction

Is the military revolution a useful paradigm for global history? The model was developed primarily in a European context, and scholars have suggested that it's an "artificial construct" that "expresses Eurocentric assumptions as opposed to being based in historical proof."[1] This chapter assesses the military revolution model in light of evidence from East Asia, arguing that although that evidence does present challenges, the model remains useful and robust because it helps focus our comparisons of Europe and East Asia, drawing scholarly attention to phenomena such as infantry drills, fortification techniques, and state centralization. It also draws our attention to the vital role that sustained interstate warfare plays in stimulating military and social innovation and, perhaps paradoxically, intercultural adoption. Military revolution theorists have focused on interstate warfare in Europe, but sustained levels of warfare between competing states also took place in other areas, and when we turn our attention to various "warring states" periods in East Asia, we find that levels of military innovation correspond with levels of warfare. Indeed, it may even make sense to speak of military revolution as a global process, which began in East Asia during the warlike 1100s, 1200s, and mid 1300s and redounded to Europe in the 1300s and 1400s, where the process of military innovation accelerated and then ramified thence throughout the rest of the world, as Europeans brought their technologies and techniques to colonies and trading posts. Throughout this period, gun-based warfare stimulated the cross-cultural transfer of military technologies and techniques in many parts of the world, particularly during times of greater sustained warfare. The Portuguese maritime empire played a key role in this process.

What is the Military Revolution? A historiographical reconnaissance

What do we mean by "military revolution"? There are nearly as many variants of the military revolution thesis as there are scholars who discuss it, but most of these variants contain some version of the same core argument: in Europe during some period between 1300 and 1800, there took place momentous military changes, which affected not just military affairs but also society and politics more generally. These changes were associated with the ever-increasing use of gunpowder weapons, especially guns. Beyond this general framework, there is little agreement. Scholars disagree about the timing, the causation, and even many of the particular phenomena themselves.

The idea that gunpowder caused deep changes in European society, politics, and culture has deep roots, going back to Francis Bacon, with variants of the idea espoused by Adam Smith and Karl Marx, among others.[2] The military revolution model in its current form, however, was first introduced by historian Michael Roberts (1908–96), whose 1955 inaugural lecture at Queen's University in Belfast, Ireland, was titled "The Military Revolution: 1560–1660."[3] It was published the following year and might not have had much influence if not for Sir George Clark, who lauded it in his seminal book *War and Society in the Seventeenth Century* (1958), helping establish Roberts's military revolution concept as part of the canon of early modern European history.[4]

Roberts focused on tactics, arguing that the spread of firearms – primarily muskets – led to new types of infantry formations. Previously, infantry units tended to march in thick squares, such as the famous Spanish tercio or the Swiss pike square. The spread of firearms, on the other hand, selected for formations that spread soldiers out in wider and thinner lines, because such formations allowed more gunners to shoot at a time and thereby concentrate fire on the enemy.

Key to this development were countermarch techniques. There were many types, but in essence, the practice allowed groups of gunners to compensate for the fact that early guns were slow to load (it could take up to two minutes to reload after firing) by taking turns shooting and loading. In this way, they could keep a constant hail of projectiles flying at the enemy. Generally, the technique called for a soldier to fire, march in good order to the back of their file, and then reload while the next soldier in the file fired, a cycle that they repeated. (The term *file* refers to the row of soldiers in which the soldiers march, with a number of side-by-side files making up the complete formation.) The idea is that the first soldier will be ready to fire again once the rest of his file has fired and he finds himself once again at the front of the line.

The idea seems simple, but it was difficult to implement in practice. For one thing, there were many choices to be made, each of which affected the efficacy of the technique. Once a soldier fires, should he march to the back of his individual file? Or should the soldiers of each file march together to one side or the other and then to the back? Or is it better if they divide in half, one half marching to the left and one to the right? How far apart do the files need to be? How many soldiers should each file contain?

The distance between idea and execution can be glimpsed in the rich records that Dutch armies left during the period that they were working out the details, in the late sixteenth and early seventeenth centuries. These sources have allowed us to reconstruct in detail the birth of the Dutch countermarch technique – which many historians believe to be the first modern European countermarch technique.[5] It was a long process.

Even once the details of the technique had been worked out, one still had to train soldiers to implement it properly, which was far more difficult than one might guess. Plans and intentions tend to dissolve under fire, and it's one thing to understand a plan and another to practice it when someone's shooting at you or cavalrymen are thundering toward you with naked swords. Practice fields rarely look like battlefields, and orders conveyed during battle are rather less clear than orders conveyed in a rehearsal. For this reason, one had to train gunners strictly and obsessively.

This required constant practice, so commanders drilled soldiers regularly, using music: soldiers were supposed to march, fire, and reload in strict rhythm, moving to the beat of drums. Critics made fun of the idea of soldiers' moving in time like dancers. In a letter in which one of the early European champions of the technique described it to his cousin, he asked that it not be shown around too widely "because it may cause and give occasion for people to laugh."[6]

The ridicule was worth it, as an early historian from the Netherlands noted:

> The beginnings were very difficult, and many people felt, because it was all so unusual, that it was odd and ridiculous [*lacherlich*]. They were mocked by the enemy, but with time the great advantages of the practices became clear . . . and eventually they were copied by other nations.[7]

Of course, to train an army day after day, one needs that army to stay together day after day, rather than being disbanded after a war or campaign, as frequently happened in the European medieval period. Therefore, a permanent standing army is likely a precondition for the effective use of firearms in battle.

Alternately, one might argue that firearms exerted selective pressure on governmental forms that could sustain standing armies. Roberts argued that guns haphazardly led to larger and more-permanent armies, which selected for larger and more-centralized state apparatuses. He believed that a key period for this process was the century between 1560 and 1660, primarily in northern Europe and particularly in the Netherlands and Sweden.

Michael Robert's military revolution model was carried forth by Geoffrey Parker. Whereas Roberts focused primarily on Sweden, Parker studied the armies of Habsburg Spain, in its war with the United Provinces of the Netherlands. He found that some of Roberts's arguments didn't jibe with the evidence in his sources. He included these criticisms in a draft of his dissertation, and it turned out that one of his dissertation readers was Roberts himself, which caused Parker some anxiety.[8] But Roberts was generous, advising Parker to develop his critique and publish it as a standalone article.[9] That article eventually became a series of lectures on the Military Revolution, delivered at Cambridge's Trinity College in 1984. The lectures in turn became a book: the seminal *Military Revolution*.[10]

Geoffrey Parker's take on the Military Revolution is different from Roberts's. Although Parker agreed that new firearm tactics were vital – specifically the countermarch (or, as Parker often referred to it, "volley fire") – he places more emphasis on cannons. To him, a key development in European warcraft was the emergence of mobile field artillery, which began to be adopted on a mass scale in the late 1400s and the early 1500s. These cannons made it possible, due to their lightness and power, to quickly direct destructive firepower at medieval walls. Previous cannons were far larger, and although they too could destroy walls, they were much more difficult to transport, and their rate of fire was lower because they took so long to cool. Mobile artillery made it possible for an army to quickly deploy guns against a fortification, changing the balance of military power from defence to offence and making forts and strongholds far more vulnerable than before.

In response, as Parker showed, leaders began building new fortresses. The artillery fortress, or *trace italienne*, is at the heart of Parker's argument. With its thick earth-filled walls and angled bastions, it allowed defenders to create a dense web of crossfire, eliminating the so-called dead zones where attackers could shelter from guns. The *trace italienne* was highly effective, and the balance of power shifted back to defenders.

More importantly for Parker, artillery fortresses caused the cost of warfare to rise. Not only were they expensive to build and garrison, but they were also expensive to capture, as swifter bombardments were replaced by longer sieges. Attackers required larger forces to surround the enemy fortress and drive away reinforcements. These armies also frequently had to remain in position for many months.

Thus, for Parker, the dramatic increase in the size of armies and the expense of war was due less to the tactical revolution that Roberts outlined and more to the revolution in fortification. The artillery fort was the primary driver of the trend towards larger army sizes, which was in turn a driver of state centralization, not to mention fiscal innovations such as those that allowed the Dutch state to borrow at interest to fund its war against the Habsburgs.

There have been major debates about the extent to which Parker was right about this and whether army size was correlated with the spread of the artillery fortress, but for our purposes here, another issue is more significant: the impact of the Military Revolution on European expansion.[11]

Parker's book was subtitled "Military Innovation and the Rise of the West," and his focus on the role of European military prowess in European colonialism is one of the reasons his book was so influential. His thesis is that techniques and technologies that developed during the European military revolution gave Europeans a significant edge beyond Europe, arguing that they help explain how Europeans

managed to conquer thirty-five percent of the world's land by 1800, before indus-
trialization revolutionized travel and warfare.[12]

Parker made three specific arguments. First, he argued that European drilling
practices – in particular the countermarch technique – provided an edge in field
battles: "The combination of drill with the use of firearms to produce volley fire,
perfected through constant practice, proved the mainstay of western warfare – and
the key to western expansion – for the next three centuries."[13] Second, he argued
that the European ship of the line, sturdy and filled with heavy artillery, provided an
advantage on the seas. Third, he argued that the artillery fortress allowed Europeans
to effectively defend land against their enemies, both on the borders of Europe,
where they helped stop the "Islamic tide," and overseas, where they allowed Europeans to create enduring coastal footholds, which gave them local power, attracting
alliances and traders:

> The invention and diffusion of the "Italian style" of fortification thus repre-
> sented an important step in the West's continuing – perhaps unique – ability
> to make the most of its smaller resources in order, first, to hold its own and,
> later, to expand to global dominance.[14]

Parker's model for the Military Revolution has been extremely influential, generating debate and inspiring new scholarship. Much of the debate has centred on
the timing. For instance, Jeremy Black has argued that the most revolutionary
aspects of the military transformation of Europe took place later than Parker argues:
1660–1710, when, Black argues, tactics changed most dramatically.[15] Black has also
suggested that the Military Revolution is not an effective explanation for European
expansion, because warfare is quite context dependent: in many circumstances,
European techniques offered little help.[16]

In a more satisfying critique, Clifford Rogers argued that there were five separate military revolutions:[17]

(1) an infantry revolution in the fourteenth century;
(2) an artillery revolution in the fifteenth century;
(3) a fortifications revolution in the sixteenth century;
(4) a fire weapons revolution between 1580 and 1630;
(5) a dramatic increase in the size of European armies between 1650 and 1715.

There are major debates about when and why army sizes increased. And there
are significant debates about causation: did the military innovations associated with
Parker's military revolution cause the rise of the centralized state, or did the centralized state make possible those innovations?

But for our purposes here, the most intriguing recent debates focus on the Military Revolution in Asia. Scholars such as Gábor Ágoston,[18] Peter Lorge,[19] Kenneth
Chase,[20] Hyeok Hweon Kang,[21] and I myself,[22] among others, have widened the
scope of the Military Revolution, suggesting that phenomena associated with the

Military Revolution in Europe were also present in Asia.[23] A particularly instructive case is East Asia.

What does evidence from East Asia tell us about the Military Revolution?

If the Military Revolution in Europe was precipitated by gunpowder weapons, then we must consider that gunpowder weapons had a much longer history in East Asia than in Europe. There is a notion, strongly rooted, that gunpowder led quite quickly and naturally to guns, as though the weapons that preceded the gun weren't worth considering. The gun was the thing, the story goes, and Europeans rapidly mastered the technology, ahead of others. For instance, world historian William McNeill wrote, in his seminal book *Pursuit of Power*, that

> even if the idea of the gun as well as the gunpowder reached Europe from China, the fact remains that the Europeans very swiftly outstripped the Chinese and every other people in gun design, and continued to enjoy a clear superiority in this art until World War II.[24]

Even Asianists have long held similar views.[25]

Yet to understand gunpowder weapons and the role that they played in military innovation, we must pay close attention to their emergence in East Asia. It's a story that is much stranger than one might guess.

Gunpowder warfare emerged during a period that I've referred to as the Song Warring States Period, when East Asia was divided between large, powerful states, which were locked into a long-term competitive balance (960–1279), with bouts of intensive warfare succeeded by periods of tense coexistence.[26] This sustained interstate competition stimulated the development of gunpowder warfare much in the way that interstate competition in early modern Europe stimulated the military developments that Roberts, Parker, and others have discussed as part of the military revolution.

Yet the starting points of these two processes were much different, because Europeans received guns and gunpowder as part of a ready-made package, whereas East Asians started from scratch. Imagine that you didn't know what a gun was but that you knew how to make a mixture that could create terrifyingly intense flames. Would you think first of using that fire to propel something like a rock or a pellet? Probably not. The warmakers of the early gunpowder age first adapted gunpowder not to hurl missiles but to create super-charged fire weapons to burn enemy soldiers, ships, and forts. The gun emerged only gradually, towards the end of this period of intense innovation.

Early gunpowder recipes weren't powerful enough to create the rapid gaseous expansion necessary to propel projectiles. Gunpowder was invented in the 700s at the latest and used in warfare soon thereafter (it was called fire medicine, or 火藥, which is still in use in mandarin Chinese today). In modern chemical terms, it has three basic components. The most important one is a nitrate, ideally potassium nitrate (KNO$_3$). A nitrate, formed of nitrogen atoms linked to carbon and lots of oxygen, make possible hot and rapid combustion because it provides its own oxygen for the reaction. The other two components are sulphur and carbon (usually in the form of charcoal). Modern black powders usually contain 75 per cent nitrates, 15 per cent charcoal powder, and 10 per cent sulphur, but early recipes had different ratios: the number of nitrates was often lower than ideal (nitrates were usually the most expensive component). In addition, powdersmiths added extraneous ingredients that seemed to them to aid the burning, especially oils, pitches, and resins.[27]

So early gunpowder recipes were useful not for explosive or propulsive qualities but for conflagration, and the first widely adopted gunpowder weapon was a variation on the venerable fire arrow, which the Chinese and their neighbours had used for centuries, shooting them at enemy structures to try to burn them down. But the interstate competition of the Song Warring States Period led to rapid experimentation, resulting in an explosion of strange devices. For instance, early gunpowder was delivered by animals. For instance, it was attached to pheasants, in the hope that they might land in enemy encampments and set them afire, and to oxen, to create "thundering fire oxen," which would stampede towards enemy positions.

In these many experiments, certain devices became more prominent, leading to the three key weapons of the early gunpowder age: the bomb, the rocket, and, most importantly, the fire lance, ancestor to the gun. Although primitive versions of the fire lance merely spewed sparks from a hollow paper tube or gourd, later versions came to approximate weapons that we might recognize as proto-guns, as people began adding rocks and caltrops to the gunpowder in their chambers. It eventually became clear that these projectiles could fly farther and do more damage than the flames themselves, so the fire lance evolved into a true gun.

But drawing a clear line between a gun and a fire lance isn't easy. In essence, a gun is a device that uses a propellant such as gunpowder to fire a projectile from a tube. Fire lances were gun-like, but a gun proper is generally considered to have a metal chamber with a projectile that more fully occludes the barrel. A fire lance had considerable "windage," which is to say that a great deal of the gas produced in the gunpowder reaction escaped past the projectile or projectiles. In contrast, a gun minimizes windage: the expanding gas can't escape past the projectile and thus imparts more of its energy to it.

Evidence suggests that guns proper emerged in East Asia – among the Chinese and their neighbours – in the 1200s, around four or five hundred years after the invention of gunpowder.[28] Why did it take so long? Partly because the powder recipe took a long time to refine: early powder mixtures were good at burning but less good at propelling or exploding. But also partly because of technical challenges: a gun barrel must be strong and smoothly bored to be effective. In addition, it seems likely that warmakers had trouble imagining that gunpowder's most revolutionary application would be to hurl the most ancient of weapons: a rock.

Did guns transform East Asian warfare and society? Yes and no. Warfare was indeed transformed, but not the same way as in Europe, and the differences are striking and illuminating. Guns really began to spread quickly in the 1300s, when the Mongol Yuan dynasty (1279–1368) faltered. By the 1350s, guns became a key part of the huge armies vying in China as various states contended for supremacy, including the group that would establish the Ming dynasty. This period – 1350 to 1450 – can be viewed as another warring states period, and it too saw rapid military innovation. The state that won these wars, which eventually became the Ming dynasty, was successful in part because of its extensive and effective use of firearms. Although the Ming had established their dynasty in 1368, war continued, as they sought to eliminate their rivals and consolidate their territory. Firearms became increasingly central. By 1380, records indicate that 10 per cent of Ming soldiers were gunners, a far higher percentage than in Western Europe. Indeed, given that the Ming armies had more than a million soldiers, there were likely at least 100,000 gunners in the Ming armed forces. By the mid 1400s, the percentage of gunners in the Ming armed forces increased to 33 per cent, far exceeding European figures at that time.

Europeans had received guns and gunpowder by the 1320s at the latest, but, in comparison to East Asians, they used few guns in field warfare until around 1500. Why did the Chinese excel with guns on battlefield, and why didn't Europe? Were Chinese guns superior? Probably not in any significant way.

What the Chinese did better was use guns in concert because they already had countermarch techniques and standing armies. Countermarch techniques had been a consistent part of China's military tradition from ancient times, applied to the crossbow, a mainstay of Chinese warfare and a weapon that shares with early guns a slow loading time. Clear records of the use of countermarch techniques in crossbow warfare can be found in military manuals from the Tang dynasty (618–907), the dynasty during which gunpowder first began spreading for military use, and during the Song Warring States Period.[29] It's not clear when precisely East Asian soldiers first applied the technique to firearms, but it was certainly by the mid to late 1300s.

So why were Chinese – and, most likely, other East Asian powers – able to implement countermarch techniques for firearms on a mass scale so much earlier than Western Europeans were? The most likely answer is that China – and most of the other East Asian polities that Chinese states competed with – had already developed states with standing armies. European states, in contrast, were more primitive and generally lacked standing armies, basing the recruitment of warriors on feudal relations.

Military revolution theorists have suggested that the gun actually helped bring about the standing army and the centralized state in Europe, but evidence from Asia should lead us to be cautions about such claims. As historian Peter Lorge argues, such claims may get the causality backwards: Europe needed to become more like China before it could fully use firearms, because in order to train soldiers in countermarch techniques, one needed constant drilling, which meant that one needed permanent standing armies, which in turn required a certain degree of state centralization.[30] Still, firearms may have exerted selective pressure in Europe, hastening the end of feudalistic structures and the rise of centralized states.

Of course, no such development was needed in East Asia, because centralized states already existed. From this perspective, China was simply more advanced than Europe, meaning that it was farther along on the developmental path that scholars like Victor Lieberman have determined was a long-term underlying trend throughout Eurasia: towards fewer but increasingly more centralized political units per given region.[31] Indeed, European state formation and centralization and early modernization would most likely have occurred even without guns.

There is another curious puzzle in global military history: why didn't the Chinese and their neighbours develop siege artillery? Although the Chinese were better than Europeans at using firearms, they didn't tend to use big guns. In contrast, Europeans and their neighbours – particularly the Ottomans – developed powerful artillery that was capable of battering down castle walls. Indeed, in the decades before firearms were adopted on a mass scale in Europe, artillery became a mainstay of Western European armed forces.

Why did Chinese warmakers not build artillery? Was the Chinese culture of war inimical to siege warfare? Were Chinese metallurgical techniques worse? Did they lack metals? Scholars have suggested these possibilities. But evidence doesn't seem to support these claims. Chinese warmakers often conducted sieges, had plenty of metal, and had access to metallurgists as good as or better than those in Europe.[32]

So why did Europeans build wall-smashing artillery, whereas the Chinese did not? The reason is probably simple: traditional European walls were much thinner and more brittle than traditional Chinese walls were. In the middle of the twentieth century, a European fortification expert wrote, "In China . . . the principal towns are surrounded to the present day by walls so substantial, lofty and formidable that the medieval fortifications of Europe are puny in comparison."[33] European walls were made of stone and tended to be between 1.5 metres and 3 metres wide. In contrast, Chinese walls were usually between 10 metres and 20 metres wide at the base and five metres to ten metres wide at the top, wide enough for a three- or four-lane roadway. So when you shot a cannon at a medieval European wall, you had a good chance of breaching it. A traditional Chinese wall would have withstood even the most effective guns of the late medieval and early modern period. Even in the modern period, European artillerists found the prospect of bombarding Chinese walls unsettling. In 1860, officers of the British army got a close look at Beijing's outer walls and doubted that their artillery would be able to breach them.[34]

Traditional Chinese walls were so thick and well-constructed that battering them with guns wasn't expedient, especially given how expensive large guns were to construct, transport, and operate. European and Ottoman bombards required at least a hundred pounds of powder for a single shot, and powder was expensive. As late as the sixteenth and seventeenth centuries, when European artillery pieces had decreased in size and increased in effectiveness, firing a single artillery shot could cost the equivalent of a month's wages for an ordinary infantry soldier.[35] There was little sense in wasting money and effort in attacking impervious walls and thus little impetus for making large guns in China. Eventually, as artillery spread, Europeans adapted and began building the artillery fortresses that are such a key part of Parker's model, and their walls were quite similar to Chinese walls: lower, thicker, earthen, sloped, although Europeans added bastions, making possible the artillery fortress's effective in-depth defence.

That transition took place in the 1400s, when another divergence was taking place in Europe: the development of what scholars have come to call the "classic" gun: longer, thinner, and tapered towards the muzzle. This new design, which reached its end around the end of the 1400s, made for lighter, faster-firing (because faster-cooling), and likely more-accurate guns. When scholars talk about the ways that Europeans "perfected" guns, this is presumably what they have in mind, because this classic form remained in use through the eighteenth century.

Why did the classic gun design emerge in Europe but not China, where gunpowder was born? Here again, data from East Asia is instructive. During the 1300s and 1400s, Chinese guns also tended with time to become thinner and longer.[36] That development stopped, however, around the mid 1400s, when Chinese gun designs became quite conservative, with less innovation over time. Why? We can't know for sure, and we must keep in mind the paucity of the data (the many types of guns make generalizations difficult), but to the extent that this trend can be ascertained, its cause can likely be found in the falling incidence of warfare in China in the mid fifteenth century, when European wars were increasing in frequency and magnitude.[37]

The core of the military revolution model holds that continual warfare and interstate competition in Europe drove innovation. Parker talks about a "challenge-and-response" dynamic, a term he borrows from other social scientists.[38] Scholars have often suggested (but not Parker himself), that China was "unified," which led to "stagnation, whereas Western Europe was divided into competitive states, driving competition."[39]

But although China did have relatively long periods of "unification," it also saw extended periods of disunity and frequent warfare, and those periods are longer and more intense than nonspecialists appreciate. During those periods of intense warfare in and around China, we see the most rapid military innovation in East Asia. Gunpowder developed as a powerful weapon during the Song Warring States Period. After the Song dynasty fell in 1279, there was a period of relative "unity" during the Mongol Yuan dynasty, but starting in the middle of the fourteenth century, as the Yuan collapsed and new states vied for supremacy, warfare increased. That warfare lasted for around a century, from 1350 to 1450, and it was intense, driving the development and spread of the gun, which became a core part of the Chinese military, with special administrative structures devoted to firearm production, provisioning, and drilling. The year 1450 saw a relative (but certainly not absolute) lull in warfare, but after 1550, China entered a new period of intense warfare, which lasted at least through 1683. That period, 1550 to 1683, was, according to scholar Sun Laichen, perhaps the most warlike period in East Asian history, and during it, unsurprisingly, Chinese warmakers innovated and imported madly, when Chinese gun designs and practices changed rapidly.[40]

Portugal played a signal role in that process, because Portuguese mariners were a key vector for the guns – small and large – that Chinese warmakers adopted and adapted so avidly in the sixteenth and seventeenth centuries. Some episodes are well known, such as the role that Portuguese experts played in the Ming dynasty's defence against Manchu incursions in the 1620s and 1630s and the role that Portuguese mariners played in the diffusion of Portuguese muskets in Japan.[41] But other episodes are only now being understood, such as the role played by Portuguese seafarers in the spread of guns in China during the sixteenth century.

Consider, for example, the so-called *folangji*, or "Frankish cannon," which began being adopted in China in the early 1500s. Clearly, they were being imported into China by 1518 at the latest, and evidence suggests that by 1519 they were present in the armoury of the great Ming philosopher Wang Yangming, who wrote about them and whose acceptance of them from a friend became the subject of a poetry exchange among Ming literati.[42] One of the major spurs towards their widespread adoption was a series of conflicts between Portuguese mariners and Ming forces in 1521 and 1522.[43] The Ming commander in those conflicts, Wang Hong, quickly recognized the efficacy of Portuguese breech-loading cannons and proposed their adoption on an empire-wide scale. In a decade, they were bristling from the Great Wall itself. Importantly, they were not just slavishly copied. From the beginning, they were adapted and adopted, merging with Chinese styles. The great Ming General Qi Jiguang (1527–88) categorized Frankish cannons into six types, by length, weight of ammunition, and powder charge.[44] The Folangji cannon was, in effect, nativized to China, becoming a part of the Ming arsenal, and although many of the subtypes came to have their own names (e.g. shooting star cannon, peerless general great gun, etc.), the term *folangji*, or "Frankish cannon," remained in use, a sign of its origin among the Portuguese.[45]

Portuguese mariners also seem to have been involved in the widespread adoption of European-style (or Western-Eurasian–style) arquebuses and muskets in East Asia, as Portuguese mariners brought such guns to East and Southeast Asia in the 1500s. The story of Portuguese influence on the adoption of the musket in Japan is well known: in 1543, a group of Portuguese visitors showed up in Tageshima Island, in southwestern Japan, and showed their arquebuses to local leaders, who quickly grasped their utility and rapidly copied them, so that they spread throughout Japan and became a mainstay of warfare in Japan's warring states period.[46] But less well known is that arquebuses spread at the same time in coastal China, and the vector was the same: Portuguese mariners.[47]

East Asian adoption of Western guns was not slavish imitation – particularly, it seems, in China. For example, the "Frankish guns" adopted from the Portuguese inspired a wide variety of Chinese subtypes. A Ming dynasty official named Weng Wanda (翁萬達, 1498–1552), for example, invented the vanguard gun (先鋒炮), basing it on the Frankish gun but modifying it for use on horseback by making it shorter and faster-loading and equipping it with a matchlock mechanism. As he wrote, it was "copied from the Frankish gun but with modifications."[48] Zhao Shizhen (趙士楨, 1552–1611) developed a cross between a Portuguese gun and a Turkish musket, and Qi Jiguang championed a version of the Frankish gun designed to destroy enemy ships.[49]

East Asians also innovated in terms of drilling techniques. Indeed, it seems to be the case that arquebuses may have first been used in countermarch techniques not in Europe or Japan, as is usually averred, but in China. Qi Jiguang describes arquebus countermarch techniques in a drill manual from 1560, nearly forty years before Maurice of Nassau implemented the technique in the Netherlands.[50] The Koreans also employed countermarch techniques with arquebuses and muskets.

Conclusions

Evidence from East Asia provides plenty of perspective on the military revolution debate. During "warring states periods," East Asians innovated quickly, much as European warmakers did during the early modern period. The gun itself emerged during the Song Warring States Period, and it became a mainstay of Chinese armies during the period of early Ming warfare (1350–1450). A period of relative stagnation followed, as military conflicts in China decreased for a century, but the "Age of Warfare" of 1550 to 1683 led to a new period of dramatic military innovation, in which Western European arms, initially brought by Portuguese mariners, were adopted and adapted throughout East and Southeast Asia.

Yet in China at least, the gun does not seem to have brought about state centralization, as it is claimed to have done in Europe. This difference suggests that perhaps the military revolution model gets the causation backwards: centralized states were not brought about because of the adoption of the gun but rather helped make the adoption of the gun possible.

This is certainly the case with the use of handheld guns on the battlefield. Firearms (as opposed to artillery) could play a significant role in battlefield warfare only insofar as they were deployed by carefully drilled units who could effectively fire in turns by using countermarch-style techniques. This required extensive drilling, which required some kind of a permanent or long-standing army, which required some kind of a centralized state. East Asian polities – particularly China – had a long tradition of centralized states with standing armies. So whereas collective drill atrophied in Europe during the so-called Middle Ages, it remained a core part of East Asian warfare, facilitating the use of firearms.

Does that mean that we must reject one of the military revolution's most significant claims, to wit that state centralization was fostered by military competition and, more specifically, by the adoption of the gun? Not necessarily. The gun did quite possibly exert selective pressure on state centralization in Europe. After all, Parker and other sophisticated military revolution theorists do not claim that the causality went only one way. As he has noted, there were likely reciprocal influences: a double spiral of causation.[51]

In any case, sustained warfare in Europe from 1400 to well past 1800 no doubt played a significant role in European history, driving military innovation. But we must also be attentive to periods of sustained warfare in other places. Keeping in mind how difficult it is to measure levels of warfare, it does seem to be the case that China's military past falls into a pattern: periods of warfare alternating with periods of less warfare, with military innovation occurring most rapidly during periods of warfare.

As the field of history becomes increasingly global, we will increasingly see the globalization of the military revolution idea itself. Is it perhaps useful to talk about a global military revolution, from the 1200s through 1800 or so, driven by guns as they redounded through Eurasia, perhaps with different rates of innovation in different areas correlating with varying rates of warfare?

One index of global military revolution would be the rapid spread of military technology and techniques, and the gun is a key example. The gun certainly spread quite rapidly throughout Eurasia and many parts of Africa after its development in East Asia in the 1200s, being adopted in Europe by the early 1300s. As global interconnection increased, innovations spread increasingly rapidly, a process that accelerated after Vasco da Gama rounded the Cape of Good Hope in 1497. The Portuguese played a key role in this transcultural borrowing, and the spread of military technologies and techniques can be seen as an index of Portuguese influence in global history.

Notes

1 Frank Jacob and Gilmar Visoni-Alonzo, *The Military Revolution in Early Modern Europe: A Revision* (London: Palgrave Macmillan, 2016), 1. Jacob and Visoni-Alonzo aren't alone in their frustration with the military revolution model. See, for example, Stephen Morillo, "Symposium Review: Tonio Andrade, *The Gunpowder Age*," *Journal of Chinese History* 2 (2018): 417–37, 429; Andrew Ayton and J.L. Price, *The Medieval Military Revolution: State, Society, and Military Change in Medieval and Early Modern Europe* (London: I.B. Tauris, 1995), 17; Geoff Mortimer, "Was There a Military Revolution?" in *Early Modern Military History, 1450–1815*, ed. Geoff Mortimer (New York: Palgrave Macmillan, 2004), 3.
2 Tonio Andrade, *The Gunpowder Age: China, Military Innovation, and the Rise of the West in World History, 900–1900* (Princeton, NJ: Princeton University Press, 2016), 115–16; Bert S. Hall, *Weapons and Warfare in Renaissance Europe: Gunpowder, Technology, and Tactics* (Baltimore: The Johns Hopkins University Press, 1997), 2; Clifford Rogers, "The Idea of Military Revolutions in Eighteenth and Nineteenth Century Texts," *Revista de História das Ideias* 30 (2009): 395–415; Adam Smith, *An Inquiry into the Nature and Causes of the Wealth of Nations*, vol. 2 (Oxford: Clarendon Press, 1869), 292.
3 Michael Roberts, *The Military Revolution, 1560–1660: An Inaugural Lecture Delivered Before the Queen's University of Belfast* (Belfast: M. Boyd, 1956).
4 Sir George Clark, *War and Society in the Seventeenth Century* (Cambridge: Cambridge University Press, 1958).
5 See especially Olaf van Nimwegen, *The Dutch Army and the Military Revolutions, 1588–1688*, trans. Andrew May (Woodbridge: The Boydell Press, 2010), 100–12; Geoffrey Parker, "The Limits to Revolutions in Military Affairs: Maurice of Nassau, the Battle of Nieuwpoort (1600), and the Legacy," *The Journal of Military History* 71, no. 2 (2007): 331–72. But see also J.P. Puype, "Victory at Nieuwupoort, 2 July 1600," in *Exercise of*

Arms: Warfare in the Netherlands, 1568–1648, ed. Marco van der Hoeven (Leiden: Brill, 1997), 69–112.

6 Willem Lodewijk letter to Maurice of Nassau describing the "countermarch," December 1594, in Koninklijke Huisarchief, The Hague, MS A22-1XE-79, last two pp., cited in Parker, "The Limits to Revolutions in Military Affairs," 331–72, 339.

7 Everhard van Reyd, *Histoire der Nederlantscher Oorlogen begin ende Voortganck tot den Jaere 1601* (Leeuwarden: Gilbert Sybes, 1650), 162.

8 Parker's dissertation, revised, was published as *The Army of Flanders and the Spanish Road* (Cambridge: Cambridge University Press, 1972).

9 Geoffrey Parker, "The 'Military Revolution' 1560–1660 a Myth?," *The Journal of Modern History* 48, no. 2 (1976): 196–214.

10 Geoffrey Parker, *The Military Revolution: Military Innovation and the Rise of the West*, 2nd ed. (Cambridge: Cambridge University Press, [1988] 1996).

11 A classic critique of Parker's position concerning the relationship between the artillery fortress and army size is in John A. Lynn, "The *Trace Italienne* and the Growth of Armies: The French Case," in *The Military Revolution Debate: Readings on the Military Transformation of Early Modern Europe*, ed. Clifford Rogers (Boulder, CO: Westview Press, 1995), 169–99.

12 Parker, *Military Revolution*, 5.

13 Geoffrey Parker, *Cambridge Illustrated History of Warfare* (Cambridge: Cambridge University Press, 2008), 391.

14 Geoffrey Parker, "The Artillery Fortress as an Engine of European Overseas Expansion, 1480–1750," in *City Walls: The Urban Enceinte in Global Perspective*, ed. James Tracy (Cambridge: Cambridge University Press, 2000), 386–416.

15 Jeremy Black, *A Military Revolution? Military Change and European Society, 1550–1800* (Basingstoke: Palgrave Macmillan, 1991).

16 Jeremy Black, *Beyond the Military Revolution: War in the Seventeenth-Century World* (New York: Palgrave Macmillan, 2011). J.C. Sharman makes a similar argument. See, for example, J.C. Sharman, "Myths of Military Revolution: European Expansion and Eurocentrism," *European Journal of International Relations* 24 (2018): 491–513.

17 Clifford Rogers, "The Military Revolutions of the Hundred Years War," *The Journal of Military History* 57, no. 2 (1993): 241–78.

18 Gábor Ágoston, *Guns for the Sultan: Military Power and the Weapons Industry in the Ottoman Empire* (Cambridge: Cambridge University Press, 2005).

19 See especially Peter Lorge, *The Asian Military Revolution: From Gunpowder to the Bomb* (Cambridge: Cambridge University Press, 2008).

20 Kenneth Chase, *Firearms: A Global History* (Cambridge: Cambridge University Press, 2003).

21 Tonio Andrade, Hyeok Hweon Kang, and Kristen Cooper, "A Korean Military Revolution? Parallel Military Innovations in East Asia and Europe," *Journal of World History* 25, no. 1 (2014): 51–84.

22 Andrade, *Gunpowder Age*.

23 See also Richard M. Eaton and Philip B. Wagoner, "Warfare on the Deccan Plateau, 1450–1600: A Military Revolution in Early Modern India?" *Journal of World History* 25 (2014): 5–50.

24 William H. McNeill, *The Pursuit of Power: Technology, Armed Force, and Society Since A.D. 1000* (Chicago: University of Chicago Press, 1982), 81.

25 For instance, this schema is epitomized in the problematic but still-excellent book *Firearms*, by Kenneth Chase, which attempts to answer the question in the following title: "Why Was It Europeans Who Perfected Firearms When It Was the Chinese Who Invented Them?" Chase, *Firearms*, 1–2.

26 Andrade, *Gunpowder Age*, 15–28.

27 On early gunpowder formulas and weapons, see Andrade, *Gunpowder Age*, 15–54.

28 Ibid., 44–54.

29 Quan Li 李筌, *Shen ji zhi di tai bai yin jing* [神機制敵太白陰經] (Shanghai Shang wu yin shu guan, 1937 [originally from c. 759AD], juan 6 卷六, "Jiao nu tu bian" [教弩圖篇], 149.

30 Peter Lorge, *The Asian Military Revolution*, 20–22.

31 Victor Lieberman, *Strange Parallels: Southeast Asia in Global Context, c. 800–1830, Volume 1: Integration on the Mainland* (New York: Cambridge University Press, 2007); Victor Lieberman, *Strange Parallels: Southeast Asia in Global Context, c. 800–1830, Volume 2: Mainland Mirrors: Europe, Japan, China, South Asia, and the Islands* (New York: Cambridge University Press, 2009). For my perspective on Lieberman, see review of Strange Parallels, Tonio Andrade, "Victor Lieberman, Strange Parallels," *Featured Review: American Historical Review* 117, no. 4 (2012): 1173–76.

32 See Andrade, *Gunpowder Age*, 95–96.

33 Sidney Toy, *A History of Fortification: From 3000 BC to AD 1700* (London: William Heinemann, 1955), 181.

34 Joseph Edkins, "Peking," in *Journeys in North China, Manchuria, and Eastern Mongolia, with Some Account of Corea*, ed. Alexander Williamson, vol. 2 (London: Smith, Elder & Company, 1870), 313–92, 317.

35 Jack Kelly, *Gunpowder: Alchemy, Bombards, and Pyrotechnics: The History of the Explosive That Changed the World* (New York: Basic Books, 2004), 78.

36 Andrade, *Gunpowder Age*, 107–12.

37 Ibid., 113–14.

38 Parker, *Cambridge Illustrated*, 5–8.

39 This idea is as old as social science itself, going back to Montesquieu and animating the works of Karl Marx and Max Weber. See Andrade, *Gunpowder Age*, 1–8.

40 Sun Laichen, "The Century of Warfare in Eastern Eurasia, c. 1550–1683," paper delivered at the International Workshop, Globalization from East Asian Perspectives, Osaka University, Osaka, Japan, 15017, March 2016, accessed 20 November 2019, https://e5014332-b984-4691-84f1-f81f4a4f4021.filesusr.com/ugd/0b4e0c_b40f4fbce7074af0b0f91aeffd5060d7.pdf.

41 See, for instance, Teresa Sena, "Powerful Weapons in the Service of Trade and God: Macau and Jesuit Support for the Ming Cause, 1620–1650," *Daxiyangguo* [大西洋國] 15 (2010): 177–240.

42 Andrade, *Gunpowder Age*, 137–41.

43 Tonio Andrade, "Cannibals with Cannons: The Sino-Portuguese Clashes of 1521–1522 and the Early Chinese Adoption of Western Guns," *Journal of Early Modern History* 19 (2015): 1–25; Cf. Vitor Gaspar Rodrigues, "Confrontos militares navais nos 'mares do sul e da China': Razões does primeiros insucessos das armadas Portuguesas," in *Actas XIII Simpósio de História Marítima* (Lisbon: Academia de Marinha, 2016), 79–88, esp. 84–88.

44 Wang Zhaochun 王兆春, *Zhong guo huo qi shi* [中國火器史] (Beijing: Junshi kexue chubanshe, 1991), 126.

45 On the various varieties of Frankish cannons and on the way that traditional Chinese firearms were re-engineered along the lines of the new guns, see Zhaochun, *Zhong guo huo qi shi* [中國火器史], 126–34.

46 António Galvão, *Tratado dos diversos e desvayrados caminhos,* excerpted in Murai Shosuke, "A Reconsideration of the Introduction of Firearms to Japan," *Memoirs of the Research Department of the Toyo Bunko* 60 (2002): 19–38. For translations of the two major Japanese accounts of this episode, see Olof G. Lidin, *Tanegashima: The Arrival of Europe in Japan* (Copenhagen: Nordic Institute of Asian Studies, 2002), chs. 2–3. Delmer M. Brown, "The Impact of Firearms on Japanese Warfare, 1543–98," *Far Eastern Quarterly* 7, no. 3 (1948): 236–53, 239. For a detailed discussion of units and their proportions in the seventeenth century, see Matthew Keith, "The Logistics of Power: The Tokugawa Response to the Shimabara Rebellion and Power Projection in 17th-Century Japan" (PhD diss., Ohio State University, Columbus, 2006).

47 Andrade, *Gunpowder Age*, 166–87. To be sure, we have evidence that the Portuguese weren't the only vector. Other peoples who had come into contact with Western-style guns also adopted them avidly, and early examples likely arrived in Japan and China via Southeast Asian mariners, who kept up lively trade with both of these East Asian countries. See, for instance, Udagawa Takehisa 宇田川武久, *Teppo denrai: heiki ga kataru kinsei no tanjo* [鉄砲伝来: 兵器が語る近世の誕生] (Tokyo: Chuo Koronsha, 1990). But in both China and Japan, the Portuguese are specifically named as the bringers of the new, eagerly adopted weapons.
48 Cited in Andrade, *Gunpowder Age*, 142.
49 Ibid.
50 Ibid., 173–81.
51 Parker, *Military Revolution*, 158–59.

BIBLIOGRAPHY

Ablancourt, Nicolas Perrot d'. *Mémoires de Monsieur d'Ablancour, envoyé de sa majesté trés chrêtienne Louis XIV, en Portugal, contenant l'histoire de Portugal depuis le traité des Pyrenées de 1659 jusqu'à 1668*. Paris, 1701.

Ágoston, Gábor. *Guns for the Sultan: Military Power and the Weapons Industry in the Ottoman Empire*. Cambridge: Cambridge University Press, 2005.

———. "Firearms and Military Adaptation: The Ottomans and the European Military Revolution, 1450–1800." *Journal of World History* 25, no. 1 (2014): 85–124.

Akveld, Leo, ed. *Machtsstrijd om Malakka: De reis van VOC-Admiraal Cornelis Cornelisz. Matelief naar Oost-Azië, 1605–1608*. Zutphen: Walburg Pers, 2013.

Allsen, Thomas T. "The Circulation of Military Technology in the Mongolian Empire." In *Warfare in Inner Asian History (500–1800)*, edited by Nicola Di Cosmo, 265–93. Leiden: Brill, 2002.

Almeida, Manuel Lopes d', ed. *Notícias da aclamação e de outros sucessos*. Coimbra: Biblioteca da Universidade, 1940.

Almeida, Manuel Lopes d', and César Pegado, eds. *Livro segundo do registo de cartas dos Governadores das Armas (1653–1657)*. Coimbra: Biblioteca da Universidade, 1940.

Alpoim, José Fernandes Pinto. *Exame de Artilheiros*. Lisbon: Oficina de José Antonio Plates, 1744.

———. *Exame de Bombeiros*. Madrid: Oficina de Francisco Martinez Abad, 1748.

Alves, Jorge Manuel dos Santos. *O domínio do norte de Samatra: A história dos sultanatos de Samudera-Pacém e de Achém, e das suas relações com os Portugueses, 1500–1580*. Lisbon: Sociedade Histórica da Independência de Portugal, 1999.

———. "Samatra." In *História dos portugueses no Extremo Oriente*, edited by A.H. de Oliveira Marques, vol. 1, bk. 2, 77–124. Lisbon: Fundação Oriente, 2000.

Amaral, Ilidio do. *O reino do Congo, os mbundu (ou Ambundos), o reino dos ngola (ou de angola) e a presença portuguesa de finais do seculo XV a meados do seculo XVI*. Lisbon: IICT, 1996.

———. *O consulado de Paulo Dias de Novais: Angola no último quartel do século XVI e primeiro do século XVII*. Lisbon: IICT, 2000.

Amin, Entji. *Sja'irPerang Mengkasar: The Rhymed Chronicle of the Macassar War*. Edited by C. Skinner. Verhandelingen Van Het Koninklijk Instituut Voor Taal-, Land- En Volkenkunde, vol. 40. 's-Gravenhage: Nijhoff, 1963.

Amzalak, Moses Bensabat. *As relações diplomáticas entre Portugal e a França no reinado de D. João IV (1640–1656)*. Lisbon: Universidade Nova de Lisboa, 1934.

Andaya, Leonard Y. *The Heritage of Arung Palakka: A History of South Sulawesi (Celebes) in the Seventeenth Century*. Verhandelingen van het Koninklijk Instituut voor Taal-, Land- en Volkenkunde, vol. 91. The Hague: Nijhoff, 1981.

———. *The World of Maluku: Eastern Indonesia in the Early Modern Period*. Honolulu: University of Hawai Press, 1993.

Andrade, Tonio. *Lost Colony: The Untold Story of China's First Great Victory Over the West*. Princeton, NJ: Princeton University Press, 2011.

———. "Victor Lieberman, Strange Parallels." *Featured Review: American Historical Review* 117, no. 4 (2012): 1173–76.

———. "Cannibals with Cannons: The Sino-Portuguese Clashes of 1521–1522 and the Early Chinese Adoption of Western Guns." *Journal of Early Modern History* 19 (2015): 1–25.

———. *The Gunpowder Age: China, Military Innovation, and the Rise of the West in World History*. Princeton, NJ: Princeton University Press, 2016.

Andrade, Tonio, Hyeok Hweon Kang, and Kirsten Cooper. "A Korean Military Revolution? Parallel Military Innovations in East Asia and Europe." *Journal of World History* 25, no. 1 (2014): 51–84.

Andrews, Keneth R. *Elizabethan Privateering 1585–1603*. Cambridge: Cambridge University Press, 1966.

Anonymous. "Dajiangjunpao" [大将军炮 Encyclopaedia]. *Baike Baidu* (blog), 2019. https://baike.baidu.com/item/%E5%A4%A7%E5%B0%86%E5%86%9B%E7%82%AE.

Araujo, Renata Malcher de. *As Cidades da Amazónia no século XVIII. Belém, Macapá e Mazagão*. Porto: FAUP, 1998.

Armas, Duarte de. *Livro das fortalezas*. Lisbon: Arquivo Nacional da Torre do Tombo, 1990.

Aubin, Jean. "L'apprentissage de l'Inde. Cochin 1503–1504." In *Le Latin et l'Astrobe: Recherches sur le Portugal de la Renaissance, Son Expansion en Asie et les Relations internationales*, vol. 1, 49–110. Lisbon and Paris: Centre Culturel Calouste Gulbenkian, Comissão Nacional para as Comemorações dos Descobrimentos Portugueses, 1996.

———. "Le capitaine Leitão: un sujet insatisfait de D. João II." In *Le Latin et L'Astrolabe. Recherches sur le Portugal de la Renaissance, Son Expansion en Asie et les Relations Internationales*, edited by Jean Aubin, vol. 1, 309–69. Lisbon and Paris: Centre Culturel Calouste Gulbenkian, Comissão Nacional para as Comemorações dos Descobrimentos Portugueses, 1996.

Ayton, Andrew, and J.L. Price, eds. *The Medieval Military Revolution: State, Society and Military Change in Medieval and Early Modern Europe*. London: I.B. Tauris Publishers, 1995.

Azedo, Matias José Dias. *Compendio militar: escrito segundo a doutrina dos melhores autores para instrusão dos discipulos d'Academia Real de Fortificasão, Artilheria, e Dezenho*. Lisbon: Regia Tipografia Silviana, 1796.

Baião, António. *História quinhentista (inédita) do Segundo Cêrco de Dio*. Coimbra: Imprensa da Universidade, 1927.

Balasubramaniam, R. *The Saga of Indian Cannons*. New Delhi: Aryan Books International, 2008.

Barroca, Mário. "Tempos de resistência e de inovação: A arquitectura militar portuguesa no reinado de D. Manuel I (1495–1521)." *Portvgalia* 24 (2003): 95–118.

Barros, Edval de Souza. *Negócios de Tanta importância: O Conselho Ultramarino e a disputa pela condução da guerra no Atlântico e no Indico (1643–1661)*. Lisbon: CHAM, 2008.

Battisti, Eugenio, and Mazzino Fossi. "Casali Giovanni Vincenzo." *Dizionario Biografico degli Italiani* 21 (1978).

Beaujard, Philippe. *The Worlds of the Indian Ocean: A Global History, vol. 2, from the Seventh Century to the Fifteenth Century CE.* Cambridge: Cambridge University Press, 2019.

Bebiano, Rui. "Organização, teoria e prática da guerra." In *Nova História de Portugal, vol. 7: Portugal da Paz da Restauração ao ouro do Brasil*, edited Avelino de Freitas de Meneses, 130–47. Lisbon: Presença, 2001.

Bethencourt, Francisco, and Kirti Chaudhuri, eds. *História da Expansão Portuguesa, vol. 1: A Formação do império (1415–1570).* Lisbon: Temas e Debates, 1998.

Bicalho, Maria Fernanda. *A Cidade e o Império: o Rio de Janeiro no Século XVIII.* Rio de Janeiro: Civilização Editora, 2003.

Birmingham, David. *Portugal and Africa.* Lisbon: Documenta histórica, 2003.

Black, Jeremy. *A Military Revolution? Military Change and European Society, 1550–1800.* Basingstoke: Palgrave Macmillan, 1991.

———. "European Overseas Expansion and the Military Revolution." In *Technology, Disease, and Colonial Conquests, Sixteenth to Eighteenth Centuries: Essays Reappraising the Guns and Germs Theories*, edited by George Raudzens, 1–30. Leiden: Brill, 2001.

———. *European Warfare, 1494–1660.* London and New York: Routledge, 2002.

———. *Kings, Nobles and Commoners: States and Societies in Early Modern Europe.* London: I.B. Taurus, 2004.

———. *Rethinking Military History.* London and New York: Routledge, 2004.

———. *War: A Short History.* London: Continuum, 2009.

———. *Beyond the Military Revolution: War in the Seventeenth Century World.* London: Palgrave Macmillan, 2011.

———. "Patterns of Warfare, 1400–1800." In *The Cambridge World History, vol. 6: The Construction of a Global World, 1400–1800 CE, Part 2, Patterns of Change*, edited by Jerry H. Bentley, Sanjay Subrahmanyam, and Merry E. Wiesner-Hanks, 29–49. Cambridge: Cambridge University Press, 2015.

Blanco, Maria Manuela Sobral. "Os holandeses e o império português do Oriente: 1595–1641." BA diss., 2 vols., University of Lisbon, Lisbon, 1974.

Bonney, Richard, ed. *Economic Systems and State Finance.* Oxford: Clarendon Press, 1995.

———, ed. *The Rise of the Fiscal State in Europe, c.1200–1815.* Oxford: Oxford University Press, 1999.

Bonney, Richard, and William M. Ormrod. "Introduction: Crises, Revolutions and Self-Sustained Growth: Towards a Conceptual Model of Changes in Fiscal History." In *Crises, Revolutions, and Self-Sustained Growth: Essays in European Fiscal History, 1130 1830*, edited by William M. Ormrod, Margaret Bonney, and Richard Bonney, 1–21. Stamford: Shaun Tyas, 1991.

Borges, Maria do Carmo Mira. *Os Portugueses e o Sultanato de Macaçar no Século XVII.* Cascais: Câmara Municipal de Cascais, 2005.

Borschberg, Peter. *The Singapore and Melaka Straits: Violence, Security and Diplomacy in the 17th Century.* Leiden: KITLV Press, 2010.

Bouchon, Geneviève. "Un monde qui Change." In *Histoire de l'Inde Moderne, 1480–1950*, edited by Claude Markovitz, 15–28. Paris: Fayard, 1994.

———. "Les Musulmans du Kerala à l'époque de la Découverte Portugaise." In *Inde Découverte, Inde Retrouvée, 1498–1630. Études d'histoire indo-portugaise*, 56–75. Lisbon and Paris: CCCG, CNCDP, 1999.

Boxer, Charles Ralph. "The Action Between Pater and Oquendo, 12 September 1631." *The Mariner's Mirror* 45, no. 3 (1959): 179–99.

———. *Francisco Vieira De Figueiredo: A Portuguese Merchant-adventurer in South East Asia, 1624–1667.* Verhandelingen Van Het Koninklijk Instituut Voor Taal-, Land- En Volkenkunde, 52. 's-Gravenhage: Nijhoff, 1967.

————. "A Note on Portuguese Reactions to the Revival of the Red Sea Spice Trade and the Rise of Atjeh, 1540–1600." *Journal of Southeast Asian History* 10, no. 3 (1969): 415–28.

————. "The Papers of Martin de Bertendona, a Basque Admiral of Spain's Golden Age, 1586–1604." *The Indiana University Bookman* 10 (1969): 3–23.

————. *The Portuguese Seaborne Empire, 1415–1825.* London: Hutchinson, 1969.

Boxer, Charles Ralph, and J.A. Frazão de Vasconcelos. *André Furtado de Mendonça, 1558–1610.* Lisbon: Agência Geral do Ultramar, 1955.

Brahim, Boutaleb. "Azemmour." In *Regard sur Azemmour.* Rabat: Marsam, 2008.

Brásio, António, ed. *Monumenta Missionária Africana África Ocidental*, vol. 15. Lisbon: Agência Geral do Ultramar, 1952–1958.

Braun, Georg, Frans Hogenberg, and Simon Novellanus. *Civitates Orbis Terrarum*, vol. I. Cologne: Philippus Galleus, 1572.

Brewer, John. *The Sinews of Power: War, Money, and the English State, 1688–1783.* New York: Alfred Knopf, 1989.

Brito, Bernardo Gomes de, ed. *História Trágico-Marítima*, vol. 2. Lisbon: Edições Afrodite, 1972.

Brito, Pedro de. "Knights, Squires and Foot Soldiers in Portugal During the Sixteenth-Century Military Revolution." *Mediterranean Studies* 17 (2008): 118–47.

Brown, Delmer M. "The Impact of Firearms on Japanese Warfare, 1543–98." *Far Eastern Quarterly* 7, no. 3 (1948): 236–53.

Bueno, Beatriz Piccolotto Siqueira. *Desenho e desígnio: O Brasil dos engenheiros militares, 1500–1822.* São Paulo: Universidade de São Paulo, 2011.

Bulbeck, David. "Construction History and Significance of the Makassar Fortifications." In *Living Through Histories: Culture, History and Social Life in South Sulawesi*, edited by Kathryn Robinson and Mukhlis Paeni, 67–106. Canberra: Australian National University, Jakarta: National Archives of Indonesia, 1996.

Burhan-i-Massir. "History of the Nizam Shahi Kings of Ahmadnagar by Ali-Ibn 'Azizullah Tabataba." Translated by T. Wolseley Haig. *The Indian Antiquary* XLIX–LI (August 1921).

Bury, John. "Francisco de Hollanda, a Little Known Source for the History of Fortification in the 16th Century." *Arquivos do Centro Cultural Português* 14 (1979): 163–202.

————. *Two Notes on Francisco de Holanda.* London: Warburg Institute, 1981.

Cadornega, António de Oliveira. *História das Guerras de Angolanas*, vol. 3. Lisbon: Agência Geral das Colónias, 1940–1942.

Cámara Muñoz, Alicia. "El ingeniero cortesano: Tiburzio Spannocchi de Siena a Madrid." In *"Libros, caminos y días": el viaje del ingeniero*, edited by Alicia Cámara Muñoz and Bernardo Revuelta Pol, 11–42. Madrid: Fundación Juanelo Turriano, 2016.

Cámara Muñoz, Alicia, Rafael Moreira, and Marino Viganò. *Leonardo Turriano: ingeniero del rey*. Madrid: Fundación Juanelo Turriano, 2010.

Cardim, Pedro. " 'Nem tudo se pode escrever': Correspondencia diplomática e información 'política' en el Portugal del seiscientos." *Cuadernos de Historia Moderna: Anejos* 4 (2005): 95–128.

Cardoso, José Luís. "Pombal, o terramoto e a política de regulação económica." In *O Terramoto de Lisbon: Impactos Históricos*, edited by A.C. Araújo et al., 165–81. Lisbon: Horizonte, 2007.

Carita, Rui. *O escudo do Reino: A Fortaleza de São Julião da Barra.* Lisbon: Ministério da Defesa Nacional, 2007.

Castro, Tiago Machado de. "Bombardeiros na Índia: Os homens a as artes da artilharia portuguesa (1498–1557)." MA diss., University of Lisbon, Lisbon, 2011.

Cénival, Pierre, ed. *Les Sources Inédites de l'Histoire du Maroc: Première Série – Dynastie Sa'dienne.* Archives et Bibliothèques de Portugal (Julliet 1486–Avril 1516), vol. I. Paris: Paul Geuthner, 1934.

Centenero de Arce, Domingo. "Soldados portugueses en la Monarquía católica, soldados castellanos en la India Lusa." In *Portugal na Monarquia Hispânica: Dinâmicas de integração e de conflito*, edited by Cardim Leonor Freire Costa Pedro and Mafalda Soares da Cunha, 47–72. Lisbon: Centro de História de Além-Mar, 2013.

Chaby, Cláudio de. *Synopse dos decretos remetidos ao extincto Conselho de Guerra*, vol. 8. Lisbon: Imprensa Nacional, 1892.

Charney, Michael W. *Southeast Asian Warfare, 1300–1900.* Leiden: Brill, 2004.

Chase, Kenneth. *Firearms: A Global History to 1700.* Cambridge: Cambridge University Press, 2003.

Chaves, Castelo Branco, ed. *O Portugal de D. João V visto por três forasteiros*, 2nd ed. Lisbon: Biblioteca Nacional, 1989.

Chaves, Luís. *D. Pedro II.* Lisbon: Empresa Nacional de Publicidade, 1959.

Cheng, Ziyi 程子頤. "Wubei yao lüe shisi juan (1632)" [武備要畧十四卷 (1632)]. In *Siku jin hui shu congkan: Zibu; di ershiba ce muci* [四庫禁燬書叢刊. 子部; 第二十八冊目次], 1–498. 北京: 北京出版社, 2000.

Chunqiu Zhanguo 春秋戰國. "Ye Meng Xiong's Cannons." *Great Ming Military* (blog), April 17, 2015. http://greatmingmilitary.blogspot.com/2015/04/ye-meng-xiongs-cannons.html.

Cid, Pedro de Alboim Inglez. *A Torre de S. Sebastião da Caparica e a arquitectura militar do tempo de D. João II.* Lisbon: Edições Colibri, 2007.

Ciermans, Jan. *Disciplinae Mathematicae.* Traditae Anno Institutae Societatis Iesu Seculari A.P. Ioanne Ciermans Soc. Iesu. Matheseos Professor. Louanii: apud Euerardum de VVitte.

Cippola, Carlo. *Guns, Sails and Empires: Technological Innovation and the Early Phases of European Expansion 1400–1700.* New York: Pantheon Books, 1965.

Clark, George. *War and Society in the Seventeenth Century.* Cambridge: Cambridge University Press, 1958.

Clifford, Timothy Robert. "The Rules of Prose in Sixteenth-Century China: Tang Shunzhi (1507–1560) as an Anthologist." *East Asian Publishing and Society* 8, no. 2 (2018): 145–82.

Clulow, Adam. *The Company and the Shogun: The Dutch Encounter with Tokugawa Japan.* New York: Columbia University Press, 2014.

Cobos, Fernando. "Dessins de fortification dans 'Os desenhos das antigualhas' du Portugais Francisco de Holanda (1538–1540)." In *Atlas Militaires Manuscrits Européens (XVIe–XVIIe siècles): Actes des 4es journées d'étude du Musée des Plans-Reliefs*, 1–48. Paris: Ministère de la Culture et de la Communication, 2003.

———. "Una visión integral de las Escuelas y los escenarios de la fortificación española de los siglos XVI, XVII y XVIII." In *Actas IV Congreso de Castellología, Madrid 2012*, 1–48. Madrid: Associacíon Española de Amigos de los Castillos, 2012.

Coelho, Possidónio Martins Laranjo, ed. *Cartas dos governadores da província do Alentejo a El-Rei D. João IV e a El-Rei D. João VI*, vol. 3. Lisbon: Academia Portuguesa da Hístoria, 1940.

Colenbrander, H.T., ed. *Jan Pietersz. Coen: Bescheiden Omtrent Zijn Bedrijf in Indië*, vol. 1. 's-Gravenhage: Nijhoff, 1919.

Colín, Francisco. *Labor evangélica de los obreros de la Compañía de Jesús en las Islas Filipinas.* Edited by Pablo Pastells. Barcelona: Imprenta y Litografía de Henrich y Compañia, 1904.

Commelin, Isaac. *Begin Ende Voortgangh, Van De Vereenighde Nederlantsche Geoctroyeerde Oost-Indische Compagnie etc.* Amsterdam: Johannes Janssonius, 1646.

Conceição, Margarida Tavares da. *Da vila cercada à praça de guerra: Formação do espaço urbano em Almeida.* Lisbon: Livros Horizonte, 2002.

————. *Da cidade e fortificação em textos portugueses (1540–1640)*. Lisbon: Nota de Rodapé Edições, 2015.

————. "Le langage militaire des ingénieurs et des fortificateurs portugais (c. 1480–1580)." In *Les mots de la guerre dans l'Europe de la Renaissance*, edited by Marie Madeleine Fontaine and Jean-Louis Fournel, 141–68. Genève: Librairie Droz, 2015.

Cook, Weston. *The Hundred Years War of Morocco: Gunpowder and the Military Revolution in the Early Modern Muslim World*. Boulder, CO: Westview Press, 1994.

Correia, Gaspar. *Lendas da Índia*. Edited by Manuel Lopes de Almeida, vol. 4. Porto: Lello e Irmão, 1975.

Correia, Jorge. *Implantação da cidade portuguesa no Norte de África: Da tomada de Ceuta a meados do século XVI*. Porto: FAUP, 2008.

————. *Implantation de la ville portugaise en Afrique du Nord: de la prise de Ceuta jusqu'au milieu du XVIe siècle*. Porto: FAUP, 2008.

Correia, Jorge, and Ana Lopes. "L'espace urbain d'Azemmour pendant la domination portugaise: Bilan de la première mission." In *Portugal e o Magrebe: Actas do 4º Colóquio de História Luso-Marroquina/Actes du IV Coloque d'Histoire Maroco-Lusitanienne (Proceedings)*, 199–212. Lisbon and Braga: Centro de História de Além-Mar da Universidade Nova de Lisbon e da Universidade dos Açores, Centro de Investigação Transdisciplinar "Culturas, Espaço e Memória" da Universidade do Minho, 2011.

Correia, Vergílio. *Lugares Dalêm: Azemôr, Mazagão, Çafim*. Lisbon: Tipografia do Anuário Comercial, 1923.

Cortés, Fernando. *Subsidios documentais para o estudo das fortificacões de Évora e de outras praças militares alentejanas nos inicios da Guerra da restauração*. Évora: Bolseira de Doutoramento do Programa HERITAS, 1986.

Cortesão, Jaime. *Alexandre de Gusmão e o Tratado de Madrid*, vol. 3. Lisbon: Livros Horizonte, 1984.

Corvisier, André. *Armées et sociétés em Europe de 1494 à 1789*. Paris: Presses Universitaires de France, 1976.

Cossart, Brice. "Les artilleurs et la Monarchie Catholique: Fondements technologiques et scientifiques d'un empire transocéanique (1560–1610)." PhD diss., European University Institute, Florence, 2016.

————. "Los artilleros a escala de la Monarquía Hispánica: el salto cuantitativo de las armadas atlánticas." In *Estudios sobre Guerra y Sociedad en la Monarquía Hispánica: Guerra marítima, estrategia, organización y cultura militar (1500–1700)*, edited by Enrique García Hernán and Davide Maffi, 205–23. Valencia: Albatros, 2017.

————. "Producing Skills for an Empire: The Seville School of Gunners During the Golden Age of the Carrera de Indias." *Technology and Culture* 57 (2017): 459–86.

————. "Un nouveau paradigme de l'apprentissage technique: Les écoles d'artilleurs de Philippe II d'Espagne." In *Mobilités d'ingénieurs en Europe, XVᵉ–XVIIIᵉ siècle. Mélanges en l'honneur d'Hélène Vérin*, edited by Stéphane Blond, Liliane Hilaire-Pérez, and Michèle Virol, 185–98. Rennes: Presses Universitaires de Rennes, 2017.

Costa, Fernando Dores. "Crise financeira, dívida pública e capitalistas: 1796–1807." MA diss., New University of Lisbon, Lisbon, 1992.

————. "Os problemas do recrutamento militar no final do século XVIII e as questões da construção do Estado e da nação." *Análise Social* XXX, no. 130 (1995): 121–55.

————. "Formação da força militar durante a Guerra da Restauração." *Penélope* 24 (2001): 87–119.

————. "A participação portuguesa na Guerra da Sucessão de Espanha." In *O Tratado de Methuen (1703)*, edited by José Luís Cardoso et al., 71–96. Lisbon: Horizonte, 2003.

————. "O estatuto social dos militares." In *Nova História Militar de Portugal*, edited by António Manuel Hespanha, vol. 2, 93–101. Lisbon: Círculo de Leitores, 2004.

————. "O século XVIII." In *Nova História Militar de Portugal*, edited by António Manuel Hespanha, vol. 2, 187–90. Lisbon: Círculo de Leitores, 2004.

————. "Recrutamento." In *Nova História Militar de Portugal*, edited by António Manuel Hespanha, vol. 2, 68–93. Lisbon: Círculo de leitores, 2004.

————. *Insubmissão: Aversão ao serviço militar no Portugal do século XVIII*. Lisbon: Imprensa de Ciências Sociais, 2010.

————. "Sobre os militares estrangeiros na Guerra da Restauração." In *Dinámica de las fronteras em periodos de conflicto: El Imperio español*, edited by M.A. Melón Jiménez et al., 71–86. Cáceres: Universidad de Extremadura, 2019.

Costa, João Paulo Oliveira. "O Império Português em Meados do século XVI." In *Mare Nostrum: Em busca de Honra e Riqueza nos séculos XV e XVI*, 165–208. Lisbon: Temas e Debates, 2013.

Costa, João Paulo Oliveira, and Vitor Luís Gaspar Rodrigues. *Conquista de Goa – 1510–1512: Campanhas de Afonso de Albuquerque*, vol. 1. Lisbon: Tribuna da História, 2008.

Costa, Leonor Freire. "Fiscal Innovations in Early Modern States: Which War Did Really Matter in the Portuguese Case?" GHES Working Paper No. 40. Gabinete de História Económica e Social, Lisbon, 2009.

Costa, Leonor Freire, António Castro Henriques, and Nuno Palma. "Portugal's Early Modern State Capacity: A Comparative Approach." Unpublished manuscript.

Costa, Leonor Freire, Pedro Lains, and Susana Münch Miranda. *An Economic History of Portugal, 1143–2010*. Cambridge: Cambridge University Press, 2016.

Couto, Diogo do. *Da Ásia de Diogo do Couto: Dos feitos que os portugueses fizeram no descobrimento dos mares e terras do Oriente*, vol. 5, 12. Lisbon: Regia Officina Typografica, 1780–1788.

Couto, Matheus do. *Tractado de Architectura que leo o Mestre e Architecto Matheus do Couto o velho no Anno de 1631*. Lisbon: Biblioteca Nacional de Portugal, Códice 946, 2013.

Cruz, Maria Augusta Lima. "Os Portugueses em Azamor (1513–1541)." BA diss., University of Lisbon, Lisbon, 1967.

————, ed. *Documentos Inéditos para a História dos Portugueses em Azamor*. Lisbon: Arquivos do Centro Cultural Português, 1970.

————. "Exiles and Renegades in Early Sixteenth Century Portuguese India." *Indian Economic and Social History Review* 23, no. 3 (1986): 249–62.

————. "Du discours euphorique à la réalité: la conquête portugaise d'Azemmour." In *La Présence Portugaise au Maroc et les relations actuelles entre les deux pays*, 45–54. Mohammadia: Anajah Al Yadidah, 2009.

Cruz, Miguel Dantas da. *Um império de conflitos: O Conselho Ultramarino e a defesa do Brasil*. Lisbon: ICS, 2015.

————. "From Flanders to Pernambuco: Battleground Perceptions in the Portuguese Early Modern Atlantic World." *War & History* 26, no. 3 (July 2019): 316–41.

Cruz Villalón, María. *Ciudades y núcleos fortificados de la frontera hispano-lusa: El territorio de Extremadura y Alentejo. Historia y patrimonio*. Cáceres: Universidad de Extremadura, 2007.

Cummings, William. *A Chain of Kings: The Makassarese Chronicles of Gowa and Talloq*. Bibliotheca Indonesica, vol. 33. Leiden: KITLV Press, 2007.

Cunha, D. Luís da. *Instruções políticas*. Edited by Abílio Diniz Silva. Lisbon: CNCDP, 2001.

Cunha, Mafalda Soares da. *A Casa de Bragança, 1560–1640: Práticas senhoriais e redes clientelares*. Lisbon: Editorial Estampa, 2000.

Cunha, Rui Maneira. *As medidas na arquitectura, séculos XIII–XVIII: O estudo de Monsaraz.* Casal de Cambra: Caleidoscópio, 2003.

Dardess, John W. *Ming China, 1368–1644: A Concise History of a Resilient Empire.* Lanham: Rowman & Littlefield Publishers, Inc., 2012.

Delson, Roberta Marx. "The Beginnings of Professionalization in the Brazilian Military: The Eighteenth Century Corps of Engineers." *The Américas* 51, no. 4 (April 1995): 555–74.

———. "Para o entendimento da educação colonial: O papel das academias militares no Brasil colonia." In *Coletânea de Estudos Universo Urbanístico Português 1415–1822*, edited by Helder Carita and Renata Malcher de Araujo, 225–42. Lisbon: CNCDP, 1998.

Demerson, Paulette. "Correspondence diplomatique de François Lanier resident de France à Lisbonne (1642–1644)." *Arquivos do Centro Cultural Calouste Gulbenkian* 32 (1993): 509–70.

———. "Correspondance diplomatique de François Lanier resident de France à Lisbonne (1642–1644), Pt. 1 (1642)." *Arquivos do Centro Cultural Calouste Gulbenkian* 33 (1994): 739–822.

De Ville Tolozano, Antonio. *Do Governador das Praças, por Antonio de Ville Tolozano: Traduzido na lingua portugueza por ordem de Sua Magestade. Obra muyto util & necessaria não so para os governadores das Praças; mas tambem para todos os officiaes de guerra, que quizerem aprender a doutrina Militar, & as suas obrigações principalmente nos presidios.* Translated by Manuel da Maia. Lisbon: António Pedroso Galram, 1708.

Dias, Paulo. "A conquista de Arzila pelos Portugueses – 1471." MA diss., New University of Lisbon, Lisbon, 2015.

Dias, Pedro. *História da Arte Luso-Brasileira: Urbanização e Fortificação.* Coimbra: Almedina, 2004.

Dickson, P.G. *Financial Revolution in England: A Study in the Development of Public Credit.* London: Palgrave Macmillan, 1967.

Domingues, Francisco Contente. "The State of Portuguese Naval Forces in the Sixteenth Century." In *War at Sea in the Middle Ages and the Renaissance*, edited by John B. Hattendorf and Richard W. Unger, 187–97. Woodbridge: The Boydell Press, 2003.

———. "Em guerra com o Mundo, por todo o Mundo (1580–1668)." In *História Militar de Portugal*, edited by Nuno Severiano Teixeira, 273–90. Lisbon: Esfera dos Livros, 2017.

Domínguez Nafría, Juan Carlos. *El Real y Supremo Consejo de Guerra (siglos XVI–XVIII).* Madrid: Centro de Estudios Políticos y Constitucionales, 2001.

Duffy, Christopher. *Siege Warfare: The Fortress in the Early Modern World, 1494–1660.* London: Routledge, 1979.

Dutra, Francis A. "Matias de Albuquerque: A Seventeenth-Century *capitão-mor* of Pernambuco and Governor-General of Brazil." PhD diss., New York University, New York, 1968.

Eaton, Richard M., and Phillip B Wagoner. *Power, Memory, Architecture: Contested Sites on India's Deccan Plateau, 1300–1600.* New Delhi: Oxford University Press, 2014.

———. "Warfare on the Deccan Plateau, 1450–1600: A Military Revolution in Early Modern India?" *Journal of World History* 25 (2014): 5–50.

Edkins, Joseph. "Peking." In *Journeys in North China, Manchuria, and Eastern Mongolia, with Some Account of Corea*, edited by Alexander Williamson, vol. 2, 313–92. London: Smith, Elder & Company, 1870.

Elbl, Martin. "Portuguese Urban Fortifications in Morocco." In *The Urban Enceinte in Global Perspective*, edited by James D. Tracy (Ed. City Walls). Cambridge: Cambridge University Press, 2000.

Elliott, John H. "The Spanish Monarchy and the Kingdom of Portugal, 1580–1640." In *Conquest and Coalescence*, edited by Mark Greengrass, 48–67. London: Edward Arnold, 1991.

———. "A Europe of Composite Monarchies." *Past and Present* 137 (1992): 48–71.

———. *Imperial Spain, 1469–1716*. London: Penguin Books, 2002.

Eltis, David. *The Military Revolution on Sixteenth Century Europe*. London: I.B. Taurus, Academic Press, 1995.

Encarnação, Marcelo Augusto Flores Reis da. "A batalha de Toro." PhD diss., University of Porto, Porto, 2011.

Enthoven, Victor. *Zeeland en de opkomst van de Republiek: handel en strijd in de Scheldedelta, c. 1550–1621*. Leiden: Luctor et Victor, 1996.

Epstein, Stephan R. "Craft Guilds, Apprenticeship and Technological Change in Preindustrial Europe." *The Journal of Economic History* 58, no. 3 (1998): 684–713.

Fara, Amelio. *Il Sistema e la Città, Architettura Fortificata dell'Europa Moderna dai Tratati alle Realizzazioni, 1464–1794*. Génova: Sagep Editrice, 1989.

Faria, Alice Santiago. "O papel dos luso-descendentes na Engenharia Militar e nas obras públicas em Goa ao longo do século XIX." In *Goa: Passado e Presente*, edited by A. Teodoro de Matos and J. Teles e Cunha, vol. 1, 225–37. Lisbon: Centro de Estudos dos Povos e Culturas de Expressão Portuguesa da Universidade Católica Portuguesa and CHAM, 2012.

Faria, Manuel Severim de. *Notícias de Portugal*. Edited by Francisco Lourenço Vaz. Lisbon: Colibri, 2003.

Faucherre, Nicolas, Pieter Martens, and Hugues Paucot, ed. *La genèse du système bastionné en Europe (1500–1550)*. Navarrenx: Cercle Historique de l'Arribère, 2014.

Feddersen, Carl Frederik. "Principled Pragmatism: VOC Interaction with Makassar 1637–68, and the Nature of Company Diplomacy." PhD diss., Leiden University, Leiden, 2016.

Fernandes, Mário Gonçalves, ed. *Manuel de Azevedo Fortes (1660–1749) Cartografia, Cultura e Urbanismo*. Porto: GEDES, 2006.

Fernandes, Valentim. *Description de la côte d'Afrique de Ceuta au Sénegal par Valentim Fernandes (1506/1507)* [*A Descripçam de Ceuta por sua Costa de Mauritania e Ethiopia pellos Nomes Modernos Prosseguindo as Vezes Algūas Cousas do Sartão da Terra Firme*]. Translated by Pierre de Cénival and Th. Monod. Paris: Librairie Larose, 1938.

Ferreira, Nuno Alexandre Martins. "Luís Serrão Pimentel (1613–1679): Cosmógrafo Mor e Engenheiro Mor de Portugal." MA diss., University of Lisbon, Lisbon, 2009.

Ferreira, Roquinaldo. "O Brasil e a arte da guerra em Angola (sécs. XVII e XVIII)." *Estudos Históricos* 39 (2007): 3–23.

Figueiredo, Luciano Raposo de Almeida. *Rebeliões no Brasil Colônia*. Rio de Janeiro: Zahar, 2005.

Filipiak, Kai. "Der Bauernaufstand des Deng Maoqi 1448/1449 als Audrück einer Zäsur in der Geschichte der Ming-Dynastie." *Monumenta Serica* 54 (2006): 119–48.

———. *Krieg, Staat Und Militär in Der Ming-Zeit (1368–1644): Auswirkungen Militärischer Und Bewaffneter Konflikte Auf Machtpolitik Und Herrschaftsapparat Der Ming-Dynastie*. Wiesbaden: Harrassowitz Verlag, 2008.

———. "'Saving Lives' – Lü Kun's Manual on City Defense." *Journal of Chinese Military History* 1 (2012): 139–88.

Fontoura, Otília Rodrigues. *Portugal em Marrocos na época de D. João III: abandono ou permanência*. Funchal: Centro de Estudos de História do Atlântico, 1998.

Fortes, Manuel de Azevedo. *Representação a Sua Magestade sobre a forma e direcção que devem ter os Engenheiros para melhor servirem ao dito Senhor neste Reyno, e nas suas conquistas*. Lisbon: Officina de Matias Pereira da Silva, 1720.

———. *Tratado do Modo o mais Facil, e o mais exacto de fazer as Cartas Geográficas*. Lisboa Occidental: Officina de Pascoal da Sylva, 1722.

———. *O Engenheiro Portuguez: dividido em dous Tratados, Tomo Primeyro que Comprehende a Geometria Pratica sobre o Papel, e sobre o Terreno: o Uso dos Instrumentos Mais Necessarios aos Engenheiros: o Modo de Desenhar e Dar Aguadas nas Plantas Militares e no Appendice a Trigonometria Rectilinea, Tomo Segundo que Comprehende a Fortificação Regular, e Irregular: o Ataque e Defensa das Praças; e no Appendice o Uso das Armas de Guerra*, vol. 2. Lisbon: Officina de Manuel Fernandes da Costa, 1728–1729.

———. *Evidencia Apologética, e critica sobre o primeyro, e segundo tomo das Memórias Militares*. Lisbon: Officina de Miguel Rodrigues, 1733.

———. *Oração Académica*. Coimbra, 1739.

———. *Lógica Racional, Geometrica e Analytica*. Lisbon: Officina José António Plates, 1744.

Foster, William. *Letters Received by the East India Company from Its Servants in the East, Transcribed from the 'Original Correspondence' Series of the India Office Records*, vol. 3, 1615. London: Sampson Low, Marston& Company, 1899.

Françozo, Mariana. "Global Connections: Johan Maurits of Nassau-Siegen's Collection of Curiosities." In *The Dutch in Brazil*, edited by M. Van Groesen, 105–23. New York: Cambridge University Press, 2014.

Franke, Herbert. "Siege and Defense of Towns in Medieval China." In *Chinese Ways in Warfare*, edited by Frank A. Kierman, 151–201. Cambridge, MA: Harvard University Press, 1974.

Franzini, Marino M. *Reflexões sobre o Actual Regulamento do Exército de Portugal*. Lisbon: Imprensa Régia, 1820.

———. "Considerações acerca da renda total da nação portuguesa." *Revista Universal Lisbonense* 24 (March 2, 1843): 293–97.

Garcia, João Carlos, ed. *A Nova Lusitânia. Imagens Cartográficas do Brasil nas colecções da Biblioteca Nacional*. Lisbon: CNCDP, 2001.

Garcia, José Manuel. *O Terrível: A Grande Biografia de Afonso de Albuquerque*. Lisbon: Esfera dos Livros, 2017.

Garza, Andrew de la. *The Mughal Empire at War: Babur, Akbar and the Indian Military Revolution, 1500–1605*. London and New York: Routledge, 2016.

Glete, Jan. *War and the State in Early Modern Europe: Spain, the Dutch Republic and Sweden as Fiscal-Military States, 1500–1660*. London and New York: Routledge, 2002.

Godinho, Vitorino M. *Mito e Mercadoria: Utopia e Prática de Navegar, séculos XIII–XVIII*. Lisbon: Difel, 1990.

Goertz, R.O.W. "Attack and Defense Techniques in the Siege of Chaul, 1570–1571." In *II Seminário Internacional de História Indo – Portuguesa, Actas*, edited by Luís de Albuquerque and Inácio Guerreiro, 265–92. Lisbon: IICT, 1985.

Góis, Damião. *Crónica do Felicíssimo Rei D. Manuel*, vol. 4. Coimbra: Imprensa da Universidade, 1949–1955.

Goldstone, Jack. *Why Europe? The Rise of the West in World History, 1500–1850*. New York: McGraw-Hill, 2009.

Gomes, José Joaquim da Costa. *Colecção de leis da dívida pública portuguesa*. Lisbon: Imprensa Nacional, 1883.

Gomes, Saul. *D. Afonso V*. Lisbon: Círculo de Leitores, 2006.

Gómez-Centurión Jiménez, Carlos. *Felipe II, la empresa de Inglaterra y el comercio septentrional (1566–1609)*. Madrid and España: Editorial Naval, 1988.

Gonçalves, Nuno Simão. "O projecto para a fortaleza da ilha de Moçambique atribuído a Miguel de Arruda." MA diss., University of Coimbra, Coimbra, 2011.

González de León, Fernando. *The Road to Rocroi: Class, Culture and Command in the Spanish Army of Flanders, 1567–1659.* Leiden and Boston: Brill, 2009.

Goodman, David C. *Power and Penury: Government, Technology and Science in Philip II's Spain.* Cambridge: Cambridge University Press, 1988.

———. *Spanish Naval Power, 1589–1665: Reconstruction and Defeat.* Cambridge and New York: Cambridge University Press, 1997.

Gorrochategui Santos, Luís. *The English Armada: The Greatest Naval Disaster in English History.* London: Bloomsbury Academic, 2018.

Green, Toby. *The Rise of the Trans-Atlantic Slave Trade in Western Africa, 1300–1589.* Cambridge: Cambridge University Press, 2012.

Gruzinski, Serge. *Les quatre parties du monde: Histoire d'une mondialisation.* Turin: Éditions de La Martinière, 2004.

Guillot, Claude. "Les Portugais et Banten (1511–1682)." *Revista de Cultura* 13–14 (1991): 80–91.

Guilmartin, John F. "The Military Revolution: Origins and First Tests Abroad." In *The Military Revolution Debate: Readings on the Military Transformation of Early Modern Europe,* edited by Clifford J. Rogers, 299–333. Boulder, CO: Westview Press, 1995.

Guinote, Paulo, Eduardo Frutuoso, and António Lopes. *Naufrágios e outras perdas da 'Carreira da Índia,' séculos XVI e XVII.* Lisbon: Grupo de trabalho do Ministério da Educação para as Comemorações dos Descobrimentos Portugueses, 1998.

Gunn, Steve, David Grummitt, and Hans Cools. "War and the State in Early Modern Europe: Widening the Debate." *War & History* 15, no. 4 (September 2008): 371–88.

———. "War and the Emergence of the State: Western Europe, 1350–1600." In *European Warfare, 1350–1750,* edited by Frank Tallett and D.J.B. Trim, 50–73. New York: Cambridge University Press, 2010.

Haecker, Charles. "'Dirty Little Wars' in Northern Mexico and the American Southwest." In *Partisans, Guerillas, and Irregulars: Historical Archaeology of Asymmetric Warfare,* edited by Steven Smith and Clarence Geier, 140–58. Tuscaloosa: The University of Alabama Press, 2019.

Hale, John Rigby. *Renaissance Fortification: Art or Engineering?* London: Thames and Hudson, 1979.

———. "The Development of the Bastion, 1440–1534, an Italian Chronology." In *Renaissance War Studies,* 1–31. London: The Hambledon Press, 1983 (first edition 1965).

Hall, Bert S. "The Changing Face of Siege Warfare: Technology and Tactics in Transition." In *The Medieval City Under Siege,* edited by Ivy A. Corfis and Michael Wolfe, 257–75. Woodbridge: Boydell Press, 1995.

———. *Weapons and Warfare in Renaissance Europe: Gunpowder, Technoogy and Tactics.* Baltimore, MD: Johns Hopkins University Press, 1997.

Hasanuddin. "Forts on Buton Island: Centres of Settlement, Government and Security in Southeast Sulawesi." In *Forts and Fortification in Wallacea: Archaeological and Ethnohistoric Investigations,* edited by Sue O'Connor, Andrew McWilliam, and Sally Brockwell, 187–210. Acton: ANU Press, 2020.

Headrick, Daniel. *The Tools of Empire: Technology and European Imperialism in the Nineteenth Century.* Oxford: Oxford University Press, 1981.

Heintze, Beatrix. *Angola nos séculos XVI e XVII. Estudos sobre Fontes, Métodos e História.* Luanda: Kilombelombe, 2007.

Henriques, António Castro. "State Finance, War and Redistribution in Portugal, 1249–1527." PhD diss., University of York, York, 2008.

———. "Uma dívida oceânica." *Revista Contraste* 36 (2011): 12–16.

———. "Plenty of Land, Land of Plenty: The Agrarian Output of Portugal (1311–20)." *European Review of Economic History* 19, no. 2 (2015): 149–70.

Henriques, António Castro, and Nuno Palma. "Comparative European Institutions and the Little Divergence, 1385–1800." EHES Working Paper No. 117. European Historical Economics Society (EHES), Paris, 2019.

He Rubin 何汝賓. "Bing lu (1606)" [兵錄 (1606)]. In *Siku jin hui shu congkan: Zibu; di jiu ce muci* [四庫禁燬書叢刊. 子部; 第九册目次], 303–767. 北京: 北京出版社, 2000.

Hespanha, António Manuel. *As Vésperas de Levithan – Instituições e Poder Político, Portugal – séc. XVII.* Coimbra: Almedina, 1994.

———. "As finanças da Guerra." In *Nova História Militar de Portugal*, edited by António Manuel Hespanha, vol. 2, 176–87. Lisbon: Círculo de Leitores, 2004.

———. "Conclusão: guerra e sistema de poder." In *Nova História Militar de Portugal*, edited by António Manuel Hespanha, vol. 2, 359–66. Lisbon: Círculo de Leitores, 2004.

———. "Introdução." In *Nova História Militar de Portugal*, edited by António Manuel Hespanha, vol. 2:9–33. Lisbon: Círculo de Leitores, 2004.

———, ed. *Nova História Militar de Portugal*, vol. 2. Lisbon: Círculo de Leitores, 2004.

———. *Filhos da Terra: Identidades mestiças nos confins da expansão portuguesa.* Lisbon: Tinta da China, 2019.

Heywood, Linda, and John Thornton. *Central Africans, Atlantic Creoles, and the Foundation of the Americas, 1585–1660.* Cambridge: Cambridge University Press, 2007.

Hoffman, Philip. *Why Did Europe Conquer the World?* Princeton, NJ: Princeton University Press, 2015.

Holanda, Francisco de. *Da Ciência do Desenho . . .* Edited by José da Felicidade Alves. Lisbon: Livros Horizonte, (1571) 1985.

———. *Álbum dos Desenhos das Antigualhas.* Edited by José da Felicidade Alves. Lisbon: Livros Horizonte, (1571) 1989.

Hoof, J.P.C.M van. "Fortifications in the Netherlands." *Revue Internationale d'Histoire Militaire* 58 (1984): 97–126.

IJzerman, J. "Het Schip 'De Eendracht' Voor Makasser in December 1616: Journaal Van Jan Steijns." *Bijdragen Tot De Taal-, Land- En Volkenkunde Van Nederlandsch Indië* 78 (1922): 343–72.

Iria, Alberto, ed. *Cartas dos Governadores do Algarve (1638–1663).* Lisbon: Academia Portuguesa da História, 1978.

Isaba, Marcos de. *Cuerpo enfermo de la milicia española.* Madrid: Ministerio de Defensa, 1991.

Isla, Lazaro de la. *Breve tratado de artillería, geometría y artificios de fuegos.* Madrid: Viuda de Pedro Madrigal, 1595.

Isselt, W.E. van Damn van. "Mr. Johan van Dam en zijne tuchtiging van Makassar in 1660." In *Bijdragen tot de Taal- Land- en Volkenkunde van Nederlands-Indië* 60, no. 1 (1908): 1–44.

Jacob, Frank, and Gilmar Visoni-Alonzo. *The Military Revolution in Early Modern Europe: A Revision.* London: Palgrave Macmillan, 2016.

Jacobs, Hubert, ed. *Documenta Malucensia*, vol. 2. Rome: Jesuit Historical Institute, 1980.

———. *The Jesuit Makasar Documents (1615–1682).* Monumenta Historica Societatis Jesu, 134. Rome: Jesuit Historical Institute, 1988.

Jesus, Roger Lee de. "O Segundo Cerco de Diu (1546): Estudo de História Política e Militar." MA diss., University of Coimbra, Coimbra, 2012.

———. "Afonso de Albuquerque e a primeira expedição portuguesa ao Mar Vermelho (1513)." *Fragmenta Historica – História, Paleografia e Diplomática* 1 (2013): 121–41.

———. "Abastecer a Guerra noutro Oceano: o Armazém das Armas de Goa em 1545–1546." In *Nos 600 da conquista de Ceuta: Portugal e a creação do primeiro sistema mundial*, edited by Francisco Contente Domingues and Jorge Silva Rocha, 169–220. Lisbon: Comissão Portuguesa de História Militar, 2015.

———. "Gunpowder, Firepower and the Portuguese in the Indian Ocean (Sixteenth Century)." In *India, the Portuguese and Maritime Interactions, vol. 1: Science, Economy and Urbanity*, edited by Pius Malekandathil, Lotika Varadarajan, and Amar Farooqui, vol. 1, 220–31. New Delhi: Primus Books, 2019.

Jonge, J.K.J. de, ed. *De opkomst van het Nederlandsch gezag in Oost-Indië (1595–1610): Verzameling van onuitgegeven stukken uit het Oud-Koloniaal Archief*, vol. 3. 's-Gravenhage: Martinus Nijhoff, 1865.

Joshi, P.M. "Relations Between the Adilshahi Kingdom of Bijapur and the Portuguese at Goa During the Sixteenth Century." *New Indian Antiquary* II (1939–1940): 359–68.

Kamen, Henry. *The Duke of Alba*. New Haven, CT: Yale University Press, 2004.

Karra, Azzeddine, and Teixeira, André. "Fouilles archéologiques à Azemmour: Questions historiques et premières Constatations." In *Portugal e o Magrebe: IV Coloque d'Histoire Maroco-Lusitanienne (Proceedings)*, 177–90. Lisbon and Braga: Centro de História de Além-Mar, Centro de Investigação Transdisciplinar 'Culturas, Espaço e Memória,' 2011.

Keith, Matthew. "The Logistics of Power: The Tokugawa Response to the Shimabara Rebellion and Power Projection in 17th-Century Japan." PhD diss., Ohio State University, Columbus, 2006.

Kelly, Jack. *Gunpowder: Alchemy, Bombards, and Pyrotechnics: The History of the Explosive That Changed the World*. New York: Basic Books, 2004.

Kennedy, Paul. *The Rise and Fall of Great Powers*. London: Unwin Hyman, 1988.

Keuning, J., ed. *De tweede schipvaart der Nederlanders naar Oost-Indië onder Jacob Cornelisz. van Neck en Wybrant Warwijck, 1598–1600*, 5 vols. 's-Gravenhage: Martinus Nijhoff, 1938–1949.

Khan, Iqtidar Alam. *Gunpowder and Firearms: Warfare in Medieval India*. New Delhi: Oxford University Press, 2004.

Kingra, Mahinder S. "The Trace Italienne and the Military Revolution During the Eighty Years' War, 1567–1648." *The Journal of Military History* 57, no. 3 (1993): 431–46.

Knaap, Gerrit. "Headhunting, Carnage and Armed Peace in Amboina, 1500–1700." *Journal of the Economic and Social History of the Orient* 46, no. 2 (2003): 165–92.

Knaap, Gerrit, Henk den Heijer, and Michiel de Jong. *Militaire geschiedenis van Nederland: Oorlogen overzee; militair optreden door compagnie en staat buiten Europa, 1595–1814*. Amsterdam: Boom, 2015.

Laichen, Sun. "The Century of Warfare in Eastern Eurasia, c. 1550–1683." Paper Delivered at the International Workshop, Globalization from East Asian Perspectives. Osaka University, Osaka, Japan, March 17, 2016. Accessed November 20, 2019. https://e5014332-b984-4691-84f1-f81f4a4f4021.filesusr.com/ugd/0b4e0c_b40f4fbce7074af-0b0f91aeffd5060d7.pdf.

Laporan penelitian ekskavasi Situs Tirtatayasa, Banten, and Buton Benteng Wolio. *NPO Association of Asian Cultural Properties Cooperation*. Indonesia: Pusat Penelitian dan Pengembangan Arkeologi Nasional, March 2007.

Lee, Wayne, ed. *Empires and Indigenes: Intercultural Alliance, Imperial Expansion, and Warfare in the Early Modern World*. New York: New York University Press, 2011.

———. "Projecting Power in the Early Modern World: The Spanish Model?" In *Empires and Indigenes: Intercultural Alliance, Imperial Expansion, and Warfare in the Early Modern World*, edited by Wayne Lee, 1–16. New York: New York University Press, 2011.

Leitão, Henrique et al. *Sphaera Mundi: A Ciência na Aula da Esfera. Manuscritos científicos do Colégio de Santo Antão nas colecções da BNP.* Lisbon: BNP, 2008.

Lemau de la Jaisse, Pierre. *Carte générale de la monarchie françoise.* Paris: Author, 1733.

Lemos, Brito de. *Abecedário Militar.* Lisbon: Pedro Craesbeeck, 1631.

Lenihan, Pádraig, ed. *Conquest and Resistence: War in Seventeenth Century Irland.* Leiden: Brill, 2001.

Lenk, Wolfgang. *Guerra e Pacto Colonial: A Bahia contra o Brasil Holandês (1624–1654).* São Paulo: Alameda, 2013.

Lenman, Bruce P. "Introduction: Military Engineers from Polymath Courtiers to Specialist Troops." In *Military Engineers and the Development of the Early-Modern European State,* edited by Bruce P. Lenman, 1–43. Dundee: Dundee University Press, 2013.

———, ed. *Military Engineers and the Development of the Early-Modern European State.* Dundee: Dundee University Press, 2013.

Li, Quan 李筌. *Shen ji zhi di tai bai yin jing* [神機制敵太白陰經]. Shanghai Shang wu yin shu guan, 1937.

Lidin, Olof G. *Tanegashima: The Arrival of Europe in Japan.* Copenhagen: Nordic Institute of Asian Studies, 2002.

Lieberman, Victor. *Strange Parallels: Southeast Asia in Global Context, c. 800–1830, Volume 1: Integration on the Mainland, Volume 2: Mainland Mirrors: Europe, Japan, China, South Asia, and the Islands.* New York: Cambridge University Press, 2007–2009.

Lim, Ivy Maria. *Lineage Society on the Southeastern Coast of China: The Impact of Japanese Piracy in the Sixteenth Century.* Amherst: Cambria Press, 2010.

———. "From Haijin to Kaihai: The Jiajing Court's Search for a Modus Operandi Along the South-Eastern Coast (1522–1567)." *Journal of the British Association for Chinese Studies* 2 (2013): 1–26.

Lindgren, Jan. "Men, Money, and Means." In *War and Competition Between States,* edited by Philippe Contamine, 129–62. Oxford and New York: Oxford University, 2000.

Liu, Yonghua. "The World of Rituals: Masters of Ceremonies (Lisheng), Ancestral Cults, Community Compacts, and Local Temples in Late Imperial Sibao, Fujian." PhD diss., McGill University, Montreal, 2003.

Lobato, Manuel. *Política e comércio dos portugueses na Insulíndia: Malaca e as Molucas de 1575 a 1605.* Macao: Instituto Português do Oriente, 1999.

Lokhandwala, M.F., trans. *Zafar ul Walih bi Muzaffar wa Alhi – An Arabi History of Gujarat by Hajji ad-Dabir,* vol. 2. Baroda: Oriental Institute, 1970.

Lopes, Ana. "(A)cerca de Azamor. Estruturas militares ao manuelino." MA diss., University of Minho, Braga, 2009.

Lorge, Peter A. *The Asian Military Revolution: From Gunpowder to the Bomb.* Cambridge: Cambridge University Press, 2008.

Loureiro, F. de Sales, ed. *Uma jornada ao Alentejo e ao Algarve.* Lisbon: Horizonte, 1984.

Loureiro, Rui. "O encontro de Portugal com a Ásia no século XVI." In *O confronto do olhar: O encontro dos povos na época das navegações portuguesas, séculos XV e XVI: Portugal, África, Ásia, América,* edited by António Luís Ferronha, 155–211. Lisbon: Caminho, 1991.

Lucca, Denis de. *Jesuits and Fortifications: The Contribution of the Jesuits to Military Architecture in the Baroque Age.* Leiden: Brill, 2012.

Lynn, John A. "Food, Funds, and Fortresses: Resource Mobilization and Positional Warfare in the Campaigns of Louis XIV." In *Feeding Mars: Logistics in Western Warfare from the Middle Ages to the Present,* edited by John A. Lynn, 137–59. Boulder, San Francisco and Oxford: Westview Press, 1993.

―――. "Recalculating French Army Growth During the Grand Siècle, 1610–1715." In *The Military Revolution Debate: Readings on the Military Transformation of Early Modern Europe*, edited by Clifford J. Rogers, 117–47. Boulder, CO: Westview Press, 1995.

―――. "The *Trace Italienne* and the Growth of Armies: The French Case." In *The Military Revolution Debate: Readings on the Military Transformation of Early Modern Europe*, edited by Clifford J. Rogers, 169–99. Boulder, CO: Westview Press, 1995.

―――. *Giant of the Grand Siècle: The French Army – 1610–1715.* Cambridge: Cambridge University Press, 1997.

Magalhães, Joaquim Romero. "As estruturas políticas de unificação." In *História de Portugal*, edited by Joaquim Romero Magalhães, vol. 3, 61–114. Lisbon: Círculo de Leitores, 1993.

―――. "Dinheiro para a Guerra: as Décimas da Restauração." *Hispania* LXIV–1, no. 216 (2004): 157–82.

―――. "As Estruturas Sociais de Enquadramento da Economia Portuguesa de Antigo Regime: os concelhos." In *Concelhos e Organização Municipal na Época Moderna: miúnças 1*, 11–39. Coimbra: Imprensa da Universidade de Coimbra, 2011.

Mallett Michael E., and John R. Hale. *The Military Organisation of a Renaissance State: Venice c.1400 to 1617.* Cambridge: Cambridge University Press, 2006.

Manesson-Mallet, Allain. *Les Travaux de Mars ou la fortification nouvelle tant régulière, qu'irrégulière*, vol. 3. Paris, 1671.

―――. *Les Travaux de Mars ou la fortification nouvelle tant régulière*, vol. 3. Paris, 1684–1685.

Marino, Viganò. *"El Fratin mi ynginiero": I Paleari Fratino da Morcote, ingegneri militari ticinesi in Spagna (XVI–XVII secolo).* Bellinzona: Casagrande, 2004.

Marques, A.H. de Oliveira, ed. *História dos portugueses no Extremo Oriente*, vol. 1, bk. 2. Lisbon: Fundação Oriente, 2000.

Marshall, P.J. "Western Arms in Maritime Asia in the Early Phases of Expansion." *Modern Asian Studies* 14, no. 1 (February 1980): 13–28.

Martin, Colin, and Geoffrey Parker. *The Spanish Armada: Revised Edition.* Manchester: Manchester University Press, 1999.

Martínez Torres, José Antonio. "Politics and Colonial Discourse in the Spanish Empire: The African Atlantic Possessions, 1575–1630." In *Jahrbuch für Geschichte Lateinamerikas 51*, 113–48. Köln: Böhlau Verlag, 2014.

Martini, Francesco di Giorgio. *Tratatto di architettura ingegneria e arte militare.* Presentation by Corrado Maltese. Milan: Edizioni il Polifilo, 1967.

Mathew, K.S. *Shipbuilding, Navigation and the Portuguese in Pre-Modern India.* London: Routledge, 2018.

Matos, Gastão de Mello de. *Nicolau de Langres e a sua obra em Portugal.* Lisbon: Comissão de História Militar, 1941.

Matos, João Barros. "Do mar contra terra: Mazagão, Ceuta e Diu, primeiras fortalezas abaluartadas da expansão portuguesa." PhD diss., University of Sevilla, Sevilla, 2012.

Matos, Luís. "La Victoria contro Mori e le presa di Azimur." *Boletim Internacional de Bibliografia Luso-Brasileira* I, no. 2 (1960): 214–22.

Mattoso, José, and Mafalda Soares da Cunha, eds. *Portuguese Heritage Around the World: South America*, vol. 4. Lisbon: Calouste Gulbenkian Foundation, 2010.

McNeill, William. *The Pursuit of Power: Technology, Armed Force, and Society Since A.D. 1000.* Chicago: Chicago University Press, 1982.

Mello, Evaldo Cabral de. *Olinda Restaurada: Guerra e Açúcar no Nordeste, 1630–1654.* Rio de Janeiro: Topbooks, 1998.

―――. *Um Imenso Portugal. História e Historiografia.* São Paulo: Editora 34, 2002.

Memorial Histórico de España. *Cartas de Algunos PP. de la Compañía de Jesús sobre los sucesos de la monarquía entre los años de 1634 y 1648*, vol. XIII–XIX. Madrid, 1861–1864.

Mendiratta, Sidh Losa. "Dispositivos do Sistema Defensivo da Província do Norte do Estado da Índia, 1521–1739." PhD diss., University of Coimbra, Coimbra, 2012.

Meneses, D. Luís de. *História do Portugal Restaurado*, vol. 2. Lisbon: na Officina de João Galrão, 1679–1698.

———. *História de Portugal Restaurado*, vol. 4. Porto: Livraria Civilização, 1946.

Menezes, José Luiz Mota, and Maria do Rosário Rosa Rodrigues. *Fortificações Portuguesas no Nordeste do Brasil: séculos XVI, XVII e XVIII*. Recife: Pool Editorial, 1986.

Meuwese, Mark. *Brothers in Arms, Partners in Trade: Dutch-Indigenous Alliances in the Atlantic World 1595–1674*. Boston: Brill, 2012.

Miller, Joseph. *Kings and Kinsmen: Early Mbundu States in Angola*. Oxford: Clarendon Press, 1976.

Millinger, James Ferguson. "Ch'i Chi-Kuang Chinese Military Official: A Study of Civil-Military Roles and Relations in the Career of a Sixteenth Century Warrior, Reformer, and Hero." PhD diss., Yale University, New Haven, CT, 1968.

Ministerie Van Koloniën, Bataviaasch Genootschap Van Kunsten En Wetenschappen, and Nederlandsch-Indische Regeering. *Dagh-register Gehouden Int Casteel Batavia Vant Passerende Daer Ter Plaetse Als over Geheel Nederlandts-India*, vol. 1, 1624–29. 's-Gravenhage: Nijhoff; Batavia: Landsdrukkerij, 1887.

Monsaingeon, Guillaume. *Vauban, 1633–1707, un militaire très civil: lettres*. Paris: Scala, 2007.

Monteiro, A. Saturnino. *Batalhas e Combates da Marinha Portuguesa*, vol. 7. Lisbon: Sá da Costa, 1996.

Monteiro, João Gouveia. *A Guerra em Portugal nos finais da Idade Média*. Lisbon: Editorial Notícias, 1998.

———. *Os Castelos Portugueses dos finais da Idade Média: Presença, perfil, conservação, vigilância e comando*. Lisbon: Edições Colibri, 1999.

———. "The Evolution of the Army." In *War in the Iberian Peninsula, 700–1600*, edited by Francisco García Fitz and João Gouveia Monteiro, 227–29. Abingdon and New York: Routledge, 2018.

Mora-Figueroa, Luís. "Transformações artilheiras na fortificação tardo-medieval." In *Simpósio Internacional sobre Castelos*, edited by Isabel Cristina Ferreira Fernandes, 651–58. Lisbon: Colibri, 2001.

Mora Piris, Pedro. *La Real fundición de bronces de Sevilla, siglos XVI a XVIII*. Seville: Escuela superior de ingenieros, 1994.

Moree, Perry, ed. *Dodo's en galjoenen – de reis van het schip Gelderland naar Oost-Indie, 1601–1603*. Zutphen: Walburg Pers, 2001.

Moreira, Rafael. "A Arquitectura Militar do Renascimento em Portugal." In *A Introdução da Arte da Renascença na Península Ibérica, Actas do Simpósio Internacional*, 281–305. Coimbra: Epartur – Universidade de Coimbra, 1981.

———. "Arquitectura Militar." In *História da Arte em Portugal, O Maneirismo*, edited by Vítor Serrão, 137–52. Lisbon: Alfa, 1986.

———. "Do Rigor Teórico à Urgência Prática: A Arquitectura Militar." In *História da Arte em Portugal, O Limiar do Barroco*, edited by Carlos Moura, 67–86. Lisbon: Alfa, 1986.

———, ed. *História das Fortificações Portuguesas no Mundo*. Lisbon: Alfa, 1989.

———, ed. *A construção de Mazagão: Cartas inéditas 1451–1542*. Lisbon: IPPAR, 2001.

Moreira, Rafael, and Miguel Soromenho. "Engenheiros Militares Italianos em Portugal (séculos XV-XVI)." In *Architetti e Ingegneri Militari Italiani all'estero dal XV al XVIII secolo*.

Dall'Atlantico al Baltico, edited by Marino Viganò, vol. 2, 109–31. Roma and Livorno: Istituto Italiano dei Castelli – Sillabe, 1999.

Moreno, Diogo de Campos. *A Bahia no livro do Sargento-mor: Livro que dá razão do estado do Brasil 1612*. Salvador: Centro de Estudos Bahianos, (1609) 1968.

Morillo, Stephen. "Symposium Review: Tonio Andrade, *The Gunpowder Age*." *Journal of Chinese History* 2 (2018): 417–37.

Mortimer, Geoff. "Was There a Military Revolution?" In *Early Modern Military History, 1450–1815*, edited by Geoff Mortimer. New York: Palgrave Macmillan, 2004.

Mostert, Tristan. "'Ick vertrouwe dat de werelt hem naer dien op twee polen keert': De VOC, de rijksbestuurder van Makassar en een uitzonderlijk grote globe." In *Aan de overkant: ontmoetingen in dienst van VOC en WIC (1600–1800)*, edited by Lodewijk Wagenaar, 77–96. Leiden: Sidestone Press, 2015.

———. "Scramble for the Spices: Makassar's Role in European and Asian Competition in the Eastern Archipelago Up to 1616." In *The Dutch and English East India Companies: Diplomacy, Trade and Violence in Early Modern Asia*, edited by Adam Clulow and Tristan Mostert, 25–54. Amsterdam: Amsterdam University Press, 2018.

Mujabuddawat, M. *Laporan Penelitian Arkeologi Menelusuri Jejak Benteng Tradisional di Pulau Seram dan Kepulauan Ambon Lease*. Ambon: Balai Arkeologi Maluku, 2018, Unpublished.

Munck, Bert de. *Technologies of Learning: Apprenticeship in Antwerp Guilds from the 15th Century to the End of the Ancien Régime*. Turnhout: Brepols, 2007.

Munck, Bert de, Steven L. Kaplan, and Hugo Soly, eds. *Learning on the Shop Floor: Historical Perspectives on Apprenticeship*. Oxford and New York: Berghahn Books, 2007.

Murteira, André. "A Carreira da India e as incursões neerlandesas no índico occidental e em águas ibéricas de 1604–1608." In *O Estado da India e os Desafios Europeus: Actas do XII Seminario Internacional de História Indo-Portuguesa*, edited by João Paulo Oliveira e Costa and Vitor Luis Gaspar Rodrigues, 457–501. Lisbon: Centro de História de Além-Mar, 2010.

———. "The Military Revolution and European Wars Outside of Europe: The Portuguese-Dutch War in Asia in the First Quarter of the Seventeenth Century." *The Journal of Military History* 84 (April 2020): 511–35.

Nayeem, M.A. *External Relations of the Bijapur Kingdoms (1489–1686 A.D.) (A Study in Diplomatic History)*. Hyderabad: Sayeedia Research Institute, Bright Publishers, 1974.

———. *The Heritage of the Adil Shahis of Bijapur*. Hyderabad: Hyderabad Publishers, 2008.

Nazzaro, Barbara, and Guglielmo Villa. *Francesco di Giorgio Martini: Rocche, Città, Paesaggi*. Rome: Edizione Karpa, 2004.

Needham, Joseph, Ping-yü Ho, Gwei-djen Lu, and Ling Wang. *Science and Civilization in China. Volume 5: Chemistry and Chemical Technology. Part 7: Military Technology: The Gunpowder Epic*. Cambridge: Cambridge University Press, 1986.

Newitt, Malyn. "The Portuguese Nobility, and the Rise and Decline of Portuguese Military Power, 1400–1650." In *The Chivalric Ethos and the Development of Military Professionalism*, edited by D.J.B. Trim, 89–115. Leiden: Brill, 2003.

———. *A History of Portuguese Overseas Expansion 1400–1668*. New York: Routledge, 2005.

———. "Portuguese Amphibious Warfare in the East in the Sixteenth Century (1500–1520)." In *Amphibious Warfare 1000–1700: Commerce, State Formation and European Expansion*, edited by D.J.B. Trim and Mark Charles Fissel, 103–21. Leiden and Boston: Brill, 2011.

Nimick, Thomas G. "Ch'i Chi-Kuang and I-Wu County." *Ming Studies* 1 (1995): 17–29.

Nimwegen, Olaf van. *The Dutch Army and the Military Revolutions, 1588–1688*. Translated by Andrew May. Woodbridge: The Boydell Press, 2010.

Nunes, Leonardo. *Crónica de Dom João de Castro*. Edited by J.D.M. Ford. Cambridge: Harvard University Press, 1936.

O'Connor, Sue, Andrew McWilliam, and Sally Brockwell, eds. *Forts and Fortification in Wallacea: Archaeological and Ethnohistoric Investigations*. Acton: ANU Press, 2020.

Oliveira, Mário Mendonça de. *As Fortificações portuguesas de Salvador quando cabeça do Brasil*. Salvador: Fundação Gregório de Matos, 2004.

Paar, Edwin. "Jan Ciermans: Een Bossche vestingbouwkundige in Portugal." *De Brabantse Leeuw, Jaargang* XLIX (2000): 201–16.

———. "O sistema fortificado de Elvas no panorama da arquitectura militar europeia da época." *Monumentos* 28 (2008): 52–57.

Parker, Geoffrey. *The Army of Flanders and the Spanish Road – 1567–1659, the Logistics of the Spanish Victory and defeat in the Low Countries' Wars*. Cambridge: Cambridge University Press, 1972.

———. "The 'Military Revolution' 1560–1660 – a Myth?" *The Journal of Modern History* 48, no. 2 (1976): 196–214.

———. "In Defense of the Military Revolution." In *The Military Revolution Debate: Readings on the Military Transformation of Early Modern Europe*, edited by Clifford J. Rogers, 337–65. Boulder, CO: Westview Press, 1995.

———. *The Military Revolution: Military Innovation and the Rise of the West, 1500–1800*, 2nd ed. Cambridge: Cambridge University Press, (1988) 1996.

———. "The Artillery Fortress as an Engine of European Overseas Expansion, 1480–1750." In *City Walls: The Urban Enceinte in Global Perspective*, edited by James D. Tracy, 386–416. Cambridge: Cambridge University Press, 2000.

———. "The Artillery Fortress as an Engine of European Overseas Expansion, 1480–1750." In *Success Is Never Final: Empire, War and Faith in Early Modern Europe*, 192–221. New York: Perseus Books Group, 2002.

———. "The Limits to Revolutions in Military Affairs: Maurice of Nassau, the Battle of Nieuwpoort (1600), and the Legacy." *The Journal of Military History* 71, no. 2 (2007): 331–72.

———. *Cambridge Illustrated History of Warfare*. Cambridge: Cambridge University Press, 2008.

———. *Emperor: A New Life of Charles V*. New Haven, CT and London: Yale University Press, 2019.

Parker, Geoffrey, and Sanjay Subrahmanyam. "Arms and the Asian: Revisiting European Firearms and Their Place in Early Modern Asia." *Revista de Cultura-Review of Culture* 26 (2008): 12–48.

Parrott, David. "The Utility of Fortifications in Early Modern Europe: Italian Princes and Their Citadels, 1540–1640." *War in History* 7, no. 2 (2000): 127–53.

———. *Richelieu's Army: War, Government and Society in France, 1624–1642*. Cambridge: Cambridge University Press, 2001.

———. *The Business of War: Military Enterprise and Military Revolution in Early Modern Europe*. Cambridge and New York: Cambridge University Press, 2012.

Paulino, Francisco de Faria, ed. *A arquitectura Militar na Expansão Portuguesa*. Porto: Comissão Nacional para as Comemorações dos Descobrimentos Portugueses, 1994.

Pearson, M.N. *Merchants and Rulers in Gujarat: The Response to the Portuguese in the Sixteenth Century*. New Delhi: Nunshiram Manoharlal, 1976.

Peers, Douglas. "Revolution, Evolution, or Devolution: The Military Making of Colonial India." In *Empires and Indigenes: Intercultural Alliance, Imperial Expansion, and Warfare in the*

Early Modern World, edited by Wayne Lee, 81–106. New York: New York University Press, 2011.

Pelúcia, Alexandra. *Martim Afonso de Sousa e a sua linhagem*. Lisbon: CHAM, 2009.

———. *Afonso de Albuquerque. Corte, Cruzada e Império*. Lisbon: Temas e Debates, 2016.

Pepper, Simon, and Nicolas Adams. *Firearms and Fortifications: Military Architecture and Siege Warfare in Sixteenth-Century Siena*. Chicago: University of Chicago Press, 1986.

Pereira, Daniela Nunes. *A evolução urbanística de Lagos (séculos XV-XVIII)*. Faro: Direcção Regional de Cultura do Algarve, 2017.

Pereira, João Cordeiro. "O Orçamento de Estado Português no Ano de 1527." In *Portugal na Era de Quinhentos. Estudos Vários*, 159–210. Cascais: Patrimonia Historica, 2003.

Pfeffinger, Johann Friedrich. *Fortificaçam Moderna, ou recompilaçam de differentes methodos de fortificar, de que usão na Europa os hespanhoes, francezes, italianos & hollandezes: Com um Dicionario aphabetico dos termos militares, Offensa, e Defensa das Praças, construcçoens de batarias, e minas, e forma de aquartelar exercitos. Composta na lingua franceza por Mr. Pfeffinger, & traduzido por ordem de Sua Magestade que Deus guarde*. Translated by Manuel da Maia, vol. 2. Lisbon: Officina Real Deslandesiana, 1713.

Picard, Christophe. *La Mer et les musulmans d'Occident au Moyen Age, VIII–XIIII siècle*. Paris: Presses Universitaires de France, 1997.

———. *L'océan Atlantique musulman: De la conquête arabe à l'époque almohade. Navigation et mise en valeur des côtes d'al-Andalus et du Maghreb occidental (Portugal-Espagne-Maroc)*. Paris: Éditions Maisonneuve & Larose, 1997.

Pimentel, Luís Serrão. *Methodo Lusitanico de Desenhar as Fortificaçoens das Praças Regulares, & Irregulares, Fortes de Campanha e Ovtras Obras Pertencentes a Architectura Militar Distribuido em Duas Partes Operativa, e Qualificativa*. Lisbon: Antonio Craesbeeck de Mello, 1680.

Pinto, João da Rocha. "Marte no Oceano Índico: antropologia da arte da guerra dos portugueses no Oriente, 1497–1525 (Afonso de Albuquerque, a invenção do poder naval e a construção do primeiro sistema mundial)." PhD diss., New University of Lisbon, Lisbon, 1997.

Pinto, Paulo Jorge de Sousa. *Portugueses e malaios: Malaca e os sultanatos de Johor e Achém, 1575–1619*. Lisbon: Sociedade Histórica da Independência de Portugal, 1997.

Pinto, Pedro. "Folha de receita e despesa do Reino para 1543." *Fragmenta Historica* 1 (2013): 161–64.

———. "Folha de receita e despesa do Reino para 1563." *Fragmenta Historica* 1 (2013): 169–72.

Pirani, Cenan. "The Military Economy of Seventeenth Century Sri Lanka: Rhetoric and Authority in a Time of Conquest." PhD diss., University of California, Berkeley, 2016.

Pirinu, A. "La traça del fratin: il progetto dei fratelli Palearo Fratino per il forte di S. Filippo a Setubal e per la collina di S. Giuliano ad Alghero." *Archeologia medievale* XXXVI (2009): 195–210.

Pissarra, José Virgílio. *Chaul e Diu – 1508 e 1509 – O domínio do Índico*. Lisbon: Tribuna da História, 2002.

———. " 'Navios de remo' and 'Navios orientais.'" In *História da Marinha Portuguesa: Navios, Marinheiros e Arte de Navegar, 1500–1168*, edited by Francisco Contente Domingues, 71–109, 125–36. Lisbon: Academia de Marinha, 2012.

———. "O Galeão Português e o desenvolvimento das marinhas oceânicas. 1518–1550." PhD diss., University of Lisbon, Lisbon, 2016.

Porras Gil, María Concepción. *La organización defensiva española en los siglos XVI–XVII: Desde el río Eo hasta el Valle de Arán.* Valladolid: Universidad de Valladolid, 1995.

Prado, Diego de. *La obra manual y pláctica de artillería.* Madrid: Biblioteca Nacional de Madrid, MSS 9024, 1591.

Prado y Tovar, Diego de. *Encyclopaedia de fundición de artillería y su plática manual.* Cambridge: Cambridge University Library, 1603.

Puntoni, Pedro. "As guerras no Atlântico Sul: A restauração (1644–1654)." In *Nova História Militar de Portugal,* edited by António Manuel Hespanha, vol. 2, 282–91. Lisbon: Círculo de Leitores, 2004.

———. "'The BarbariansWar': Colonization and Indigenous Resistance in Brazil (1650–1720)." In *Resistance and Colonialism. Insurgent Peoples in World History,* edited by Nuno Domingos, Miguel Bandeira, and Jerónimo Ricardo Roques, 153–73. Cham, Switzerland: Palgrave Macmillan, 2019.

Puype, J.P. "Victory at Niewupoort, 2 July 1600." In *Exercise of Arms: Warfare in the Netherlands, 1568–1648,* edited by Marco van der Hoeven, 69–112. Leiden: Brill, 1997.

Pyrard, François. *Voyage de Pyrard de Laval aux Indes orientales (1601–1611) . . .* Edited by Xavier de Castro, vol. 2. Paris: Chandeigne, 1998.

Qaisa, Ashan Jan. *Indian Response to European Technology and Culture, AD 1498–1700.* New Delhi: Oxford University Press, 1988.

Qi Jiguang 戚继光. "Ji xiao xinshu (1560)" [纪效新书 (1560)]. In *Chuangshi cangshu – zi ku – bingshu* [传世藏书-子库-兵书], edited by Zhang Xinqi 张新奇, 967–1103. 海南: 海南国际新闻出版中心, 1995.

———. "Lianbing shi ji (1571)" [练兵实纪 (1571)]. In *Chuangshi cangshu – zi ku – bingshu* [传世藏书-子库-兵书], edited by Zhang Xinqi 张新奇, 1105–204. 海南: 海南国际新闻出版中心, 1995.

Rau, Virgínia Robertes, and María Fernanda Gomes da Silva. *Os Manuscritos do Arquivo da Casa de Cadaval respeitantes ao Brasil,* vol. 2. Coimbra: Universidade de Coimbra, 1956–1958.

Raudzens, George. "Military Revolution or Maritime Evolution? Military Superiorities or Transportation Advantages as Main Causes of European Colonial Conquests to 1788." *Journal of Military History* 63 (July 1999): 631–41.

Rego, António da Silva, ed. *Gavetas da Torre do Tombo,* vol. I. Lisbon: Centro de Estudos Históricos Ultramarinos, 1960.

Reid, Anthony. "Sixteenth Century Turkish Influence in Western Indonesia." *Journal of Southeast Asian History* 10, no. 3 (1969): 395–414.

———. *Southeast Asia in the Age of Commerce, 1450–1680,* vol. 2. New Haven, CT: Yale University Press, 1988–1993.

———. "A Great Seventeenth Century Indonesian Family: Matoaya and Pattingalloang of Makasar." In *Charting the Shape of Early Modern Southeast Asia,* edited by Anthony Reid, 126–54. Singapore: Institute of Southeast Asian Studies, 2000.

———. "The Rise of Makassar." In *Charting the Shape of Early Modern Southeast Asia,* edited by Anthony Reid, 100–25. Singapore: Institute of Southeast Asian Studies, 2000.

———. "Early Modernity as Cosmopolis: Some Suggestions from Southeast Asia." In *Delimiting Modernities: Conceptual Challenges and Regional Responses,* edited by Sven Trakulhun and Ralph Weber, 123–42. London: Lexington Books, 2015.

Resende, Vasco. *A Sociedade da Expansão na época de D. Manuel I: mobilidade, hierarquia e poder entre o Reino, o Norte de África e o Oriente.* Lagos: Câmara Municipal, 2006.

———. "L'Orient islamique dans la culture portugaise de l'époque moderne, du voyage de Vasco de Gama à la chute d'Ormuz (1498–1622)." PhD diss., École Pratique des Hautes Études, Paris, 2011.

Restall, Matthew. *Seven Myths of the Spanish Conquest*. Oxford: Oxford University Press, 2003.

Reyd, Everhard van. *Histoire der Nederlantscher Oorlogen begin ende Voortganck tot den Jaere 1601*. Leeuwarden: Gilbert Sybes, 1650.

Ricard, Robert. "Sur la chronologie des fortifications portugaise d'Azammūr, Mazagan et Safi." In *Congresso do Mundo Português*, vol. 3. Lisbon: Comissão Executiva dos Centenários, 1940.

Ricklefs, Merle, and P. Voorhoeve. *Indonesian Manuscripts in Great Britain: A Catalogue of Manuscripts in Indonesian Languages in British Public Collections*. Oxford: Oxford University Press, 1977.

Ridjali. *Historie Van Hitu: Een Ambonse Geschiedenis Uit De Zeventiende Eeuw*, edited by Hans Straver, Chris van Fraassen and Jan van der Putten. Utrecht: Landelijk Steunpunt Educatie Molukkers, 2004.

Rivara, J.H. da Cunha, ed. *Archivo portuguez oriental*, vol. 1, bk. 2. Nova Goa, 1876.

Roberts, Michael. *The Military Revolution, 1560–1660: An Inaugural Lecture Delivered before the Queen's University of Belfast*. Belfast: M. Boyd, 1956.

———. "The Military Revolution, 1560–1660." In *The Military Revolution Debate: Readings on the Military Transformations of Early Modern Europe*, edited by Clifford J. Rogers, 13–35. Boulder, CO: Westview Press, 1995.

Rodrigues, Ana Maria. "The Black Death and Recovery, 1348–1500." In *An Agrarian History of Portugal, 1000–2000: Economic Development on the European Frontier*, edited by Dulce Freire and Pedro Lains, 45–68. Leiden and Boston: Brill, 2017.

Rodrigues, Miguel Geraldes. "Between West Africa and America: The Angolan Slave Trade in the Portuguese and Spanish Atlantic Empires (1560–1641)." PhD diss., European University Institute, Florence, 2019.

Rodrigues, Teresa. *História da População Portuguesa: das longas permanências à conquista da modernidade*. Porto: Afrontamento, 2008.

Rodrigues, Vitor Luis Gaspar. "A evolução da arte da guerra dos portugueses no Oriente (1498–1622)." PhD diss., vol. 2, IICT, Lisbon, 1998.

———. "A guerra na Índia." In *Nova História Militar de Portugal*, edited by António Manuel Hespanha, vol. 2, 198–223. Lisbon: Círculo de Leitores, 2004.

———. "Armas e Equipamentos de Guerra Portugueses no Oriente nas Primeiras Décadas de Quinhentos." *Revista de Cultura* 26 (2008): 43–55.

———. "Reajustamentos da Estratégia militar naval do 'Estado da India' na viragem do século XVI para o XVII." In *O Estado da India e os Desafios Europeus. Actas do XII Seminario Internacional de História Indo-Portuguesa*, edited by João Paulo Oliveira e Costa and Vitor Luis Gaspar Rodrigues, 443–56. Lisbon: Centro de História de Além-Mar, 2010.

———. "The 'Easternisation' of the Portuguese Fleets in the Asian Seas During the 16th Century: Causes and Consequences." In *Gujarat and the Sea*, edited by Lotika Varadarajan, 221–50. Vadodara: Darshak Itihas Nidhi, 2011.

———. "Mestres-Fundidores Portugueses na China." In *Portugal – China: 500 anos*, edited by Miguel Castelo Branco, 158–63. Lisbon: Babel, 2014.

———. "Confrontos militares navais nos 'mares do sul e da China': Razões does primeiros insucessos das armadas Portuguesas." In *Actas XIII Simpósio de História Marítima*, 79–88. Lisbon: Academia de Marinha, 2016.

Rodríguez Hernández, Antonio José. *Los tambores de Marte: el reclutamiento en Castilla durante la segunda mitad del siglo XVII (1648–1710)*. Valladolid: Universidad de Valladolid-Castilla Ediciones, 2011.

Rogers, Clifford J. "The Military Revolutions of the Hundred Years War." *The Journal of Military History* 57, no. 2 (1993): 241–78.

———, ed. *The Military Revolution Debate: Readings on the Military Transformation of Early Modern Europe*. Boulder, CO: Westview Press, 1995.

———. "The Military Revolution in History and Historiography." In *The Military Revolution Debate: Readings on the Military Transformations of Early Modern Europe*, edited by Clifford J. Rogers, 1–10. Boulder, CO: Westview Press, 1995.

———. "The Military Revolutions of the Hundred Years War." In *The Military Revolution Debate. Readings on the Military Transformation of Early Modern Europe*, edited by Clifford R. Rogers, 55–93. Boulder, CO: Westview Press, 1995.

———. "The Idea of Military Revolutions in Eighteenth and Nineteenth Century Texts." *Revista de História das Ideias* 30 (2009): 395–415.

Rossa, Walter. *Beyond Baixa: Signs of Urban Planning in Eighteenth Century Lisbon*. Lisbon: IPPAR, 1998.

Rossa, Walter, and Luísa Trindade. "1514 El Jadida 1541: Le vicende della fondazione di una città marocchina." In *Il cantiere della città: strumenti, maestranze e tecniche dal medioevo al novecento*, edited by Aldo Casamento, 103–20. Roma: Edizioni Kappa, 2014.

Rouffaer, G.P., and J.W. Ijzerman, eds. *De eerste schipvaart der Nederlanders naar Oost-Indië onder Cornelis de Houtman, 1595–1597: journalen, documenten en andere bescheiden*, 3 vols. 's-Gravenhage: Martinus Nijhoff, 1915–1929.

Roy, Kaushik. *Military Transition in Early Modern Asia, 1400–1750*. London: Bloomsbury, 2014.

Russell-Wood, Anthony. *The Portuguese Empire 1415–1800: A World on the Move*. Baltimore: John Hopkins University Press, 1998.

Ryor, Kathleen. "Wen and Wu in Elite Cultural Practices During the Late Ming." In *Military Culture in Imperial China*, edited by Nicola Di Cosmo, 219–42, 367–71. Cambridge, MA: Harvard University Press, 2009.

Saldanha, António Vasconcelos de. *As capitanias do Brasil – Antecedentes, desenvolvimento e extinção de um fenómeno atlântico*. Lisbon: CNCDP, 2001.

Salgado, Augusto, and João Pedro Vaz. *Invencível Armada – 1588 – A participação portuguesa*. Lisbon: Tribuna da História, 2004.

Sanceau, Elaine. "A ordenança no Porto no reinado de D. João III." *Boletim Cultural da Câmara do Porto* 29, no. 3–4 (1966): 504–44.

Sanceau, Elaine, and Maria de Lourdes Lalande. *Colecção de São Lourenço*, vol. 3. Lisbon: CEHU, JICU, IICT, 1973–1983.

Sanger, Victoria. "Vauban urbaniste: l'exemple de Brest." In *Vauban et ses successeurs dans les ports du Ponant et du Levant, Brest et Toulon. Actes du colloque de Brest, 16–19 mai 1996 et Toulon, 8–11 mai 1997*. Paris: Association Vauban, 2000.

Santos, Catarina Madeira, and Vitor Rodrigues. "Fazer a guerra nos Trópicos: aprendizagens e apropriações. Estado da Índia e Angola, séculos XVI e XVIII." In *VI Jornadas Setecentistas*, 57–66. São Paulo: Minas Gerais, 2005.

Santos, Horácio Madureira dos. *Catálogo dos decretos do extinto Conselho de Guerra*, vol. 9. Lisbon: Gráfica Santelmo, 1957–1976.

Santos, João Marinho dos. *A Guerra e as Guerras na Expansão Portuguesa (séculos XV e XVI)*. Lisbon: GTMECDP, 1998.

Santos Pérez, José Manuel. "Brazil and the Politics of the Spanish Hapsburgs in the South Atlantic (1580–1640)." *Portuguese Literary & Cultural Studies: The South Atlantic, Past and Present* 27 (2015): 104–20.

Sarkar, Jagadish Narayan. *The Art of War in Medieval India*. New Delhi: Munshiram Manoharlal, 1984.

Schäpper, Antoinette. "Build the Wall: Village Fortification, Its Timing and Triggers in Southern Maluku, Indonesia." *Indonesia and the Malay World* 47, no. 138 (2019): 220–51.

Schaub, Jean-Frédéric. *Le Portugal au temps du Comte-Duc d'Olivares (1621–1640). Le conflit de juridictions comme exercice de la politique.* Madrid: Casa de Velázquez, 2001.

Schoorl, Pim. "Het 'eeuwige' verbond tussen Butonen de VOC, 1613–1669." In *Excursies in Celebes: Een Bundel Bijdragen Bij Het Afscheid Van J. Noorduyn Als Directeur-secretaris Van Het Koninklijk Instituut Voor Taal-, Land- En Volkenkunde,* edited by Harry A. Poeze and Pim Schoorl, 21–61. Leiden: KITLV Uitgeverij, 1991.

Schouten, Wouter. *De Oost-Indische Voyagie Van Wouter Schouten.* Edited by Michael Breet and Marijke Barend-van Haeften. Zutphen: Walburg Pers, 2003.

Schwartz, Stuart. "The Voyage of the Vassals: Royal Power, Noble Obligations, and Merchant Capital Before the Portuguese Restoration of Independence, 1624–1640." *American Historical Review* 96, no. 3 (June 1991): 735–62.

———. *Da América Portuguesa ao Brasil.* Lisbon: Difel, 2003.

Seguí Beltrán, Andreu. "La administración de la artillería del Reíno de Mallorca en el siglo XVI." *Bolletí de la Societat Arqueològica* 69 (2013): 143–57.

Segunda relaçam verdadeyra da marcha, e operaçoens do Exercito da Provincia de Alentejo governado pelo Marquez das Minas D. Antonio Luis de Sousa, dos Conselhos de Estado, & Guerra delRey nosso Senhor, & Governador das Armas da dita Provincia; rendimento da Praça de Alcantara, & diversaõ intentada pelo inimigo na Praça de Elvas. Lisbon: na Officina de Antonio Pedrozo Galram, 1706.

Selesky, Harold. "Colonial America." In *The Laws of War – Constraints on Warfare in the Western World,* edited by Michael Howard, G. Andreopoulos, and M. Shulman, 59–85. London and New Haven, CT: Yale University Press, 1994.

Sena, Teresa. "Powerful Weapons in the Service of Trade and God: Macau and Jesuit Support for the Ming Cause, 1620–1650." *Daxiyangguo* [大西洋國] 15 (2010): 177–240.

Sepúlveda, Cristovão Aires de Magalhães. *História orgánica e política do exército portuguez: provas,* vol. 17. Lisbon: Imprensa Nacional, 1902–1932.

Serrão, José V. "O quadro humano." In *História de Portugal,* edited by António Manuel Hespanha, vol. 4, 49–69. Lisbon: Círculo de Leitores, 1993.

———. "População e rede urbana em Portugal nos séculos XVI–XVIII." In *História dos municípios e do poder local (dos finais da Idade Média à União Europeia),* edited by César Oliveira, 63–77. Lisbon: Círculo de Leitores, 1996.

Sharman, J.C. "Myths of Military Revolution: European Expansion and Eurocentrism." *European Journal of International Relations* 24, no. 3 (2018): 491–513.

———. *Empires of the Weak: The Real Story of European Expansion and the Creation of the New World Order.* Princeton, NJ: Princeton University Press, 2019.

Shea, W.R. "Descartes in the Philosophical Haven of the Netherlands." *Canadian Journal of Netherlandic Studies* VI, no. i (Spring 1985): 61–85.

Sheikh, Samira. *Forging a Region: Sultans, Traders, and Pilgrims in Gujarat, 1200–1500.* Oxford: Oxford University Press, 2009.

Shosuke, Murai. "A Reconsideration of the Introduction of Firearms to Japan." *Memoirs of the Research Department of the Toyo Bunko* 60 (2002): 19–38.

Shunzhi Tang 唐顺之. "Wu Bian (Before 1560)" [武编 (Before 1560)]. In *Chuangshi cangshu – zi ku – bingshu* [传世藏书-子库-兵书], edited by Zhang Xinqi 张新奇, 1205–503. 海南: 海南国际新闻出版中心, 1995.

Silva, Álvaro Ferreira da. "Finanças Públicas." In *História Económica de Portugal (1700–2000),* edited by Pedro Lains and Álvaro Ferreira da Silva, vol. 1, 237–61. Lisbon: Imprensa de Ciências Sociais, 2005.

Silva, António Castanheira da. "Praça de guerra de Estremoz – a formação (1640–1690)." MA diss., New University of Lisbon, Lisbon, 2019.

Smith, Adam. *An Inquiry into the Nature and Causes of the Wealth of Nations*, vol. 2. Oxford: Clarendon Press, 1869.

Soromenho, Miguel. "Manuel Pinto de Vilalobos, da Engenharia Militar à Arquitectura." MA diss., New University of Lisbon, Lisbon, 1991.

Soromenho, Miguel, and Lucas Branco Ricardo. "The Architectural Career of Filippo Terzi in Portugal (1577–1597)." In *Da Bologna all'Europa: Artisti bolognesi in Portogallo (secoli XVI–XIX)*, edited by Sabine Frommel and Micaela Antonucci, 101–23. Bologna: Bologna University Press, 2017.

Soromenho, Miguel, et al. *A Ciência do Desenho. A Ilustração na Colecção de Códices da Biblioteca Nacional*. Lisbon: BN, 2001.

Sousa, Augusto Fausto de. "As fortificações no Brasil." *Revista do Instituto Histórico e Geográfico Brasileiro* XLVIII, pt. II. (1885): 5–140.

Sousa, Bernardo Vasconcelos e. "O sangue, a cruz e a coroa: a memória do Salado em Portugal." *Penélope* 2 (1989): 27–48.

Sousa, Frei Luís de. *Anais de D. João III*. Lisbon: Sociedade Propagadora dos Conhecimentos Úteis, 1844.

Sousa, Luís Costa e. *A arte na Guerra: A arquitectura dos campos de batalha no Portugal de Quinhentos*. Lisbon: Tribuna da História, 2008.

———. *Campanha de Etiópia, 1541–1543: 400 Portugueses em socorro do Preste João*. Lisbon: Tribuna da História, 2008.

———. *Construir e Desconstruir a Guerra em Portugal, 1568–1598*. Lisbon: Instituto de Estudos Superiores Militares, 2016.

———. "The War on Land." In *War in the Iberian Peninsula, 700–1600*, edited by Francisco García Fitz and João Gouveia Monteiro, 241–56. Abingdon and New York: Routledge, 2018.

Sousa, Luís Costa e, and Vítor Rodrigues. "The 16th Century (1495–1600)." In *War in the Iberian Peninsula*, edited by Francisco García Fitz and João Gouveia Monteiro, 241–66. London and New York: Routledge, 2018.

Stafford, Ignace. "La Architectura Militar." In *Varias obras mathematicas compuestas por el. P. Ignacio Stafford mestre de mathematica en el collegio de S. Anton de la Compañia de Jesus y no acavadas por causa de la muerte del dicho padre. . .*, fl.s 505–642. Lisbon: Biblioteca Nacional de Portugal, Códice 240, 1638.

Stapel, Frederik Willem. *Het Bongaais Verdrag*. Groningen: Wolters, 1922.

Stavros, Matthew. "Military Revolution in Early Modern Japan." *Japanese Studies* 33, no. 3 (2013): 243–61.

Storrs, Christopher. *War, Diplomacy and the Rise of Savoy, 1690–1720*. Cambridge: Cambridge University Press, 1999.

Subrahmanyam, Sanjay. "Holding the World in Balance: The Connected Histories of the Iberian Overseas Empires, 1500–1640." *American Historical Review* 112, no. 5 (2007): 1359–85.

———. *The Portuguese Empire in Asia, 1500–1700: A Political and Economic History*, 2nd ed. Oxford: Wiley-Blackwell, 2012.

Swart, Erik. "'Qualifications, Knowledge and Courage': Dutch Military Engineers, c. 1550-c. 1660." In *Military Engineers and the Development of the Early-Modern European State*, edited by Bruce P. Lenman, 47–70. Dundee: Dundee University Press, 2013.

Swope, Kenneth M. "Clearing the Fields and Strengthening the Walls: Defending Small Cities in Late Ming China." In *Secondary Cities and Urban Networking in the Indian Ocean Realm, c. 1400–1800*, edited by Kenneth R. Hall, 123–54. Lanham: Lexington Books, 2008.

Tallett, Frank. *War and Society in Early Modern Europe, 1495–1715*. London and New York: Routledge, 1992.

Tenace, Edward. "A Strategy of Reaction: The Armadas of 1596 and 1597 and the Spanish Struggle for European Hegemony." *The English Historical Review* 118, no. 478 (2003): 855–82.

't Hart, Marjolein. "The Emergence and Consolidation of the 'Tax State.' II: The Seventeenth Century." In *Economic Systems and State Finance*, edited by Richard Bonney, 281–93. Oxford: Clarendon Press, 1995.

Thomaz, Luís Filipe F.R. *De Ceuta a Timor*. Lisbon: Difel, 1994.

———. "Os portugueses nos mares da Insulíndia no século XVI." In *De Ceuta a Timor*, 567–80. Lisbon: Difel, 1994.

———, ed. *Aquém e além da Taprobana. Estudos luso-orientais à memória de Jean Aubin e Denys Lombard*. Lisbon: CHAM, 2002.

———. "O malogrado estabelecimento oficial dos portugueses em Sunda e a islamização da Java." In *Aquém e além da Taprobana. Estudos luso-orientais à memória de Jean Aubin e Denys Lombard*, edited by Luís Filipe F.R. Thomaz, 381–607. Lisbon: CHAM, 2002.

Thompson, Irving A.A. "Money, Money and Yet More Money! Finance, the Fiscal-State, and the Military Revolution: Spain, 1500–1650." In *The Military Revolution Debate: Readings on the Military Transformation of Early Modern Europe*, edited by Clifford J. Rogers, 273–98. Boulder, CO: Westview Press, 1995.

Thompson, William R. "The Military Superiority Thesis and the Ascendancy of Western Eurasia in the World System." *Journal of World History* 10, no. 1 (Spring 1999): 143–78.

Thornton, John K. "The Art of War in Angola, 1575–1680." *Comparative Studies in Society and History* 30, no. 2 (1988): 360–78.

———. *Warfare in Atlantic Africa, 1500–1800*. London: University College London Press, 1999.

———. "Firearms, Diplomacy, and Conquest in Angola: Cooperation and Alliance in West Central Africa, 1491–1671." In *Empires and Indigenes: Intercultural Alliance, Imperial Expansion, and Warfare in the Early Modern World*, edited by Wayne Lee, 167–91. New York: New York University Press, 2011.

Tilly, Charles. *The Formation of Nation States in Western Europe*. Princeton, NJ: Princeton University Press, 1975.

———. *Coercion, Capital, and European States, AD 990–1990*. Cambridge, MA: Wiley-Blackwell, 1990.

Tong, James W. *Disorder Under Heaven: Collective Violence in the Ming Dynasty*. Stanford, CA: Stanford University Press, 1991.

Torgal, Luís Reis. *Ideologia Política e Teoria do Estado na Restauração*. Coimbra: Biblioteca Geral da Universidade, 1981.

Toy, Sidney. *A History of Fortification: From 3000 BC to AD 1700*. London: William Heinemann, 1955.

Udagawa, Takehisa 宇田川武久. *Teppo denrai: Heiki ga kataru kinsei no tanjo* [鉄砲伝来: 兵器が語る近世の誕生]. Tokyo: Chuo Koronsha, 1990.

Vala, Margarida Helena de la Féria. "Os engenheiros militares no planeamento das cidades: Entre a Restauração e D. João V, 1640–1750." PhD diss., University of Lisbon, Lisbon, 2007. http://hdl.handle.net/10451/578.

Valladares, Rafael. *La rebelión de Portugal 1640–1680*. Valladolid: Junta de Castilla y León, 1998.

———. "Las dos guerras de Pernambuco: La armada del conde da Torre y la crisis del Portugal hispánico (1638–1641)." In *El Desafío Holandés al Dominio Ibérico en Brasil en el Siglo XVII*, edited by José Manuel Santos Pérez and George Cabral de Souza, 33–66. Salamanca: Ediciones Universidad de Salamanca, 2006.

———. *La conquista de Lisboa. Violencia militar y comunidad política en Portugal, 1578–1583.* Madrid: Marcial Pons, 2008.

———. *A conquista de Lisbon: 1587–1583.* Lisbon: Texto Editores, 2010.

Varadarajan, Lotika. "Positioning Gujarat as a Medieval Mercantile Centre: Contours and Context." In *Port Towns of Gujarat*, edited by Sara Keller and Michael Pearson, 9–17. New Delhi: Primus Books, 2015.

Varnhagen, Francisco Adolfo. *História Geral do Brazil.* Rio de Janeiro: Em casa de E. e H. Laemmert, (1854–1857) 1877.

Vasconcelos, Luís Mendes de. *Arte Militar dividida em três partes . . .* Termo de Alenquer: Por Vicente Alvarez, 1612.

Veen, Ernst van. *Decay or Defeat? An Inquiry into the Portuguese Decline in Asia, 1580–1645.* Leiden: Research School of Asian, African and Amerindian Studies, Universiteit Leiden, 2000.

Vellozo, Diogo da Sylveyra. *Arquitetura Militar ou Fortifcação Moderna.* Edited by Mário Mendonça de Oliveira. Salvador: Edufpa, (1743) 2005.

Veloso, Queiroz. *D. Sebastião: 1554–1578.* Lisbon: Empresa Nacional de Publicidade, 1935.

Vilalobos, Manuel Pinto de. *Tractado do Uzo do Pantometra de Desenhar as Forteficasoins assim do lado do Polygono exterior para fora, como do lado do Polygono exterior pera dentro nas figuras tanto regulares como irregulares pello Methodo de Luís Serrão Pimentel. . .* Lisbon: Biblioteca Nacional de Portugal, Códice 13201, *c.* 1690.

Vila-Santa, Nuno. "Revisitando o Estado da Índia nos anos de 1571 a 1577." *Revista de Cultura-Review of Culture* 36 (2010): 88–112.

———. *Entre o Reino e o Império. A Carreira político-militar de D. Luís de Ataíde 1516–1581.* Lisbon: ICS, 2015.

Villes et Tribus du Maroc. Casablanca: Éditions Frontispice, 2002.

Virol, Michèle. *Vauban: de la gloire du roi au service de l'état.* Seyssel: Champ Vallon, 2003.

Viterbo, Francisco Sousa. *Dicionário Histórico e Documental dos Arquitectos, Engenheiros e Construtores Portugueses*, vol. 3. Lisbon: INCM, 1988.

Walton, Steven A. "The Art of Gunnery in Renaissance England." PhD diss., University of Toronto, Toronto, 1999.

Wang Minghe 王鸣鹤. *Deng tan bi jiu (1599)* [登坛必究 (1599)], vol. 20–24. 中国兵书集成, Zhongguo bingshu jicheng. 北京: 解放军出版社, 1990.

Wang, Zhaochun 王兆春. *Zhong guo huo qi shi* [*中國火器史*]. Beijing: Junshi kexue chubanshe 军事科学出版社, 1991.

Wendt, Helge, ed. *The Globalization of Knowledge in the Iberian Colonial World.* Berlin: Edition Open Access, 2016.

Wernham, Richard B. *After the Armada: Elizabethan England and the Struggle for Western Europe, 1588–1595.* Oxford: Oxford University Press, 1984.

———. *The Return of the Armadas: The Last Years of the Elizabethan War Against Spain, 1595–1603.* Oxford: Oxford University Press, 1994.

White, Eugene. "From Privatized to Government-Administered Tax Collection: Tax Farming in Eighteenth Century France." *The Economic History Review* 57, no. 4 (November 2004): 636–63.

White, Lorraine. "Guerra y revolución militar en la Iberia del siglo XVII." *Manuscrits* 21 (2003): 63–93.

———. "Strategic Geography and the Spanish Habsburg Monarchy's Failure to Recover Portugal, 1640–1668." *The Journal of Military History* 71 (April 2007): 373–409.

Winius, George D. "Portuguese as Players on a South Asian Stage." In *Portugal, the Pathfinder. Journeys from the Medieval Toward the Modern World 1300-ca.1600*, edited by George D. Winius, 191–212. Madison: Hispanic Seminary of Medieval Studies, 1995.

Witkam, H.J. "Jean Gillot (1614–1657): Un ingeniero de Leiden muerto en Olivenza." In *Encuentros/Encontros de* Ajuda, vol. 3. Badajoz: Diputación Provincial de Badajoz, 1997.

Xu Baolin 许保林. *Zhongguo bingshu tonglan* [中国兵书通览]. 北京: 解放军出版社, 1990.

Yun-Casalilla, Bartolomé. "Introduction: The Rise of the Fiscal State in Eurasia from a Global, Comparative and Transnational Perspective." In *The Rise of the Fiscal States: A Global History, 1500–1914*, edited by Bartolomé Yun-Casalilla and Patrick K. O'Brien, 1–35. Cambridge and New York: Cambridge University Press, 2012.

———. "Social Networks and the Circulation of Technology and Knowledge in the Global Spanish Empire." In *Global History and New Polycentric Approaches: Europe, Asia and the America in a World Network System*, edited by Manuel Pérez García and Lucio De Sousa, 275–91. Basingstoke: Palgrave Macmillan, 2018.

———. *Iberian World Empires and the Globalization of Europe 1415–1668*. Basingstoke: Palgrave Macmillan, 2019.

Yun-Casalilla, Bartolomé, and Patrick O'Brien, eds. *The Rise of Fiscal States: A Global History, 1500–1914*. Cambridge: Cambridge University Press, 2012.

Zhao, Fengxiang 赵凤翔. "Mingdai folangjichong hexin jishu tezheng jiqi zhuanbian yanjiu" 明[代佛郎机铳核心技术特征及其转变研究]. *Ziran bianzhengfa tongxun* [自然辩证法通]讯 39, no. 3 (2017): 31–39.

Zheng Cheng 郑诚. "Fagong kao – 16 shiji chuan Hua de Oushi qianzhuang huopao jiqi yanbian" [发熕考 – 16 世纪传华的欧式前装火炮及其演变]. *Ziran kexueshi yanjiu* [自然科学史研究] 32, no. 4 (2013): 504–22.

Zheng Ruozeng 鄭若曽. *Chou hai tu bian (1562)* [籌海圖編 *(1562)*]. Edited by Li Zhizhong 李致忠. 北京: 中華書局, 2007.

Zhenyu Feng 冯震 宇. "Lun folangji zai Mingdai de bentuhua" [论佛郎机在明代的本土化]. *Ziran bianzhengfa tongxun* [自然辨证法通讯] 34, no. 3 (2012): 57–62.

Zhou Weiqiang 周维强. *Folangjichong zai Zhongguo* [佛朗机铳在中国]. 北京: 社会科学文献出版社, 2013.

Zúquete, A.E. Martins. *Nobreza de Portugal*, vol. 3. Lisbon: Editorial Enciclopédia, 1960–1961.

Zurara, Gomes Eanes de. *Chronica do descobrimento e conquista de Guiné*. Paris: Officina Typographica de Fain e Thunot, 1841.

INDEX

Page numbers in *italics* indicate figures and bold indicate tables in the text.